Ireland, the United Nations and the Congo

'Libera nos a malo'
('Deliver us from evil')

Motto suggested for the 35th Irish Battalion by Lt Col. A.G. Cullen. NAI DFA 305/384/2 Pt V, Cullen to Maj. Gen. Collins Powell, 17 Oct. 1961. Elisabethville, the capital of Katanga, was contracted to 'E-ville' in ONUC correspondence.

Ireland, the United Nations and the Congo

A military and diplomatic history, 1960–1

MICHAEL KENNEDY

AND

ART MAGENNIS

FOUR COURTS PRESS

Typeset in 10.5pt on 12pt Dante by
Carrigboy Typesetting Services for
FOUR COURTS PRESS LTD
7 Malpas Street, Dublin 8, Ireland
www.fourcourtspress.ie
and in North America for
FOUR COURTS PRESS
c/o ISBS, 920 NE 58th Avenue, Suite 300, Portland, OR 97213.

First published 2014
Paperback reprint 2017

A catalogue record for this title is available
from the British Library.

ISBN 978–1–84682–656–6

Printed in Ireland
by SPRINT-Print, Dublin.

Contents

Abbreviations

ANC	Armée Nationale Congolaise
Brig.	Brigadier
Brig. Gen.	Brigadier General
Capt.	Captain
CMD	Command
Col.	Colonel
Comdt	Commandant
DEA	Department of External Affairs
FO	Foreign Office
Gen.	General
GMT	Greenwich Mean Time
Lt	Lieutenant
Lt Col.	Lieutenant Colonel
Lt Gen.	Lieutenant General
MA	Military Archives, Cathal Brugha Barracks, Dublin
Maj.	Major
Maj. Gen.	Major General
MNC	Mouvement Nationale Congolais
NAI	National Archives of Ireland, Dublin
NLS	National Library of Sweden, Stockholm
OC	Officer Commanding
ONUC	Organisation des Nations Unies au Congo
Pte	Private
RH	Bodleian Library of Commonwealth and African Studies, Oxford (Rhodes House)
SCOMEP	Sub-Command Eastern Provinces
TNA	The National Archives, Kew, London
Tpr	Trooper
UAR	United Arab Republic
UCDA	University College Dublin Archives
UN	United Nations
UNA	United Nations Archives, New York
UNEF	United Nations Emergency Force
UNFICYP	United Nations Force in Cyprus
UNIFIL	United Nations Interim Force in Lebanon
UNOGIL	United Nations Observer Group in Lebanon
UNTSO	United Nations Truce Supervision Organization
UTC	Co-ordinated Universal Time

List of maps and plates

Maps

Plates *(between pages 128 and 129)*

21 Capt. Cyril McQuillan, Platoon Commander, Support Platoon, B-Company, 35th Battalion, with Indian troops who were co-located with B-Company in Nyunzo, north Katanga, November 1961.

22 Lt Col. Hugh McNamee, Col. Jonas Waern and Lt Col. S.S. Maitra, Elisabethville, 1961.

23 A Bren gun crew digging in, Jadotville, September 1961.

24 Camouflaged A-Company position, Jadotville, September 1961.

25 A burned out bus, part of Comdt Pat Cahalane's ambushed patrol, outside Radio College, Elisabethville, September 1961.

26 Capt. Mark Carroll points to where a Katangese anti-tank projectile hit Comdt Pat Cahalane's Ford armoured car, Elisabethville, September 1961.

27 Comdt Pat Quinlan, OC A-Company, 35th Battalion.

28 Lt Col. Hugh McNamee, unknown Gurkha captain, Lt Col. S.S. Maitra, Elisabethville, September 1961.

29 Frank Aiken being briefed by Comdt John Keane while Lt Col. Hugh McNamee and a 35th Battalion Chaplin listen, Elisabethville, September 1961.

30 Jack Conway, Conor Cruise O'Brien, Frank Aiken, Freddie Boland and Con Cremin, Idlewild Airport, New York, late 1950s.

31 Irish Ford armoured cars and Willys jeeps at 35th Battalion Headquarters, Elisabethville, 1961.

32 Irish ONUC troops with a Swedish SKP m/42 Armoured Personnel Carrier, Elisabethville, August 1961.

Credits

1, 2, 3, 5, 6, 7, 10, 18, 21, 28 and 29 are reproduced with the permission of Col. Seamus Condon and of Military Archives, Cathal Brugha Barracks Dublin; 4 and 8 are reproduced with the permission of the family of the late Capt. Jack Browne (37th Battalion, ONUC); 30 is reproduced with the permission of University College Dublin Archives Department and the family of the late Frank Aiken; 9, 11, 12, 14, 15, 16, 19, 20, 23, 24, 27 are reproduced with the permission of Leo Quinlan; 13, 17, 22, 25, 26, 31 and 32 are from Comdt. Art Magennis' personal collection.

Acknowledgments

This book originates in a personal memoir by Comdt Art Magennis of his service with the 35th Irish Battalion in Organisation de Nations Unies au Congo (ONUC) in the Congolese province of Katanga. Dr Michael Kennedy developed the memoir into an entirely new text by combining Magennis' eye-witness account with in-depth archival research. The result is military and diplomatic history; an Irish perspective on a defining moment in the history of the United Nations, the Cold War and modern Africa. Except where the memoir is quoted, what follows was written and researched by Michael Kennedy. Kennedy's drafts were read and commented on by Magennis and were the subject of wider discussions with groups of ONUC veterans – these comments and discussions being worked back into the text. The original Magennis memoir can be consulted at Military Archives at Cathal Brugha Barracks, Dublin.

Many people gave advice and assistance and we would particularly like to thank the ONUC veterans who talked about their experiences in Congo: Lt Gen. Bill Callaghan, Capt. Noel Carey, Sgt Tim Carey, Col. Jim Condon, Col. Phelim Connolly, Comdt Liam Donnelly, Brig. Gen. James Farrell, Lt Col. Colman Goggin, Tpr Bill Maher, Sgt James McCafferty, Col. Michael Moriarty, Tpr John O'Mahony, Col. Terry O'Neill, Brig. Gen. Patrick Purcell, Brig. Gen. Tom Quinlan, Capt. Tommy Ryan and Col. Michael Shannon.

As always Military Archives was magnificently helpful and we thank Hugh Beckett, Lisa Dolan, Noelle Grothier, Comdt Pádraic Kennedy, Comdt Victor Laing, Capt. Stephen MacEoin and Pte Adrian Short for their assistance. At the National Archives of Ireland Eamon Mulally, Paddy Sarsfield, Mary Chaney and Ken Robinson delivered box upon box of essential Department of External Affairs files. At University College Dublin Archives, Seamus Helferty, Orna Somerville and Kate Manning guided the way through the collections in their care.

The United Nations Archives, New York, The National Archives, Kew, Rhodes House Library, Oxford and the National Library of Sweden, Stockholm, provided critical sources underpinning the book. Martin Fanning and his colleagues at Four Courts Press were, as always, a pleasure to work with. We received strong personal support from many people – our most sincere thanks go to Edward Bourke, Peter Browne, Edward Burke, Brendan Culleton, Dr David Dickson, Dr Noel Dorr, Comdt Terry Fleming, Sarah Gearty, Lt Col. Dan Harvey, Fr Pat Hudson OFM, Lar Joye, Alan Kennedy, Kitty Kennedy, the late Col. Frank Lawless, Dr Donal Lowry, Dr Eoin Magennis, Tim Magennis, Dr Ivar McGrath, Dr Deirdre McMahon, Professor Rory Miller, Professor Michael Mulqueen, Dr Conor Mulvagh, Simon Nolan, Dr Alanna O'Malley, Dr Kate O'Malley, Dr Kevin O'Sullivan, Declan Power, Lt Col. Pat Power, Leo Quinlan, Dr Susannah Riordan and Airman Michael Whelan. We would particularly like to thank Col. Richard Heaslip for his suggestion that we might consider working together – this book came from that suggestion.

Key people mentioned in the text

Adoula, Cyrille	Prime Minister of Congo, 1961–4
Aiken, Frank	Irish Minister for External Affairs, 1957–69
Berendsen, Ian	United Nations Representative in Elisabethville, Aug. 1960–Mar. 1961
Boland, Frederick H.	Irish Ambassador to the United Nations, 1956–64
Boland, Kevin	Irish Minister for Defence, 1957–61
Buckley, Lt Col. Mortimer	OC 32nd Irish Battalion, ONUC, July 1960–Jan. 1961
Bunche, Ralph	UN Under Secretary for Special Political Affairs; Special Representative of the UN Secretary General in Congo, July–Aug. 1960
Bunworth, Lt Col. Richard	OC 33rd Irish Battalion, ONUC, Aug. 1960–Jan. 1961
Byrne, Col. Henry 'Harry'	OC 9th Brigade (ONUC), 1960–1; Commander, SCOMEP, 1960
Collins Powell, Lt Gen. Seán	Chief of Staff of the Irish Defence Forces, 1961–2
Cordier, Andrew	Executive Assistant to the UN Secretary General
Cremin, Cornelius 'Con'	Secretary, Department of External Affairs, Dublin, 1958–63
Créner, Henri	Belgian Consul General, Elisabethville
Dayal, Rajeshwar	Representative of the UN Secretary General in Congo, Sept. 1960–May 1961
Dean, Sir Patrick	British Ambassador to the United Nations, 1960–4
Dixon, Sir Pierson	British Ambassador to the United Nations, 1954–60
Dumontet, Georges	UN Secretary General's Representative in Katanga, Mar.–May 1961 and Dec. 1961–Jan. 1962
Dunnett, Denzil	British Consul General, Elisabethville, 1961–2
Egge, Lt Col. Bjorn	Military Information Officer, ONUC, Katanga, 1961
Evans, George	British Consul General, Elisabethville, 1957–61
Gizenga, Antoine	Head of the secessionist government in Stanleyville, 1961; Deputy Prime Minister of Congo, 1961–2
Hammarskjöld, Dag	Secretary General of the United Nations, 1953–61
Hogan, Lt Col. Michael	OC 36th Irish Battalion, ONUC, Dec. 1961–May 1962
Home, Alexander 'Alec' Lord	British Foreign Secretary, 1960–3
Ivan Smith, George	Head of the UN Press Service in Katanga
Kasavubu, Joseph	President of Congo, 1960–5
Khiari, Mahmoud	Chief of Civilian Operations, ONUC, 2 Sept. 1961–Sept. 1962
Kjellgren, Col. Anders	OC, ONUC, Southern Katanga
Lemass, Seán	Irish Taoiseach (Prime Minister), 1959–66

Linner, Sture	Chief of Civilian Operations, ONUC, July 1960–Sept. 1961; Officer-in-Charge, ONUC, May 1961–Jan. 1962
Lumumba, Patrice	Prime Minister of Congo, June–Sept. 1960
McCarthy, Col. Justin	Deputy Chief of Staff and Chief of Operations, ONUC, Leopoldville, 1960
MacEoin, Lt Gen. Seán	Force Commander, ONUC, Jan. 1961–Mar. 1962
McNamee, Lt Col. Hugh	OC, 35th Irish Battalion, ONUC, Aug.–Dec. 1961
MacNeill, Lt Col. Olaf	OC, 35th Irish Battalion, ONUC, July–Aug. 1961
Mobutu, Col. Joseph	Chief of Staff of the ANC, took control in Congo in September 1960; formally relinquished power in August 1961, though still wielding considerable influence; President of Congo (Zaire), 1965–97
Munongo, Godefroid	Katangese Minister of the Interior, 1960–3
Muké, Gen. Norbert	Commander of the Katangese Gendarmerie
O'Brien, Conor Cruise	UN Secretary General's Representative in Katanga, June–Dec. 1961
O'Neill, Col. Eugene	OC, 34th Irish Battalion, ONUC, Jan.–July 1961
Quinlan, Comdt Patrick	OC, A-Company, 35th Irish Battalion, ONUC
Raja, Brig. K.A.S.	OC, ONUC, Katanga, Mar. 1961–Apr. 1962; OC, 99th Indian Independent Brigade
Riches, Derek	British Ambassador to Congo, Sept. 1961–3
Rikhye, Maj. Gen. Indar Jit	Military Adviser to the UN Secretary General, 1957–67
Rosen, Maj. Sven	Chief of Staff, Sector-B, ONUC, Elisabethville
Scott, Sir Ian	British Ambassador to Congo, 1960–1
Sendwe, Jason	Leader of the Balubakat
Spaak, Paul Henri	Belgian Foreign Minister, 1961–6
Thant, U	Secretary General of the United Nations, 1961–71
Tshombe, Moïse	President of Katanga, 1960–3
Urquhart, Brian	UN Secretary General's Representative in Katanga, 1961
von Bayer, Lt Stig	Interpreter with ONUC
von Horn, Gen. Carl	Supreme Commander, ONUC, July–Dec. 1960
Waern, Col. Jonas	OC of Southern Katanga, later Sector-B, ONUC, Katanga, June 1961–May 1962

Notes on editorial method

Time zones, sunrise and sunset in Congo and Katanga

UTC is the primary global time standard. It is equivalent to Greenwich Mean Time (GMT). Ireland is on UTC during winter and is one hour ahead of UTC during summer. Congo has two time zones. Its capital, Kinshasa (Leopoldville), is one hour ahead of UTC. Katanga's capital, Lubumbashi (Elisabethville), 1,600 kilometres to the southeast, is two hours ahead of UTC. New York, the location of the UN Secretariat, is five hours behind UTC in winter and four hours in summer. At midday in Dublin it is early afternoon in Katanga and early morning in New York. The suffix 'Z' is used to designate a time given in UTC and the suffix 'B' for the time zone two hours ahead of UTC.

In Congo daybreak and nightfall occur rapidly regardless of season. Dawn is between 0500 and 0630 local time and dusk 1800 to 1930.

Irish military organization

Irish ONUC battalions ranged in size from 464 to 730 personnel all-ranks, and were commanded by a lieutenant colonel who was responsible to the commander of the local sector or command who was in turn responsible to the ONUC Force Commander. Two or more battalions brought together for tactical purposes formed a brigade, commanded by a colonel.

Battalions were divided into three infantry companies (A, B and C) plus a headquarters company and a support company, with additional attachments such as an armoured car group being added to some battalions.

Companies, containing approximately 150 men, were commanded by a commandant. Each company formed a semi-autonomous unit with its own support, logistics and transport elements.

Companies broke down into three platoons plus a weapons support platoon, each of approximately 32 men and commanded by a captain or lieutenant. Platoons broke down into sections of about 8 men, each commanded by a corporal.

Armoured car groups were organized into four sections of two armoured cars per section and, like a company, were commanded by a commandant. A trooper in a cavalry unit is the equivalent of a private in an infantry unit.

Footnote style

In addition to detailing archive, collection, sender, recipient and date, footnotes that refer to teleprinter messages also include the serial number and, where relevant, the time of each communication. For example, 'UNA S/840/2/4, ELLEO 748, O'Brien to Linner, Khiari and MacEoin, 2000Z, 27 Aug. 1961' footnotes teleprinter message 'ELLEO 748' from Conor Cruise O'Brien to Sture Linner, Mahmoud Khiari and Lt Gen. Seán MacEoin sent at 2000GMT on 27

August 1961, which can be located in UN archives in file S/840/2/4. 'ELLEO' was the designator for Elisabethville to Leopoldville teleprinter traffic and '748' the number of the message.

1 Congo, 1960–1

The name of the state

Today's 'Democratic Republic of the Congo' was from 1908 to independence in 1960 known as 'Belgian Congo'. From 1960 to 1964 the country was known as 'République du Congo', which translates into English as 'Republic of the Congo' or 'Republic of Congo'.

To the north-west of 'République du Congo' the neighbouring 'French Congo' also gained independence in 1960 and chose the similar name Republic of Congo. To avoid confusion the countries were then known respectively as 'Congo-Leopoldville' and 'Congo-Brazzaville', after their respective capital cities.

In 1965 République du Congo became the Democratic Republic of Congo, which became Zaire in 1971 and the Democratic Republic of the Congo, or simply DRC, in 1997.

The République du Congo/Congo-Leopoldville/Republic of the Congo/ Republic of Congo of 1960 to 1964 is referred to in the text below as 'Congo' and has been left in contemporary quotes as 'the Congo', this latter form also being used in the title of the book. Thus 'Congo' as referred to below is not to be confused with Congo-Brazzaville, today's Republic of the Congo.

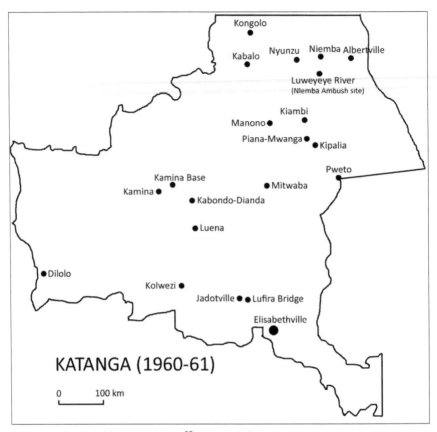

2 Katanga, 1960–1

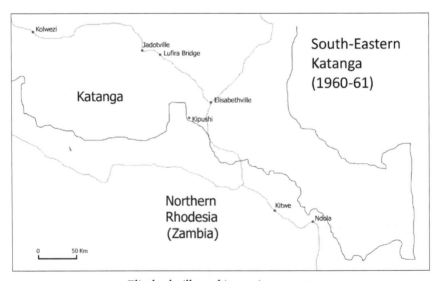

3 Elisabethville and its environs, 1960–1

'There is nothing like the Congo. You will thank God for that'[1]

IN JULY 1960 the 32nd Infantry Battalion of the Irish Defence Forces joined Organisation des Nations Unies au Congo (ONUC), the recently established United Nations peacekeeping operation in the newly independent central African state of Congo. In 1960, Congo had a population of 13 million Congolese and 100,000 European, mainly Belgian, settlers. With a vast territory of 700,000 square miles it was eighty times larger than Belgium, from which it gained independence on 30 June 1960. In the days after independence the newly installed and inexperienced government of Prime Minister Patrice Lumumba began to collapse and Lumumba ultimately sought Soviet support. The Eisenhower administration in Washington was increasingly fearful that Congo would become a Cold War flashpoint and tried to keep the Congolese government Western-oriented to prevent the Soviet Union from gaining a foothold in the country. Meanwhile, in an attempt to stabilize Congo, Belgium quickly deployed troops across its former colony. The UN swiftly intervened through ONUC to support the independence of Congo, to enable the Belgian troops to withdraw and to try to keep the Cold War rivals out of the growing Congolese power vacuum.

Involvement in ONUC was the Irish Defence Forces' first large-scale overseas deployment and its first comprehensive experience of UN peacekeeping. From July 1960 to May 1964 almost 6,200 Irish soldiers served with ONUC. For the 32nd Battalion and its successors, and for the UN and its Secretary General Dag Hammarskjöld, ONUC was a step into the unknown. In summer 1960 Ireland and other ONUC contributors had little idea what lay ahead; neither had the UN Secretariat. The Irish Defence Forces joined the UN on a steep learning curve where the ideal of UN intervention to maintain peace was tested against the realities of peacekeeping in a failing state, as in central Africa Irish soldiers went into combat for the first time since 1923.

ONUC lacked a clearly defined mission and followed a changing mandate. The force was tasked to keep the peace in Congo but how it was to do this in practical terms was unclear. Peacekeeping was a new and underdeveloped concept in 1960. It was not mentioned in the United Nations Charter, was not a term used during the UN action in the Korean War, and first came into being with the UNEF force in Sinai in 1956. The deployment of international troops to Congo in July 1960 was initially intended to provide security for the UN civilian mission in the country, allowing Belgian forces to withdraw and local forces to re-organize. There was no expectation that ONUC would act other than in self-defence. Yet its mission evolved from peacekeeping into what is often called 'peace-enforcement', a misleading term for what is more properly called 'war', as, fourteen months into its deployment, lightly armed ONUC troops found themselves at war with local forces in the southeastern Congolese province of Katanga.

Katanga was the most significant of a number of provinces to secede from the control of the central Congolese government in Leopoldville after independence. Rich in copper and uranium, and pro-Western in the Cold War, Katanga was supported in a variety of covert and overt ways by Belgium, Britain, the Rhodesian Federation and France, and by elements in the United States. They coveted the province's mineral wealth and saw an independent Katanga as a bulwark against the spread of Communism in Africa. In the face of considerable opposition, from July 1960 to August 1961 the UN sought by political means to cajole Katanga back under the umbrella of the central Congolese government in Leopoldville. The intention of the UN in Katanga through the second half of 1961 was clear – Katanga's secession was to be brought to an end. The American-sponsored government of Cyrille Adoula came to power in Leopoldville in August 1961. The Kennedy administration saw a united, stable, pro-Western Congo under Adoula as central to preventing the development of Communism in central Africa. The UN and Adoula began to work in parallel towards ending Katanga's secession. Ultimately, and to the annoyance of the superpowers, the UN unilaterally undertook military measures to end Katanga's secession. The most notorious of these measures, Operation Morthor, took place in Elisabethville, Katanga's capital city, in mid-September 1961.

Operation Morthor ended in failure and international controversy for the UN with military stalemate in Elisabethville and the Katangese government still in control of their province. Conscious of losing American and British support at a time when he had no Soviet support, Hammarskjöld distanced himself from Morthor. His senior colleagues in the UN Secretariat would later follow this line. However, they knew in advance that the operation would take place and that Hammarskjöld had authorized it. Under British and American pressure Hammarskjöld attempted to broker a ceasefire in Katanga; these efforts ended when he was killed as his aircraft crashed en-route to the negotiations.

The September fighting and Hammarskjöld's death shook the UN to the core. The Congo crisis had already placed Hammarskjöld under extreme personal strain during a period where he was also under direct Soviet pressure to resign. He had maintained strict overall personal command of ONUC and emerges from UN records on Congo and from his personal papers not as the neutral international civil servant with 'a halo, which is visible for a considerable distance', but as a calculating, pro-Western and at times Machiavellian operator – a side of his personality rarely commented on by his biographers.[2] Under Hammarskjöld's initiative the UN had arrived in Congo in July 1960 full of optimism that it could bring the ailing Congo back from the brink. After Morthor, and Hammarskjöld's death, the idealistic zeal of the previous summer vanished, to be replaced by fatigue and anxiety. Shortly before his death

Hammarskjöld described Congo as 'the sort of a problem-challenge that does stay in one's blood'.[3] His bringing the UN into Congo led the organization 'into a nightmare of great power rivalry, post-imperial chicanery and lethal score settling by the Congolese politicians'.[4] ONUC frustrated superpower and former colonial power interests and agendas in Congo and Katanga. Hammarskjold's actions worked contrary to their designs. Never again would the superpowers allow the UN, or its Secretary General, to wield such independent power.

ONUC's experience in Katanga had near fatal consequences for the UN system. It ground the UN and ONUC down, and, although a ceasefire in Katanga was agreed in late September 1961, the UN remained determined to end the province's secession. In early December 1961 substantial fighting erupted in Elisabethville after Katangese forces attempted to block UN freedom of movement. The UN response, Operation Unokat, in which Irish forces played a significant part, was more robust than Morthor. During Unokat ONUC surrounded Elisabethville, putting Katanga on the defensive. As a result of this operation, and growing United States pressure, Katanga's President Moïse Tshombe renounced the province's secession on 21 December 1961, but the secession did not end outright until 15 January 1963. The last ONUC troops departed from Congo in June 1964.

While there are many accounts of ONUC and the Congo crisis and studies of the role of the Irish Defence Forces in ONUC, this account concentrates on Defence Forces actions in Katanga, in particular on small-unit operations in Elisabethville during 1961.[5] It looks at events on the ground from the tactical perspective of Irish ONUC battalions and places them in their international, military, diplomatic and political contexts, with particular reference to how these actions were determined by the interests of the Irish government and the UN Secretariat. It situates these within the overall Cold War context of the Congo crisis.[6] The global tensions and crises of the Cold War often seemed very distant to ONUC forces in Katanga where instead the frictions and ill-feeling of local politics and the daily strains of peacekeeping predominated.

Involvement in ONUC was a major step forward for the Irish Defence Forces. In the doldrums since the end of 'the Emergency' of 1939 to 1945, it had become a garrison army lacking a sense of purpose. Service with ONUC provided a mission with an international sense of purpose at a time when Ireland, independent only since 1922 and joining the UN only in 1955, was expanding the parameters of its foreign policy outside the traditional concerns of British–Irish relations. However, involvement in ONUC exposed problems in Irish military training. Battalions deployed to Congo often lacked the experience necessary, particularly in early deployments, to undertake other than policing operations. Lightly armed peacekeepers were ultimately tasked to undertake military operations in often-hostile environments for which they were not properly equipped or briefed. The Defence Forces rarely trained in large formations and initial Irish ONUC battalions formed so quickly that team training was impossible. Senior officers did not know, or sometimes chose not to follow, best practice in operations. This was covered up by keeping men in the dark or by taking chances. Initially at least, little effort was made by the Defence Forces to learn from the experience of ONUC service and many veterans spoke of the lack of debriefing after returning to Ireland.

Irish forces in Katanga operated within the international structure of ONUC under Swedish control at brigade level (often known as 'sector' level) and above this under Indian control at command level. There were differences of military experience, practice and operating procedure, not to mention linguistic and temperamental differences, between these forces. For the Defence Forces, participation in ONUC was the first step in a long process of developing structures and procedures suitable for involvement in peacekeeping operations. If some of the responses of Irish contingents to events in Congo seem ill-conceived, it is well to remember what a step into the unknown Irish participation in ONUC was, and to recall the long and steep learning curve it began for the UN, as well as for the Defence Forces. Today's Irish peacekeepers have up-to-date equipment, specialist training, suitable uniforms and considerable understanding of the terrain they operate in. The journey to this point began in the rushed deployment of ONUC in the summer of 1960.

United Nations peacekeeping is often lauded as the most important international task of the Irish Defence Forces and a task for which the Irish temperament seems ideally suited. The defence forces of a neutral state that sees itself as having experienced colonization by a great power and having a missionary zeal – in Africa and beyond – would seem ideally suited to such UN operations. Yet there is reason to be critical of Dublin's Congo policy and its attitude towards ONUC. This is not because Dublin despatched battalions of ill-prepared troops into unknown territory – that was common practice across ONUC contributors and the UN Secretariat. It is rather because once Irish troops were despatched to Congo, Dublin showed little interest in them or in Congo except via declaratory rhetoric that served to bolster Ireland's position at the United Nations. Ireland's contribution to ONUC allowed the state to honour the obligations of UN membership. With Irish soldiers serving in Congo, Africa had never before been so important to Irish foreign policy. Yet after their deployment the Irish government did not seek greatly to understand the position Irish troops were in as part of ONUC or how they were faring in Congo. Only when Irish troops were in danger did Dublin show any real concern about their situation. Minister for External Affairs Frank Aiken actively sought to limit Dublin's understanding from Irish ONUC contingents of how events in Congo were developing because he felt that to ask them directly about UN operations would be disloyal to the UN.

Such idealism was commendable but ultimately naive and counterproductive, as, with communications with Congo difficult, it left the Irish civilian and military authorities largely in the dark on the operation of ONUC and reliant on second-hand and often inaccurate information. Though the Irish Permanent Mission to the UN was in close touch with other delegations and the Secretariat, it never got a clear insight into the Congo crisis. The UN, for which read Hammarskjöld, kept material received from ONUC largely to itself. When it came to supplying this material onwards the UN proved unable to provide the 'rapid and accurate information' required.[7] Ordinary UN delegates in New York were kept on the outside, even if they felt they had close connections with the Secretariat. Those, like the Irish UN mission, who had no independent sources of information from Congo, were often unaware of what ONUC was doing.

Ireland's ambassador to the UN during the Congo crisis, Frederick Boland, described ONUC as 'a matter of day-to-day, and even hour-to-hour impro-visation'.[8] Lt Col. Richard Bunworth, OC of the 33rd Irish Battalion, explained that 'above all else we lacked experience, and consequently it was difficult for us to visualize what a UN peacekeeping mission entailed'.[9] The same can be said for the UN; peacekeeping was a relatively untried concept in the summer of 1960. The idealistic enthusiasm of that summer gave way to deepening crisis. Congo collapsed and ONUC and the UN were sucked further into that crisis. In essence ONUC 'lacked every element that history now says is necessary for a successful peacekeeping mission'.[10] ONUC's four years in Congo ended 'peacekeeping's brief age of innocence'.[11] The mission became 'an operation that a generation of UN officials wanted to forget, or, if not forget, then never to repeat'.[12]

CHAPTER I

Intervention

Establishing ONUC

ON 30 JUNE 1960 Congo gained independence from Belgium. Soon afterwards the army, the 25,000-strong Force Publique, mutinied and it became clear that the incoming administration of Prime Minister Patrice Lumumba lacked experience of government. Many hoped that the unrest caused by the mutiny would fizzle out, but panic bred panic, attacks on Europeans spread and an exodus to Belgium began among the European population. The mutiny should have been anticipated as independence had brought no change to conditions of service in the Force Publique. It was allied to a deeper feeling that Belgium remained insistent on clinging to Congo. The façade of independence began to crumble and on the night of 9–10 July Belgian troops intervened to restore order. In Elisabethville, the capital of the southeastern province of Katanga, there was near panic. Belgian units held the airport and patrolled from the city to the nearby Northern Rhodesian border. Many officials from the Union Minière du Haut Katanga, the massive Belgian-owned copper mining conglomerate that had mines in the city area, and which was the major source of income for Katanga and of power in the province, left for the security of Northern Rhodesia.

Because of its mineral wealth Katanga was Congo's most economically developed province. It held almost 60 per cent of the world's cobalt reserves and almost 10 per cent of global copper deposits. It also had a large supply of uranium, a vital component in nuclear weapons. Powerful business concerns in Belgium with major interests in Katanga, in particular the Societé Générale bank and Union Minière, considered that following Congolese independence the creation of an independent Katanga was indispensable for the security of their shareholders. British businesses also had a substantial share in Union Minière and there were also those in Britain who favoured an independent Katanga securely controlled from Elisabethville.

Supported by these powerful interests provincial premier Moïse Tshombe declared Katanga's independence on 11 July 1960. Tshombe was pro-Western in the Cold War and Katanga's secession was covertly supported by Belgium, though no state formally recognized Katanga's independence. Brussels despatched military and civilian advisors to assist Tshombe. The province was 'all that the Belgians intended the Republic of the Congo should be, and still intended it should become'.[1] The Katangese premier had other ideas; Tshombe was pro-Belgian and was surrounded by Belgian advisors, but in Elisabethville as president of Katanga he was the sovereign ruler.

After Brussels' military intervention anti-Belgian feeling hardened in Congo as unrest spread. On 12 July Lumumba and Congolese president Joseph Kasavubu requested that the United Nations, of which Congo had become a member on 7 July, provide military assistance to 'protect the national territory of the Congo against the present external aggression which is a threat to international peace'.[2] United Nations Secretary General Dag Hammarskjöld realized that the ongoing instability in Congo would cause geopolitical, economic and regional volatility across Africa and could make the country a Cold War flashpoint. There was simply too much at stake internationally to leave Congo unassisted. Hammarskjöld did not desire any UN undertaking in the country requiring the use of force and anticipated despatching officers from the existing UNTSO mission in Gaza to assist re-organizing the Congolese army. Aware that food shortages were looming he also envisaged sending technical assistance to Congo but quietly ignored requests for military assistance.

On 13 July, on receipt of information from Ralph Bunche, his Special Representative in Congo, Hammarskjöld changed his mind. To Bunche, who was more opposed than Hammarskjöld to sending military forces to Congo, the country was deteriorating daily and 'only a "third military presence", which must be international in character, could now save the situation'.[3] Time was required to reform the Force Publique and an interim force was necessary to protect the European population and enable Belgian troops to withdraw. Hammarskjöld hoped the Security Council would swiftly decide to send a UN force to Congo. He would ask two or three African states to provide the core of the force, along with one European, one Asian and one transatlantic power. The troops would stay for a short period and remain resolutely neutral. ONUC was established the following day at an emergency meeting of the Security Council on 14 July 1960. France and Britain abstained, but the US and the USSR approved the resolution that also called on Belgium to withdraw its troops. ONUC would not interfere in internal Congolese politics. However, by their very presence in Congo ONUC would soon become, like it or not, a party to the internal political environment.

The use of article 99 of the UN Charter by Hammarskjöld to bring the Congo crisis to the Security Council on his own initiative was unusual.[4] ONUC was conducted by the Secretary General in a personal capacity. Hammarskjöld kept power to himself and rarely delegated authority beyond trusted key advisors. Secretary General since 1953, some believed Hammarskjöld 'had come to believe not only that the United Nations needed him, but that he and the UN had become one'.[5] He and his team 'moved fast, planned big and worked endlessly to assemble a force from the ends of the earth'.[6] The UN would hold the fort while Congo readied itself for statehood. ONUC would stabilize Congo and fill a potential regional power vacuum as Cold War adversaries and former European colonial powers in Africa circled to move into Congo for their own strategic and selfish ends.

Hammarskjold requested Tunisia, Morocco, Mali and Guinea to provide one battalion each for ONUC, and one in reserve. The Congolese government upset Hammarskjöld's arithmetic by asking Ghana for a contingent. ONUC deployed on 16 July 1960 as Tunisian and Ghanaian troops arrived in Leopoldville under the command of Gen. Henry Alexander, Chief of the Ghanaian Defence Forces. Lumumba and Kasavubu expected the UN to be an ally. Instead Alexander kept Belgian and Congolese forces apart. He did ensure however that the Force Publique co-operated with ONUC. A sign of the military-civilian distrust to come within ONUC, Bunche told journalists that he knew nothing about this agreement between Alexander and the Congolese. After Alexander proclaimed himself temporary Force Commander Hammarskjöld gave Bunche complete control of military matters in Congo. The UN was now operating on unfamiliar ground. ONUC began as a technical civilian mission dropped into Congo without a solid operational plan. It was now developing a military component under civilian control under the direct command of the Secretary General.

Ireland contributes to ONUC

Ireland's permanent mission to the United Nations sent an urgent telegram to Dublin on 14 July explaining that Hammarskjöld was establishing ONUC under the overall command of Swedish general Carl von Horn, who was serving with UNTSO in Jerusalem. Von Horn would take his orders directly from Hammarskjöld.[7] ONUC was likely to be confined to African states, but the possibility existed 'that other neutrals may be invited to join later'.[8] Dublin replied asking whether it was likely that Ireland would be approached to participate in ONUC. Pending a response, the Department of External Affairs instructed the Government Information Bureau to let it be known that Ireland had not been asked, but 'if we were, the request would be considered'.[9]

ONUC personnel soon numbered almost 5,000, but the UN needed twice that number. Hammarskjöld now approached non-African governments for assistance. Mindful of the need for a 'neutral European battalion',[10] on the evening of Saturday 16 July he requested that Ireland provide a battalion 'with light arms and equipped with normal supporting services' to join ONUC at the earliest possible date as part of the broadening of the force.[11]

The Department of External Affairs knew little about Congo; Ireland had no diplomatic mission in Leopoldville, its nearest embassy was Lagos, Nigeria, 1,800 kilometres away, and reports from New York contained simply what could be obtained through UN channels. Dublin lacked, and would continue to lack, good first-hand information on Congo, though Irish ambassador in Brussels, Denis McDonald, provided what he could glean from Belgian sources, in particular from British ambassador to Belgium Sir John Nicholls, who had Irish ancestors. There was little attempt to get information from other missions. Writing later to Sir Ian Maclennan, the British ambassador in Dublin, the Foreign Office remarked that the Irish embassy in London never discussed Congo with them.[12] Maclennan replied that no one at External Affairs discussed Congo with him either. Dublin's understanding of events in Congo was often limited to newspaper reports.

On the morning of Sunday, 17 July, Minister for Defence Kevin Boland rang the Chief of Staff of the Defence Forces, Maj. Gen. Seán MacEoin, with news of

Hammarskjöld's request and asked him to come to a hastily arranged meeting at Army Headquarters. The Defence Forces Plans and Operations Section had given little attention to large-scale UN deployments, envisaging that the Defence Forces could send no more than a reinforced company overseas – a force of between 250 and 300 men. MacEoin found the request for a full battalion – close to 650 men – 'staggering', but mindful of low morale in the Defence Forces and conscious of what he later called 'the sense of a lack of purpose in our minds' he suggested to Boland that Hammarskjöld's request be accepted.[13]

Officials from External Affairs and the Department of Defence met urgently to consider Ireland's contribution to ONUC. Tours of duty were to be limited to six months because of the prevailing tensions and climatic conditions in Congo. External Affairs began consultations with the UN Secretariat on the requirements of troops going to Congo. Evidence of the hasty origins of ONUC is the simple list of equipment suggested by the UN to Dublin. Troops were to bring 15 to 20 days rations, tents, bedding, cooking equipment and light arms. Indicative of the expected policing nature of the mission the Secretariat added that it would not be necessary to take too much ammunition. On arrival in Congo the UN would provide short trousers and shirts and UN helmets and armbands. Prior vaccination against smallpox, yellow fever, tetanus and typhoid was essential. Mosquito nets and water purifiers were recommended, New York suggesting that 'the men can boil the water before drinking if it is not provided'.[14] The despatch of an advance party to prepare the way for the battalion was not 'essential', but a small one was 'desirable'.[15]

The Secretariat was vague on the weapons the Irish battalion might bring. It was not necessary to take mortars, machine-guns or tear-gas grenades, 'but if it has them as part of its normal equipment, it could take them'.[16] There were some omissions from the UN list, External Affairs adding that soldiers 'would have to be protected from the sun' and they should 'take fatigue dress in order to be fully covered until they get "browned"'.[17] No details were given on communications or transport requirements though 'it would be much better if the unit could bring these with it'.[18] No one knew that Irish soldiers were not issued with tropical kit and had no suitable uniform for overseas service. They were to travel to the equatorial heat of Congo in their heavy Irish service dress. Whatever uncertainty the Defence Forces were facing into with their first overseas deployment, the United Nations was on a similarly steep learning curve and its preparations were as amateur. Dublin's and New York's accounts show that officials on each side had no detailed understanding of the situation in Congo, ONUC requirements or the equipment in use by the Irish Defence Forces, the majority of which dated from the Second World War.

Minister for External Affairs Frank Aiken brought Hammarskjöld's request for troops to cabinet on 19 July. He explained that Congo faced 'a state of near anarchy' and ONUC was being despatched to restore order.[19] Under the UN Charter it was 'incumbent' on Ireland to comply with Hammarskjold's request. Aiken felt it was 'desirable in the interests of the development along peaceful lines of the emerging states of Africa and the preservation of good relations between Europe and that continent that European countries should be associated with this effort to maintain peace and stability in the Congo'. He also emphasized the danger of Africa falling under the Communist sphere of influence. The choice of European states that could serve in Congo was limited and it was desirable that Ireland should play an active role in the force. The cabinet agreed to Hammarskjöld's request, empowered Aiken and Boland to take steps to comply with it, and the government prepared to rush legislation through the Oireachtas to enable Irish soldiers to undertake UN service. By the evening of 19 July the Secretary General's office knew that an Irish battalion would be despatched to Congo. The terms were vague, to 'assist in the preservation of order and protection of lives and property'; terms thought to preclude active intervention in hostilities between the parties in Congo.[20]

In the Dáil, Taoiseach Seán Lemass explained that Hammarskjöld had requested Irish involvement in ONUC as the state occupied a 'special position' in world affairs because of its impartial stance at the UN and its 'national traditions and outlook'.[21] Irish troops would 'command the confidence of all parties' to the conflict. This mantra of Ireland's experience of being colonized and of never having had an empire has since become a national article of faith in Irish involvement in peacekeeping. In Congo though, those among whom the Irish were to be deployed saw one European as the same as another, and were unaware of Ireland's long difficult relationship with Britain. Significantly, Lemass stressed that Irish ONUC troops would not be under Irish government control on UN deployment. This stance would be strictly adhered to, sometimes with negative consequences. He also emphasized that the force could not enforce specific political solutions or influence the political balance; it would 'have no role to play in any problem of a political nature in the Congo'.[22] Lemass added that if the force were used for actions not covered by the Security Council resolution it would be withdrawn. Newspaper reports explained that the battalion was going to Congo 'not to fight a war, but to carry out police action on behalf of the United Nations'.[23] It was a 'most politic remedy' to the growing disorder in Congo, but subsequent events in Katanga were to show how far from reality this view would be.[24]

As word spread that an overseas mission was in the offing Kevin Boland told Lemass that the number of soldiers who had indicated their intention to volunteer was 'much more than adequate'.[25] Each of the four military commands into which the Defence Forces was divided would provide one company for the Congo battalion. In total 3,000 out of the 9,000 serving officers and men in the Defence Forces volunteered for duty with ONUC. This 'tremendous response' to the request for troops was 'fantastic' and MacEoin thought 'to hell with it, whether they are well prepared or not, it's worth the chance to give seven or eight hundred men the opportunity of this experience'.[26] He caught the mood of the time, the 'can-do' attitude prevailing at the UN towards Congo during summer 1960. Then it seemed that Hammarskjöld's energy and optimism would carry the day for ONUC and Congo.

CHAPTER 2

The learning curve

ONUC enters Katanga

BY EARLY AUGUST 1960 Belgian troops were withdrawing from Congo with ONUC troops taking their place and ensuring local security. After Tshombe refused them access to Katanga, gaining ONUC peaceful entry into the province became Hammarskjöld's objective. Tshombe feared the UN would side with Lumumba and move to end Katanga's secession. There was little chance of this. Following heated exchanges Lumumba and Hammarskjöld disagreed over ONUC's purpose in Congo. Hammarskjöld hoped to end Katanga's secession peacefully by political means, but Lumumba expected ONUC to assist the ANC, the Armée National Congolaise (formerly the Force Publique), in ending Katanga's secession. Their talks were difficult and Hammarskjöld thought Lumumba 'a very unsatisfactory figure'.[1] Relations between the two men broke down irretrievably through summer 1960 and the Secretary General felt it would be impossible to get Lumumba to meet Tshombe. It was as difficult in Katanga. A fed-up Bunche reported to Hammarskjöld after difficult negotiations with Katangese officials and their Belgian advisers that there was 'no assistance or support for the UN effort ... and no attempt to interpret it honestly, was forthcoming from any, repeat, any source in the province'.[2] Hammarskjöld was also bitter about the role played by local Belgians in Katanga and felt they had sabotaged the UN operation in the province. He sought a Security Council resolution to enable ONUC to enter Katanga. If agreement could be reached with Tshombe, Hammarskjöld envisaged ONUC forces deploying to the province, allowing Belgian troops to withdraw to their base at Kamina in central Katanga and from there to withdraw completely from Congo.

ONUC's entry into Katanga was to be peaceful, but Bunche was worried about Tshombe calling out what he called 'the painted-face, spear-carrying warriors' who could 'arouse the crowds and set off a conflict', causing UN troops to retaliate in self-defence.[3] Dublin instructed the Secretariat that it wished to be consulted before Irish troops were included in any ONUC force entering Katanga 'against the active opposition' of Elisabethville.[4] On 8 August Hammarskjöld got his Security Council resolution. It called for Belgium to withdraw from Katanga, declared the necessity of ONUC entering Katanga and reaffirmed that the UN would not influence internal Congolese affairs. Hammarskjöld departed for Elisabethville and Frederick Boland learned confidentially from Hammarskjöld's executive assistant Andrew Cordier that with Tshombe's concurrence the

Secretary General would lead an advance force of 220 Swedish troops into Elisabethville on 12 August.

Despite this success Hammarskjöld felt Congo's future looked 'very bad and worsening'.[5] The delay getting into Katanga reduced ONUC's momentum across the country. Lumumba was incensed that Hammarskjöld led ONUC into Katanga without an accompanying representative from Leopoldville. He called for the withdrawal of African units from ONUC in protest. Hammarskjöld told African contributors to ONUC that if they supported Lumumba he would pass his personal mandate for ONUC over to the Security Council with the suggestion that the mandate would then become a much tougher operation allowing for the use of force.

Though UN policy remained to reintegrate Katanga into Congo the UN appeared to recognize Tshombe's government when ONUC entered Katanga. ONUC had agreed with Elisabethville that after its deployment primary responsibility for provincial security would remain with the Katangese. ONUC was unable to interfere in local security arrangements. This was a particular problem in north Katanga where Katangese Gendarmerie and the Baluba tribe were engaged in a civil war. ONUC tried to keep the sides apart but was not an effective intermediary and Irish peacekeepers were drawn into the conflict.

The 32nd Battalion in Kivu and Katanga

The 689 Irish soldiers chosen for ONUC service became a new battalion, the 32nd Infantry Battalion, under the command of Lt Col. Mortimer 'Murt' Buckley. From Brussels McDonald reported that King Baudouin was 'delighted with the response in Ireland to the UNO appeal for a contingent of forces. He said that they were "the best troops we had" and said we should send all those who volunteered!'[6] The Irish ambassador to France reported that the deployment was welcomed in NATO circles as a 'splendid gesture' and 'a step of major significance in our post-war history'. It gave a

> positive and valuable content to our attitude of being non-committed, which is certainly not neutrality, much less 'neutralism', but may perhaps be expressed by the Swedish word 'alliansfrihet', or freedom from alliances, and means … that we endeavour to judge issues on their individual merits and to take a constructive attitude without reference to prior commitments, save, of course, the United Nations Charter itself.[7]

Led by Buckley and watched by emotional crowds the 32nd Battalion paraded through Dublin on 27 July as Lemass took the salute. The battalion then flew from Baldonnell military airport in American Air Force transports and the first contingent arrived at Goma in northeast Kivu province on 29 July to a peaceful reception from an excited local population.[8] With the exception of B-Company which flew to Kindu, 250 miles to the southwest, the complete 32nd Battalion arrived in Goma by 31 July. Battalion Operations Officer Comdt M.J. O'Brien reported how 'the people see in our arrival hopes for a new deal which will improve their lot'.[9] Until mid-November 1960 the battalion operated in Kivu, principally in Goma, Kindu and Bukavu. It then redeployed almost 600 miles to the south to Kamina Base and Kaminaville in central Katanga where, until January 1961, it was responsible for base security, the security of Kilubi power station to the north and guarding trains en-route to Luena to the south.

The 32nd Battalion spent much time calming apprehensive local communities and showing a UN presence in trouble spots. As it was thinly spread the battalion often could only maintain a token presence in key areas. Patrols visited populated areas, especially those garrisoned by ANC troops, as frequently as possible and met with local leaders to deal with problems. The battalion also worked with the World Health Organization and gathered intelligence for the ONUC Force Commander. This intelligence role concerned estimating the order of battle, locations and strengths of ANC forces and any remaining Belgian forces, and gathering information on road and rail infrastructure.

The 32nd Battalion Unit History considered that 'by and large the population of Kivu province displayed a great friendliness towards the 32nd Battalion ... the ANC on the whole were pretty well behaved'.[10] Battalion officers made useful liaison contacts with the Ugandan police and the King's African Rifles and discussed security within Kivu and border security between Congo and Uganda. Their Ugandan contacts felt that the Irish 'seem to have gained the confidence of the Congolese Administration, though the Force Publique continue to remain suspicious of them'.[11] Nevertheless Irish morale suffered as the battalion saw little real soldiering in Kivu, and the lack of provisions from home also caused morale to flag. A British intelligence report summarized that Irish troops were 'good but their morale is dropping. The troops are not keen on overseas service'.[12]

The 32nd Battalion had a peaceful tour of duty. Yet its Unit History offered salutary advice for those who thought that Irish troops, coming from a country that had suffered colonization, would be acceptable in Congo: 'The intransigence of [the ANC] was due to a large extent to ignorance, fear and a wide distrust of white men in general – to them all white men were Belgians and all Belgians were enemies'.[13] The 33rd Battalion would find out to its cost in north Katanga that other local forces shared this attitude.

The 33rd Battalion in north Katanga

On 30 July Hammarskjöld requested a second battalion from Ireland to improve ONUC's military capability and ensure a greater balance between African and non-African elements in the force. He explained to Lemass that in choosing troops from Europe, the UN was limited to Swedish and Irish troops due to political and technical considerations. The Department of External Affairs wanted to accept Hammarskjöld's request. The Department of Defence wanted to wait until the experience of the 32nd Battalion became clearer. Resources were strained by ONUC deployment and two battalions were all the Defence Forces could hope to send to Congo. MacEoin knew there would be problems in the

Defence Forces with almost 1,400 troops overseas, but he balanced that against the possibility that the Congo deployment would be short-lived and the chance of overseas service was worth taking while it lasted.

Aiken emphasized Hammarskjöld's point to cabinet when seeking approval for the second battalion, explaining that due to Cold War alliances and the colonial past of many European states, the choice facing the UN was limited. He added that if the UN failed in Congo there would be 'disastrous consequences for the Congo and Africa' and 'the value of the organisation as a mediator may be compromised and the danger to world peace correspondingly increased'.[14] On 4 August the cabinet agreed to provide a second ONUC battalion. Lemass told Hammarskjöld that Ireland 'keenly appreciate[d] your difficulties' and was 'anxious to cooperate to the utmost in helping you meet them'.[15] The new battalion, the 33rd Infantry Battalion, would deploy to Congo as quickly as possible.

With a second Irish battalion Congo-bound the question arose of the overall control of the 32nd and 33rd Battalions. When two or more battalions are grouped tactically together they form a brigade and brigade-level control for the two Irish ONUC battalions was now required. In early August Col. Harry Byrne was posted to ONUC Headquarters in Leopoldville and was subsequently appointed OC 9th Brigade, comprising the 32nd and 33rd Battalions. Byrne's command expanded when in mid-August ONUC Force Commander Gen. von Horn placed him in charge of a new sub-command at Elisabethville that had responsibility for Katanga and Kivu – an area the size of France – known as Sub-Command Eastern Provinces (SCOMEP).[16] SCOMEP was to 'provide adequate assurance to the Belgian and African population' of Katanga and Kivu that 'the UN will provide an ample measure of security and prevent panic' in the area.[17] Given the delicate negotiations required to get ONUC into Katanga, the appointment of an Irish officer to head SCOMEP was a significant sign of UN confidence in Irish abilities. Byrne commanded a combined force of Swedish, Moroccan, Malian, Ethiopian and Irish soldiers numbering in excess of 4,800.

Even at this early stage the Irish military were learning the lessons of UN deployment. External Affairs asked Irish diplomats in New York to 'request UN in light of experience first battalion to advise any changes necessary in organization, equipment and supply arrangements of second battalion to ensure that it is suitable for its purpose'.[18] Conscious of the growing public interest in Ireland in ONUC, the Department of Defence asked for 'periodic official information from ONUC HQ on supply position, health and morale of Irish troops'.[19] Irish Liaison Officer with ONUC Lt Col. F.E. Lee suggested to the Defence Forces Director of Plans and Operations that the 33rd Battalion should bring long-range radio equipment capable of operating over 1,000 miles and that it should not bring Vickers machine-guns or 81mm mortars. Lee was correct when it came to communications, but his decision on weapons had a serious impact on the ability of the 33rd Battalion to operate in a robust manner and Lee's 'advice was to prove faulty as the history of [the 33rd Battalion] and later units was to prove'.[20] Lee was on firmer ground when he suggested that each company in the new battalion 'should be fully self-contained and tactically loaded in aircraft fully armed', he also explained that twenty landrovers or jeeps were required per battalion and tropical kit should be issued in Ireland.[21]

On 17 August, the 706 officers and men of the 33rd Battalion, under the command of Lt Col. Richard Bunworth, departed for Congo. The battalion was initially bound for Kivu, but with ONUC having just entered Katanga it was instead sent to Kamina Base in central Katanga. After some days at Kamina Base they moved to northeast Katanga replacing a mutinous Malian battalion in the town of Albertville (now Kalemie) on the shores of Lake Tanganyika. Thereafter the battalion operated from Albertville and Manono, 250 kilometres southwest of Albertville, between Baluba and Katangese Gendarmerie within the north Katanga civil war zone.

A-Company 33rd Battalion under the command of Comdt Louis Hogan remained at Kamina Base, eventually taking it over from its Belgian commander on 29 August. The Irish takeover was a significant event as with it all Belgian troops left Katanga, though this left the UN to find a way to remove Belgian technicians and advisors who remained and also to remove the former Belgian officers who commanded the Gendarmerie. A-Company was later joined at Kamina by C-Company, 32nd Battalion and a Swedish company as SCOMEP strengthened the base's defences and created the Kamina Base Group from these companies in anticipation that the ANC might try to seize the airbase. Kamina Base Group operated from September to November 1960, after which the 32nd Battalion provided the overall defence of Kamina Base. In the Defence Forces' journal *An Cosantóir* Capt. R.A. Hinchy recalled A-Company 32nd Battalion, who were responsible for ground and runway defence, 'toiling always against time in the blinding heat and glare reflected from the white tarmac' when an aircraft was expected, and B-Company and C-Company 'standing their lonely night vigil in remote clearings in the bush' guarding the perimeter.[22] Hinchy added that 'a stream of reports' arrived at Kamina Base 'detailing in the most alarming terms Baluba strengths and operations in the villages to the North and East of Kamina'.[23]

In late August the Baluba rebellion against Elisabethville spread across northern Katanga. As responsibility for order in northern Katanga rested with the Gendarmerie, and as ONUC could not intervene in internal conflict, the UN was powerless to act. The 33rd Battalion had little prior knowledge of the situation in northern Katanga or of 'the delicate balance' there between Jason Sendwe's Balubakat party and Tshombe's Conakat party and their armed forces.[24] They as yet knew nothing 'of the extreme savagery with which they would meet each other on frequent occasions'.[25] As Col. Justin McCarthy, ONUC Deputy Chief of Staff and Chief of Operations, explained:

> The situation in Northern Katanga has gradually been deteriorating for some weeks as a result of antagonism between the Gendarmerie and the local Congolese (mainly Baluba and Balubakat tribes). This antagonism has arisen because of the harsh and brutal measures adopted by the Gendarmerie in repressing lawlessness by the local people, and in turn the

almost barbaric actions displayed by the tribesmen against members of the Gendarmerie in reprisal.[26]

The 33rd Battalion received no political briefing before leaving Dublin. They did not know that north Katanga was generally Balubakat and the south Conakat. It was clear to them nevertheless that Katanga was in a disturbed state. As 33rd Battalion units moved northeast from Kamina the nearly 600 kilometres to Albertville they encountered 'a great wake of pessimism' that 'engulfed' those they met; 'stories and rumours were rife, especially amongst the European population' of disturbances in Albertville.[27] The battalion could not stop Gendarmerie attacks, it could not help the European population and it could not help the Baluba. The 33rd Battalion was forced to adopt a 'policy of negotiation and non-use of force' – a policy which would cost the battalion nine fatalities in November near the village of Niemba.

In the weeks after its deployment to Albertville the 33rd Battalion's presence did have a positive impact on local life as calm returned to the city. This was a honeymoon period and later in their deployment the 33rd Battalion encountered open hostility from European and African populations. Further afield they deployed 250 kilometres southwest from Albertville to the town of Manono and the village of Piana-Mwanga a further 60 kilometres southeast to guard a power station. The battalion also undertook long-range patrols and train guards from Albertville west to Kabalo and further southwest to Kamina.

Lumumba now had 'only one thought in his head – how to get his hands on Katanga'.[28] ANC forces had already intervened in the civil war in Kasai province to the west of Katanga, but they ran out of steam. Lumumba felt a further military adventure would strengthen Leopoldville and allow it to deal with Tshombe. ANC troops invaded northern Katanga in late August 1960, their movements threatening the position of the 32nd Battalion as they moved. In response, on Hammarskjöld's instructions, military commanders across Congo were given authority to intervene to maintain law and order. Maintaining control of airfields was of specific concern and the 32nd Battalion blocked runways at Goma and Kindu airports to prevent ANC troops taking off. They sought clarification from SCOMEP on the use of force. SCOMEP replied that 'troops are entitled to use force in self-defence. Self-defence applies to holding positions which are necessary for the UN forces'.[29] The ANC invasion petered out and a ceasefire was declared, but tension remained high as civil war continued between pro-Tshombe and Baluba forces.

In discussion with 'an authoritative informant' on the night of 4 September, Frederick Boland learned that Lumumba's overthrow was imminent.[30] The following day central government disintegrated further in Congo, as Kasavubu dismissed Lumumba and Lumumba fired Kasavubu. Boland concluded a despatch to Dublin that Congo was 'heading for a situation in which nothing short of a UN trusteeship will avert disaster'. But 'no one can see far ahead. The future is still very obscure and uncertain'. Boland was correct. On 14 September ANC Chief of Staff Col. Joseph Mobutu seized power in a coup in Leopoldville, placing Lumumba under house arrest. In the Cold War divide the West backed Kasavubu and Mobutu, while the Soviets backed Lumumba. Hammarskjöld thought that Lumumba was an 'outstanding political leader, but he was highly neurotic and dangerous'.[31] Following a Western, anti-Communist and anti-Lumumba line, the Secretary General considered that 'the UN must safeguard itself so far as possible against the possibility that Lumumba may emerge as the victor. But his future plans [were] based on the assumption that this can be prevented, and that a government with which it is possible to do business on a reasonable basis may emerge'.[32] A complex constitutional crisis with immense Cold War ramifications was played out in Leopoldville over the coming months. The UN hoped to get Congo's parliament to meet, but legislature and executive were paralyzed.

Tension continued to rise in north Katanga. In mid-September 140 men from B-Company 33rd Battalion commanded by Comdt Pearse Barry found themselves in a hostile situation in Manono where they controlled the airport and patrolled the town. Manono was the Tshombe government's administrative centre in the Baluba area of north Katanga and when it was occupied by Baluba forces the Gendarmerie refused to retreat. The town was also the location of the Geomines tin mine, an offshoot of Union Minière, and was of strategic economic value. Bunworth flew to Manono to assess the situation, bringing with him a reinforcement platoon. Barry had plans to protect the local European population and he negotiated the evacuation of the pro-Tshombe administration. This annoyed the Baluba who could not understand why the Irish had not shot those who had killed many Baluba. Anti-UN feeling ran high and it was a difficult time for B-Company.

After the Baluba uprising in Manono B-Company patrols tried to develop goodwill and show a UN presence to bring stability back to the area. 33rd Battalion units in Albertville did likewise. West of Albertville on the road south from Niemba Irish long-range patrols passed through burned-out villages and encountered a jittery local Baluba population, many of whom had formed armed war parties hostile to ONUC. On 4 October a patrol under Comdt Keogh, passing west by train from Albertville to Nyunzu, was stopped sixty miles west of Albertville close to Niemba station by an extremely aggressive and volatile 500-strong Baluba war party and was forced to return to Albertville. ONUC reported 'situation in Niemba bad. The railway and the road are blocked … patrol is in need of helicopter for observation of the area'.[33]

A further attempt by Keogh's patrol to reach Nyunzu by road came up against the same Baluba war band but reached Niemba on 6 October, finding the town ablaze, ransacked and abandoned. On 8 October 33rd Battalion Head-quarters instructed Lt Kevin Gleeson and his No. 2 Platoon from A-Company, 33rd Battalion, to garrison Niemba. Gleeson wrote to his wife – 'imagine yourself in a "ghost town" with 38 others and surrounded by madmen'.[34] Cpl James Lynch noted in his diary that 'all the shops in the village were burnt out … the place smelt of death'.[35] A patrol under Capt. Flynn continued south to Kiambi following the trail of destruction left by the Baluba, encountering groups of hostile Baluba at roadblocks and in towns. 'The Long Patrol', as Flynn's patrol became known, returned to Albertville via Pweto on 13 October, covering 1,200 miles over nine days and seeing the impact on the local population of the civil war in northern Katanga. As 'The Long Patrol' was underway an Irish train guard moving from Kamina to Albertville learned of the sack of Niemba after halting at Kabalo on 6 October. In Kabalo the situation was tense. Baluba attacked the town on 9 October and the Irish heard of numerous murders and atrocities. A fortnight later an Irish patrol searched Kabalo and saw 'the full extent of Baluba depredations'.[36] They reported that 'Belgian houses had been looted … houses belonging to alleged Conakats had been razed and if the Balubas were to be believed, their inhabitants liquidated'.[37]

On 17 October Col. Byrne, Hammarskjöld's military advisor Gen. Rikhye, UN Representative in Katanga Ian Berendsen and Tshombe agreed to establish two neutral zones in north Katanga, one including Nyunzu, Kabalo and Manono, with Irish and Ethiopian troops placed in the zones. The UN hoped the Gendarmerie would not attack Baluba within these zones and ONUC would defend certain areas within the zones and keep infrastructure open. However, to the Baluba ONUC troops were protecting Katangese interests, and to the European population the UN did nothing to disarm the ANC and other hostile elements. It was a hopeless task. As Byrne put it: 'In an area where the white man is anathema to the Balubakat warrior it has been difficult to depend upon the Blue Helmet and UN goodwill as a means of protection'.[38] The neutral zones simply indicated the greatest danger zones in northern Katanga and, Tshombe hoped, transferred 'the Katanga situation into [UN] hands when he had lost control, hoping no doubt that we will fall into the trap of imitating the methods of his Gendarmerie'.[39]

North Katanga remained tense with 'bloody encounters' between Baluba and Gendarmerie.[40] A goodwill tour by Byrne and Balubakat leader Sendwe brought some respite, but the area remained volatile. The twenty-strong 33rd Battalion post at Piana-Mwanga under Capt. Harry Gouldsborough undertook foot and jeep patrols to let locals see that ONUC was friendly and 'tried to impress upon them that while UN troops were there to help them continue a normal way of life, they also intended there would be NO fighting in the area'.[41] The Piana-Mwanga outpost was in a very volatile region of northern Katanga and patrols into surrounding areas encountered great hostility and considerable danger. On a patrol to Kiambi Gouldsborough and Tpr Kealy accompanied the local Balubakat leader through roadblocks manned by tribesmen 'and could hear the Swahili word for "KILL" being shouted'.[42] A night patrol of seven all-ranks in one jeep twenty miles south to the village of Kipaila to secure the local ferry encountered hostile tribesmen when at a large roadblock Baluba refused to let the patrol pass. The patrol 'saw many campfires in the bush and soon there seemed to be hordes of tribesmen yelling and shouting all around. They appeared to have been drinking palm wine and were in a most unfriendly mood'.[43] After negotiation the patrol was allowed through to Kipaila accompanied by Baluba warriors. One member of the patrol, battalion chaplain Father Shinnors, 'said afterwards that he was saying his last prayers'.[44]

On receiving a report from Gouldsborough that the village of Kronkole, 80 kilometres to the southeast of Piana-Mwanga, had been wiped out by the Gendarmerie, Lt Vincent Blythe led a patrol to investigate. They left Manono on 4 November in two pick-ups and experienced considerable difficulty en-route getting by felled trees and over broken bridges. ONUC patrols in this region were cautious and 'where bridges were broken or roads were blocked' patrols would 'halt the jeep 200 to 300 yards from the obstacle and the Post Commander covered by a Gustav man went forward to investigate while the remainder of the patrol covered them both'.[45] Only when the commander was satisfied that the area was safe would the patrol move forward. A final broken bridge was impassable and the patrol moved forward on foot the last four kilometres to Kronkole.

Kronkole, located between Balubakat and Conakat territories, was deserted and burned out and 'seemed to have been abandoned in a great hurry as cooking pots, beds, chairs, manioc, etc. were left behind in the houses'.[46] There had been no fighting and there were no dead or wounded. Blythe brought the patrol back to Manono by a different route and 'found the local Balubakat population very much on the defensive'. On their return journey they again had to repair bridges and make detours. The patrol was once surrounded by 'some fifty armed natives' who, after discussions with the patrol's interpreter, produced the timbers of a bridge the patrol needed to cross. Blythe's small patrol was extremely lucky as events near Niemba days later showed.

Niemba

In early November Lt Gleeson's platoon in Niemba reported roadblocks being constructed near their outpost. Gleeson knew his men were tense as the atmosphere deteriorated in the town. Unknown to them a strong group of Baluba warriors was operating in their vicinity. Bunworth ordered patrols north from Manono and south from Niemba to clear Baluba roadblocks. On the morning of 7 November, Comdt Barry took a patrol north from Manono and Comdt P.D. Hogan moved south from Niemba. Hogan's twenty-strong patrol was reinforced by twenty men from Gleeson's platoon. By midday they reached a dismantled bridge on the River Luwuyeye at an area known as Tundula, encountering armed Baluba close by.[47] Repairing the bridge would take several hours and Bunworth ordered Hogan back to Albertville.[48]

Gleeson was ordered to reconnoitre the same route the following day. With ten men in a Land Rover and a pickup truck Gleeson set off at 1330 for Tundula and the bridge on the Luwuyeye River with instructions to then move south to Kinsukulu. Gleeson had no radio and when his patrol failed to return by 2100 a search party led by Lt Jeremiah Enright set out from Albertville.[49] They were joined by two helicopters and an aircraft. They expected that Gleeson's return had been delayed by roadblocks. Enright's patrol arrived at the Luwuyeye River crossing at 0630 on 9 November and found spent rounds, arrows, blood and five bodies. A shocked Pte Joseph Fitzpatrick emerged from the bush. He explained that at 1500 the previous day Gleeson's patrol had been ambushed by a hostile

Baluba party who were waiting for them at the bridge.[50] In the ensuing skirmish the Irish 'defended stubbornly and when [there was] no further hope of concentrated action scattered into bush which borders [the] road on both sides'.[51] Baluba killed 9 of the 11 members of the patrol who in turn had killed 15 Baluba and wounded 10. These were the same Baluba that Hogan had encountered.

News of the ambush arrived in Leopoldville mid-morning on 9 November and was immediately sent to New York. Dublin was informed directly by the 33rd Battalion. Rikhye cabled Hammarskjöld of the 'tragic news' and the Secretary General replied that the ambush was 'shocking and tragic'.[52] A UN spokesman in Leopoldville, quoting Sendwe, suggested that the Baluba thought the Irish were Belgian members of the Gendarmerie. Byrne and his Irish colleagues at SCOMEP were 'surprised' by this statement as 'for at least six weeks no Gendarmerie patrol had been in [the] area of [the] ambush and that road had been regularly patrolled by Irish troops'.[53] The 1961 trial of a number of those involved in the ambush showed that the Baluba were waiting to ambush an Irish patrol. This was borne out by contemporary accounts that showed that Gleeson had attempted to parley with the tribesmen, but he and his patrol were 'immediately fired upon by many arrows from either side of the road. Most of the patrol including the officer were hit and injured immediately. Officer ordered men to take cover and fire. It appears patrol overwhelmed by numbers'.[54] This was a premeditated ambush, not a chance event. The Baluba in charge of the ambush, ex-Premier Sergeant Lualaba, had placed his men in ambush positions at the bridge. The Baluba chief in the area, Kasanga-Niemba, told Lualaba's men 'ou bien les soldats irlandais rebrousseront chemin, ou bien c'est la guerre et vous vaincrez ou vous mourez'.[55]

After picking up Fitzpatrick, Enright reported large numbers of Baluba close by in the bush, and, having radio contact with Albertville, he was instructed to return to Niemba. The following afternoon two search patrols, one an Irish-Ethiopian group and the other a 37-strong Irish patrol led by Capt. Crowley recovered the bodies Enright and his men had located. A final patrol, another Irish-Ethiopian force, led by Hogan, returned to the ambush site on 10 November and made contact with the second ambush survivor, Pte Thomas Kenny. They recovered three more bodies.[56]

Also on 10 November an Irish patrol south of the ambush site encountered ten wounded Baluba who had participated in the ambush and recovered the vehicles used by Gleeson's patrol. The patrol 'met a confusing situation amongst the villagers on the road to Kabeke, ranging from bewilderment to hostility. The Chief of Kiambi stated that people now accepted that there was a clash between Niemba Baluba and the UN.'[57] Edward Burke's suggestion that the Baluba were suspicious of white soldiers and the UN is most plausible, in particular his point that 'the Baluba would certainly have resented the Irish for removing their roadblocks, guarding the trains and assets of Katangan companies and the contact they had with the Gendarmerie.'[58] The 33rd Battalion evacuated Niemba on 11 November. The men at Niemba had become nervous, the area remained volatile and there was a high likelihood of a Baluba attack.

Byrne cabled Berendsen on 9 November after receiving news of the ambush that 'our horizon is clouded on this day of anguish'.[59] There was talk of sending Byrne back to Dublin for debriefing. Though he did not return, Hammarskjöld thought it was a good idea as following the 'recent extremely bad luck of Irish contingent ... and need for early action by Irish authorities on [the] provision of a replacement battalion' a short trip to Dublin would be a good move.[60] Hammarskjöld was worried that the ambush might lead to Ireland's withdrawal from ONUC. The Niemba ambush was the largest Defence Forces loss of life during ONUC deployment. There was a national outpouring of grief as the dead were returned to Dublin for burial. Half a million people lined the route of the funeral procession. However, despite Hammarskjöld's fears, the Irish contingent was not withdrawn.

Discussing what had happened at Niemba with Hammarskjöld Rikhye explained that Gleeson and his men 'walked into the ambush due [to] inadequate caution and training'. He emphasized that their 'action thereafter [was] very brave' and added that while he had 'every confidence in Irish to improve, in view of anti-European attitude of tribesmen, it [was] desirable to employ non-European troops with more experience' in north Katanga.[61] Niemba showed the Defence Forces that weapons, training and tactics needed to be modernized to meet the conditions of UN service. Gleeson's patrol had been too trusting of the Baluba. They had left their most significant weapons – two Bren light machine-guns – out of reach. The patrol was too small in number and weak in armament, had no radio communications and once engaged with the Baluba had become separated. It was not prepared for what it encountered and was caught off guard. Yet Gleeson was acting in accordance with UN orders not to use force, to talk with locals and to adopt a friendly demeanour. The experience of the 33rd Battalion in north Katanga shows that an ambush similar to Niemba could have happened on any number of occasions.

The Irish attitude to patrolling became more assertive after Niemba. In a later interview Enright, by then a brigadier general, explained that 'we weren't going to permit anything like that to happen again'. Referring to a platoon advance on a hill he explained – 'when we got near the top of the hill, there was a lot of dense growth there, we opened fire before we moved up to ensure nobody was there, our attitude had changed. We were prepared to fire.'[62] SCOMEP's attitude changed too. After Niemba Byrne issued 'Directive No. 4' to all unit commanders stressing they were to 'be prepared to meet attack at all times' and that 'men should be imbued with the offensive spirit so that they will be mentally prepared should the occasion arise'.[63] Posts were to 'be capable of destroying any attack' and patrols 'should be sufficiently strong to deter any attempt at attack'. In particular patrol commanders were to 'prepare a battle drill and instruct all ranks what to do in the event of being ambushed. An ambush is most likely to take place at a road block'. Niemba was never mentioned, yet the ambush pervaded what Byrne had written.

The tone of the memorandum and the orders to adopt a 'firmer and more vigilant attitude ... in the face of armed tribesmen' annoyed some of Byrne's colleagues, in particular Rikhye.[64] Rikhye also exchanged strong words with Berendsen over the latter's call for 'a full appraisal of our pacification methods' of the 'primitive and barbaric tribesmen' in north Katanga.[65] Rikhye retorted that ONUC should follow 'peaceful means', go no further than maintaining full alert and showing 'the maximum display of force possible'.[66] Berendsen replied that he 'was certainly not proposing indiscriminate use of force by UN troops which moreover our units would not be prepared to apply'.[67] Byrne was asked to amend his more aggressive instructions.

After Niemba there was quiet resolve in Ireland to remain in ONUC. On 14 November the UN requested that Dublin replace its two ONUC battalions with one battalion in January 1961. The cabinet agreed to send a new battalion, the '34th Irish Battalion', but the implementation of the decision would depend on the circumstances in Congo which were 'so fluid as to counsel prudence in definitively committing ourselves to send a new contingent.'[68] On 3 December Dublin informed the Secretariat that the 34th Battalion would be sent to Congo to replace the 32nd and 33rd Battalions. Lemass telegrammed Aiken in New York that the new battalion would go 'unless, between now and date of departure, conditions so change as to require reconsideration'.[69] There had been much talk in late 1960 of national contingents being withdrawn from ONUC, but Ireland remained committed to the operation. Dublin advised the UN that the new battalion would be ready for duty on 10 January 1961. The UN expected that it would initially be located at Kamina Base and Kaminaville. Such was the pressure on the Defence Forces caused by this deployment that many in the 34th Battalion had only finished basic training when they found themselves en-route to Congo.

The lessons of six months with ONUC

After Niemba the 33rd Battalion regrouped in Albertville, and the 32nd Battalion remained at Kamina. The 34th Battalion would not arrive until January 1961. The rotation of battalions should have led to an examination of the lessons of six months in Congo. Though small changes were made from battalion to battalion based on experience gained, learning from overseas missions was not in the culture of the 1960s Defence Forces. No attempt was made to debrief contingents on their return from Congo. There was no discussion of the political and military lessons of ONUC service or the fundamental lesson that, as B-Company, 33rd Battalion found out in north Katanga, the 'United Nations meant nothing to the Congolese people ... they had never heard of the organisation'.[70] If they had not heard of the UN, there was little chance they had heard of Ireland and that furthermore 'whites, even white UN troops, were not welcome'.

Lessons from ONUC service were learned painstakingly slowly. Defence Forces' service dress was made of a heavy fabric known as 'Bull's Wool', which was completely unsuitable for the tropics. The experience of battalions in Congo of these uniforms and the incidence of heatstroke caused by its weight made provision of light-weight tropical uniforms for the 34th Battalion essential. The Department of Defence had been 'badly let down by the UN' as the tropical kit it provided was poor quality.[71] Unable to solve this problem speedily, the 34th and later the 35th Battalion while dropping the 'Bull's Wool', wore these ill-fitting poor-quality UN-issue uniforms with a consequent negative impact on morale.

The manner of deployment of battalions was queried. More comprehensive advance parties were needed to allow the quicker deployment of battalions on arrival in Congo. Each battalion should deploy en masse to one location and re-organize thereafter, not fly in to several different locations. Key headquarters personnel tended to be loaded onto the first flight from Ireland and this would incapacitate the battalion should that aircraft be lost. Individual aircraft instead should be loaded tactically, allowing self-contained companies to deploy in combat formation if required. This was sorted out and the 36th Battalion later successfully deployed under fire in combat formation on arrival in Elisabethville in December 1961.

More attention needed to be given to headquarters staff and the 33rd Battalion Unit History highlighted that superior units should not be staffed 'at the expense of field units'.[72] This led to a doubling up of posts at battalion headquarters and of headquarters ceasing to function smoothly. The practice was not ended and when it came to the crunch in Elisabethville in September 1961, 35th Battalion Headquarters was seriously depleted when hostilities broke out, as officers had been deployed to higher posts without replacement from Ireland. Communications by radio had been problematic and signals personnel were required in the advance party to identify and sort out hitches. Indian operators kept the Irish battalions in touch with ONUC Headquarters in Leopoldville but battalions needed their own rear radio links. At unit level, Niemba showed that small patrols with no radio communications would not suffice. Language deficiencies at all levels were flagged and the shortage of interpreters was clear. Language courses were run during deployments, but no long-term language training was established during or after ONUC deployment when even a conservative assessment suggested that a basic proficiency in French would be useful in international missions. Related was the need for all battalion members to receive a detailed political briefing on the area they were being deployed to and to show greater awareness of political intelligence. Many simply did not realize it was significant; one officer recalling how an important move by Tshombe from Elisabethville in September 1961 had taken place 'without as much as a word from Irish troops' located nearby.[73]

The 32nd and 33rd Battalions had taken too few Land Rovers and no heavy transport. Long wheel-base Land Rovers were suggested as a solution, though their value on narrow Congolese roads was debatable. The 33rd Battalion suggested taking ten Land Rovers and five jeeps. More training in driving and patrolling was required and the 33rd Battalion took matters into its own hands by developing a motorized patrolling procedure. It was not until the 36th Battalion deployed in December 1961 that greater numbers of jeeps were added to battalion transport. In a wider context no attempt was made to adapt standard procedures and training from the experience of operating on the ground in Katanga.

After Niemba the possibility arose of deploying armoured cars to Congo. This had first arisen in September 1960 as an 'armoured car squadron [of] mixed Landswerks and Ford cars would be acceptable for use in Leopoldville'.[74] Initially the Defence Forces were against sending armoured cars to Congo because it would reduce operational capacity in Ireland. Niemba changed this. When MacEoin visited Irish troops in Congo after Niemba, the 33rd Battalion recommended deploying armoured cars, machine-guns and mortars and he accepted their points. On 1 December 1960 the Director of Cavalry, Col. J.K. Cogan proposed to MacEoin the deployment of an armoured car group with the 34th Battalion of three armoured car troops each with two Landswerks and two Land Rovers. Due to a shortage of crews for the Landswerks, the Ford armoured car was substituted as it was a vehicle on which all armoured car crews had trained.[75] The deployment of the Fords was agreed; the armoured car contingent of the 34th Battalion, commanded by Comdt Joe Foley, was an integral part of 34th Battalion HQ Company under the operational control of Battalion Headquarters. From the 35th Battalion onwards the 'Armoured Car Group' became a company with its own commander within the battalion.

Team training by sections and platoons had not been possible pre-departure to Congo due to the manner in which battalions formed up. In many cases only personal weapons training had been undertaken and experience with ONUC showed that NCOs and men should have fired their weapons recently, as they might be have to defend themselves in an emergency. The experience of both battalions showed that the standard issue Defence Forces infantry rifle – the .303" No. 4 Lee Enfield – needed to be replaced by a fully automatic weapon. The Carl-Gustav 9mm sub-machine-gun got good recommendations and the 33rd Battalion reduced the number of Lee Enfields and brought more Gustavs. However the Gustav was suitable only for close-quarters combat, the 35th Battalion Unit History commenting that 'targets beyond 100 yards were out of effective range'.[76] It lacked the punch of weapons like the 7.62mm FN automatic rifle with which the Katangese Gendarmerie were armed. While the 33rd Battalion brought ten more Bren light machine-guns than the 32nd, it did not use them when they were vitally needed at Niemba. The 35th Battalion regarded the Bren as 'invaluable' and 'quite effective' at ranges up to 1,000 yards.[77] The mistake of not bringing heavy weapons such as the Vickers machine-gun and the 81mm mortar would not be repeated. The 35th Battalion took over the 81mm mortars of the 34th Battalion and found them 'a most effective weapon' during Operation Morthor as they had the weight and volume that the 60mm mortar lacked.[78] Overall most Irish equipment stood up fairly well to tropical conditions, but it was out of date and unsuitable for modern warfare. It was not until the 35th Battalion arrived in Katanga in July 1961 armed with FN automatic rifles and 84mm anti-tank guns that there was any improvement in the armament of Irish ONUC contingents.

Concern over some of these matters was apparent in a memorandum prepared for cabinet on deploying the 34th Battalion.[79] It flagged the need for additional training, the provision of a proper course of vaccinations and the issuing of tropical kit. But it did not deal with the provision of modern weapons.

The points gathered together above come mainly from Battalion Unit Histories, documents often prepared in hindsight. In late 1960 and early 1961 the main concerns of the Defence Forces were the provision of uniforms and bedding for Irish ONUC contingents and the despatch of armoured cars in the aftermath of Niemba. There is little real evidence of learning, either strategic or tactical, in the Defence Forces or the Department of Defence, from Ireland's first six months in Congo. While the Congo crisis would take a dramatic turn for the worse over the next six months as the factors that led to the eventual clash between the UN and Katanga fell into place, there was little to indicate that Irish peacekeepers were aware of the changed environment in which they were operating. That would change in April 1961 when the 34th Battalion deployed to Elisabethville.

CHAPTER 3

Deepening crisis

A S 1960 ENDED, Congo teetered on the brink of anarchy with no legitimate government in Leopoldville and Lumumba under house arrest. He escaped on 27 November, was arrested in Kasai en route to his political base in Stanleyville, and returned to Leopoldville a prisoner. The UN did not act. In Katanga Tshombe remained firmly in control supported by Belgian advisors and with his military forces commanded by Belgian ex-officers. He found time to make an official overseas visit, his first, to Brussels in early December. While Congo faced ongoing crises, Katanga consolidated its position.

By December 1960 ONUC was also in trouble. The withdrawal of national contingents reduced its size by one-third; and von Horn was increasingly unsuitable as Force Commander. Britain's ambassador to the UN Sir Patrick Dean advised von Horn's replacement with an officer who would strengthen ONUC. A 'broader and more practical understanding' of ONUC and 'a sympathetic rather than a governessy relationship with the Congolese' were required.[1] The new Force Commander had to make his 'presence and leadership felt' and develop good relations with Leopoldville. Hammarskjöld should 'forget about colour' and not restrict himself to officers already in Congo. ONUC needed someone who was 'suitably neutral', possibly with an Afro-Asian background, 'with experience of civil affairs administration who will exercise effective authority and inspire confidence in the Congo and abroad'.[2] Dean conveyed these points 'urgently' to Hammarskjöld, explaining that the UN would face serious criticism if they appointed 'a General with virtually no serious military experience'.[3] Hammarskjöld admitted he had problems selecting von Horn's replacement. The new Force Commander would have to overcome the strong Indian influence in ONUC headquarters and Hammarskjöld wanted a man of 'authority and experience who also is reasonably non-controversial nationality-wise'.[4] On 4 December Dayal suggested 'the Irish General McGowan [sic] who is here on tour ... an immediate decision is necessary ... we are building up to an immediate crisis both military and political.'[5] Hammarskjöld's close advisor Andrew Cordier got back in touch with Dean for 'any confidential information about the Irish General Maceion [sic]'.[6]

An Irish Force Commander

The Chief of Staff of the Irish Defence Forces Major General Seán MacEoin visited Irish ONUC units in December 1960 to assure them of the support they were receiving in Ireland and to see how they were equipped for UN service. During the visit MacEoin came to Dayal's notice. Dayal felt MacEoin had the toughness to bring order to ONUC that von Horn lacked. The British embassy in Dublin investigated MacEoin's background. They concluded that having been Chief of Staff for a year he was 'well suited for the appointment' as he had completed 'a major re-organisation of the army' and had overseen the despatch of two 'composite battalions' to Congo.[7] In personality MacEoin was 'pleasant and well educated'.[8] Professionally he showed 'the absence of any marked tendency to become flustered and the ability to command willing and loyal service'.[9] The embassy also learned that MacEoin was 'rather tense and is not very popular with the Irish Army', but this was kept for London's eyes only.[10] London's suggestions on potential force commanders, including MacEoin, were passed on to Hammarskjöld 'for his private information', Dean being told that 'it would be most awkward for us, and I imagine for him, if there were to be an indication that subsequent approaches to Governments were the result of anything but his personal inspiration'.[11]

MacEoin returned to Dublin on 12 December having told Dayal that he was willing to succeed von Horn. However a formal approach to Dublin was required, as there might be constitutional difficulties for the Irish government. Hammarskjöld approached Dublin to release MacEoin for a year's duties as ONUC Force Commander. Aiken was willing, but Lemass took charge and sought MacEoin's personal view. On 15 December, having received a report from Lemass, the cabinet agreed to MacEoin's appointment. There was no public announcement, but to ensure cross-party support Lemass confidentially informed Fine Gael leader James Dillon and Labour leader Brendan Corish, asking them to keep MacEoin's appointment secret until its formal announce-ment. Lemass added that as Force Commander MacEoin would 'act on the directions and advice of the Secretary General and will have no responsibility to the Irish Government'.[12]

To the *Irish Times* MacEoin's appointment brought Ireland 'into the front rank of countries carrying the terrible burden of the United Nations in the Congo'.[13] It added that 'few people will envy him the job; but at the same time, there can be no doubt that the appointment honours Ireland'.[14] MacEoin's appointment was confirmed by the United Nations on 21 December. He would command 20,000 soldiers from eighteen nations and be directly responsible to Hammarskjöld. Sources in New York said that MacEoin had accepted the post only after receiving guarantees that he would have full authority in Congo to take whatever action he saw fit. This was contrasted with von Horn who refused to take action against Congolese forces and dissident Afro-Asian ONUC contingents.[15] The *Irish Independent* editorialized that 'such a command could well become a nightmare'.[16] MacEoin was taking over 'a top-heavy HQ ... which gives soft jobs to too many officers and is both out of touch and unable to exercise effective [word undeciphered]'.[17] Full-scale civil war in Congo loomed and with it the possibility of outside intervention. Aiken thought the situation 'menacing'.[18]

MacEoin was 'greatly honoured' by the appointment, but he was an untried entity.[19] His re-organization of the Defence Forces had been a small-scale operation; he had no experience of operational command of a unit larger than a battalion. Despite serving in the Defence Forces during the Second World War he had no combat experience and was primarily a staff officer. The military structure he commanded in Ireland was less than half the size of ONUC, but to his credit he was not von Horn and he had significant international support and peer approval.

In London the Foreign Office and the War Office were anxious to meet MacEoin to give him the '"the situation as we see it" and not what we think the UN "ought (or ought not) to do"'.[20] Britain thought MacEoin would follow their interests. Their expectations of MacEoin taking a subservient line were dispelled when the 'keen-eyed, broguey' general passed through London. He had a 'friendly, but ... distinctly wary manner' and seemed 'to be in no hurry' for the officials he met to become his advisers.[21] The British explained that the UN mission in Congo was not 'a sort of protectorate and indeed a suitable object on which to try out various laudable theories'; MacEoin countered 'that his great object was on the contrary to finish the job at the earliest possible moment'.[22]

The Director of Military Intelligence regarded MacEoin as 'a first-class soldier and thought there were good prospects that he would do an excellent job'. Foreign Secretary Lord Home felt MacEoin's attitude was 'encouraging' and he hoped MacEoin had not come too late to make a difference.[23] London hoped MacEoin would get Hammarskjöld to approach the problems of Congo and ONUC in a freer manner and not keep acting 'by steps which may appear hesitant and sometimes devious'.[24] Political decisions taken by ONUC in Leopoldville were 'not being passed on to troops on the ground in the form of clear understandable orders'.[25] This was due not only to von Horn, but also to the military and political influence of Rikhye and Dayal at ONUC Headquarters as a result of which the 'normal chain of command [was] being short-circuited'.[26]

By late January MacEoin's 'influence had still to make itself felt' and the Rikhye–Dayal axis still prevailed.[27] MacEoin got caught in military-civilian rows with Dayal over executive authority and the interpretation of instructions. Hammarskjöld felt unable to replace Dayal because this would undermine Indian support for ONUC; Dayal was increasingly biased in favour of Lumumba but would have to remain in place. There were poor relations between Dayal and Kasavubu, and Leopoldville kept Dayal at arm's length. Accordingly the UN Secretariat was 'frequently without information' as to what was happening in Congo and Hammarskjöld was often 'misled by false reports from Dayal'.[28] MacEoin knew of Dayal's behaviour and tried to correct his reports, but Dayal refused to accept the amendments. Under Anglo–American pressure Hammarskjöld called Dayal to New York for consultations, but he remained reluctant to do anything that might upset Delhi or the Afro–Asian members of the UN Congo Advisory Committee. Dayal was eventually replaced in May 1961 by a Swede, Sture Linner. With Dayal out of the picture Mobuto, a fellow-soldier, felt that 'MacEoin "with his hands free" was easy to work with'.[29]

MacEoin was a 'modest, shrewd, tough and realistic soldier', yet he was unable to put ONUC in order.[30] This was his first international mission and his first overseas posting. As Force Commander he found his hands tied by his political colleagues and masters. He arrived in Leopoldville to face the formidable Rikhye–Dayal machine unaided. He had no advisors and no diplomatic or political support from Dublin. He appointed his own staff officers, but like their commander they too were on their first overseas postings and had limited United Nations experience.

In April 1961 Rikhye suggested that MacEoin take personal command of all UN operations in Katanga, a proposal showing his belief in the Force Commander. In Leopoldville MacEoin was burdened by immense amounts of routine communications from New York. He left affairs in the provincial ONUC commands largely to their commanding officers. A confidential 'UK Eyes Only' document from September 1961 concluded that ONUC had 'an indifferent Force HQ, incapable of efficient planning and resolute command'.[31] Bunche's remark that MacEoin ran an 'infinitely more amateur, irresponsible, incompetent and totally disorganised' headquarters in Leopoldville than von Horn was harsh. However both remarks were product of the dates they were made – after the failure of Operation Morthor in September 1961.[32] The Irish ambassador in Washington reported in late September that the *Washington Post* considered MacEoin 'out of his depth, and often ignorant of where his forces were or what they were doing'.[33] The Indian commander in Katanga, Brigadier Raja, regarded MacEoin as 'useless' and disliked the Force Commander's interference in his area of control, in the months after Morthor.[34] The Indians saw themselves as battle-hardened and knew that MacEoin had not previously held active military command in theatre.

After September 1961 until his departure from Congo in March 1962 MacEoin acquired 'a very poor' or 'not a very good' military reputation.[35] However between January and September 1961 he oversaw ONUC as expected by New York and got involved in the complex relationships underpinning ONUC. He was not greatly criticized for his actions. Harold Macmillan hoped that MacEoin would make ONUC 'more effective and purposeful'.[36] He gave ONUC commanders across Congo the autonomy to implement the mission's mandate. MacEoin's staff officers implemented his decisions, yet his personal actions are evident across a range of ONUC activities, and if the accusation is made that he was out of the loop during Operation Morthor, the counter-argument can be made that he exerted his influence thereafter. Indeed MacEoin later maintained that he had been 'largely sidelined and ignored' by the Secretary General's Special Representative in Elisabethville, Conor Cruise O'Brien after O'Brien's arrival in Katanga in June 1961.[37] In the political atmosphere of ONUC HQ it is nevertheless clear that MacEoin's comparative lack of international experience compared to men like Rikhye and Dayal put him at a disadvantage. MacEoin was able to keep ONUC running, but he was not able to carry out the restructuring that his supporters hoped for. In the pressure-cooker atmosphere of Leopoldville, bogged down with logistics, numbers and structures, MacEoin was caught in a delicate high-level balancing act between the forces underpinning ONUC.

The Irish intelligence deficit on Congo

Irish ambassador to Great Britain Hugh McCann assumed that Dublin would 'obtain private reports' from MacEoin on the Congo crisis.[38] The Secretary of the Department of External Affairs Con Cremin replied that McCann was mistaken. It was Irish policy, Cremin explained, that when governments placed themselves in the hands of the UN 'they should act solely through the UN'.[39] This meant that Irish soldiers in Congo were 'detached entirely from our control'. Dublin knew that other countries ignored this, but Ireland would not do so. It was an honourable attitude, but it left the Irish authorities in the dark about Congolese affairs and culpable of wilful ignorance because of an idealistic desire to follow principle.

Not all in External Affairs thought in this manner. Paul Keating, in a minute to Conor Cruise O'Brien on the prevailing anti-UN mood in British press reports, emphasized that 'we have no established means of checking their veracity. The returned officers from Congo might be helpful in this regard if their professional scruples do not inhibit their commenting on their colleagues in other armies, or else lead them to be unduly hostile to their civilian rivals'.[40] When Comdt Fergus Fleming, an army intelligence officer, was attached to ONUC Headquarters, Eamon Gallagher and Keating at External Affairs agreed to suggest to the Department of Defence that Fleming 'should be requested to report back to that Department but also for the information of this Department on the situation in the Congo'.[41] Keating explained that though the UN frowned on this practice, providing the information was not used to criticize ONUC decisions and because 'of the Irish lives at stake' it was not unreasonable 'to secure an unbiased account of the situation'. Ireland had 'no diplomatic representation in the Congo and no other source of information on what is occurring there than the guarded reports of the UN and possibly tendentious mess stories unless we use a member of our forces'. He doubted 'that any other country would pass up this intelligence opportunity'.[42] Sean Ronan passed Keating's minute on to O'Brien noting that this was an infringement of UN rules and that the Department of Defence 'would not be favourably disposed towards the idea', though in November 1960 he and Cremin had spoken to a high-ranking officer returned from Congo.[43] Ronan recommended that Keating's proposal be dropped. Defence felt that approaching officers on UN service would break UN regulations and 'amount to a breach of loyalty by officers to their commanding officer'.[44] They 'had some scruples in the matter' and disliked any direct approach from External Affairs to the military.[45] Though there is considerable evidence of officers serving with ONUC reporting to Army Headquarters, the material, mainly local intelligence reports, did not filter through to External Affairs and Aiken remained 'inclined not to depart from our existing practice of not seeking reports from our officers in the Congo'.[46] However correct, it was a lost opportunity.

The 34th Battalion

The 34th Battalion, led by Lt Col. Eugene O'Neill, mustered at the Curragh Camp, Co. Kildare on 4 January 1961. They were told by Aiken that they carried with them 'all the prayers of threatened humanity that your tour of duty will bring the Congolese people nearer to peaceful and stable life under ordered and representative government'.[47] A reference in the speech to the 'arduous service' awaiting the battalion was crossed out of the final version, perhaps with the deaths at Niemba in mind. Niemba was on the minds of the 34th Battalion; its men were conscious that they would do their utmost not find themselves caught in the same position as Gleeson's patrol. The 626 officers and men of the 34th Battalion were accordingly better armed than their predecessors. Instead of the .303" Lee Enfield rifle nearly all were armed with Carl Gustav sub-machine-guns. The weapon had not previously been issued to other ranks in Irish ONUC battalions.

Four Ford armoured cars were sent with the 34th Battalion. Built by Thompsons of Carlow during the Second World War, weakly armoured and poorly armed they gave the impression of power to those who knew no better, but were no match for modern armoured vehicles. The Fords were armed with a single turret-mounted Vickers .303" water-cooled machine-gun, and had a 3-tonne chassis with an armoured hull made of boiler plating. The Ford's Vickers machine-gun caused concern as its ball mounting, while flexible, led to difficulties holding the gun stable when firing. The OC of the Cavalry Depot, Lt Col. Johnny Stapleton, well known for his ingenuity, rose to the occasion. He stabilized the gun by fixing brake shoes left and right of the mounting, connecting them by cable to motorcycle brake levers mounted on the Vickers' handgrips. When the system was tested at the Glen of Imaal weapons range it worked satisfactorily. The same could not be said for the car's armour plating, which could not withstand .303" ball or armour-piercing rounds fired at 100 yards. Ball ammunition produced an inside blister to the armour plating, while armour piercing rounds did what they were designed to do. As the 34th Battalion's mission was to keep the peace, not to fight a war, these results were deemed acceptable.

Further modifications to the Fords included replacing with metal tracks the wooden trench planks carried on the hull, fitting searchlights and ending the dangerous practice of carrying two spare jerry cans of petrol on the exterior. Reports from the 34th Battalion later outlined two major operational problems with the Fords in the harsh climate of Congo. First, the high temperatures made the cars unbearably hot inside. Second, dust from unpaved roads and tracks clogged the carburettor air filters, a situation exacerbated when the vehicles travelled in convoy. The question of air conditioning was raised in a Dáil question to Kevin Boland. The minister prevaricated, answering that the Fords were 'serviceable and are being used for patrol duties'.[48] To overcome air conditioning problems interior fans were fitted and extra air filters were included in spares kits.

As a result of Niemba the role envisaged for the Fords was supporting infantry patrols in hostile territory. In reality only greater training in patrol and ambush drills could assist infantry patrols, yet the deployment of armoured cars suggested to hostile elements that Irish troops were not to be taken on lightly.

The Fords were later used for quelling riots and patrolling tense urban areas. Unaware of the Ford's limitations, other ONUC commanders thought of them 'as armoured cars in the ordinary sense, i.e. with a gun to deal with enemy armour'.[49] In the September and December 1961 fighting in Elisabethville the Fords were used largely as infantry support weapons. They should have operated in pairs as a section giving comprehensive protection to each other, but they often operated alone with infantry protection. While they might give heightened visibility to the Irish ONUC presence and impress locals, Katangese Gendarmerie commanders knew they were of little military value and could easily be destroyed. To counter this threat the Fords often operated in conjunction with jeep-mounted anti-tank guns.

The February Resolution

In early January 1961 Hammarskjöld visited Leopoldville and found 'a mood of confidence'.[50] The UN hoped the recall of parliament and the reestablishment of central authority in Leopoldville would soon be possible. On 17 January, reports arrived from Elisabethville airport that Swedish troops had seen three prisoners, one of whom was a badly beaten Lumumba, arrive under tight security. The prisoners were quickly driven away and ONUC did not intervene. To External Affairs this was a 'most serious development'; it showed co-operation between Mobutu and Tshombe and the implications were 'ominous'. Dublin expected 'very serious Afro-Asian and Soviet Bloc reactions'.[51] External Affairs argued that 'the present "line-up" in the Congo may lead to civil war. Roughly speaking two of the six provinces (Leopoldville and Equator) are held by Kasavubu–Mobutu, two (Oriental and Kivu) by Lumumba supporters, and Katanga and Kasai are each controlled mainly by other groups'.[52] Within Katanga there was civil war and conditions remained 'extremely unsettled'.[53] In January 1961 Elisabethville declared the October 1960 neutral zones in north Katanga void and reoccupied them. 'Unpredictability', External Affairs concluded, was the only certainty facing Congo.

ONUC, now reduced to 14,000 men, was dangerously thin on the ground and its military position would become intolerable once further units departed in late February. Hammarskjöld was worried about finding replacements. Bunche informally asked Frederick Boland whether, in addition to the 34th Battalion, a reinforced infantry company or a further Irish battalion could be deployed to replace the departing contingents. Cremin discussed Bunche's request with Lemass and Aiken. At cabinet Minister for Defence Kevin Boland 'was quite sympathetic'.[54] Lemass was 'definitely opposed'.[55] The feeling around the cabinet table was that Ireland could not undertake this request because of the tense situation on the Northern Ireland border following the murder of a Northern Ireland policeman by the IRA. Aiken was 'personally sorry that we could not meet a further request now',[56] but the cabinet followed Lemass. Despatching another battalion to Congo would be 'unwise and impolitic' considering domestic security requirements.[57] It was Lemass, not the public face of Ireland's engagement with the UN, Aiken, who took the critical decisions.

On 1 February the UN Security Council discussed the deepening Congo crisis. Resolutions were tabled against the treatment of Lumumba, and Hammarskjöld explained that ONUC was protecting Congo against external military interference and was assisting the maintenance of internal law and order to enable the establishment of a stable democratic government. He specifically excluded the possibility of ONUC using force and hoped that moral suasion would be successful. Boland reported scepticism in New York 'as to the soundness of this belief'.[58] The future of ONUC looked bleak as mission fatigue set in. The initial unity of purpose among UN members over ONUC was breaking down, having been eroded by a combination of Cold War rivalries, Afro-Asian dissensions, local ambitions and a widening unwillingness to accept commitments. It was only due to the dogged determination of Hammarskjöld and his staff that ONUC continued to exist.

New ideas on Congo emerged. On 6 February United States ambassador in Dublin, Scott McLeod, informed Aiken of a new approach on Congo being developed by President Kennedy.[59] This approach aimed to nurture Congolese independence. The new administration in Washington wished for a broadly based government in Leopoldville with Joseph Iléo as Prime Minister, with the UN controlling all military elements in Congo and improving UN civilian operations to assist the Congolese establish a civilian government. McLeod explained that Washington gave 'particular weight' to Ireland's views on Congo. Aiken instead explained his solution to McLeod. Aiken also hoped to see a broadly based Congolese government, but he disliked the American commitment to appointing one named individual as prime minister. He thought a provisional government with a long mandate followed by elections might stabilize the country. Then Aiken made an unusual suggestion. To remove the motivation for international intervention in Congo Aiken suggested creating a United Nations corporation to buy out foreign, particularly Belgian, interests in the country. Naively Aiken wanted Belgium to then use its knowledge of Congo to assist the United Nations. The UN could then, with the support of the civilian government and the consent of Belgian interests, disarm the various armed forces in the state. Boland tactfully suggested that Aiken's plan was 'rather far out of the range of present thinking' about Congo.[60] Aiken remained deeply concerned about Congo and asked Boland to provide him with daily reports on developments. One report usefully synopsized Boland's view that 'the solution of the Congo problem supported by most delegations nowadays embraces four elements – the summoning of Parliament, the release of Mr Lumumba from Katanga, the "neutralisation" of the ANC and the stopping of all forms of outside intervention.'[61] Hammarskjöld desired the neutralization of the ANC first and felt that this could be done without resort to force with 'a unanimous or at least an unopposed decision of the Security Council'; but Boland was less certain, telling Dublin that there was 'a great deal of scepticism in the UN corridors on this score'.[62]

A meeting of the Security Council was fixed for 13 February. The situation changed dramatically as rumours spread and 'everyone at the UN [was] waiting for definite news with regard to Lumumba.'[63] Boland reported that 'if in fact Mr Lumumba is dead, his demise will have an adverse effect on the negotiations now proceeding at the UN with a view to an agreed solution on the Congo problem'. On 13 February Katangese Minister for the Interior Godefroid Munongo announced that Lumumba had been murdered in Katanga. The Security Council met in a mood of gloom. Aiken was shocked and told Hammarskjöld that the Security Council should issue a unanimous appeal for calm. Even western opinion, usually critical of Lumumba, was dismayed. The entire United Nations effort in Congo was 'called seriously into question, faith in Hammarskjöld was shaken, and Soviet demands for his dismissal became insistent'.[64] Lemass wrote to Khrushchev in support of the United Nations and Hammarskjöld, condemning Lumumba's killing. Ireland's government and people gave their 'firm support' to the United Nations resolutions on Congo and to Hammarskjöld's implementing them.[65] Boland anticipated that Lumumba's death would 'sharpen antagonisms, provoke atrocities and spread civil war'.[66] There was little chance now of the formation of a stable Congolese government and the outlook remained extremely uncertain. The Soviets might be anxious to improve their relations with the incoming Kennedy administration, but Moscow would not endanger its 'leadership of the more extreme wing of the Afro–Asian bloc by adopting a line which appears "softer" than theirs' over Congo.[67]

Hammarskjöld had to get Congo on the road to political stability before the General Assembly opened in autumn 1961. He had to have a success to secure his embattled position from Soviet criticism. After Lumumba's death the United Nations needed to act. Dayal advised Hammarskjöld to obtain Security Council authority to take measures in Congo 'if necessary by means of force' as it was 'imperative to stem the tide of turbulence'.[68] The Security Council reconvened on 16 February to face a strong Soviet attack on Hammarskjöld. Hammarskjöld refused Soviet calls to resign and defended his position with United States support. There was now no chance of arriving at an agreed resolution. Aiken remained convinced that his ideas on Congo could provide a way forward, and Boland carefully told Cremin that 'the thinking at present in UN circles is not such as to provide a good context in which to urge the proposals made' in the Minister's memorandum.[69] He added that in Hammarskjöld's view Aiken's proposals 'do not bear closely on the immediate problems' of which the most significant was the likelihood of civil war. The main problems in New York were the 'threat to the United Nations' and the 'danger of an East–West clash'. Boland concluded that 'President Kennedy's assertion that America would not stand quietly by while foreign intervention takes place in the Congo' is particularly significant. Cremin told the American ambassador in Dublin that Ireland endorsed the American viewpoint on 'the importance of standing behind the United Nations, both generally and in regard to the Congo'.[70]

India wanted the Security Council to give the UN authority to take firm action to restore political and military stability in Congo. Prime Minister

Jawaharlal Nehru believed that 'if necessary the UN should use force to give effect to its policies' in Congo.[71] Delhi put forward a resolution condemning Lumumba's murder, demanding control of Belgian military personnel in Katanga and authorizing ONUC to use force to prevent civil war. Lumumba's murder was a turning point for India in the Congo crisis. Thereafter it supported greater UN involvement in Congo and gave consideration to sending combat troops if 'convinced that they will be used rightly for the freedom of the Congo people and not to support the gangster regimes that function there'.[72] By this Nehru meant Kasavubu as much as Tshombe.

Yet Tshombe cared little. He and his cabinet did not read the foreign press and international reaction to Lumumba's murder passed them by. A confidential report from the Irish ambassador in Brussels added that Belgium was 'determined to extend all moral support to the Belgian colonists in their efforts to maintain the real control of Katanga, even at the cost, if necessary, of destroying the Congo politically and economically'.[73] In Elisabethville the mood was confident. Tshombe awaited the future with equanimity; British Consul George Evans thought the Katangese president might say that with Lumumba dead 'things have never looked better for Katanga'.[74] Above all, Tshombe 'did not care a hoot for the UN'.[75]

On 21 February the Security Council passed Resolution 161, a tripartite resolution tabled by the UAR, Ceylon and Liberia, which India had played a lead role in drafting. It urged that the United Nations 'take immediately all appropriate measures to prevent the occurrence of civil war in the Congo, including arrangements for ceasefire, the halting of all military operations, the prevention of clashes, and the use of force, if necessary, in the last resort'.[76] All Security Council members supported the resolution, except France and the USSR. It gave a stronger and clearer framework for UN actions in Congo and gave enhanced powers and functions to ONUC, allowing it a more active role in preventing disorder. The Soviet effort to oust Hammarskjöld and weaken the UN was rejected decisively through Resolution 161 and with his new mandate Hammarskjöld obtained the overwhelming support of the Afro–Asian and non-Communist members of the UN. The resolution halted the Afro–Asian slide away from ONUC and

> had no parallel in UN history. The Council had authorized a 'non-threatening' peacekeeping force, neither mandated nor equipped to fight a campaign, to adopt an enforcement role without first determining that a threat existed, still less the adoption as a first expedient of non-military coercive measures such as economic sanctions. It also left the command and control of such an enforcement operation in the virtually unfettered hands of the Secretary General.[77]

The immediate reaction to the resolution was subdued in the aftermath of Lumumba's death, yet after February 1961 ONUC was on an entirely new footing. In Hammarskjöld's view force could now be used 'when all other efforts' had failed.[78] From February to August 1961 Hammarskjöld and his colleagues nevertheless tried to use quiet diplomacy to achieve reconciliation in Congo, but their being prepared to ultimately use force is clear in their correspondence. The sweeping implications of Resolution 161 and how ill-prepared ONUC was to use force did not emerge until late August 1961.

CHAPTER 4

Conflict in Katanga

AFTER LUMUMBA'S death and the February resolution, a sequence of events commenced which brought the UN and Katanga to war. There was nothing inevitable about the two sides coming to blows, but the battle of wills between ONUC and Tshombe intensified as pressure on the UN for the implementation of the February resolution grew and this led eventually to armed conflict. Certain developments are, in hindsight, waypoints leading to the September clash between ONUC and Katanga. The arrival in Katanga of Indian forces with recent combat experience changed ONUC's demeanour from peacekeeping to a more offensive outlook. ONUC's subsequent use, with Hammarskjöld's approval, of these Indian troops to threaten Tshombe increased tension when they were sent to north Katanga. By summer 1961 the civil war in north Katanga had also placed ONUC on a collision course with Tshombe who was intent on recapturing the area. As the Indians gained control of north Katanga their presence further increased Katangese government fear of Indian intentions across the province. Hammarskjöld's patience with Tshombe weakened and Irish diplomat Conor Cruise O'Brien was sent to Elisabethville in June as the Secretary General's Special Representative to implement the February resolution. O'Brien sought to repatriate the non-Katangese military and civilian officials supporting Tshombe's government and began a high-stakes initiative to return Katanga to Leopoldville's control. O'Brien's actions, the presence and attitude of the Indians across Katanga, and Hammarskjöld's changing outlook towards Katanga, all in the face of Tshombe's intransigence, placed the UN and Katanga on a collision course.

Indian troops for ONUC

After the passage of the February resolution and with ONUC now permitted to use force in the last resort, Hammarskjöld sought further troops for ONUC. The mission needed twenty-five battalions and only had sixteen available. India was rumoured to be prepared to help. The Indian government was 'thinking furiously about the request for Indian troops in the Congo. It was a big decision; compliance would be difficult, but the Indian Government [was] fully aware that the whole question of the future of the United Nations not only in the Congo but altogether was involved.'[1] As the leading Asian non-aligned state, India did not want to appear uninterested in Africa. It had long-term African interests and wished to keep the newly independent states of Africa conscious that it was an important country with which to develop economic and political relations.

Despite the senior roles of Rikhye and Dayal in ONUC, until spring 1961 India sent only small non-combat units to Congo. Hammarskjöld's request for troops brought Indian involvement in ONUC to a higher level. London and Washington were supportive of India's increased involvement in the mission as it 'would greatly help to hold the UN operation together and keep the other Afro–Asians behind it. It would also widen the gap between them and the Soviet position and stiffen those who have been reluctant to support Mr Hammarskjöld because of the Soviet attitude.'[2] Hammarskjöld ultimately asked India for a brigade of troops for ONUC. Nehru agreed because 'he was convinced that without UN forces the Congo would go to pieces and might lead to direct conflict between Russia and the United States.'[3] India sent a brigade of 4,700 personnel, including 3,000 combat troops, hoping that the February resolution would be implemented speedily. Nehru later explained that when India decided to send forces to Congo 'they went in to do a job of work'.[4] Forcefully he added that it would be necessary for ONUC to stage 'a small show of force' in one or two places 'if the Congolese were to be brought to co-operate'.[5]

The arrival of battle-hardened Indian units with combat experience to join Swedish and Irish contingents who were primarily peacekeepers shifted the balance of military power in ONUC. The Indians even suggested bringing tanks to Congo. Hammarskjöld opposed this because of 'the psychological effect of their arrival ... tanks are an offensive weapon, primarily designed to dominate any military situation.'[6] As ONUC intelligence officer Col. Bjorn Egge concluded, the Indian contingent perceived its task 'as an ordinary military fighting job. They had not been properly briefed on the basic idea and the special procedures of UN peacekeeping.'[7]

The 34th Battalion at Kamina

Little had been heard in Ireland of the 34th Battalion since its deployment to Kamina Base. Journalist Ray Moloney explained that they 'laughingly call themselves "The Phantom Battalion"' as unlike the 32nd and 33rd Battalions their activities were not headline-making.[8] They settled in and were finding their way around 'without being lost all the time'.[9] Battalion commander Lt Col. Eugene O'Neill took over as Kamina Base commander on 1 March. Katanga was divided into three ONUC regions – Northern Katanga (Brigadier Ward (Nigeria)), Southern Katanga (Col. Kjellgren (Sweden)) and Kamina Base. O'Neill was now one of the top three UN officers in Katanga. The majority of the 34th Battalion defended the over 100 square miles of the vast Kamina airfield. It was made up of 'wide, well-laid roads, avenues of pleasant, well-built houses, giant hangars, workshops and superb runways that can land and take off the biggest jetplanes'.[10] Earlier in the Congo crisis the base had been busy as Belgian paratroopers arrived and Belgian civilian refugees departed. Now a transhipment depot for relief supplies being flown to famine areas in Kasai it was being run down and had a desolate air.

The 34th Battalion was under direct control from ONUC Headquarters in Leopoldville for the defence of Kamina Base. For secondary tasks it was controlled by South Katanga Command from Elisabethville. These tasks included stationing a platoon at Kilubi power station and a company at Luena on the railway from Kamina south to Elisabethville. Air and road reconnaissance patrols southeast from Kamina Base towards the town of Kabondo-Dienda found villages burned out following sharp exchanges between Gendarmerie and Baluba. B-Company 34th Battalion was interposed to try to keep the peace and persuaded the local Baluba, who had fled into the bush, to return to their villages. Outside Kamina the 34th Battalion patrolled 'as a threat and a reassurance' during periods of inter-tribal tension.[11] Contacts were developed with pro-Tshombe forces and with local Baluba. The battalion band toured 'so that the people may recognise the Irish troops as friends'. Intelligence officers compiled information on local Gendarmerie strengths and monitored inter-tribal relations and relations with Elisabethville.

34th Battalion morale continued 'very high despite difficult conditions.'[12] Defence Forces Adjutant-General Col. P.J. Hally visited the battalion for St Patrick's Day to assess 'the efficiency, the discipline and the welfare arrangements of the Irish contingent'.[13] He told reporters that the 34th battalion was 'fit, alert and the morale is high', adding that relations between the Irish troops and the local population were excellent.[14] The St Patrick's Day celebrations passed successfully with Mass, a dinner at Kamina Base with twenty-five nationalities present, hurling matches and an evening barbeque with local dancers and drummers. A few weeks later, on Easter Sunday, 2 April 1961, troops from the 32nd Battalion under the command of Lt Col. Buckley and the 33rd Battalion under the command of Lt Col. Bunworth paraded through Dublin. It was their first public parade since returning from Congo and the men wore their newly-awarded United Nations Congo service medals. Public interest in ONUC remained high in Ireland.

The Indian Brigade

The deployment to Katanga of the Indian Independent Brigade Group headed by Brigadier K.A.S. Raja was a turning point for ONUC. It would eventually form one-third of ONUC and its strength gave India leverage to press for the strong implementation of the February resolution. This worried ONUC contributors including Ireland as, with Dayal not yet departed and Nehru holding increasingly fixed views on Congo, it seemed to be the beginning of implicit Indian trusteeship over the country. From mid-March 1961 Indian troops began arriving in large numbers in Congo building up ONUC as African contingents withdrew. Though Indian Defence Minister Krishna Menon 'was at pains to declare' the troops were peacekeepers, the inclusion of Gurkha units indicated that 'this Indian expeditionary force means business and will use its weapons if need be'.[15] Anti-Indian statements from the Katangese government on the arrival of Indians at Kamina Base 'caused unrest among Katangese officials, both military and civilian, in Kaminaville'.[16] They considered it the precursor of military action against Katanga.

Tshombe feared the arrival of the Indians. There was a long-standing antipathy between Katangans and Indians and no Indians were admitted to Congo under Belgian rule. The British consul general in Elisabethville claimed that 'being able to survive at African standards of living but nevertheless being far shrewder in business than Africans, an immigration of Indians would mean a fatal setback to African advancement'.[17] O'Neill explained in more detail that

> There is very real opposition to the presence of Indians. This is nothing new. It is largely historical. The Indians followed the Arab Slave traders in Africa in the last century. They are the merchants, the moneylenders and the shopkeepers of East Africa. They are looked upon as the Jews were looked on in central Europe. Furthermore, Mr Nehru's policies, his left-wing socialism, are at variance with the views of the Katanga Government. And finally, Mr Dayal is generally noted throughout the Congo as the epitome of all that is evil![18]

In late March Tshombe sent troops into north Katanga against the Baluba. ONUC had a mandate under the February resolution to keep the two sides apart. MacEoin told Hammarskjöld that he expected Tshombe to move on Manono, the capital of north Katanga, to prevent the establishment of a Baluba state in the area. The town had been occupied by ANC forces since January 1961 and as March ended 34th Battalion intelligence officers reported a build-up of Gendarmerie nearby. MacEoin, Ward, Kjellgren, O'Neill and UN representative in Katanga Georges Dumontet met Tshombe to convey their concerns. MacEoin emphasized that any Katangese attack on Manono would breach the February resolution and 'merit the gravest sanction of the UN'.[19] Tshombe explained that he had no intention of attacking Manono. Katangese forces nevertheless took Manono on 30 March. The town fell with little fighting and the ANC offered no resistance. Neither did Nigerian UN troops in the area. The UN next threatened Tshombe that if his forces moved north from Manono, ONUC would move Indian forces to north Katanga. MacEoin hoped that Tshombe would not risk a direct clash with the Indians and that 'a firm stand against Tshombe's Gendarmerie may succeed, even if UN troops are outnumbered'.[20] Hammarskjöld agreed as 'the threat to do so ... can in our view, be honestly upheld'.[21] Yet he refrained from taking a harder line fearing that it might 'result in more serious friction and breakdown of law and order'.[22] Hammarskjöld nevertheless felt it 'imperative' that the UN 'take every step to prevent civil war in North Katanga'.[23] He even suggested that the UN take offensive action, telling MacEoin that ONUC should immediately recapture any ground lost 'even if this requires resort to force'.[24]

Indian troops moved to Kamina Base as a result of the fall of Manono. The 3/1 Gurkha Rifles started arriving from 1 April and Lt Col. Maitra, OC of 1st

Gurkha Battalion, took command of the base from O'Neill. Hammarskjöld believed that the Indian deployment to Kamina needed to proceed to 'get [the] full psychological impact' of their arrival in Katanga.[25] Locals staged protests, but only 2,000 of the expected 50,000 arrived. The demonstration was called off though the entrance to the base was blocked. Three Irish armoured cars under the command of Capt. Raymond Whyte stood by with the Gurkhas to respond should an attack occur. Even if there were women and children in the vanguard of any attack Whyte said he 'would not hesitate in opening fire'.[26]

The arrival of the Indians created problems for the isolated Irish units at Kilubi and Luena. The unit at Kilubi could not be relieved as 'the Katanga authorities state that any movement from the Base by the Indians will be looked upon as an act of war'.[27] The Indians might get to Kilubi, probably by sending a company-strength force. They would relieve the Irish but O'Neill was worried that the small Irish force would be ambushed on the return journey. The African ONUC interpreter at Kilubi had been given a message for the Irish there not to leave the post. The company at Luena was 'completely cut off', but having maintained good relations with the locals 'they are being boycotted but no harm is being done to them'. They were 'remaining cool' and were in radio contact. O'Neill was 'trying to have them brought out by rail before some other bubble bursts'.

Confrontation at Elisabethville airport

Tshombe felt tricked as the Indian presence in Katanga expanded. On the night of 1–2 April Gendarmerie blocked the runway at Elisabethville airport and took over the control tower to prevent any surprise landing by Gurkhas. All was defused after a phone call from ONUC to Munongo, however the runway was again blocked the following night and after an ultimatum to remove the obstacles was ignored Swedish troops reoccupied the airport. An agreement on joint control was reached, but during 4 April Tshombe roused local mobs and 'several thousand Africans, mostly armed with clubs, spears, etc.,' marched on the airport and smashed windows and tore down UN flags.[28] Gendarmerie and police removed the hostile crowd, which was part-led by Belgians. Hammarskjöld personally instructed the improvement of airport defenses and suggested that the 34th Irish Battalion were the 'most appropriate reinforcement'.[29] MacEoin ordered that they be flown to Elisabethville early the next morning.

On 5 April MacEoin and Kjellgren met with Tshombe and his cabinet. At the same time A-Company and B-Company of the 34th Battalion, approximately 300 troops, arrived in Elisabethville and re-occupied the airport. MacEoin warned Tshombe that he had ordered this action, but the arrival of the Irish still 'caused great consternation.'[30] The first company arriving assumed they would go directly into action. The men had trained for this and 'their action on arrival at the airport nearly began the war again'.[31] One unnamed soldier told journalists that we got overnight orders to move to Elisabethville, where the Swedish troops were in trouble. It was battle order and we loaded into our planes, DC4s. On the flight we got our instructions for action on the airfield.

We touched down at Elisabethville on April 5th, and as soon as the propellers stopped swinging we jumped from the planes and took up defence positions with guns at the ready.

We eyed them and they eyed us.[32]

By nightfall A-Company and B-Company and a portion of HQ-Company had arrived and 'the Gendarmerie were extremely nervous'.[33] O'Neill warned his men 'not to appear too warlike'. To keep the temperature down MacEoin decided not to deploy Irish armoured cars in Elisabethville as 'this would be sufficient to have the war start again, and if the mob came we would either have to fire or give them the airport'. To defuse tension Irish troops shared tea with Katangese airport guards 'who were so jittery and afraid they were likely to open up at any moment'. To counter local propaganda portraying the UN as communist the Irish played to their spiritual strength – 'Our chaps go to Mass almost to a man daily. The Company Commanders say evening prayers in the various camps and some Congolese, most of whom are Catholics, join in. Many Belgians attend our Masses now.'[34]

With the Irish in place Hammarskjöld told Mekki Abbas and MacEoin that they were entitled to bring Indian troops to Elisabethville if the circumstances in their judgment indicated such a move was wise.[35] MacEoin advised Tshombe that he would do so if the Katangese further interfered with UN operations. A concerned Tshombe was 'reassured' by Kjellgren and Dumontet that no Indians were on the way for the moment.[36] Future moves of UN troops 'would be governed by moves of the Gendarmerie'.[37]

Joint UN/Katangese control of Elisabethville airport was agreed, the flare-up of early April was forgotten and the atmosphere in Elisabethville improved. Tshombe met O'Neill and, with the arrival of Indian troops in mind, 'in a friendly mood, joked: "no more surprises I hope?"' 'There will be no surprises at all', O'Neill replied.[38] One company of ONUC troops now permanently occupied Elisabethville airport, with a company from each ONUC battalion in the city ready to support them. MacEoin considered the airfield 'the vital ground at Elisabethville'.[39] He ordered that in the event of the UN losing control of it the location was to be 'immediately retaken ... using force if necessary'.[40] There was agreement that no further Katangese or UN troops would be sent to the airport without advance notice being given. The Katangese stationing of a 75mm gun at the airport perimeter warned the UN not to move Indian forces to Elisabethville.

The UN position was precarious, Rikhye wrote to Hammarskjöld that 'the initiative is with Katanga ... militarily we are weaker and what we have gained so far is through bluff not force'.[41] Attempting to ratchet up tension, Tshombe boycotted the UN in Elisabethville and harassed ONUC by depriving troops of water, electricity and banking facilities. Fearing the worst, O'Neill had his men fill water containers nightly. He attempted to get the 34th Battalion armoured car group to Elisabethville as they would 'be vital here in the event of a clash'.[42] Initially opposed, on 10 April MacEoin relented and ordered the infantry and armoured car components of the 34th Battalion still at Kamina Base to join with forces at Luena and move to Elisabethville. The British consul reported that with the arrival of this group in the city the UN was 'flexing its muscles'.[43]

Parallel with the move, though not related, the Defence Forces agreed that there was 'an urgent need' to equip the 34th Battalion with FN automatic rifles, replacing their ageing Lee Enfields.[44] The 32nd Battalion judged the Lee Enfield 'inadequate for the conditions of modern warfare. While it is robust and trouble-free it is seriously lacking in fire power.'[45] The FN was a new weapon for the Defence Forces and while in use internationally, including in Congo by the Katangese, it was its description as 'the latest NATO-type' rifle which caught the attention of the Irish media; a story External Affairs anxiously damped down.[46] 84mm anti-tank guns were also being despatched to the 34th Battalion and later 'gave a very necessary sense of security in the face of the Katangese Gendarmerie Armoured Cars' and were 'most useful in dealing with enemy pockets located in buildings and in [an] anti-personnel role'.[47]

O'Neill was concerned by an order to arrest a group of mercenaries when their jet arrived at Elisabethville airport. He explained to Defence Forces Chief of Staff Major General Seán Collins Powell that the arrival of an airliner at Elisabethville was 'like steamer day on the Aran Islands', there would be about 1,500 people at the airport and if Irish UN troops moved on the mercenaries 'there would certainly be an incident and a demonstration' by crowds aided by Gendarmerie and police.[48] O'Neill asked for instructions to follow if such a crowd attempted to take over the airport and Kjellgren gave O'Neill 'clear' orders – 'I should shoot on the crowd'. These orders were countered by Georges Dumontet, the UN civil chief in Elisabethville. O'Neill angrily told Dumontet and Kjellgren that 'they must be aware of the consequences of any actions'; the 34th Battalion would 'hold the airport as ordered. We will not allow any Irish soldier to be killed. In order to do this it may be necessary to open fire'. Faced with the possibility of further mob action at Elisabethville airport, O'Neill explained to the white Gendarmerie officers 'that we intend to shoot them first'. He added that if there was 'a rush on my men by an armed and crazy mob we will have to use perhaps machine-guns'. ONUC HQ in Leopoldville was 'asked for a decision as the machine-gunning of a mob, even an armed one, may not be in line with UN policy'. The Katangese government cancelled the mercenaries' arrival; however O'Neill regularly faced such scenarios. He had to work out how to react and how Tshombe might react, noting that these were 'some of the very tricky problems which must be faced … and then it may all be a bottle of smoke!'

Visiting the 34th Battalion Irish Liaison Officer Capt. Fogarty found Elisabethville airport 'completely calm with no tension whatsoever'.[49] B-Company was bivouacked in cramped and inadequate conditions at the terminal, yet there was 'a marked sense of discipline in this Company and Guards and Sentries were quite impressive and extremely alert. Indeed the entire Company was on its toes'. Food was good, despite the facilities available and 'there was a general air of cheerfulness and lightheartedness'. A-Company and 34th Battalion Tactical HQ were located 1¼ miles west of the airport at Sabena Villas on the main road to Elisabethville. The troops in this location were also under canvas, 'not a very pleasant place to be in a torrential downpour' Fogarty commented, and were dealing with the aftermath of the Swedish troops who had previously held the position having removed almost everything on their departure, an action which was 'deeply resented'. Conditions for the 34th Battalion did not improve and by mid-May they were still under canvas and sleeping on stretchers.[50] Their move to 'The Factory', a large empty factory on the outskirts of Elisabethville was, relatively speaking, an improvement, but was far from adequate. Headquarters Company was located in the Swedish Camp, four miles south of the airfield on the outskirts of the city. Fogarty reported that the battalion was widely dispersed, a problem O'Neill also raised. Writing of the behaviour of his men, O'Neill had

> never seen soldiers in better form. They are in wonderful spirits and most willing. We have not had a charge since we came here. The work here is most demanding. For days there has been a shortage of beer and minerals. The population are anti-UN. The men of B-Coy have not left their half-acre in 14 days. All troops are prohibited from visiting the city. We must be exceptionally tough on sentries and we have ceremonial guard mounting 4 times daily – this is to impress onlookers.[51]

O'Neill knew his forces were spread out, but 'nevertheless as our mission is to hold the airport it is essential that we remain where we are'.[52] A-Company and B-Company had Bren medium machine-guns and 81mm mortars, and Fogarty expected that the imminent arrival of the armoured cars from Kamina 'would greatly strengthen and reinforce this battalion and make the seizure of the Airfield a very tough proposition for any Katangese forces'.[53] The Swedes lent the Irish 84mm anti-tank guns 'against the cannon mounting armoured cars and the light AA guns of the Gendarmerie'.[54] The Irish also borrowed trip-mines from the Swedes. Training was prioritized and Fogarty saw platoons moving around the airfield engaged in bayonet and anti-riot drill. The Irish were given lectures on anti-riot tactics by a Norwegian officer and O'Neill informed Dublin that his men had 'done some training in mob drill using hurleys for every second man'.[55] Tear gas grenades were issued and respirator drill was 'the order of the day'. 'Great stress' was being laid on physical fitness and troops were playing football with locals at the airport. There was 'NO sign whatever of any hostility' towards Irish troops at the airport or in Elisabethville and despite their preparation for the worst 34th Battalion officers were 'optimistic that with careful handling the situation will again return to normal'.[56]

Kjellgren was not so optimistic and drew up an operational order for Elisabethville envisaging a continued Katangese boycott of ONUC, further demonstrations and riots, the taking of UN personnel hostage and attacks on UN positions at the airport and in the city. In this scenario the 'greatest importance' was attached to holding the airport and keeping it open for UN traffic.[57] The 10th Swedish Battalion would 'stand by ready to go to the airport to reinforce the troops there or to counterattack'. The 34th Battalion would hold the airport and block the main roads leading to the airport 'to ensure that [the] airfield remains in UN control, come what may'.[58] Two bazooka sections and three dogs with handlers were detached to the Irish battalion for these duties. O'Neill noted that the dogs were trained to kill.[59] Pre-planned positions were set out and it was for O'Neill to order them to be occupied. Operational orders explained that 'the use of force is authorised after parleying has failed, whenever there is danger to UN personnel or property. Although discretion is essential in the use of force, whenever the circumstances justify it, commanders at all levels must use their initiative and take action'.[60] Gendarmerie, police, or mobs were 'to be halted at outer positions and told that they have no access to airport. UN troops [to] show weapons ready for firing'.[61] Responsibility for what might follow would rest with the Katangese 'for challenging UN authority and for any armed clash'. Mobs would be warned, fired on with tear gas, and given the opportunity to withdraw. If direct fire had to be opened a limited number of men, not exceeding one section, were authorized to fire one round each at the mob leaders. Only as 'a very final step' if UN positions were about to be overwhelmed could the 'full shooting strength of troops' be resorted to.[62]

Katanga: April to May 1961

Meanwhile in northern Katanga in early April Gendarmerie moved northwest from Manono towards Kabalo. Ethiopian ONUC troops engaged them outside Kabalo stopping the advance and killing 80 Katangese after sinking a barge with mortar rounds and picking off the survivors with machine-gun fire. Hammarskjöld believed that 'the psychological impact in Katanga was good as the tendency to believe that the UN could be pushed around with impunity had been checked'.[63] The Kabalo incident raised tension in Katanga, which took time to subside, but it did not stop the fighting. Where ONUC could not maintain a presence Baluba and Katangese continued to skirmish. Hammarskjöld favoured the re-establishment of UN control over north Katanga, starting with Manono and Albertville, by recreating local neutral zones. The Secretary General proposed using Indian forces to strengthen ONUC in the area before getting external forces to withdraw. If this failed Hammarskjöld advised MacEoin to 'consider military action.'[64] Hammarskjöld, MacEoin and Abbas agreed that ONUC now 'must clear the whole of North Katanga and keep it as a neutral zone.'[65]

While these moves were ongoing the United Nations General Assembly voted on 15 April for a resolution calling on Belgian and other foreign military and paramilitary personnel and political advisors not under United Nations command to withdraw from Congo within three weeks. ONUC made no secret that it expected shortly to round up white Gendarmerie personnel. The worsening situation in north Katanga damaged the relationship between the

United Nations and Tshombe. Hammarskjöld became increasingly hostile towards the Katangese president after the Gendarmerie took Manono and UN policy in Katanga was now 'much coloured by emotional dislike of Tshombe'.[66] To Elisabethville it seemed that the UN was partisan, with ONUC attacking Katangese forces, but not the ANC forces occupying north Katanga. In fact the Katangese action in north Katanga in part persuaded Leopoldville to sign an agreement with the United Nations on 17 April through which Kasavubu and the UN made up. The 15 April resolution, the UN–Leopoldville agreement and the formation of a new government in Belgium with Paul Henri Spaak as foreign minister opened the possibility of implementing the February resolution and beginning the repatriation of unauthorized personnel from Katanga.

On 24 April Tshombe attended a conference at Coquilhatville, a continuation of earlier discussions at Tananarive on Congo's future. He withdrew after Baluba leader Jason Sendwe was admitted. Tshombe was then arrested by the Leopoldville authorities. The reaction in Elisabethville was 'incredulous and bewildered' but the population settled down in a 'subdued mood.'[67] Local feeling was that Tshombe might lose rather than gain support following his arrest. But Tshombe was 'firmly established and on good terms with his ministers ... now using the Belgians rather than vice-versa'.[68] Much of his success came from his knowledge of Katanga through his business interests and the solid support of his Lunda people and the tribes which formed his Conakat party. He was seen by many Europeans as 'a moderate of no small charm who frankly acknowledges his own limitations'.[69] Yet while Tshombe might listen to them courteously and sometimes even accept advice 'at all times he remains the President and a president with considerable determination and single-mindedness of purpose'. His sole objective was independence for Katanga.

Tshombe's incarceration occurred at the same time as Georges Dumontet became UN Special Representative in Katanga. Dumontet subtly explained to Katangese leaders that it was 'undignified' for African politicians to be surrounded by foreign advisers and he ridiculed that he was only able to meet Katangese leaders when Belgians were present.[70] Dumontet hit a chord with the aggressively anti-Belgian Godefroid Munongo who, with Tshombe jailed, emerged as Katanga's leading figure. He was 'intelligent, very hard working and conscientious, though without Tshombe's magnetic personality'.[71] Backed by his Belgian adviser Victor Tignée, Munongo was very much in charge in Elisabethville. On meeting Munongo and Tignée in Albertville some months earlier, officers from the 33rd Irish Battalion thought them 'a thoroughly bad pair'.[72] The expectation that Katanga would collapse in Tshombe's absence proved groundless.

When doubts were expressed about Katanga's continued independence Munongo emphasized that an attack on Katanga would be met with 'scorched earth tactics'.[73] But the energetic and ruthless Munongo would negotiate on individual issues and informed Hammarskjöld there could be movement on implementing the February resolution if Tshombe was released. He realized that co-operation with the UN would allow the removal of certain troublesome

Belgian advisors from Katanga. Munongo became more conciliatory towards the United Nations and acted cautiously, not wanting to provoke ONUC to act against mercenaries in north Katanga. Under Munongo's influence the recruiting of mercenaries halted and the boycotting of UN troops relaxed.

The UN military build up in Katanga continued; by late April ONUC had 7,000 troops in the province. In early May MacEoin intensified ONUC operations in north Katanga, moving Indian troops there from Kamina to repatriate Katangese mercenaries. Hammarskjöld expected ONUC to have complete control of north Katanga by early June. But his desire to solve the Katanga problem by action in north Katanga could jeopardize the stability of south Katanga. Hammarskjöld nevertheless remained 'reasonably confident about the Katanga situation'.[74] He was now co-operating closely with Kasavubu and hoped to create conditions whereby the Congolese parliament could meet. Linner had recently telexed Hammarskjöld from Leopoldville that 'we have reached a stage where the future of our activities, looked at from here, looks brighter than it has perhaps been for some time'.[75] The Congolese government was becoming more co-operative, trying to sort out their own affairs and Linner hoped that ONUC could increase its collaboration with Kasavubu.

The Indians soon took overall control of north Katanga. Where Tshombe had opposed the presence of Indian UN troops in Katanga outside Kamina, Munongo was more amenable. He agreed that a contingent of Gurkhas move to Manono on 8 June after MacEoin agreed to establish a unified ONUC command for Katanga. This was welcomed by the Katangese as proving that the UN had no intention of dividing the province. The establishment of Katanga Command was announced simultaneously by the UN and Elisabethville who proclaimed the move as the UN's recognition of Katanga and its territorial integrity. This the UN denied.

ONUC began in early June to re-organize the Katangese gendarmerie under the February resolution by removing Belgian and foreign personnel and replacing them by French-speaking ONUC officers. The Katangese government, Munongo explained to MacEoin, welcomed 'assistance from UN in providing senior officers for the interim period until they would be able to take over themselves'.[76] This was 'encouraging' and indicated that Munongo was 'behaving sensibly and working towards a more friendly relationship with the United Nations'.[77] Munongo co-operated far more than had seemed likely, but it was unclear if this would lead to 'appreciable headway' being made towards a rapprochement between Elisabethville and Leopoldville.[78] But taking first things first, with Munongo in control Elisabethville was 'superficially less intransigent to the United Nations'.[79]

Norwegian Lt Col. Bjorn Egge assisted the Katangese authorities reforming the Gendarmerie and advised on 30 June that 512 foreigners of all ranks in the Gendarmerie should be removed, suggesting that 460 replacements were needed from ONUC if all foreigners were withdrawn. This was impolitic as the UN could not support a Gendarmerie that was upholding Katangese independence. Belgium in any case rejected Egge's proposals. In practical terms the number of

ONUC personnel required was not available. The Secretariat felt that the Katangese were playing for time and had no intention of implementing the February resolution.

Conor Cruise O'Brien

In May 1961 Sture Linner, ONUC Chief of Civilian Operations, became 'Officer in Charge' in Congo with all soldiers and civilians in ONUC subordinate to him. Tunisian diplomat Mahmoud Khiari took charge of the civilian operation and political contact work. Khiari was 'a consummate politician who rarely hit the headlines because he performed his main negotiating services in softness and silence behind the scenes'.[80] He became ONUC's eminence grise. ONUC also required a new man in Katanga. In mid-May 1961, at Hammarskjöld's request, Aiken agreed to release Conor Cruise O'Brien from the Department of External Affairs, where he was an Assistant Secretary in the Political Section with responsibility for UN affairs, to take up a senior post in the Political Division of the UN Secretariat. Dublin specifically asked that O'Brien not be assigned immediately to Katanga. Hammarskjöld accordingly reassigned O'Brien to duties in Katanga in June 1961 where he replaced Dumontet as the Secretary General's Special Representative. The 'charming, slightly pugnacious, black-suited-diplomat' knew his task was to implement the February resolution.[81]

Hammarskjöld's exact rationale for selecting O'Brien is unclear. The Secretary General's interest in O'Brien's literary works has been noted by some to explain his interest in O'Brien. In February 1961, when the United Nations first requested O'Brien's release for service in Congo, Hammarskjöld's executive assistant Andrew Cordier referred to *Maria Cross*, a collection of essays on Catholic writers, as one of O'Brien's 'excellent books'.[82] However O'Brien's performance as a member of the Irish UN delegation was also a driving factor in his choice. Cordier highlighted O'Brien's 'excellent career in government and also in literature'. O'Brien had a sense of originality in both that appealed to Hammarskjöld and had showed 'clear thinking and independent judgment' and an 'ability to appreciate the Afro–Asian point of view.'[83] By May 1961 the UN was actively seeking a replacement for Dumontet and Hammarskjöld was limited to the choice of an official from a European neutral state to act as his special representative in Katanga.[84] He had appointed Linner, a Swede, to Leopoldville; therefore he could not appoint another Swede to Elisabethville. Coming from another European neutral state, and one that was unswervingly loyal to the UN, O'Brien was, Hammarskjöld felt, the right man for Katanga. Alan James has suggested that in Katanga O'Brien 'would be in the business of executing policy, not making it', but if Hammarskjöld really thought so he had appointed the wrong man.[85] In the Irish diplomatic service O'Brien often displayed a tendency to bypass normal channels of authority and act on his own initiative. Hammarskjöld's judgement over O'Brien's suitability as his representative in Katanga and the basis of his decision to appoint O'Brien remain unclear, nevertheless they can be called into question as O'Brien had no practical experience of African affairs.

As to O'Brien's own motivation, the British ambassador in Dublin, Sir Ian Maclennan considered that to say O'Brien was '"anti-Colonial" is no doubt true, though I had not thought of him as being so rabidly so, but merely as taking the views which you might expect of an Irish intellectual with academic interests and no firsthand experience of any Colony'.[86] Maclennan continued that 'what is unfortunate is that O'Brien's anti-Colonial views may have been strongly reinforced by his Irish Republican views on Partition ... O'Brien has been emotionally biased against any kind of devolution of authority to Katanga even within a Congo Federation'. Katanga was often portrayed in the British and Irish press as 'the Ulster of the Congo' and O'Brien's Irish political upbringing and his international experience suggested correctly that he would have little tolerance of Katanga's desired independence from Congo.[87] Reading himself into his brief at the Secretariat O'Brien got 'an ill-defined sense of uneasiness' about the UN's activities in Congo.[88] He considered that many in New York, including Hammarskjöld's personal circle, lacked a clear picture of what was happening in Congo and were not adequately informed to take worthwhile decisions. This was to become a leitmotif of the UN's Congo policy through 1961.

O'Brien arrived in Katanga on 14 June determined to implement the UN's mandate in the province. Working under Linner's overall responsibility, O'Brien's understood he had 'the necessary flexibility and margin of manoeuvre to get the work done'.[89] Later events would show this to be a very significant declaration. O'Brien explained to Munongo that he meant to end Katanga's secession. O'Brien advised Linner that 'in putting the pressure on harder as we must do, we will be faced with dangers of serious contretemps if the means at our disposal are not adequate to the demands placed on them. This is unfortunately the case at present.'[90] Soon after his arrival O'Brien realized that he and Egge faced serious problems removing foreign mercenaries from Katanga. They were 'extremely dangerous men' and he told MacEoin that 'the present position in this regard is so unsatisfactory as to be positively dangerous'. The repatriation of the Belgian political advisors had not been an easy task either and after Tshombe was released and returned to Elisabethville on 24 June the anti-ONUC mood intensified. ONUC would have to become 'a good deal tougher as regards implementing the resolutions' and O'Brien assumed 'that in no case will the Katangese authorities give us genuine and active co-operation.'[91] The forcible expulsion of foreign mercenaries and Belgian advisors was looming. O'Brien feared that ONUC, lacking the military means to act, was not up to the task of removing them.

A crowd of 10,000 had greeted Tshombe at Elisabethville airport on his release and ONUC intelligence sources reported that 2,000 of them were Europeans. They also saw that European houses from the airport to the city displayed Katangese flags, and wondered if this was 'genuine admiration for the President or it might be good business to appear loyal'.[92] As July progressed Tshombe's 'prestige and position' seemed 'unchallengeable'.[93] He told O'Brien that he would send Katangese deputies to the Congolese parliament after meeting with Kasavubu and Gizenga. Hammarskjöld accordingly felt there were good hopes of political stability following the expected meeting of parliament in Leopoldville. But there were 'prolonged and tortuous negotiations' being conducted in such a manner 'as to make it virtually impossible to find out exactly what is taking place'.[94] Tshombe, Munongo and Minister for Finance Jean Baptiste Kibwe were planning holidays, leading British consul in Elisabethville Denzil Dunnett to conclude that 'it hardly looks as if Katangan ministers expected to be taking major constitutional steps in the next month or so'. Linner was worried and speculated that due to social unrest and economic problems Mobutu might feel that from Leopoldville's perspective 'a military coup d'eclat might come in handy in diverting the preoccupation of the masses' and his forces might invade Katanga and cause widespread civil war.[95] He proposed to an astounded Hammarskjöld that ONUC

> make a show of strength in Katanga and draw the carpet from under Tshombe's and consequently Mobutu's feet by taking the whole of the province over by force, pushing out all the Belgian and French personnel quickly. I do not know if this would be politically possible from your end but time may be running short and the only language people around here understand is forceful action. MacEoin assures me that he has troops of sufficient quality and strength now in Katanga to achieve this in a relatively short time.

Here in stark terms is a signpost giving an early indication of the direction in which ONUC was moving. Dealing with Tshombe's Katanga by force was now an acceptable option for ONUC as far as the UN's most senior official in Congo was concerned.

Hammarskjöld was not impressed by Linner's proposed 'extreme departure' as it would make ONUC an 'occupation force' in Katanga. He preferred a 'harsher policy' to expel Belgian and French officers.[96] The UN also planned to disengage Tshombe from his extremist supporters. O'Brien remained hopeful. He tried to bring Tshombe and Kasavubu together in Leopoldville and get Gizenga to join them for a summit as a precursor to parliament meeting in Leopoldville. O'Brien explained to Tshombe that 'only by participation could he avert or at least reduce the risk of decision[s] inimical to Katanga being adopted'.[97] Tshombe would not go to Leopoldville, fearing a coup by Munongo and Kibwe under the growing influence of extremists encouraged by French mercenaries.

A significant step forward was the removal by ONUC of Tshombe's political advisor Georges Thyssens in early July. At the same time ONUC had to counter the growing French influence in Katanga. In Tshombe's absence Munongo had courted French interests to secure their goodwill should his rapprochement with the UN fail. A cat-and-mouse game followed through July. The Katangese played down the French influence, especially when it came to mercenaries. Information at MacEoin's disposal nevertheless suggested that French military and political interests were working in Katanga to usurp Belgian influence and gain an economic foothold in the province. France had never supported ONUC, and opinion in the French government favoured Katanga.

Like Linner, O'Brien was becoming more aggressive towards Katanga. He wrote to Linner 'that the people here will do nothing without being squeezed and to some extent frightened'.[98] It was a sure sign of things to come. Yet despite this O'Brien settled into Elisabethville easily. He was content and developing the manner of a colonial administrator, writing that he was 'enjoying life in Elisabethville very much indeed, although I have the idea that I am unlikely to win any local popularity contest'.[99] His mood verged on arrogance as he speculated to a United Nations colleague that 'fate may bring you to the Congo while I am here. In that case we will have a party and eat some Belgians ... '[1] Aware his letters were read by the Katangese he kept them short, closing one: 'the local Gestapo are in the habit of censuring [sic] the mail. I doubt myself whether they can really read it'.[2] He wrote to Munongo that his 'only goal' was the implementation of Security Council resolutions, 'the only policy that could create chaos in Katanga is precisely a policy to thwart the implementation of the resolutions'.[3] It was a warning to Katanga. Hammarskjöld, though appalled at Linner's suggestion of the use of force in Katanga, was allowing his officials in Congo greater personal initiative. O'Brien and Linner were now not averse to using force. The fate of Katanga's secession would be decided in a head-to-head clash between ONUC and Katanga in Elisabethville as the incoming 35th Irish Battalion was about to find out.

CHAPTER 5

The 35th Irish Battalion

The 35th Irish Battalion

ADDRESSING THE General Assembly on 28 March 1961 in defence of the UN and Hammarskjöld, Aiken attacked the Soviets for using the Congo crisis 'as ammunition in … a deliberate campaign against the United Nations and all that it stands for'.[1] Small states, he argued, had a duty to uphold the UN because it safeguarded their independence. Two days later Ireland had to live up to this rhetoric when the UN requested a replacement for the 34th Battalion when its tour of duty ended in June 1961. Hammarskjöld knew that more troops were needed in Congo, that ONUC must 'do the best job we can with the tools in hand', and that Katanga needed to 'receive [the] highest priority.'[2] On 18 April the cabinet in Dublin discussed Hammarskjöld's request and a further linked request for two additional infantry companies to be deployed for early service with ONUC as 'white troops were needed for the United Nations force and it is assumed that they are required in Katanga'.[3] The cabinet agreed on 21 April to provide two infantry companies to be integrated with the 34th Battalion. This became the 300-strong '1st Irish Infantry Group' which departed for Congo in late May commanded by Lt Col. John O'Donovan.[4]

The cabinet also agreed to the formation of the replacement battalion, the '35th Irish Battalion', contingent on sufficient volunteers being available. Lemass agreed a press release explaining that ONUC remained necessary 'to achieve the purposes for which it was initiated' and that consequently the 34th Battalion would be replaced.[5] On 5 May, the Chief of Staff, Maj. Gen. Seán Collins Powell, authorized the formation of the new battalion. Serving in Congo had become 'the dream of every soldier as they wished to get away from the drab routine of twenty-four hour barrack and camp duties where excitement was almost always absent'.[6] Unit commanders drew up lists of requirements and worked out what men could be spared as through June 1961 the personnel who would form the 35th Battalion were selected. As with previous battalions, the Defence Forces gave these men little background briefing on the mission they were about to undertake.

The 35th Battalion eventually comprised 626 personnel all-ranks and was to be commanded by Lt Col. C.J. Burke. On 20 May Lt Col. Olaf MacNeill replaced Burke as commanding officer. His second-in-command was Comdt Hugh McNamee. The battalion was made up of Battalion Headquarters, Headquarters

Company, A, B and C Infantry Companies and an Armoured Car Group. A-Company, commanded by Comdt Pat Quinlan, was recruited from Western Command; B-Company commanded by Comdt Alo McMahon from Southern Command; and C-Company commanded by Comdt Tom O'Neill from the Curragh Training Camp. Battalion Headquarters and Headquarters Company came from a selection of Defence Forces units. The Cavalry Corps provided personnel for the Armoured Car Group.

The OC of the Armoured Car Group was Comdt Pat Cahalane, Senior Staff Officer at the Cavalry Directorate, Curragh Camp and Capt. Art Magennis of the 1st Armoured Squadron was second-in-command. Cahalane and Magennis agreed in advance of the Armoured Car Group's deployment that Cahalane would look after the paperwork and keep the unit functioning administratively while Magennis, who had greater experience in handling armoured cars, looked after operational duties and training. The Armoured Car Group numbered 53 all-ranks – 7 officers, 18 NCOs and 28 troopers. It was divided into two Troops; the Troop commanders being Capt. Seán Hennessy of the 1st Motor Squadron, Fermoy, and Capt. Mark Carroll of the Cavalry Depot, Curragh Camp. Capt. Frank Lawless was Technical Officer and Lt Kevin Knightly and Lt Michael Considine were Section officers.

Personnel issues beset the 35th Battalion and this was particularly so at headquarters level. On deployment a significant number of senior officers were posted from Battalion HQ to South Katanga Command HQ (later Sector-B) in Elisabethville and ONUC HQ in Leopoldville. The most senior move was the August 1961 departure of battalion commander Lt Col. MacNeill to Leopoldville and his replacement as the battalion was about to go into action by Comdt (later Lt Col.) McNamee. Comdt Sean Barrett, Battalion Operations Officer, moved to South Katanga Command HQ in early July 1961. This led to Intelligence and Operations becoming a combined Section in Battalion Headquarters under Comdt John Kane, who was promoted to second-in-command after McNamee became battalion commander. Kane was not content with his combined roles, writing to Dublin that 'the drawing of the Int Offr into the Ops side of things too has taken from the time one would like to spend on Int.'[7] He was being honest and the 35th Battalion would suffer from a lack of personnel devoted solely to intelligence work. 35th Battalion HQ was severely stretched from early in the battalion's deployment. Vacant posts were filled by Battalion Headquarters doubling up duties.

35th Battalion HQ soon almost ceased to exist and no attempt was made to rebuild it with new staff officers from Ireland. This depletion raises the question of what role Headquarters was originally expected to play in the 35th Battalion and at what point it ceased to operate as an effective unit. According to Comdt Quinlan, in a swipe at Headquarters, the 35th Battalion suffered from a lack of strategic cohesion. Quinlan was 'not very happy about our Battalion plan. There is no co-ordination at Battalion level so I'm just minding my own Company.'[8] While the 35th Battalion brought with it from Ireland many differences of opinion and outlook at senior level, and also a number of ongoing resentments

35th Irish Battalion – ONUC

Officer Commanding
Lt Col. Olaf MacNeill (16 June to 26 August 1961)
Lt Col. Hugh McNamee (26 August 1961 to December 1961)

Second in Command
Comdt Hugh McNamee (16 June 1961 to 26 August 1961)
Comdt John Kane (26 August 1961 to December 1961)

Senior Headquarters Personnel
Operations Officer: Comdt J.J. Barrett[9]
Adjutant: Comdt Edward Condon
Quartermaster: Comdt J. Pierce Wheatley
Intelligence Officer: Comdt John Kane
Legal Officer: Comdt Tadhg O'Shea[10]
Assistant Operations Officer: Capt. Joe Stewart
Assistant Intelligence Officer: Capt. James Parker[11]
Communications Officer: Capt. Jerry Melinn[12]

Company Commanders and Seconds in Command

Headquarters Company	'A' Company	'B' Company	'C' Company	Armoured Car Group
OC Comdt P. J. Barry	OC Comdt Pat Quinlan	OC Comdt Alo McMahon	OC Comdt Tom O'Neill	OC Comdt Pat Cahalane
2iC Capt. Gerry Melinn	2iC Capt. Dermot Byrne	2iC Capt. Seán O'Connell	2iC Capt. Roger McCorley	2iC Capt. Art Magennis

Table 1. 35th Battalion – key posts and post holders

Company HQ	No. 1 Rifle Platoon[13]	No. 2 Rifle Platoon	No. 3 Rifle Platoon	Support Platoon[14]

Table 2. Infantry Company composition

and personal conflicts, this was not unusual as differences of opinion for a variety of reasons, some personal, some professional and some long-standing were a common feature of battalions sent overseas.

Battalion Headquarters tended to be remote from the day-to-day operations of companies, which operated as semi-autonomous units. This was particularly so if a company was operating away from Battalion Headquarters. Company commanders attended briefings at Battalion Headquarters and on return told their officers what was happening. In the strictly hierarchical structure of the Defence Forces of the 1960s MacNeill and McNamee were nevertheless far-off figures to the lieutenants and captains of the 35th Battalion. Through July and August 35th Battalion components functioned as expected but as headquarters staff were reduced discontent rose particularly with regard to the provision of intelligence at company level. Thus the 35th Battalion went into action in late August 1961 under a new commander and with its headquarters at its most depleted.

Battalion preparation, weapons and equipment

As the 35th Battalion formed up it was a busy time at the Curragh Camp for infantry units and at Fermoy Camp for cavalry units supplying the Armoured Car Group. For the Armoured Car Group as far as possible all ranks were to be qualified gunner-drivers and radio operators. As the Group came from a variety of units there was no time for it to gel or to train together before embarking for Katanga. Unlike the 35th Battalion's infantry companies, which had two weeks' basic training in Ireland, the Armoured Car Group would undertake basic training and orientation in Elisabethville. This was unfortunate and Lt Col. O'Neill had earlier warned against it:

> The next battalion must get into training for its role now. We got our chance in Kamina but we should not bank upon the chance of training here before action commences. Many of our men were virtually untrained – some were only 17/18 years old. In the new Battalion they may not get the chance to harden these men.[15]

O'Neill was primarily a staff officer and before ONUC had little experience as a battalion commander. Yet his staff experience and experience on the ground in Katanga made his reports and his suggestions among the most comprehensive sent from any Irish ONUC deployment. He made some prescient comments on the necessary armament of future ONUC battalions:

> In view of the changed conditions here, the heavy armament of our possible adversaries and the possible offensive role of the UN under the recent UN resolution it will be necessary to review the armament of the next Battalion coming out. *FN rifles will be necessary.* They *must* have bayonets. Bazookas will be a necessity in each Company. Anti-aircraft mountings for machine-guns fitted for jeeps will also be required (We are buzzed daily by spotter aircraft. They have been known to drop grenades in action against the ANC). The Swedes have steel helmets. We have only the papier-mâché one. The Swedes are also supplied with clubs and riot shields. Our men must be protected in case of mob fights. The range of

the Gustav [sub-machine-gun] is not great enough against the FN automatic rifle which is standard equipment for Gendarmerie, ANC and even police. The Swedes are sending home for a lot of extra equipment, including light tanks.[16]

The 35th Battalion brought 70 tons of equipment to Congo and took over the heavy equipment of the 34th Battalion, including its 81mm mortars. The types and numbers of the weapons taken by the battalion are given below and are a more modern array than those brought by previous battalions.

9mm Carl Gustav sub-machine-gun	374	60mm mortar	14
7.62mm FN automatic rifle	272	81mm mortar[17]	7
.38" revolver[18]	56	84mm Carl Gustav anti-tank rifle	13
.303" Bren light machine-gun Mk III	44	Energa grenade launchers	51
.303" Vickers medium machine-gun	7 (Infantry) 11 (Cavalry)		

Table 3. 35th Battalion weapons and quantities

9mm Carl Gustav sub-machine-gun	78	60mm mortar	3
7.62mm FN automatic rifle	64	84mm Carl Gustav anti-tank rifle	3
.303" Vickers medium machine-gun	2	Energa grenade launchers	17
.303" Bren light machine-gun Mk III	12		

Table 4. 35th Battalion company weapons and quantities

.303" light machine-gun (ball)	96,800 rounds	60mm mortar (smoke)	396
.303" light machine-gun (tracer)	9,680 rounds	84mm Carl Gustav anti-tank rifle	390
.303" medium machine-gun (ball)	182,000 rounds	Energa anti-tank grenades	265
.303" medium machine-gun (tracer)	28,600 rounds	No. 36 grenades	684
9mm Carl Gustav sub-machine-gun	290,304 rounds	Smoke grenades	600
7.62mm FN rifle	136,000 rounds	Lachrymatory Grenades	400
60mm mortar (high-explosive)	1,692		

Table 5. 35th Battalion ammunition stocks

Communications within and from Congo were extremely difficult and the type of equipment being used by the Defence Forces was not designed for long-range operation. Attempts were made to broadcast from the Curragh to Congo by shortwave radio, but due to interference from commercial stations the Irish broadcasts were often not picked up in Congo. The 35th Battalion kept in direct contact with Ireland via an AC12 shortwave set, another unidentified transmitter of higher power and via contacts with amateur radio operators. The Curragh station was generally out of action but some broadcasts did get through to and from Ireland. Those containing news from Ireland, especially sports results, were greatly appreciated.

Communications from New York to ONUC HQ in Leopoldville were by telex via Geneva. The Canadian armed forces were in charge of trans-Congo communications operating a thinly-spread net of ANGRC-26 radio-teletype transceivers. These operated from sectors to brigades and commands and back to ONUC Headquarters. They also operated from sector to battalion level. Over longer distances some command-level communications were provided by Indian and Irish signallers using BC610 sets supplied by the United Nations. In the 35th Battalion communications equipment was reasonably modern but basic. Radio nets could range between one and 500 miles. Signallers worked sets beyond their ranges and found inventive methods of ensuring communications in the difficult reaches of the tropical zones where radio communications were highly problematic due to distance and atmospherics.

Communication from battalion headquarters to company and armoured car group headquarters was by the Pye Wireless Set C12, a high-frequency voice and Morse transceiver with a level range of about 60 miles. Developed in the mid-1950s, it operated between 1.6 Mhz and 10.0 Mhz. This versatile set became a workhorse of Irish ONUC operations as a base set and mobile in patrols, armoured cars, trains and on occasion in aircraft. With the 35th Battalion it was 'required to do work well outside its normal function'.[19] The 32nd Battalion thought it a 'really first class set, both from the point of view of the range in communications it provided, and its serviceability throughout the entire six-month period'.[20] 32nd Battalion HQ in Goma and C-Company in Kamina established Morse communications via a C12 set over a distance of close to 550 miles.

Communication between company headquarters and platoons and armoured car sections was by Wireless Set 31, a short-range man-pack radio introduced in 1948 with a range of about five miles. 33rd Battalion found these sets adequate but not rugged enough for operation in Congo. The Wireless Set 88, also a manpack radio, introduced in 1947, was used for communication from company to platoon and mortar units. The 35th Battalion considered that both the No. 31 and No. 88 sets 'fulfilled their function' when used during the attack on The Tunnel in Elisabethville in December 1961, but only did so because they were fitted with good batteries.[21] The 36th Battalion Unit History was also critical of the role of local sets in operations as 'control was rendered difficult by complete failure of local communications'.[22]

There were no cypher systems available to ONUC forces below Command level and 35th Battalion signallers knew their network was monitored by Katangese forces. As Irish officers and signallers were not trained in code systems beyond the cumbersome Slidex system, they adopted an ad-hoc practice of speaking rapidly in Irish dialect. Irish language words were used as code words. McNamee agreed the list reproduced below containing 'code words to be used in verbal, phone, or radio messages'.[23] They were used in the almost exclusively Irish language communications between 35th Battalion HQ and South Katanga Command HQ where Comdts Barrett and O'Shea were on the staff. Comdt Kane felt that this system was necessary as 'phones are tapped here and wireless monitored.'[24] Such codes were not favoured by ONUC, in particular by Irish officers working at ONUC Headquarters in Leopoldville. Col. Quinn, MacEoin's Assistant Chief of Staff, was 'rather shocked' when Conor Cruise O'Brien suggested using Irish to pass secret information, Quinn explaining to South Katanga Command Headquarters in Elisabethville that 'allusive style or use of Irish language cannot be accepted as a means of passing classified information'.[25] The Katangese recorded messages passed 'as Gaeilge' and had them translated by Irish missionaries in Northern Rhodesia.

People		*Places*	
Gendarmerie	FCA	Katanga	Sasanach
Police	Garda	Elisabethville	Blath Cliath
Officer	Taoiseach	Jadotville	Luimneach
Civilian	Duine	Leopoldville	Londun
Belgian	Ultach	Kamina	Cill Cionnaigh
Blackman	Fear Gorm	Kasenga	Cill Dara
Whiteman	Fear Geal	Mokambo	Muileann Gearr
Indian	Fear Dearg	Albertville	Ard Macha
ONU Person	Cara (Cairde)	Goma	Gaillimh
		Bukavu	Bailebeg
Vehicles		Manono	Maghalla
Heavy Truck	Capall	Nyunzu	Nas
Light Truck, Jeep	Asal	Kolwezi	Cill Coca
Landrover		Kabalo	Corcaigh
Saloon	Madra	Dilolo	Dunmor
Aircraft	Preacan	Luluaburg	Lismor

Table 6. Ad-hoc code-words adopted by 35th Battalion

Preparing for the arrival of the 35th Battalion

Lt Col. O'Neill recommended that the 35th Battalion advance party depart for Elisabethville two weeks before the main body of the battalion and that it

> consist of operations and intelligence reps as well as Q and A. It is vital that the operational and intelligence background be fully passed on and understood. It cannot be done in a briefing. Contacts must be introduced, plans explained, rehearsed etc. It will also be necessary to have Company representatives, owing to the dispersal of our locations.[26]

The advance party of five officers and one NCO assembled in early June 1961. It was to facilitate the changeover between battalions and was headed by Comdt McNamee who was to 'learn the operational task' facing the 35th Battalion.[27] McNamee brought with him Comdt Tadhg O'Shea, Comdt T. Moynihan, Capt. Art Magennis, Capt. K. O'Halloran, Capt. E.F. Whyte and Sgt F. Linanne. They

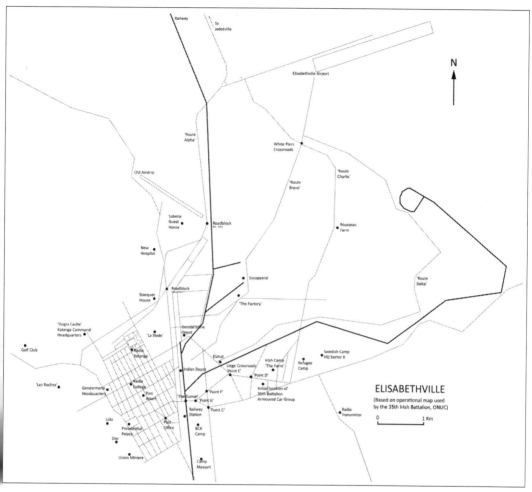

4 Elisabethville city map, 1961

left for Leopoldville on 10 June, with the battalion scheduled to depart ten days later. Shortly after takeoff they learned that an Irish diplomat now with the UN, a Dr Cruise O'Brien, was on board their flight. The Irish soldiers were travelling tourist class and O'Brien first class. McNamee asked the cabin crew to let O'Brien know that they were next door, but O'Brien did not come back to meet them. They politely put this down to their being on a night flight and that O'Brien preferred to sleep.

The advance party landed in Leopoldville just as dawn was breaking. They met MacEoin and were bound that afternoon for Elisabethville where the air temperature 'was in the thirties, but with a pleasant, dry heat, a heat much more agreeable than the warmer, damp heat of Leopoldville'.[28] At the Elisabethville airport groups of Belgians lounged, watching the arrival of the flight, sipping gin and tonic or coffee and listening to a military band. The band was 'more rhythmic than musical, trumpets and bugles galore and the percussion section competing almost violently. Their uniform was bright, almost gaudy, in the Katangan colours of red, green, black and white and their head gear sported a very elaborate cockade'. This was not the Africa that Capt. Magennis had anticipated, 'but six months of this, I thought, would suit fine. It was very far indeed from the lions, elephants and tropical jungle I had expected'.[29]

Comdt Herbie McDwyer, OC C-Company 34th Battalion, and his second in command, Capt. Roger O'Shea, met the advance party and after a quick orientation of the airport they departed for the battalion's headquarters. The airport was about three miles northeast of Elisabethville and connected to the city by a tarmac dual carriageway lined with villas surrounded by brightly flowering trees and shrubs. Elisabethville presented 'the appearance of a Belgian colonial town. Its streets are clean and swept, its residential quarters spacious and well-planned with pleasant gardens. There is plenty of traffic in the streets and, compared with Leopoldville, plenty of goods in the shops.'[30] After a drink of 'Simba', the local beer, at the Commander's Headquarters, Lt Col. O'Neill arrived and took McNamee off for a briefing. The other members of the advance party continued to the nearby headquarters of the 34th Battalion at Leopold Farm, known as 'The Farm', a large villa on Avenue des Savonniers on the eastern outskirts of Elisabethville. The following morning McNamee called a conference of the advance party and laid down tasks. Magennis was to take over the Armoured Car Group and be responsible for battalion transport, vehicle administration, fuel supply and accountancy as well as for heavy vehicle repairs outside the capability of battalion technicians.

Busy days followed ahead of the arrival of the main contingent of the 35th Battalion. The Armoured Car Group presented no problem as the vehicles and weapons being handed over by the 34th Battalion were in reasonable shape. The modifications to the Ford armoured cars to improve the efficiency of the carburettor air filters remained to be undertaken. The air filters continually clogged on dust tracks and the advance party needed to understand the operational performance of the Fords in the difficult conditions of Katanga. Sgt Steve Sullivan, senior fitter NCO of the 34th Battalion Armoured Car Group, recalled a mixed column of Swedish APCs and Irish Fords moving from Kamina to Elisabethville –

> The dust that the leading APCs threw up was like a thick fog at home. Our air filters were not able to cope with the dust. Every so often we had to stop. We cleaned the filters as best we could and then sucked out the fuel leads from the [petrol] tanks and set off again. We had a planned stop about halfway, and when the filtering process was completed and the Cook Sgt. announced he had food ready for all the fitters all I could say was 'no fucking food. What we need is a barrel of Beamish each.' But we made it to Elisabethville the following day and there is no doubt that better fuel filters are necessary.[31]

Despite making final preparations for the journey home Comdt Joe Foley, commander of the outgoing armoured car group, provided Magennis with a Landrover to familiarize himself with the city. The isolation of the 34th Battalion's Headquarters at The Farm presented a problem. Located about three miles from the airport, there was only one route available from The Farm to the airport and it was through central Elisabethville. As the 34th Battalion was preparing to leave Elisabethville Tshombe organized a demonstration, which made access to the airport along that route difficult. The 35th Battalion had to solve this dangerous situation and, with the help of Capt. Ted Sheehy, Magennis developed a second route that began as a lower-class road and turned into a deeply rutted narrow bush track. It was difficult to negotiate with a four-wheel-drive Landrover and the gradient was hazardous for the rear-wheel-drive Ford armoured cars.

One of the most difficult problems facing the advance party was how to counter off-duty boredom. Darkness fell early, around 1830, and there was little to do in the evening. From a comfortable armchair on the veranda of the Irish Officers' Mess 34th Battalion Medical Officer Comdt Elliot captured the predicament. Pointing to the star-lit sky he declared that from now to bedtime was the worst time of the day. 'Did you ever see the Southern Cross?' he asked Magennis.[32] 'Well', Elliot continued, 'now there it is, almost straight above us and watch, it keeps slowly turning, and when it has turned through 90 degrees I get up from this seat and go to bed, and that's the end of my day – every day since I arrived in this place.' With this in mind, when Comdt Gill, the 34th Battalion's Legal Officer, suggested to Magennis that he join him in a regular Tuesday evening game of bridge at the Belgian Officers' Mess at Gendarmerie Headquarters, Magennis 'jumped at the offer', later writing 'little did I know it at the time but I was to become very familiar with this location in the course of the 35th Battalion's tour of duty'. Gill was well known to the Belgians and he and Magennis were admitted without security procedures. After 'a very pleasant game' Magennis agreed with Gill that 'it was a much better evening than one spent following the gyrations of the Southern Cross across the heavens.'

The 35th Battalion arrive in Katanga

The 35th Battalion activated on Friday 16 June 1961 under Lt Col. MacNeill's command. Lemass, with Minister for Defence Boland and Minister for External Affairs Aiken, reviewed the battalion in Dublin at McKee Barracks on 19 June. The first elements of the battalion were to leave Ireland the following day. Lemass' speech was strong on rhetoric; the battalion's object was 'the promotion of brotherly relations between men … a purpose worthy of Irish soldiers'.[33] Lemass continued that 'the outlook in the Congo is rather more hopeful than it was some months ago … I hope that during your service in the Congo you will have the satisfaction of seeing the present hopeful trends developing and expanding to the benefit of the sorely tried Congolese people'.[34] Lemass ignored the situation in Katanga. Tshombe had dug himself in and could only, in reality, be ejected by force. The February resolution brought the use of force to end Katanga's secession firmly onto the United Nations' agenda. Outside a small number of senior officers, the 35th Battalion knew little about political currents in Congo or Katanga. Most thought that 'there were no political implications for us in the Congo situation; we were going there simply to restore order'.[35] The 35th Battalion would not have the satisfaction of seeing peace reign in Congo. They would play a central role in the United Nations' ill-fated attempts to end Katanga's secession. What no-one pointed out to the 35th Battalion, or to its predecessors, was that 'in the collective UN view, ONUC was in Congo to settle issues, not to be the spectator of or mediator in them'.[36]

The first elements of B-Company departed from Dublin airport on 20 June on United States Air Force Globemaster transport aircraft.[37] Phase one of the airlift comprised A-Company, B-Company, C-Company (minus),[38] Battalion HQ and HQ-Company (minus) and the Armoured Car Group. The remainder of the battalion, the final elements of HQ and HQ-Company and C-Company followed on 25 and 26 June.

The first 35th Battalion troops passed through Wheelus Air Force Base in Libya, Leopoldville and Kamina and landed at Elisabethville on 23 June. B-Company secured Elisabethville airport, allowing A-Company to arrive on 25 and 26 June and pass through to their camp at 'The Factory', a disused factory on Avenue Usoke previously used by the 34th Battalion.[39] It had been marked by the UN as 'not a suitable billet for a unit doing patrol and guard duty'.[40] Comdt Pat Quinlan, OC A-Company 35th Battalion, thought The Factory 'a shambles', adding 'it is so bad as to be degrading to any Irish soldier to ask him to sleep there'.[41] The UN suggested instead that the 35th Battalion be located in full at Leopold Farm in place of the 34th Battalion; 'well appointed and conducive to high morale', it had 'the space to concentrate two Rifle Companies, the Armoured Car Group and HQ Company' and this gave 'the necessary concentration and control for the speedy fulfilment of the primary task of the Battalion'.[42] From Leopold Farm there were routes to the airport, the buildings were in good repair and temporary accommodation could be erected. Its proximity to the Swedish 12th Battalion camp was 'tactically good and simplifies the problem of control from the Brigade point of view'.[43]

On arrival on 29 June C-Company took over security duties at Elisabethville airport from B-Company. Last to arrive was the balance of B-Company. They touched down at Elisabethville on the afternoon of 2 July, were met by a 'resounding welcome party', and moved directly into the Elisabethville city area.[44] By 1300 on 2 July the 35th Battalion was 'complete and fully operational', arriving in Elisabethville as ONUC reached a strength of 19,825.[45] The battalion's principal mission was to hold the airport and its secondary task, working with the 12th Swedish Battalion, was to maintain law and order in Elisabethville and 'interpose a force between Africans and Europeans should the former be roused to go on the war-path and seek to molest whites and burn or otherwise destroy property'.[46] 35th Battalion forces were scattered in five locations over seven miles throughout Elisabethville. A-Company was at The Factory, and B-Company and

C-Company at Elisabethville airport and Sabena Villas. The Battalion Headquarters, Headquarters Company and the Armoured Car Group were located in the east of the city at The Farm on Avenue des Savonniers.[47]

ONUC Command Structures

The 35th Battalion slotted into the ONUC command structures developed since July 1960. Its Unit History explains that 'the Battalion's overall mission was to maintain the UN presence in a secessionist and increasingly hostile Katanga. The Battalion was at all times part of a higher formation which directed its activities more or less closely'.[48] In overall command of the military aspects of ONUC was the Force Commander at ONUC HQ in Leopoldville. The successive order of ONUC precedence, dictated by Hammarskjöld, was –

1. ONUC Supreme Commander (Force Commander)
2. ONUC Chief of Staff
3. Brigade Commanders
4. Battalion Commanders (or Grade 1 Staff Officers or equivalent)
5. Company Commanders.[49]

The Congo was sub-divided into military districts or 'Commands'. Prior to July 1961 there were three Commands in Katanga – 'North Katanga', 'South Katanga' and 'Kamina Base'. In July 1961 they were merged as 'Katanga Command' with its headquarters in Elisabethville. Katanga Command came into formal existence on 5 August 1961 as 'an operational command, co-ordinating and controlling all the different command groups operating hitherto in the Province of Katanga'.[50] It was commanded by the 'coldly objective [and] entirely confident' Brigadier K.A.S. Raja who also commanded all Indian troops in Katanga.[51] Raja would oversee three major UN operations in Katanga, but according to Brian Urquhart was 'weak … and was not respected by his subordinates', many of whom were strong personalities in their own right.[52] Katanga Command was sub-divided into three 'Sectors' (A, B, and C) of which Sector-B, under Swedish control (Col. Jonas Waern, OC 12th Swedish Battalion), covered southern Katanga and Elisabethville. Elisabethville was garrisoned and the remaining areas patrolled. The military forces in the area comprised the 35th Irish Battalion, the 12th Swedish Battalion and, ultimately, a battalion of the Indian Dogra Regiment and a battalion of the Gurkha Rifles.[53]

ONUC forces in Katanga Command were to ensure the maintenance of peace in the area and through 'constant and effective patrolling' try to 'restore confidence among the local population', the overall objective being to 'render whatever assistance is possible … to bring about conditions of normalcy and relieve suffering among the people'.[54] Katanga Command would issue directives for all operations in Katanga and sector commanders would be responsible for their execution. Sector-B also ensured the security of Elisabethville airport 'at all costs', ensured the security of vital installations in the town, and maintained internal security in the event of civil disturbance.[55] Katanga Command Headquarters was entirely staffed by the Indian army and Sector-B Headquarters, also in Elisabethville, was staffed almost entirely by the Swedish army. There was considerable friction between command and sector staffs due to linguistic difficulties, outlook and training. O'Brien took the Indians to be anti-Katanga whereas the Swedes often sympathized with the Katangese and he wearily concluded 'such are the troubles of an international force'.[56]

Added to these problems were difficulties arising from differences of emphasis and opinion between UN military and civilian operations in Congo. O'Brien was Hammarskjöld's Special Representative in Katanga while in Leopoldville Linner headed UN civilian operations. O'Brien worked closely with Raja in Elisabethville and Linner and MacEoin co-existed in Leopoldville. O'Brien increasingly came under Raja's influence. The Indian wished to swiftly end the secession of Katanga. In his communications with MacEoin about the civil war in north Katanga Raja emphasized that his orders were to develop a neutral zone in the area and implement the February resolution. He wanted to avoid 'killing without reason, but if the occasion presents itself the General will give the orders necessary'.[57] MacEoin forcefully replied that 'when you have to resort to force to implement our instructions we must be informed in advance'.[58] Raja was liable to act on his own initiative and to do so without reference to his Force Commander. O'Brien was also prone to act on his own initiative and also saw his objective in Katanga as the implementation of the February 1961 resolution. A month into his posting he promised that 'Katanga is finished.'[59] The headstrong O'Brien and the belligerent Raja were a volatile combination as the 35th Battalion would soon discover.

Settling in

On 2 July Comdt Cahalane brought the officers of the Armoured Car Group together for a conference in preparation for the first Commanding Officer's conference the following day. Magennis' experience with the advance party meant that he 'began the conference with a general topographic brief, sketching out Elisabethville and its infrastructure. The 35th Battalion was very scattered over Elisabethville so an immediate intimate knowledge of the city area was essential.'[60] The only map of Elisabethville available to the UN was confined to the white European city, ignoring the African suburbs to the west and southwest. The city's main avenues and boulevards ran roughly north to south and allowed two-way traffic. The interconnecting streets ran east–west and were alternately one-way. Because of the shortage of maps, officers and NCOs needed to be familiar with street names and the location of major buildings and, driving Landrovers and civilian cars around the city, they familiarized themselves with its layout.

The 35th Battalion's primary task was to defend Elisabethville airport. The only road to the airport was via the city centre and could easily be obstructed by the Katangese. The conference agreed that the first task for the Armoured Car

Group was to undertake reconnaissance of the rough ground between the airport and battalion headquarters to see if bush tracks could be developed into alternative routes. Lt Col. MacNeill gave the 35th Battalion time get familiarized with their environment and confined his 3 July conference to emphasizing the nature of ONUC's mandate. It could only use force in self-defence and was to remain strictly impartial should Leopoldville attempt to end Katanga's secession by force. MacNeill emphasized that officers should use every occasion to repeat these conditions to their troops – 'We are here to keep the peace. No shooting unless you are fired on.' There was no expectation that the 35th Battalion 'might have to fight rather than act only as diplomats in uniform'.[61]

The following day the sun shone from a cloudless sky and the temperature was in the high twenties. Magennis doubted whether he had 'ever seen a more willing group of soldiers more anxious to get to work.'[62] There was one problem to overcome – the tropical kit issued by the UN came only in two sizes – small and large. The 35th Battalion morning parade 'resembled a scene from a Charlie Chaplin movie – small men swimming in big shirts and long trousers, and large men bursting their allocated kit at the seams.'[63] The uniform was cool cotton khaki, a welcome change from the 'bull's wool' issued in Ireland. Yet it was poor quality and in it Irish soldiers tended to 'show up unfavourably in comparison with other troops in the matter of dress'.[64] It was suitable for 'actual operations' but not for day-to-day wearing and a better-fitting uniform was required 'in the interests of morale, welfare and comfort'. The UN countered with 'surprise' that the uniforms were unsatisfactory as they were Indian Army tropical issue.[65] The 'Jungle Green' Indian uniform was 'admirable for its purpose but wholly unsuited for after-hours' and one officer suggested that the men were ashamed of being seen in it due to the lack of a 'walking-out' uniform and as a result 'are driven to frequent the less salubrious shebeens and dives'.[66]

The 35th Battalion was soon 'settling in' and reported to Dublin that morale was good.[67] It was operating to plan and as might be expected of a newly deployed force. Considerable work was required to bring the battalion's defences into shape and infantry companies dug trenches, weapons pits and command posts for local security. Armoured car and infantry reconnaissance patrols learned the topography of Elisabethville and the 35th Battalion's area of operations. They amassed information on the Gendarmerie and investigated incidents across the city. Intelligence Officer Comdt Kane assessed information from these patrols and compiled periodic intelligence reports for South Katanga HQ. 35th Battalion officers undertook 'cloth model exercises', tactical exercises without troops, to ensure they were 'familiar with the sequence of events as laid down in Plan A' – the defence of Elisabethville airport – their primary mission objective.[68] These exercises focussed on company and armoured car group actions and the overall battalion communication and medical systems involved in putting 'Plan A' into effect.

The Armoured Car Group established how to get swiftly to the airport. An armoured car section of two vehicles was located at the airport and at the nearby Sabena Villas and hardly a day passed without a call for the other cars in the group to accompany patrols around the city. Armoured Car Group preparations for 'Plan A' led to the development of the three alternative routes to the airport as routes Bravo, Charlie and Delta joined the existing route Alpha.

Still in its honeymoon period, 35th Battalion relations with other ONUC contingents were 'excellent', Kane adding that this 'makes one really believe that UN has arrived as a practical and working machine'. The Swedes provided considerable assistance and vehicles and were 'most helpful and co-operative', and the Norwegians, Indians, Danes and Italians were 'all grand fellows both on and off duty'.[69] Kane wrote to the Director of Military Intelligence in Dublin that 'we are not yet settled in enough to get into the Int business in a worthwhile manner. However we are observing the scene.'[70]

The political landscape

The 35th Battalion initially viewed Elisabethville as being under 'benevolent but omnipresent occupation' by ONUC.[71] Yet the often-changing attitude of the Katangese towards ONUC was a feature of Kane's intelligence reports. When MacNeill and battalion HQ staff visited Mokambo to establish a post to counter suspected arms smuggling across the nearby Northern Rhodesian border they were met with 'tremendous enthusiasm'. But on a return visit the reception Comdt Pat Quinlan received was 'decidedly cool'.[72] Quinlan felt that 'the change in local temperature' was officially inspired. Relations with local Belgians were 'still cool to cold', though 'NCOs and men are breaking the ice by the usual Irish soldiers' fondness for children and dogs.' The African population, bar a small minority, were 'particularly friendly … our men are on good terms with all whom they come into contact'.[73] There were a few taunts against ONUC and a group of Gendarmerie officers refused to play football with the Irish; instead the 35th Battalion played friendly matches against an African team. 35th Battalion troops settled in well and relations with local Africans were, Kane reported, 'good and improving as our troops pick up some of the local languages'.[74] Relations between Irish and Katangese forces were otherwise friendly, with the 35th Battalion using the Gendarmerie range for training and 'exchanging drinks, playing Bridge in their Mess, etc.' As yet, the Irish had 'no firm opinion as to morale, training, communications, tactics, etc., of this force.'

Relations between 'Europeans' and 'Africans' rated

> between correct thro' good to cordial. In a number of night clubs and hotels mixed parties of Africans and Whites swap drinks and talk. We have noticed white ladies dance with Africans and vice versa. Privately at times one hears whites describe the Africans as zombies and make a general jeer of the Govt and Administration. Again we have noticed vehement support by whites for President Tshombe.[75]

The Europeans were 'a mixed bag'. Diehard Belgians were 'cool – even cold' towards the UN, a 35th Battalion intelligence report adding 'they seem not to want us', but most other whites adopted a normal, sometimes even friendly, attitude towards the UN, some Belgians remarking that 'without [the] UN the whites could pack up.' Belgians

> gave the impression that they are living on borrowed time. Even while recreating themselves they do not appear to be enjoying themselves to the full. But then maybe Belgians don't enjoy themselves like we do. They appear to be on the edge, uncertain and here only in a temporary capacity.[76]

Elisabethville in July 1961 'was rife with rumours'.[77] Comdt Quinlan noticed the 'uneasy calm' over the city as tensions grew between UN forces and Katangese mercenaries.[78] There was no open hostility only a growing sense of foreboding.

There was no relaxation for the 35th Battalion as tactical training, training in riot drills and mob control was undertaken, as were arms drills and live range practices. The Armoured Car Group secured use of the Gendarmerie rifle range and had one very profitable day's training there. It was the first and only range firing practice they got in Elisabethville before hostilities broke out. A second attempt to use the range towards the end of July failed as the mood in Elisabethville worsened. Intelligence reports indicated growing unrest in the city suburbs where Tshombe's supporters were at loggerheads with the Baluba tribe as Munongo used Radio Katanga to stir up trouble between the factions. Large numbers of Baluba had come to Elisabethville to escape the civil wars in Kasai and north Katanga and obtained work with Union Minière. The major political disagreement between the central government and Tshombe's secessionist Katanga was easy to understand but tribal differences were more complex and 35th Battalion troops received no political briefing on these differences and the associated political rifts and clashes. For example, they were unaware that the Kasai Baluba and the north Katanga Baluba were separate branches of the Baluba tribe.

Capt. Magennis received a crash-course in local politics from Bill Williams who ran a quarry in Katanga and employed many locals. During July Magennis visited Williams and his family and got an insight into the politics of Elisabethville. Williams also introduced Magennis to a friend of his, a Belgian who was the local representative of the large European multinational Lever Brothers, and he also kept Magennis informed of developments in Elisabethville. Magennis then got to know Stan Zurakovsky, a Pole who ran a construction company in the city. He spoke fluent English as well as French and Swahili. These contacts provided useful information on the mood across Elisabethville. Nevertheless, looking back Magennis could not understand

> why during the six months the 35th Battalion spent in Katanga, I was never party to a political briefing on what was going on in the province other than that the Central Government in Leopoldville was using what pressure it and the United Nations could to prevent the secession of

Katanga from the Congo and to unite the Republic of Congo. With my fellow soldiers in the 35th Battalion I looked on the Baluba tribe in general as a group of thugs who had slaughtered nine Irish soldiers at Niemba.[79]

Williams 'astounded' Magennis with his view of the Baluba, pointing out that they were the most advanced economically of Congo's tribes and provided most of the clerical workforce in Elisabethville. This was news to Magennis.

The information available to senior Irish officers and officials about Congo was limited and was rarely passed down the line. The Department of External Affairs provided, with Lemass' agreement, a monthly analysis of events in Congo to senior political figures. These documents did not make their way to Irish forces in Elisabethville. Magennis thought that

> at the very least the officers should have been briefed on possible developments. If this had occurred they could have ensured that some of the events that were to happen in the near future would have been less of a surprise for them and their men.[80]

The feeling among 'some officers' of the 35th Battalion was that they were 'not being kept in the picture in respect of the general and local situation.'[81] Kane thought this 'a pity' as there were, he felt, ample opportunities for officers to be kept informed. Sector-B held regular briefings, Kane adding that a 'representative from each Company is welcome but they don't make a habit of coming', Battalion Conferences were held for 'all important events', Operations and Intelligence staff briefed sub-units and 'any officer at any time may ask a Battalion Staff Officer to brief him. He won't go away empty handed.'[82] This was the theory, the problem was that when it really counted, in the operations in August and September 1961 Katanga Command, Sector-B and 35th Battalion forces operated in a closed fashion and the practical information required by units on the ground was provided at short notice, if at all. This lack of briefing meant that the 35th Battalion was often to undertake tasks without knowledge of the difficulties that lay ahead. There may have been another reason for this closed attitude. Lt Col. Art Cullen noticed during a trip to Elisabethville before and after the fighting in September 1961 that there was 'too much loose talk, discussions and speculation by Officers, especially in the presence of NCOs' concerning UN policy, particularly its 'political' policy.[83] Cullen's view was that the Defence Forces were in Congo to carry out policy and obey orders 'and not to criticise policy or discuss orders'. The less that was explained, the less that was known and the less criticism was possible. On the other hand, without information the rumour-mill churned out misinformation. Ultimately this attitude impeded the operability of the 35th Battalion.

UN policy in Elisabethville was moving in a specific direction as O'Brien was now planning to end Katanga's secession. The federal parliament in Leopoldville was to meet in early August, though without Katangese participation. O'Brien expected it would adopt a resolution dismantling Katanga's independent institutions and requiring the Gendarmerie to withdraw from north Katanga. The UN would not 'without further authority from the Security Council employ its force to carry out such a resolution', but it would continue to implement the February resolution by diplomatic means. This would enable the UN to remove foreign political advisors and European officers from the Gendarmerie, leading to Katanga's ultimate collapse.

MacEoin presided over a meeting on 21 July with the senior UN military and civilian figures in Katanga including Raja, Waern and MacNeill. Briefing the meeting O'Brien came to the same conclusion as the 35th Battalion – the European population of Elisabethville was 'jumpy'; the Africans were 'generally calm'.[84] Tshombe appeared to be ill and the 'unpredictable' Munongo was in the ascendant and making noises about approaching the Soviet bloc. Waern estimated there were 2,000 Gendarmerie in Elisabethville and thought UN forces 'adequate to meet any Gendarmerie threat', but they would require additional troops if there was a civilian riot.

MacEoin announced that Raja would take over command of all Katanga, and that 'all military and civilian affairs would be handled from Elisabethville'.[85] Promoting an Indian to overall command of ONUC in Katanga was guaranteed to provoke Tshombe's government. One battalion of Gurkhas would move to Elisabethville, the objective being 'intimidating Tshombe and so compelling his attendance at Leopoldville with his deputies and senators; ensuring the expulsion of French, Belgian and other foreign officers from Katanga; and, coping with possible civil disturbances which might result'.[86] O'Brien and MacEoin were 'aware of past controversies over [the] entry of Indian troops into Elisabethville' and that the Katangese government 'probably thought they had succeeded' in getting an assurance that Indian troops would not be sent to Elisabethville. The move 'represented a policy of maintaining pressure on Katanga Ministers "until they realize they can no longer postpone carrying out the February 21 resolution".'[87] But Tshombe's government was unpredictable and O'Brien was 'underestimating popular Katangese support for the regime and ... inviting serious trouble by using the present position as an excuse to intensify pressure on the authorities'.[88]

Much of this politicking was unknown to the officers of the 35th Battalion who sought out off-duty haunts across Elisabethville and watched life go by. Stade de la Victoire on Avenue Saio and the Café Royale in the city centre were among the most popular. The Stade was 'a very fine location', as it had a large swimming pool.[89] The bar was 'good and served coffee and drinks, available with excellent service, by natives of course. All of this was otherwise forbidden ground to the local African population.'[90] Like Stade de la Victoire, the Café Royale in the city centre also exclusively served the white population. It was 'an ideal location to pass the time if one wished to just sit in comfort, sip coffee and watch the world go by.' Irish troops noticed an increase in Belgian mercenaries at the Café Royale during July 1961, as well as a growing number of French officers, locally known as 'Les Affreux', former soldiers who disagreed with the French government's recognition of Algerian independence. Magennis recalled that a scruffier collection of men I have never seen: they sported long unkempt hair, were unshaven and were visibly armed with knives and hand guns that they seemed to glory in everyone seeing. Believed to be on leave from north Katanga they were reputed to be well paid to make life very difficult for the Baluba, burning villages and dispersing the surviving Balubas, mostly women and children, into the deep bush.[91]

During late July another change for the 35th Battalion was that they were no longer invited play bridge at Gendarmerie Headquarters. The Belgian attitude to ONUC was hardening. In this unsettled climate Waern emphasized that 'every scrap of information in and about this city should be at once reported to higher authority' by all ONUC personnel.[92] This included any conversation with Katangese or Belgians, civilian or military on the situation in Elisabethville, reports of movements of troops or police and movement of vehicles or large crowds or bodies of civilians. Kane passed this on to 35th Battalion company commanders who were to bring it to the attention of all ranks to keep their eyes and ears open, 'personnel should not decide themselves that an item was not worth reporting. When in doubt report it.' The holiday period for ONUC in Elisabethville was about to end.

Rumpunch

B Y EARLY AUGUST 1961 ONUC had reduced the flow of mercenaries into Katanga and compiled a comprehensive list of Belgian advisors to be repatriated. Further progress was needed to remove the 512 European military personnel and mercenaries serving with the Gendarmerie. A negotiated solution to this problem was unlikely. Katangese aggression towards ONUC had increased after Tshombe's release but O'Brien nevertheless saw Katanga entering 'a reasonably hopeful phase.'[1] He had 'cause for optimism', but 'this was the Congo and the most permanent arrangement lasts for, at most, one month usually less'.[2] A Congolese national government was formed by the moderate Cyrille Adoula on 2 August. It was 'a moment of relief' for Linner, but Katangese deputies did not attend the new parliament.[3] When Adoula announced Leopoldville's intention to 'break Katanga if they didn't come to heel' there was a noticeable change in Linner's and MacEoin's outlooks.[4] With a functioning Congolese government and parliament established they resolved to end Katanga's secession and put pressure on Tshombe to attend the parliament in Leopoldville. Following the formation of Adoula's government UN–Leopoldville relations improved. Many European Gendarmerie officers, worried by the changing UN attitude, left Katanga; some felt 'that NO white officers will be left in three weeks' time'.[5]

Beneath the superficial calm in Elisabethville 'it was obvious at the time that something was brewing'.[6] Kane received a warning that 'nothing will happen immediately; keep your men occupied and alert'.[7] Unease among UN personnel increased, ONUC patrols through Elisabethville became more frequent and infantry were accompanied by armoured cars. Tshombe looked 'worried and ill at ease' and Belgians sought UN protection as 'there may be a blow-out soon against Europeans'.[8] As the climate deteriorated detailed instructions on how to respond if trouble broke out were distributed to ONUC –

> UN Forces in the Elisabethville area will secure Elisabethville airport in order to prevent its occupation or use by unauthorised personnel and maintain it open for use by UN forces and, in addition, will be prepared to take the necessary steps to maintain law and order and protect persons and property in the Elisabethville area against unauthorised interference.[9]

Airport defence was ONUC's primary priority and Elisabethville airport was to be kept open.

Tshombe maintained he was willing to negotiate with Adoula, but added that 'there could be no question of dismantling what Katanga had achieved'.[10] Tshombe and Munongo were willing to concede 'the symbols of sovereignty' but would not surrender political power and would defend Katanga against 'any outside attack'.[11] Adoula wanted a peaceful solution in Katanga. The UN did also, and was willing to help Adoula. Khiari explained to Hammarskjöld that

> for psychological reasons, it would be well to give the Katangans the impression that we are prepared to support the Central Government and that the only way for them to extricate themselves from the situation would be to arrive at a compromise with the Central Government. In my opinion, it is absolutely necessary for us to present a firm and inflexible front if we want to avoid the development of a situation in which recourse to force will be the only possibility.[12]

Khiari and MacEoin hoped to encourage Tshombe to 'normalise his situation with the Central Government without loss of face'.[13] Tshombe had 'failed to grasp the opportunities that were offered to him' and instead took any relaxation of UN intent as 'a sign of lack of determination', accordingly hardening his position.[14] Raja planned to put psychological pressure on Tshombe by having the Dogras take over from the 12th Swedish and the 35th Irish Battalions in Elisabethville. The deployment of Indian forces would be a 'deterrent and will facilitate [the] speedy settlement of [the] Katanga problem'. Indian troops carried on a 'war of nerves with Katangese troops' and

> if the Katangese troops show signs of being difficult, the Indian units, which include a Battalion of Gurkhas, hold drills with live ammunition in the streets or on the airstrips. Katangese officers are invited to watch bayonet or shooting practice or demonstration by jeep-mounted recoilless rifles.[15]

Khiari learned from Adoula that because of unrest in north Katanga caused by an aggressive foreign-led mobile group of Gendarmerie it was desirable that ONUC 'take steps to ensure the evacuation of these foreign officers and mercenaries'.[16] With Hammarskjöld's agreement MacEoin and Khiari planned an 'urgent and energetic action' against Tshombe by swooping on the mercenaries. This move would be carried out in consultation with Leopoldville under paragraph A2 of the February 1961 resolution. O'Brien, Egge and Raja would begin by asking Tshombe for the immediate withdrawal of all mercenaries in the mobile groups, the evacuation of other non-Congolese officers and the cessation of Gendarmerie operations in north Katanga. They hoped to persuade Tshombe of ONUC's determination to act if he did not. Raja was then to ensure that ONUC had the military superiority to give armed assistance in case of opposition to the plan. If Tshombe was willing to submit to Leopoldville the measures could be carried out 'with less severity'. If Tshombe refused to act, 'we should increase our pressure'. Khiari warned Hammarskjöld that 'nos representants à Elisabethville sont desireux de l'embarquer manu militari'.[17]

O'Brien remained confident that Katanga was entering a positive phase, writing to his friend Desmond Williams, Professor of Modern History at University College Dublin, that 'things are going on the whole fairly well here although some kind of bust-up is never to be excluded in this part of the world'.[18] The 'bust-up' in Katanga came on 24 August when the Sûreté (the Katangese Special Branch) arrested Raphael Bintu, the representative of South Kasai in Elisabethville. The following day as arrests of South Kasai Baluba continued about 500 Kasai Baluba sought UN protection. ONUC protested to Tshombe, but the campaign continued and there were soon 5,000 refugees in a makeshift camp between the Irish and Swedish camps in eastern Elisabethville. Women and children came in large numbers; the women carrying bags and bedding on their heads with two or three small children clinging to their long, multi-coloured dresses. Conditions were very basic:

> There was one water tap in that area and I can still see a lady taking her two small children to the tap to give them a quick shower. Undaunted by the circumstances the two laughed and splashed each other as if they were on holidays. It was soon obvious that the influx of Baluba would continue and it became necessary to move all our vehicles and equipment to the opposite end of the camp and erect a wire fence to separate our area from that of the refugees.[19]

The refugee camps became too large to be run by Swedish and Irish troops and United Nations and NGO civilian workers took control, assisted by missionaries who had fled from north Katanga. ONUC continued to provide security. The younger Baluba, known as the 'Jeunesse', sought to evade ONUC patrols and escape to get their own back on the Gendarmerie. The refugee camp 'created not only a very serious problem for the United Nations which had to protect, feed, shelter and care for' the refugees, 'but also a situation likely to lead to tribal and civil war' in Elisabethville.[20] Tshombe's refusal to co-operate over the repatriation of mercenaries, the civil war in north Katanga, and the now worsening situation in Elisabethville, as well as the need to implement the February resolution, finally pushed O'Brien and Raja into taking unprecedented measures against Katanga.

Planning Operation Rumpunch

On 24 August Adoula enacted an ordinance enabling Leopoldville to expel foreign officers and mercenaries from Katanga by force. Leopoldville sought UN assistance to implement the ordinance as it was in line with the February resolution. Hammarskjöld interpreted this as a 'call for immediate action in Katanga' and tried again to get Tshombe to meet Adoula.[21] Tshombe refused, secure in the knowledge that Katanga was financed by Union Minière, armed by its European supporters and defended by a mercenary-led military force. In the five months since the February resolution there had been no movement on repatriating foreign personnel. The UN was preparing to embark on a 'swift sharp action' against Katanga.[22] Watching events from across Congo's southern border the pro-Katanga Prime Minister of the Federation of Rhodesia and Nyasaland, Sir Roy Welensky, considered that 'the line-up for a final trial of strength with Tshombe now appears to be taking shape.'[23] Hammarskjöld instructed O'Brien to inform Tshombe that ONUC would soon commence the expulsion of non-Congolese officers and mercenaries in the Gendarmerie. This gave Tshombe a few days to co-operate before the UN took action. The UN was determined to remove the mercenaries, but it would prefer if their repatriation was undertaken by the Katangese government. If Tshombe did not act the UN would 'proceed with forceful evacuation'.[24] O'Brien hoped to meet Tshombe in Albertville to talk to him 'away from the harmful influence which surrounds him [in Elisabethville] and particularly from Munongo's surveillance'. Rumours of an imminent UN action circulated in Elisabethville and Tshombe made a hasty return from Albertville without meeting O'Brien. Indian Dogra troops moved to Elisabethville to bolster UN strength in the city.

On 26 August, aware that he was disconnected from events on the ground in Katanga, Hammarskjöld told Linner to go ahead with the round-up of mercenaries 'irrespective of our previous communication on same subject. At this distance we cannot judge the details as well as you can; we trust that everything will go well.'[25] However Linner made sure not to inform the Secretary General of the extent of the military operations ONUC was now planning as that would have 'bound his hands too tightly' regarding the forthcoming operation in Elizabethville.[26] He explained to the American ambassador in Leopoldville that he was 'paid to take risks and assume that responsibility.'[27] That day Waern received orders from MacEoin to plan for the temporary occupation of Elisabethville by ONUC. He drew up a scheme based on existing plans for control of the city should civil order break down. The city remained calm. Linner was in an 'uncompromising' mood and felt it 'necessary to keep up the pressure' on Tshombe.[28] His statements were clear – 'the United Nations would support any policy designed to reintegrate Katanga into the Congo.' He was of the view that the UN was 'at the disposition of the Central Government and ready to assist it so far as possible'.[29]

O'Brien frankly told Tshombe of the UN's 'determination [to] uphold [the] central government and ensure [the] reintegration of Katanga in Congo'.[30] He explained that Tshombe could still go to Leopoldville under UN protection, but Munongo 'vehemently opposed' this. UN officials felt that Tshombe wished to accept, but 'fear [of] Munongo's negative influence may be once more decisive'. Tshombe told the Elisabethville consular corps that O'Brien had given him an ultimatum to go to Leopoldville. O'Brien replied that he had 'invited' not 'ordered' Tshombe and had 'in very frank language' explained the dangers facing Katanga and urged him to accept Adoula's invitation to talks.[31] He explained that if Tshombe refused, the UN was prepared to move against the Gendarmerie.

ONUC now felt it had 'sufficient strength to subdue any opposition from Katanga force'.[32] O'Brien and Egge further explained to Tshombe and Munongo the 'pressure of events' bearing down on Tshombe, that 'his position would be interpreted as negative and that we would seek new instructions.'[33] The UN was ready to put pressure on the Katangese government to bring about the departure of foreign military personnel from Katanga and 'if they did not leave of their own accord United Nations troops would compel them to do so'.[34]

Despite ONUC's warnings the Katangese 'had taken decisions for which they must assume responsibility'.[35] Tshombe and Munongo told a press conference that the UN had threatened them that 'UN forces would act in support of the central government if called upon to do so'.[36] This was 'a significant distortion' of what O'Brien had said to Tshombe, but O'Brien and his colleagues felt that 'it may not be a bad thing for discussion here at present to hinge on whether or not we are about to give military aid to [the] central government against Katanga. This will serve to distract attention from our real plans and such distraction is necessary since the arrival of the Dogras has given ground for persistent speculation as to our intentions.'[37]

Planning for the UN sweep against the mercenaries continued on 26 August at a staff conference between Indian, Irish and Swedish officers at Katanga Command HQ. The commander of the 1st Irish Infantry Group also attended as it was through Kamina, where his force was based, that apprehended personnel would be evacuated. The final touches to the UN plan, codenamed Operation Rumpunch, were made on the afternoon of 27 August at a meeting at Kamina Base attended by MacEoin, Egge, Raja, UN legal adviser Vladimir Fabry, Khiari and O'Brien.

The arrival the Dogras led to 'several wild rumours circulating' across Elisabethville.[38] As night fell on 26 August the city was 'calm but tense' and a group of Irish NCOs reported the streets were more deserted than usual. They heard from Swedish units that 'all local leave was cancelled and trouble was expected in Elisabethville because of the arrival of [the] Indian detachment'.[39] They also learned from a Gendarmerie captain that 'President Tshombe was perturbed about arrival of Indians'. Tshombe's house was under a strengthened guard and all guards across Elisabethville had been doubled. Gendarmerie reinforcements were sent to Elisabethville airport to protect Katangese air force aircraft and the Air Katanga buildings. B-Company 35th Battalion observed them preparing defensive positions. The Gendarmerie occupied a position controlling the runway approach and when disturbed dispersed into the bush. A-Company at Sabena Villas and B-Company at the airport 'reported the sound of troop movement, vehicles, and digging somewhere in the bush to the WEST of the runway.'[40] Keeping the Katangese under observation, the Irish set up listening posts, which noticed that Gendarmerie activity ceased as Irish patrols passed.

The OC of the 35th Battalion, Lt Col. Olaf MacNeill, was now suddenly replaced by his second-in-command Comdt Hugh McNamee. MacNeill was sent by MacEoin to UN Headquarters in Leopoldville on 'temporary duty' on 26 August and remained there.[41] McNamee was initially Acting Officer

Commanding, being formally given command on 22 September 1961. He was 'able and tough', a highly competent officer who showed great calmness under fire in Elisabethville.[42] During the September 1961 fighting, he smoked his pipe and was 'cool as a cucumber'; one officer remembering him remarking to a trooper in Elisabethville 'Not very nice out there now, is it?' as the UN and Katangese forces fought across the city.[43] Upon assuming command on the night of 26 to 27 August, McNamee had immediately to take decisive action against the Gendarmerie at the airport.

At 0220 on 27 August McNamee ordered Comdt Pat Quinlan, O/C of A-Company, and Comdt Alo McMahon, O/C of B-Company, to prepare a combined force with a section of armoured cars 'to attack at first light and capture the party which was digging in' at the airport.[44] At first light a platoon from B-Company with armoured cars and support weapons from A-Company moved in. A further platoon from B-Company surrounded the position and a platoon from A-Company blocked roads from the airport to prevent the Gendarmerie escaping. In what was described as an 'exemplary action' B-Company captured and disarmed the Katangese force, taking two Belgian officers into custody.[45] They found two loaded mortars, a working radio set tuned to communicate with Gendarmerie Headquarters and machine-guns readied to fire. The captured European officers were sent to Kamina for repatriation. The captured weapons and ammunition were returned to the Gendarmerie personnel and they were released.

Across Elisabethville there was further Gendarmerie activity over the night of 27–28 August as roadblocks sprang up and guards were again strengthened. The Gendarmerie action at the airport was taken as a sign of things to come and Rumpunch was brought forward twenty-four hours to 0500 on 28 August.[46] Tshombe was nervous, complaining to O'Brien about his heart problems. They cannot have been helped when O'Brien and Raja asked to meet him early on 28 August as they 'were expecting an important communication' which they would deliver to him immediately upon receipt.[47]

'Rumpunch [has] gone off swimmingly'[48]

ONUC Operation Order No. 3 'Operation Rumpunch' instructed ONUC forces across Katanga to take into custody and repatriate white Gendarmerie officers and mercenaries. Egge wanted the gradual phasing out of Belgian officers and NCOs. O'Brien instead preferred a dawn swoop as a show of force to make Katanga co-operate. As Rumpunch began Tshombe would be informed, Police Commissioner Pius Sapwe would be asked to co-operate, and the commander of the Gendarmerie, Col. Norbert Muké, would be informed that the UN was not attempting to disarm the Gendarmerie. The plan in Elisabethville was to take Gendarmerie HQ and the New Hospital, locations at which white Gendarmerie officers and mercenaries were living, and occupy key communications facilities including the airport.

Troops deployed	Objective(s)	Tasks
A-Coy 35th Irish Battalion 3 APCs (Swedish) 2 armoured cars (Irish) (Col. Waern)	Gendarmerie HQ and Munongo's house.	Seize and hold Gendarmerie HQ, disarm and take into custody white officers and mercenaries, then arrange documentation and transport to airport. Surround Munongo's house, placing him under house arrest.
12th Swedish Battalion (1-Coy, 3-Coy, HQ-Coy) (Major Mide)	Radio Transmitter (Route de la Kilobelobe) and secure approaches to Elisabethville.	Seize, hold and control installation and entry and exit points to city. Establish brigade reserve force in the city centre (Parc Albert).
C-Coy 35th Irish Battalion HQ-Coy Irish Battalion 5 armoured cars (Irish) (Lt Col. McNamee)	New Hospital area.	Surround New Hospital and take into custody white officers living there, arrange documentation and transport to airport. Be prepared to move to Jadotville Junction to prevent Gendarmerie movement from that direction.
B-Coy 35th Irish Battalion A-Coy 1 Dogra Battalion One section of armoured cars (Irish) (Comdt McMahon)	Airport.	Secure Elisabethville airport in accordance with Plan A for airport and Sabena Villas companies.
Dogra Battalion less one company (Major Sukhdial Singh)	Elisabethville Post Office and Radio Katanga studio.	One Company each to seize and hold each objective.

Table 7. Operation Rumpunch – objectives of ONUC units in Elisabethville

Comdt Quinlan, OC of A-Company, 35th Battalion, learned of his Rumpunch objectives on 27 August. He would have with him three Swedish APCs and two Irish armoured cars. The first indication for the Armoured Car Group of what lay ahead was when Group OC Comdt Cahalane informed Capt. Magennis of a probable 35th Battalion operation in the near future. Magennis and his section were tasked to operate with A-Company taking Gendarmerie Headquarters because Magennis knew the layout of the building from his bridge games there. The Armoured Car Group now faced the problem of breaking through the iron gates at the entrance to the Gendarmerie building. If they were locked they would have to be rammed open. Could a Ford armoured car carry the extra weight of a battering ram? Magennis discussed this with Capt. Frank Lawless and substantial problems arose. The Armoured Car Group did not possess welding equipment and Lawless doubted if the Ford could carry much additional weight.

Magennis watched what happened next: 'One man saw a section of railway track here and another spied a heap of discarded "H-section" iron there'.[49] The following evening Lawless called Magennis over to see what another fitter had managed to procure – an oxyacetylene unit minus its oxygen cylinder. A medical officer approached the Italian military hospital for a new cylinder and that problem too was solved. The scrap metal was cut to the required size and taken to the United Nations supply stores for further work. A message to the Cavalry Workshops at the Curragh Camp, the birthplace of the Fords, asked whether the front axle could carry the weight of a battering ram. The reply was 'Okay, but no more'; construction work started immediately.[50] The resulting modification was so successful that the strengthened armoured car was one of those later handed over to the ANC when Defence Forces involvement with ONUC ended.

Magennis reported to A-Company at Sabena Villas on 27 August with his two armoured cars. He and Quinlan talked about the layout of the Gendarmerie Headquarters and about the entrance gate and capabilities of the modified armoured car to break it open. At 0045 on 28 August Quinlan issued his orders. A-Company 'would be going into action in darkness and it was absolutely essential that every man should know exactly where he was to go and what he was to do'.[51] He emphasized that they would not open fire unless first engaged and informed his men that their objective was to arrest and detain white and European officers and to hold them in a safe location. Lt Noel Carey assembled his 'No. 3 Platoon' for a briefing, instructed them 'to check all equipment, ammunition and weapons and told them to write a letter to loved ones just in case'.[52] A-Company got general absolution and 'this certainly concentrated the mind on how serious was the task in hand'.[53]

Reveille would be an hour before first light with the move on Gendarmerie Headquarters commencing at 0500 hours on 28 August. The armoured cars would lead the move to the start line and Col. Waern would accompany A-Company. The assault was 'the only job where real action was expected. On the success or failure of this mission depended the success or failure of the whole mission and, as Dr Cruise O'Brien and Brigadier Raja told [Quinlan], perhaps the UN in the Congo.'[54] When A-Company reached the entrance to Gendarmerie Headquarters they found the gates wide open. The assault moved in and the armoured cars took up positions. Quinlan led the offensive and his second-in-command Capt. Dermot Byrne travelled with Magennis and directed A-Company's infantry platoons once they were inside the Gendarmerie compound. All proceeded as planned and the infantry occupied the building. Magennis knew from previous visits the location of the Orderly Officer's post. Accompanied by a sergeant he walked in to find a young Belgian mercenary officer asleep in an armchair. Disarmed swiftly, he offered no resistance and walked quietly with Magennis to the assembly area for captured personnel.

Leaving Sgt Dan Morris in charge of the armoured cars – one covering the entrance gate and the other the officers' mess – Magennis entered the ground floor of the headquarters building and found himself in Col. Muké's magnificently-furnished office. Everything was quiet; there was no shouting, just the footsteps of an occasional passing soldier. Then Muké arrived escorted by an NCO from A-Company. He was fuming with rage. Magennis spoke no French and Muké no English, but Magennis succeeded in calming him down, gesturing that he would be brought to Comdt Quinlan. Gendarmerie Headquarters was under A-Company control by 0520. Noel Carey recalled that he and his men were 'highly elated that the operation had gone so well'; they had received no casualties and his No. 3 Platoon had arrested four mercenaries.[55]

An hour or so later two shots were fired at the front of the Gendarmerie complex from a passing civilian car. Magennis later wrote that 'it was the only firing I heard during the whole operation to take the Gendarmerie Headquarters.'[56] However Quinlan wrote that some of his men had fired inside the compound to dissuade some of the keener Gendarmerie from action.[57] A-Company remained in occupation of Gendarmerie Headquarters until midday on 28 August when the premises was returned to Katangese control.

B-Company, with a section of armoured cars, took the Air Katanga installation at Elisabethville airport. Closing the area down they ensured that telephone lines were cut and that entrances and exits to the airport were sealed off. They found no mercenaries or European officers and left the twelve Katangese soldiers at the airport with their arms.[58] C-Company, with a section of armoured cars and with a section of Military Police, accompanied by McNamee took control of the New Hospital which acted as living quarters for Belgian officers. Across the city Rumpunch was going well. Radio reports at 0550 indicated that the New Hospital was in UN hands and all was calm. A further report at 0555 indicated that the east-end transmitter was taken by the Swedes. There was no information from the Dogras at the Post Office or the Radio Katanga premises, but there were verbal reports that Gendarmerie HQ had been entered and all was quiet. Though he was not in the building, Munongo's residence was surrounded and isolated, as were all approaches to Elisabethville.

Rumpunch went according to plan and all objectives were taken peacefully with practically no resistance. Comdt Barrett signalled to Lt Col. S.K. Dhar 'that all Brigade first objectives were in our hands. No casualties reported. Good show.'[59] Some Belgians put up resistance, including a small group at the New Hospital, but most were unconcerned. A number of Katangese officers were even co-operating with the UN, having been assured that ONUC was only enforcing the February resolution. With Radio Katanga under UN control it was planned to use it to inform the population about what was happening and dispel rumours that there were ANC soldiers from Leopoldville arriving.

As promised, Raja and O'Brien paid their early morning visit to Tshombe with the intention of telling him he was not in danger and neither was Rumpunch an attempt to disarm the Gendarmerie nor bring the ANC into Katanga. The operation was the implementation of the February resolution, undertaken as O'Brien had intimated to Tshombe it would be. When O'Brien and Raja arrived at Tshombe's residence the guard told them that Tshombe had left but would return shortly. When they said they were in the process of removing the Belgian officers and the foreign mercenaries the guard became very friendly. Meeting Tshombe and the Katangese cabinet later at the Presidential Palace, O'Brien thought that Tshombe 'seemed depressed and anxious rather than angry at course of events'.[60] He accepted the UN action, though he did not like the security measures taken. At 0900 the guard on Munongo's house was lifted and telephone and radio communications across the city were restored. Katangese officers were then allowed to return to Gendarmerie Headquarters. Tshombe met with O'Brien, and during the meeting Katangese Foreign Minister Evariste Kimba read out a prepared statement to be broadcast later on Radio Katanga indicating that the Katangese government was co-operating with the UN. As Kimba was in full flow Munongo entered and shook O'Brien's hand 'in a friendly enough way and said smiling "vous m'avez fu".'[61] When the broadcast aired Tshombe explained that his government 'bows to the decisions of the United Nations'.[62] He asked the population to remain calm, explaining that Katangese would now command all levels of the Gendarmerie.

By mid-morning the first batches of mercenaries were flown to Kamina. Relations between the UN and the Katangese government seemed remarkably good in the aftermath of Rumpunch and the Katangese seemed 'to be anxious in their own interest to avoid stirring up feelings'.[63] In Elisabethville life went on as normal, though the population was suspicious. While the Gendarmerie and police co-operated, many Belgians were 'decidedly cool and obviously confused.'[64] UN security measures were lifted by mid-morning, though ONUC troops remained on alert. At midday O'Brien explained the UN's action to the Elisabethville consular corps, adding that it was based on the February resolution and Adoula's request for help to carry out the Ordinance of 24 August. By now 85 'Europeans' had been picked up and it was known that elements of the Gendarmerie had escaped into the bush with full equipment and supplies.

By early afternoon the intensive drive for apprehending non-Katangese Gendarmerie officers had ceased. A-Company had arrested ten mercenaries, B-Company eighteen, and C-Company thirteen. Of those not expelled immediately the UN relied on the Belgian consul in Elisabethville to repatriate the remainder and many simply disappeared.[65] These were serious weaknesses in Rumpunch. A further serious weakness was that the buildings and installations taken over by the United Nations were handed back to the Katangese. But these problems were not seen at the time. On the evening of 28 August Linner and MacEoin congratulated Raja and O'Brien on Rumpunch. Calling the operation 'excellent progress', they said it was 'a direct tribute to your good judgment, skill and tact'.[66] Reports from Elisabethville had 'filled all of us here with joy. We wish you continued success and please be assured of our fullest support in your endeavours.' Raja and O'Brien conveyed these congratulations to Waern and Egge, replying that all in Elisabethville 'warmly appreciate your generous message'. They were 'particularly pleased by the close and spontaneous co-operation which prevailed between the various national units in the military operations and between the civilian and military sides.'[67] To these units O'Brien and Raja proclaimed that 'Operation Rumpunch which was launched by you with vigour was hundred per cent successful and achieved our aim … Keep the flag flying.'[68] From Hammarskjöld came the message that the 'Congo Club, in congress assembled, passed unanimous vote of congratulations, gratification and sincere respect for an exceedingly sensitive operation carried through with skill and courage. We hope that results will render your task in other respects easier and increasingly constructive.'[69] Hammarskjöld was pleased, but he knew that ONUC had stretched its mandate in Rumpunch, telling Abbas that

> We have had to take some new actions on Katanga, which, if a bit bolder than usual, seem to have been very successful in cleaning up the intolerable carrying on of the Belgian and other foreign officers in the Gendarmerie. We are now more hopeful that Katanga may prove less troublesome henceforth.[70]

The UN felt that Rumpunch had removed Tshombe's military means of maintaining Katanga's secession. Bunche informed Boland that the 'elimination of foreign elements in [the] Katangese army is proceeding smoothly and rapidly according to plan.'[71] About 90 were to leave on 30 August and a hundred or so on 31 August. In Dublin Aiken was anxious to have any information which might indicate that ONUC was widening its operations. There was at this point no expectation that Rumpunch would lead to further use of force by ONUC. Raja redeployed his forces after of Rumpunch, sending a composite Swedish–Irish force of one Swedish company and B-Company 35th Battalion to Jadotville on 29 and 30 August 'to take control and prevent uprisings and untoward incident'.[72] C-Company was under orders to move to Kamina, being replaced by an Indian Dogra company at Elisabethville airport.[73] The airport was guarded by the Dogras and A-Company, 35th Battalion.

On 29 August Tshombe relieved all Belgian Gendarmerie officers of their functions. Many had gone into hiding and during a meeting of the consular corps on 29 August chaired by Belgian Consul Henri Créner, the US consul proposed that two former Belgian army colonels be tasked to get officers in hiding to re-emerge and be repatriated. O'Brien felt this would be more effective than continuing to use force. But O'Brien and Raja did not trust Créner who they felt was 'working with the Gendarmerie officers here in order to stall on the execution of the resolutions'.[74] The gentleman's agreement that Créner would look after the repatriation of mercenaries soon broke down.

Spaak protested to the UN about the measures taken against Belgian officers during Rumpunch. This caught the UN off guard and Hammarskjöld privately told Linner that it was 'surprising' that the Belgian government considered itself 'in position to protest on behalf of people regarding whom in general they have previously claimed to have no authority',[75] but he publicly responded to Spaak that UN actions were based on 'une base juridique évidente et incontestable'.[76] Approximately seventy Belgians who had taken shelter in the Belgian consulate remained to be dealt with. Créner was anxious to avoid their arrest by the UN. O'Brien intended to announce that all officers who had not handed themselves in by 30 August would be arrested. His instruction to secure the immediate departure of all foreign officers still stood and he would not exclude 'any means of obtaining this result'.[77] Agreement was reached that Créner 'would call in all remaining officers falling under the resolution and see to their prompt evacuation'.[78] Hoping to get repatriation speeded up and maintain a sense of urgency in the operation ONUC expected all Belgians in the consulate to be repatriated by 31 August.

The international press reported that the UN had the 'situation well in hand ... order will be restored come what may'.[79] But order was deteriorating in Elisabethville. On 30 August, O'Brien protested against the continuing widespread arrests of Kasai Baluba in Elisabethville. Fearing that the arrests could lead to civil war O'Brien asked Tshombe to suspend Munongo for organizing atrocities against the civilian population. Tshombe 'promised to arrange a confrontation' between the UN and Munongo.[80] Linner felt that 'no pacification or reconciliation can take place in Elisabethville before Munongo has been removed'.[81] He looked for guidance and Hammarskjöld's response was that ONUC should arrest Munongo under the February resolution 'if reliable evidence shows Munongo engaged in clear and immediate incitement' to civil war.[82]

In the short term ONUC could be happy because a substantial number of mercenaries had been apprehended during Rumpunch. The operation had been completed without loss of life and was 'a swift, bloodless coup in which there was the element of complete surprise'.[83] Tshombe bowed to UN pressure and the remaining mercenaries melted away. Raja and O'Brien grew in confidence, as did Khiari and Linner. Yet this confidence was misplaced as Rumpunch was only partially successful. As the mercenaries drifted back into Katanga it became apparent that Rumpunch had achieved little and was 'a quite inadequate remedy'.[84] With civil war a distinct possibility in Elisabethville O'Brien told Dunnett that 'the application of measures authorized by the resolution of February 21 would be continued until [the] secession ended'.[85] Tshombe correctly anticipated that, bolstered by the apparent success of Rumpunch, ONUC now 'intended to reduce Katanga by force'.[86]

CHAPTER 7

From Rumpunch to Morthor

After Rumpunch

KATANGESE MORALE lifted after Rumpunch as the Rhodesian Federation announced that its troops were ready to assist Elisabethville. Tshombe began an anti-UN propaganda campaign and Munongo armed local tribesmen in Elisabethville, inciting them to attack the South Kasai Baluba in the city. As Munongo remained in office O'Brien told Tshombe that ONUC would reduce its contact with the Katangese authorities to a minimum. Civil order began to break down in the African suburbs and numbers in the refugee camp rose to over 25,000. With rioting in the central jail, prisoners escaping, and Gendarmerie ransacking the main food depot, ONUC was worried. There was a 'grave social emergency'[1] in the camps and 'savage persecution' in Elisabethville.[2] O'Brien feared that the volatile situation would lead to riots and require a repeat of the 'desperate measures' of Rumpunch – seizing communications facilities in Elisabethville to stop anti-Baluba propaganda and arresting Munongo.[3] The disintegrating situation in Elisabethville also provided Leopoldville 'with solid reason for intervention' in Katanga.[4] This was the basis to ONUC's forthcoming follow-up to Operation Rumpunch, Operation Morthor. Yet at this point O'Brien told Linner that he did not want a repeat of Rumpunch, 'except if necessary and you so instruct for final moves involving termination of Katanga's secession'. In the 'rapidly evolving situation' O'Brien felt he still held the initiative and could maintain pressure on Tshombe.[5]

In early September enhancing central government control in north Katanga and managing the deteriorating situation in Elisabethville were O'Brien's twin concerns. O'Brien and Raja asked for support from ONUC HQ in Leopoldville to 'get a clear solution in North Katanga'.[6] They envisaged the removal of the Gendarmerie and what amounted to the 'enforced partition of Katanga', perhaps in the face of Katangese resistance. They asked that UN forces 'in Katanga generally and in North Katanga particularly, should be in such force as completely to overawe the Gendarmerie.' Raja sought permission from MacEoin to redeploy a Gurkha company from Leopoldville to Kamina. He did not want to thin out his forces in Elisabethville or in north Katanga. Gendarmerie units were 'very jumpy and touchy' without their European officers and UN forces 'must be strong to keep them in check'.[7] MacEoin refused, and after he also moved Ethiopian and Ghanaian troops from north Katanga Raja forcefully explained that the evacuation was 'politically and militarily unsound and not acceptable'.[8]

In his account of his time as Hammarskjöld's representative in Katanga, *To Katanga and back*, O'Brien played down the situation in north Katanga in early September 1961. In doing so he excluded some critical events on the road to Morthor.[9] His 1961 correspondence shows that he considered that the 'profound crises' in north Katanga and Elisabethville should be dealt with together. Planning the UN's next move, O'Brien cabled Linner that 'we should not make two bites of the Katanga cherry and that the next time we have to take firm action here, we should not hand over control to anyone not authorized by the central government'.[10] It was time for united action across Katanga and between ONUC and the Congolese government. Seeking information from his superiors on their plans for north Katanga, O'Brien asked 'if Khiari could pay us a visit ... he would be to us as a great light in our present darkness'.[11] Linner had by September 1961 delegated considerable political authority to Khiari and Khiari became a central figure in Morthor for O'Brien. In *To Katanga and back* Khiari's role was modified by O'Brien to allow O'Brien withdraw from centre stage in planning Morthor; O'Brien placed Khiari there instead. This was disingenuous. Contemporary correspondence places O'Brien firmly in the driving seat setting the policy that led to Morthor, even if Khiari delivered the final instructions to O'Brien to commence the operation.

O'Brien put pressure on ONUC HQ in Leopoldville to move again against Katanga and to do so in a more concerted effort than Rumpunch. The plan for what would become Morthor evolved in O'Brien's mind in the days after Rumpunch as he spoke openly to Khiari of ending Katanga's secession. ONUC HQ was thinking only of actions in north Katanga and the gist of O'Brien's telexes to them was to develop a wider strategy across Katanga. He advocated that ONUC and Leopoldville 'combine our action' against Katanga.[12]

The Kamina Conference: 4 September 1961

In *To Katanga and back* O'Brien set the run up to Morthor in terms that were designed to be vague. He explained that early in September he received a telegram in French from Linner beginning 'Tous ici applaudissent votre Rumpunch, mais ...' O'Brien added that 'we always took Linner in French to be Khiari.'[13] The telegram explained that while ONUC Headquarters applauded Rumpunch, the 'real objective of our endeavours was the reintegration of Katanga in the Congo and we must now press even harder towards this end'.[14] It is not clear when this telegram was sent and it appears not to have survived in the archives consulted for this book, but it was at least consistent with Khiari's thinking.

O'Brien thus implied that it was Khiari or Linner who took the lead role in the development of Morthor. However, this suggestion is undermined by a letter sent by O'Brien to Linner on 3 September which suggests that it was O'Brien, not Khiari or Linner, who began the events leading to Morthor. The letter does not appear in *To Katanga and back*. In the letter O'Brien stressed the need for 'early personal contact' between Raja, himself, MacEoin and either Linner or Khiari.

He felt the pace of events in Elisabethville had led to these five men at the centre of ONUC's Katanga policy 'getting mentally a little out of touch'.[15] O'Brien explained that he and Raja 'agreed that a clean cut finish to the secession can only be obtained in Elisabethville and by a similar action to [Rumpunch], but this time bringing in representatives of the Central Government, as provisional authority'. Here was Morthor in essence. O'Brien called on Linner and ONUC legal advisor Vladimir Fabry to establish the legal basis for a UN operation along these lines. He did not refer to Security Council resolutions, or suggest the need to make contact with Hammarskjöld. But he did explain that the UN in Katanga 'strongly feel that the prolongation of the death throes of "Independent Katanga" is a highly dangerous process'. A negotiated settlement was unlikely. UN measures in north Katanga would only lead to unrest in south Katanga and 'firm action in Elisabethville' with the Central Government taking over the apparatus of the Katangese state on a temporary basis would 'considerably increase the chances of an orderly transition'.

O'Brien suggested a meeting at Kamina Base on 4 September to agree ONUC's next moves in Katanga. Linner agreed, but he did not attend. MacEoin did not attend either.[16] So Khiari and Fabry met O'Brien 'to review the position and co-ordinate future actions'.[17] O'Brien and Raja hoped to immobilize Munongo in the expectation that Tshombe would again '"s'incliner" before such a "coup" ... this would be in accordance with the general pattern of his behaviour.' O'Brien sent his views to Khiari with a stark covering message:

> We want to finish it once and for all with 'Katanga Indépendent' and it seems to us useless to beat about the bush.
>
> It is in Elisabethville ... that we will end the secession. The last conference at Kamina gave good results. Let us meet therefore once again in Kamina, and this time for the coup-de-grace.[18]

These letters are not mentioned in *To Katanga and back*, though O'Brien did obliquely refer to his 'pressing for renewed action in Elisabethville'.[19] O'Brien was not the passive agent he suggests in the book, rather, he was setting an agenda. Just how far Raja was pressing O'Brien to take this new line is unclear and no account of the Kamina talks other than O'Brien's passing mention that they were inconclusive has come to light. A second issue that arises from this exchange is how much Hammarskjöld knew. Brian Urquhart, in his biography of Hammarskjöld mentions O'Brien's and Raja's concerns but he highlights that though Linner facilitated the Kamina meeting he did not tell Hammarskjöld of what O'Brien had proposed.[20] That may be so, but Hammarskjöld knew in considerable detail the options being proposed for Katanga in early September 1961.

Permission from Hammarskjöld

However inconclusive the Kamina talks, they led to a significant development. On his return to Leopoldville Khiari sought clearance from New York to revise

UN policy in Katanga. He and Linner told Hammarskjöld that the situation in Katanga had 'entered into a delicate state and urgently necessitated a review of our initial plan.'[21] Rumpunch had not yielded the expected results, escaped mercenaries were on the loose and the number of refugees in Elisabethville was increasing. This 'could lead to a catastrophic situation'.[22] Munongo's actions meant 'it was impossible for O'Brien to make any further progress by purely political means'.[23] It was necessary to act 'rapidly and in a determined and decisive manner'.[24]

The new policy was that Linner would brief Brussels on events in Katanga, and O'Brien would try to persuade Tshombe to end the inflammatory radio broadcasts and arrests. Tshombe would receive twenty-four hours notice to expel the remaining foreign officers. If he refused the UN would take over Radio Katanga, arrest troublemakers and prevent Katangese security forces interfering with UN work. As a result Tshombe would hopefully order Munongo's arrest. If he did not, then Leopoldville would take control of Katanga's administration. Linner and Khiari hoped that Tshombe would co-operate. This new plan became known as 9(c) from the paragraph in the document to Hammarskjöld in which it was contained. Linner and Khiari told Hammarskjöld that their proposals were made conscious that the alternative could be a central government invasion of Katanga.

Plan 9(c) was taken from O'Brien's ideas and from ONUC thinking in the aftermath of the Kamina Conference. The draft telegram Linner and Khiari planned to send to Hammarskjöld added that the plan 'may seem to exceed the mandate given to us by the UN'. However the version ultimately sent to New York made no mention of this, nor did it include the final sentence that 'this plan contains little risk, and its success, we are sure, will justify the means employed'. As Alan James succinctly put it, 'what was now proposed was the conduct, by the UN, of a Provincial coup on behalf of the Central Government'.[25] This was uncomfortably close to getting fully involved in the internal affairs of Katanga and Congo. Urquhart thought Hammarskjöld was now 'increasingly apprehensive'. After Rumpunch he knew 'of people in the field taking unauthorised decisions'.[26] Hammarskjöld wished 'to be fully informed of important military movements and events' and instructed Linner to send him 'your proposed moves and plans in advance to enable us to send our views as necessary. This would enable us to co-ordinate all our efforts.'[27]

In his initial response to Linner on 9(c) Hammarskjöld agreed that with inter-tribal violence rising the seizure of the radio station was allowed under the February resolution and he agreed in principle with much of the plan, though with the caveat that 'very much will depend on how these steps are implemented.' Hammarskjöld needed more time to consider the fundamentals of 9(c) and felt that it would 'be most unfortunate if we have to go to this point, and it would in practice amount to temporary occupation on behalf of the central government in a way which at least comes close to "interference by force" in domestic affairs.' But he agreed that if the alternative was war between Congo and Katanga 'we may have to take on the responsibility also for such "interference" as the lesser of evils'.[28] Hammarskjöld's objective remained to bring Tshombe and Adoula together for talks and for Katanga to peacefully return under Leopoldville's remit.

The UN military build-up in Elisabethville

Hammarskjöld felt that the best policy in Katanga was 'to remain strong but to sit tight, and let the medicine do its work without, if possible, new injections'.[29] In Elisabethville UN military commanders thought differently and asked MacEoin for 'more troops, transport, equipment [and] barbed wire ... to deal effectively with any eventualities in addition to dealing with the refugee problem'.[30] Raja asked MacEoin for transport to be made immediately available to fly in a company of Gurkhas from Manono to Elisabethville. This time Raja did not look for authority from MacEoin to undertake the move. The troops would start moving on 6 September. Even Hammarskjöld now seemed increasingly equivocal on future military steps, cabling Linner to see if he had 'considered reinforcing South Katanga urgently so as to be ready for any eventuality'.[31] Whatever the Secretary General might have in mind, Katanga Command was undertaking a military build-up to apply the 'new injections'. On 6 September, a week before Morthor began, Raja travelled to Kamina to meet MacEoin.[32] They decided to increase the number of ONUC troops in Elisabethville. Ultimately a battalion of Gurkhas was sent to Elisabethville before Morthor began, their deployment being completed on 9 September. A larger operation than Rumpunch could not be undertaken before the Gurkhas arrived in force. Once the Gurkhas were operational ONUC strength in Elisabethville 'would be sufficient to deal with any emergency.'[33] However despite this reinforcement ONUC still lacked the heavy equipment necessary to undertake more than policing duties; but this deficiency only became apparent once Morthor began.

As the Gurkha advance party arrived in Elisabethville troop movements within the city showed that a strong Indian-led military build-up was underway. The Dogras took over airport security from the Irish, who concentrated their forces at Leopold Farm. Irish patrols across Elisabethville were harassed continually by organized local groups. Radio Katanga broadcast daily anti-United Nations propaganda. The situation grew uglier and Sector-B undertook 'immediate plans [to] cater for the maintenance of law and order in the city of Elisabethville and the defence of the airport.' ONUC moved its headquarters from the centre of Elisabethville, where it had been the location of violent protests, to Dogra Battalion HQ on the western outskirts of the city. Plans were 'prepared to implement any decisions which may be taken regarding the assumption of control by UN of Radio Katanga and further arrests'.[34] Hammarskjöld proposed sending three additional battalions to Katanga 'as a useful backstop'. He considered that the 'psychological reaction to a reinforcement in South Katanga could be important'.[35]

From Dublin Aiken asked Boland in New York 'to find out what are the specific objectives of the UN in Katanga … and how far it is considered by UN authorities that use of force is permissible for achievement of each objective'.[36] Aiken took a poor view of what seemed to be happening in Katanga and saw 'a danger in stating the general obligation of UN forces to be "to preserve unity and territorial integrity".'[37] He was anxious lest the desire to complete the Congo operation quickly should lead ONUC to exceed the peace and order role outlined by Lemass when Irish troops were being deployed and advised acting with the utmost patience. Patience was in short supply.

Writing of this period, O'Brien explained that the Security Council had authorized the use of force in Katanga in the last resort and 'the "last resort" was almost at hand'.[38] Rhodesian Federation sources were 'reliably informed that the United Nations has prepared for stage two of its operations'.[39] They believed that O'Brien interpreted his instructions 'as being the elimination of Katanga's independence and considers anything necessary to achieve this aim to be justified.' The Foreign Office believed Rhodesian expectations of further UN action in Katanga, telling Sir Patrick Dean that Salisbury's view 'certainly chimed in with the impression Hammarskjöld gave you'.[40] The State Department instructed the United States ambassador to the United Nations Adlai Stevenson to ask Hammarskjöld 'what his future plans are' for Katanga.[41] Harold Macmillan felt it 'all too likely' that instructions from UN Headquarters were 'being misinterpreted by the man on the spot in Elisabethville'.[42] It suited Hammarskjöld for this impression to be given.

O'Brien's increasing pressure on Tshombe

O'Brien maintained pressure on Tshombe, reminding him that the 'inter-tribal hate propaganda on Radio Katanga must cease' and that if it did not, recourse to force remained an option for ONUC.[43] Meanwhile the Congolese government prepared arrest warrants for Munongo and his colleagues and decrees to legalize renewed UN action in Katanga. O'Brien requested authority from ONUC in Leopoldville to assume temporary control of Katangese communications and to apprehend Munongo as principal inspirer of the hate campaign. If there were attacks on UN personnel O'Brien told Tshombe he would hold him and his government personally responsible, warning that 'we will of course be obliged to take action'.[44] O'Brien told Linner that 'our main need now is to be able to react immediately and decisively if people get killed and badly hurt'.[45]

Demonstrations took place in central Elisabethville and Sector-B instructed that United Nations personnel in the city move in groups of not fewer than four. Leaflets were circulated portraying Irish peacekeepers as pro-Communist and arguing that Katanga's plight was similar to Ireland's under British rule. An Irish platoon-strength patrol was attacked by a stone-throwing mob on 6 September and two soldiers wounded. The Katangese parliament heard deputies call for war against the United Nations. ONUC troops were 'alert in their lines' and 'prepared to implement pre-arranged plans if a serious situation develops'.[46] Numbers in the refugee camps continued to rise as the 'increasingly violent' anti-UN campaign continued across Elisabethville.[47] Raja reported the 'situation tense but under control. All protective measures taken.'[48] Dunnett speculated that the UN would 'continue to apply whatever measures are authorised ... until Katanga's secession is ended'. He claimed that O'Brien 'has been given five weeks in which to liquidate Tshombe's government'.[49]

O'Brien met Tshombe to discuss the dangers facing Katanga and to seek his help ending the propaganda campaign and locating over 100 absent foreign Gendarmerie officers. Tshombe agreed to help, but O'Brien told Linner that 'little can be expected from Tshombe until we can assure him that we are prepared to act with determination'.[50] What O'Brien wanted was 'authority to react immediately to any incident consequent on this incitement which may involve loss of life or serious personal injury, by taking the necessary measures to terminate the agitation'.[51] He telexed Linner that 'representatives of an international organisation are obliged to exercise very great patience in such circumstances. It is clear however that our patience is open to misinterpretation.'[52] O'Brien felt that the UN must 'act decisively very soon' as otherwise 'our loss of momentum [is] inevitable.'[53] He used the argument of impending civil war in Katanga to make a case to remove Tshombe. O'Brien was trying to set up a situation where he could pounce on Tshombe and thus end Katanga's secession. He was using a dangerous situation to force a denouement.

O'Brien got his chance on 8 September when Linner left for Brussels to brief Spaak and Khiari took temporary charge of ONUC. To O'Brien 'Khiari's ascendancy in Leopoldville is a help, he being a rock of strength, equipped with wisdom of [a] serpent. We now have a Battalion of Gurkhas here ... so there is no doubt about the military situation. The political and legal situations however are still quite tricky, in New York and Leopoldville as well as here.'[54] Aiken telegrammed Boland on 9 September that 'UN force should avoid getting bogged down in hostilities against any group of Congolese secessionists'.[55] That the Indian contingent in Elisabethville was amply prepared for hostilities would become evident in the coming days.

Elisabethville remained tense. ONUC had opened fire on protestors, and Gendarmerie were 'patrolling in strength in most sectors' and at the airport were nervously expecting ONUC or ANC troops to arrive.[56] Katanga Command felt it 'desirable to have European troops for internal security duties in Elisabethville', however MacEoin refused to move further Swedish troops to the city.[57] On 9 September Tshombe announced a UN–Leopoldville plot to overthrow his government. Tension increased further. Tshombe was 'apprehensive and anxious to seek a way out'.[58] O'Brien suggested that he meet central government leaders in Kamina. If Tshombe refused O'Brien feared, or perhaps hoped, that the 'last opportunity [for the] negotiation [of a] solution [to the] Katanga crisis may have passed.' 'Further developments consequent on [the] breakdown [of] negotiations should', he wrote, 'now be discussed here on arrival Khiari.'[59] With Khiari on the move something was in the air. In addition, senior UN intelligence officer Col. Bjorn Egge was instructed to remain in Elisabethville.

Hammarskjöld maintained that 'it was untrue that any further UN operation was planned.' But he did foresee scenarios where the UN would have to act in Katanga. On 6 September he explained this to a number of UN delegations, more than likely those who were contributing to ONUC. The most favourable scenario was that Elisabethville and Leopoldville cooperate to give Katanga a form of local autonomy. Less favourable was that Leopoldville would move against Katanga or that in attempting to move against Katanga the central government would implode and chaos would ensue throughout the country. A final scenario Hammarskjöld envisaged was where the UN had 'to resort to "drastic measures", which, increasingly, would lead us to a kind of take-over of controls in various respects in Katanga.'[60] This was 'entirely against our wishes and with obvious objections in view of UN principles as we wish to maintain them.' However Hammarskjöld added that because of the 'inacceptability' of allowing the ANC invade Katanga or letting the Congolese government break down, and if devolved government for Katanga proved impossible, the 'drastic measures' option would become a possibility and the UN 'would have to assume responsibility for such a policy'. He added that the UN was 'being pushed further and further' towards 'drastic measures' because of the lack of movement on settling Katanga–Congo relations. Indeed Hammarskjöld specifically told UN delegates that they 'should anticipate developments' that would lead the UN to take greater control in Katanga. The Secretary General was preparing UN members for a difficult period ahead.

Hammarskjöld explained to Sir Patrick Dean that 'it was untrue that any further UN operation was planned.' However, the Secretary General added that 'he had given authority to Mr O'Brien and Col. Egge to take control of Elisabethville radio if the radio continued to broadcast what amounted to incitement to civil war. This action, if it had to be taken, would be justified in his view under AI ... and would of course only be taken with the agreement of the central government.'[61] Bearing these points in mind, a 'guidance' telegram that Hammarskjöld sent to Linner for O'Brien on 8 or 9 September is significant. A key sentence summarized by Urquhart reads in the original – 'Whether or not reports of preparation for, or incitement to, violence justify the use of *preventative or defensive force* by UN troops can only be answered in the light of the specific circumstances.' When it came to dealing with 'measures for the forcible apprehension and detention of individuals', for which read Godefroid Munongo, these were 'clearly justifiable in the event that they are apprehended while engaged in military action or otherwise in flagrante delicto. *In circumstances which fall short of this, the problem is a difficult one to deal with in abstracto.*'[62] Hammarskjöld was leaving the road open to local initiative. The version in Urquhart's biography strips away Hammarskjöld's vacillation and uncertainty, though he still concludes that the guidance telegram 'can have provided little comfort for O'Brien and his staff in the overcharged atmosphere of Elisabethville'.[63] Legalistic and distant, Hammarskjöld's response to 9(c) showed he was losing touch with Elisabethville.

Hammarskjöld nevertheless asked Khiari to see the instructions being formulated for O'Brien. Khiari assured Hammarskjöld that he and Linner agreed with Hammarskjöld's advice over implementing 9(c) and that there would be no deviation from O'Brien's existing instructions. Linner and Khiari now sought authority from Hammarskjöld to implement 9(c). The messages from ONUC HQ to Hammarskjöld through 8 September state and re-state the need to take urgent and decisive action in Elisabethville before it was too late. On the afternoon of 8 September Linner told Hammarskjöld that Adoula had signed the ordinances appointing provincial commissioners to replace Tshombe. O'Brien wished to proceed to arrest troublemakers and take over the radio station, but had been 'instructed to refrain from such measures until they are specifically authorised by us.' Then came the critical request to Hammarskjöld: 'The urgency, however, is increasing and we would appreciate receiving your authority to apply 9C immediately after Khiari's return'.[64] On the night of 9 September Khiari told Hammarskjöld that he had received the warrants and other documents signed by Adoula to take action in Katanga and he specifically told Hammarskjöld it was time to look at the possibility of implementing 9(c) in entirety.[65]

There has been much debate about what Hammarskjöld knew of ONUC's intentions in advance of Operation Morthor. There is no doubt that Hammarskjöld that knew a further UN operation was planned in Elisabethville and that he expected a repeat of Rumpunch. Hammarskjöld was also in no doubt that O'Brien was looking for authority to act and that ONUC and Leopoldville were acting in parallel against Katanga. Linner told Hammarskjöld that while Leopoldville had prepared 'all the ordinances and decrees necessary to legalize action' in Katanga, the Secretary General alone should know that 'we prefer to keep [the] initiative in our hands to prevent central government from enacting measures which we would not be in a position to help them implementing. However, there is complete identity of views and outwardly we are only following lead taken by government.'[66] It seems that Hammarskjöld, in New York, and Khiari and Linner, in Congo, ultimately differed in their interpretation of what the forthcoming ONUC operation would entail. After all, Linner had previously purposely kept the extent of Rumpunch from Hammarskjold and, with Khiari and O'Brien, Linner was becoming increasingly prone to taking risks with high odds.

Hammarskjöld moved in two stages on implementing 9(c). On 9 September he instructed Khiari that 'with quick changes of constellations ... you are authorized, at the moment you consider necessary, to take control of radio station'.[67] This was not a full implementation of 9(c) as he still felt that this was not legally possible for ONUC to undertake under the February resolution. Then on 10 September Hammarskjöld sent a further message to Khiari, though the cable was formally sent to Linner who was absent. The text is critical. Hammarskjöld realized that 'the speed of developments and the stage reached means that short of a change for the better in Katanga we are beyond the point of no return as regards your plans under 9C'. He continued, 'You are therefore authorised to pursue the policy'.[68] This telegram significantly alters the history of Operation Morthor. It shows that Hammarskjöld knew in advance that the UN was about to take action in Katanga and that he authorized Khiari to undertake that action. Even if he did not fully know what the move entailed, he reminded his senior officials in Congo to 'bear in mind the various views we have found necessary to express in the course of our exchange; views of principle of which we know from your own cables that you share'.[69] Views of principle often amounted to very little in the game of rising stakes being played in Elisabethville.

This interpretation of events is further supported by a confidential report from Frederick Boland to External Affairs in Dublin. Boland asked Bunche had Morthor 'been ordered by the Secretary General? I thought it might conceivably have been a local initiative. Bunche replied – "well, not exactly ordered - but authorised. We gave them the green light".'[70] He added that 'an operation involving taking over control of the entire telecoms system can hardly be mounted overnight' and would take a couple of days to organize. Boland also reported that senior UN official Heinrich Wieschoff told him that the Secretary General 'had not instructed the action in Elisabethville to take over the Radio Station but had authorised them to do so "if it proved absolutely necessary" … a wide measure of discretion was left to the UN representatives in Elisabethville.'[71] An off-the-cuff remark to Linner gave away just what Hammarskjöld knew when he mentioned 'the possible drama over the next few days'.[72] Wieschoff's remarks, Bunche's reply to Boland, and Hammarskjöld's telex and remark to Linner all say the same thing – the Secretary General gave O'Brien the green light in Katanga. This would later be denied vociferously by the UN Secretariat and subsequently by Hammarskjöld's supporters. By 'authorising' O'Brien to act in Elisabethville Hammarskjöld acted cannily. Almost a year earlier he told Andrew Cordier that 'responsible persons on the spot may permit themselves, within [the] framework of principles which are imperative, what I could not justify myself – taking the risk of being disowned when it no longer matters'.[73] Hammarskjöld's 'authorization' of O'Brien to act on his own initiative allowed Hammarskjöld to exercise plausible deniability should Morthor go wrong.

48 hours to go

O'Brien got the opportunity to act against Tshombe on 10 September when Michel Tombelaine, a senior ONUC official, was arrested at Elisabethville Post Office by Sûreté officers, one of whom was Belgian. Tombelaine was released, but O'Brien demanded the evacuation within 48-hours of all Belgian personnel from Katanga under paragraph A2 of the February resolution. In doing so O'Brien emphasized that he was 'authorized to take immediate action by force if necessary'.[74] He saw the Sûreté as 'a small time Gestapo which is disturbing rather than maintaining public order'.[75] Tshombe refused to remove the personnel. On 11 September, O'Brien again tried to convince to Tshombe to go to Leopoldville. Tshombe again refused. At the same time the central government called upon the UN to take action in Katanga. Munongo's agents, busy reporting the Indian military build-up in Elisabethville, noticed that a consignment of Congolese flags had arrived in the city. This, if they had ever doubted its actions, gave the UN game away to the Katangese. O'Brien also got two sets of loudspeakers flown from Leopoldville for his own use. O'Brien informed ONUC Headquarters in Leopoldville that he was 'gradually losing [the] initiative if it has NOT already been lost – Require clear directions as to line of action'.[76]

On 11 September, Khiari and Fabry arrived in Elisabethville and met Raja, Waern, Egge, and O'Brien. Their job, Linner told Hammarskjöld, was 'to set up program of implementation on para 9C.'[77] Khiari and Fabry delivered 'very precise and detailed instructions' on how to act against the Katangese authorities.[78] The meeting saw serious, sometimes heated, discussions as the intentions of the forthcoming UN action were decided. Waern wanted a repeat of Rumpunch, Khiari and O'Brien looked for stronger action including the arrest of senior Katangese politicians. Waern was against this. At the meeting the 'instructions, on the basis of which' a new UN action was to be prepared were handed over by Khiari.[79] He also brought the warrants from Leopoldville for Tshombe's and Munongo's arrest and the arrests of Jean-Baptiste Kibwe, Evariste Kimba and Charles Mutaka. Tshombe was only to be arrested in the last resort. Waern thought it unlikely that Munongo would be found and O'Brien agreed. Linner had earlier told Hammarskjöld that these warrants had been prepared, but not fully explained who was to be arrested.[80]

On the evening of 11 September, the plans for Operation Morthor were refined at Sector-B Headquarters. The hope was that the UN would maintain the element of surprise when it acted and those making the plans on the civilian and military sides worked on the 'understanding that this line of action had been referred to, and approved by' Hammarskjöld.[81] Although he had 'authorised', he had not strictly 'approved' the plan that ONUC in Elisabethville was developing, but he had given his senior officials in Katanga the green light to proceed. Hammarskjöld was now playing a game of bluff, telling those who sought his outlook on Katanga exactly what they wanted to hear, and not revealing to them his prior authorization of UN action in the province. O'Brien, some months earlier, when still with the Department of External Affairs, had noted that it was 'more than doubtful' whether Hammarskjöld took anyone 'into his confidence where major political matters are concerned'.[82] Meeting Boland on the afternoon of 11 September Hammarskjöld explained that, while 'the use of force had to be avoided at all costs', force remained an option 'in the very last resort'.[83] This was the very situation, the 'dramatic measures' Hammarskjöld had in mind, towards which the UN was moving.[84] He felt that

> it was difficult to define its objectives and methods fully by reference to rules and regulations. It was largely a matter of 'playing by ear'. Not only had one to play by ear, one had to play with a very delicate touch. The basic uncertainty of the Congo remained. Anything could still happen at any moment.

But Hammarskjöld again maintained that force must not be used and ONUC 'must achieve their objective by other methods – by holding vital points, controlling transport and, when required, by making shows of superior strength in critical situations.' It all sounded very much like the operation being planned. Yet Hammarskjöld concluded emphatically that 'there was no reason to think that the UN forces in Katanga or anywhere would become engaged in active hostilities.'

The Secretary General had already given authorization for Morthor when he met Boland and was giving Boland the specific message he knew Boland needed to give to Aiken. Boland suspected that he was not getting 'a completely frank picture' from the UN.[85] Hammarskjöld had similar conversations with the Dutch, Canadian, Norwegian and British ambassadors. After Morthor London considered that Hammarskjöld had not 'been guilty of duplicity', but a lot had happened between 11 and 13 September 'which requires explanation'.[86] By mid-September Foreign Office officials were 'increasingly concerned' about ONUC policy in Elisabethville.[87] They knew from Linner that 'matters were coming to a head'.[88] Rumours were rife in Elisabethville that ONUC was about to take action, but among an already rumour-ridden population this was nothing unusual.

24 hours to Morthor

On the night of 11 September, Hammarskjöld told dinner party guests in New York that the worst was over in Katanga. On 12 September he left for Congo. Linner let O'Brien know that Hammarskjöld was on his way and would be in Leopoldville from 13 to 15 September. In a friendly tone he suggested that if O'Brien felt he could travel, he could 'come on any one [of] these dates', adding 'I know SecGen will appreciate meeting you'.[89] According to Urquhart, Hammarskjöld 'certainly had no idea that any major and drastic action might be taken before he himself arrived in Leopoldville'.[90] But we now know he knew that an action was likely to take place. It is also likely that he expected nothing more than a repeat of Rumpunch. Khiari told O'Brien that 'Hammarskjöld had given authority for operations in Elisabethville, but that it would be embarrassing for him if fighting were actually going on while he was in Leopoldville'.[91] On the morning of 12 September O'Brien and Khiari held a further unproductive meeting with Tshombe, who seemed to be 'wavering and very much under the thumb of the extremists around him'.[92] Dunnett considered that Khiari's presence in Elisabethville and his and O'Brien's meetings with Tshombe were 'little more than an attempt to help the United Nations' forces to achieve surprise the next morning.'[93] As the following chapter shows, preliminary orders to prepare for Morthor had by then already been despatched to battalion commanders by Waern. When O'Brien and Dunnett spoke on the late afternoon of 12 September about a further demarche with Tshombe, O'Brien declined Dunnett's offer 'saying the matter was closed in view of the statement made at 4pm by Tshombe to a Press Conference denying that he had received a formal invitation to meet Hammarskjöld'. Dunnett told O'Brien there was still some chance of success but O'Brien ended the conversation. By 12 September he had given up on Tshombe, and with the Congolese parliament voting for action against Katanga and news of the warrants for Tshombe's and Munongo's arrest circulating, a turning point in Katanga was apparently imminent. Also on 12 September Linner told the British ambassador in Leopoldville that the UN was 'approaching the point where they would have to take further measures in Katanga in order to carry through the expulsion of foreign military personnel'.[94] Linner knew a follow-up to Rumpunch was imminent. In the week before Morthor he told Hammarskjöld of the coming 're[ab]sorbtion of Katangese secession and its integration in to the rest of Congo'.[95]

After Hammarskjöld's death it became heresy to suggest that the Secretary General had authorized what became Morthor. The record shows that in commencing Morthor, ONUC acted with Hammarskjöld's authorization, though Hammarskjöld immediately denied this once Morthor went off the rails, insisting that 'the action in Katanga had been taken by the UN officials in Elisabethville within their existing authority without any specific authorization by himself'.[96] On 5 October 1961 an *Irish Times* reporter asked O'Brien if he had acted on his own authority or under instruction. O'Brien replied that 'no local UN official would take on his own authority decisions of the magnitude of those taken here.' It was Hammarskjöld who had 'the great burden of the ultimate personal responsibility for what happened'.[97] But O'Brien's story is also problematic. He sought to apportion the blame for Morthor to Khiari and Hammarskjöld, yet it was O'Brien who was convinced from the first days of September that the UN needed to move again in Katanga, and in doing so, to end Katanga's secession. O'Brien placed the genesis of Morthor into Linner and Khiari's heads. Khiari and Linner sold O'Brien's plan to Hammarskjöld and the Secretary General authorized Khiari and ultimately O'Brien and Raja to act. O'Brien told an interviewer in 1991 that 'the historian interprets, but there are great brute facts which he can't interpret away'.[98] In explaining the origins of Morthor in *To Katanga and back* O'Brien came up against these great brute facts when grappling with the harsh realities of the impact of his own actions. UN archives show he fudged the tale of the origins of Morthor at critical points in *To Katanga and back*. The book is of course polemic, not objective history. But perhaps admitting his actions was too much for O'Brien to handle in the aftermath of the failure of Morthor and Hammarskjöld's death. Hammarskjöld is remembered as a saint in UN history, the man who died trying to patch up a botched UN operation in Katanga. History also remembers O'Brien for what he did in Katanga. He was in Hammarskjöld's words, 'the responsible person on the spot' who took too many risks. But O'Brien himself later concluded that 'what had happened to me fell, I think under the head of what is known as expendability'.[99]

Khiari told O'Brien to implement Morthor before 3pm on 13 September, the time that Hammarskjöld was due to arrive in Congo, or to wait until after the Secretary General had returned to New York. London and Washington watched

Hammarskjöld's actions carefully; all suggested that 'important decisions by the United Nations may have to be taken shortly'.[1] Khiari and Fabry left Elisabethville for Leopoldville on the afternoon of 12 September. Khiari's final words to O'Brien were 'surtout pas de demi-mesures'.[2] It was as if he was repeating O'Brien's remarks after Rumpunch: 'Cette-fois ci pour le coup de grâce'. O'Brien planned to move as soon as possible. Raja believed that the military operation against Tshombe and Munongo would take two hours maximum. O'Brien, increasingly under Raja's influence and without military experience, believed this. The final preparations for Morthor were underway. Tshombe had 'bowed' before to UN pressure, O'Brien told Khiari that if the United Nations 'acted firmly, he would bow again'.[3]

CHAPTER 8

Morthor

'These Soldiers of Peace were out for destruction'[1]

OPERATION MORTHOR aimed 'to seize *once again* vital points in Elisabethville in order to round up all Europeans, Ministers and Advisers'.[2] Col. Jonas Waern, who commanded UN forces in Elisabethville, hoped that Morthor would demonstrate to Katanga ONUC's determination to act against foreign military personnel and advisers and against Munongo's persecution of the Baluba. Morthor, like Rumpunch, would be a quick show of force to achieve limited objectives. But there was a critical difference of opinion in ONUC in Elisabethville over the operation. Waern saw Morthor as a repeat of Rumpunch, but O'Brien and Khiari saw it as the opportunity to end Katanga's secession. Through 11 September O'Brien and Khiari, backed by Raja, gained the upper hand over Waern. The UN would deny ending Katanga's secession was Morthor's objective, but 'the trend of United Nations actions in preceding weeks could point to no other conclusion'.[3]

On the morning of 12 September Elisabethville was calm. The UN military build-up continued as a further 550 Gurkhas arrived in the city. Plans for Morthor were finalized by Raja and Waern. Battalion commanders received preparatory orders at 0830 that an operation was imminent. A hint of the military preparations taking place emerges in a telegram from ONUC in Elisabethville concerning a rumour that Tshombe had recognized Mobutu as commander of the Gendarmerie. They queried this with ONUC HQ in Leopoldville, concluding that 'unless [we] receive further instructions from you, [we] assume this makes no difference to our dispositions and will proceed as arranged'.[4] Linner and MacEoin replied to Raja 'proceed as arranged'.[5] The response indicates that ONUC HQ knew that action against Katanga was imminent.

ONUC made every effort to keep Morthor secret but Katangese agents had already established ONUC's intentions. Across Elisabethville there was an increased Gendarmerie presence on the streets. Gendarmerie also occupied strategic buildings across the city including the Post Office and Radio Katanga. Linner later maintained that Khiari had compromised Morthor by secretly meeting with senior politicians in Leopoldville, 'briefing them on what was going to take place' and they leaked the news to Elisabethville.[6]

By the early afternoon of 12 September 35th Battalion Headquarters knew Morthor was imminent. At 1430 Lt Patrick Purcell, who was with the Signals Platoon in Headquarters Company, noted that 'at 4AM tomorrow we are going into action and Katanga as a separate state will be no more'.[7] The information did not filter down further at this point. The ONUC soldiers who would go into action in the early hours of 13 September had still been told nothing about Morthor. Until almost zero-hour most of the 35th Battalion assumed that they were in Elisabethville to keep the peace. B-Company and C-Company nevertheless felt that they were on the verge of combat. They anticipated that soon ONUC would undertake another round-up operation, but what was planned and when it would take place was unclear. The ultimate failure of Morthor meant that many who knew about the operation in advance later denied that they knew what was planned. In particular, MacEoin denied knowing in advance about Morthor, though he was sent a numbered copy of the operational orders late on 12 September. The UN was quick to portray Morthor as an Elisabethville affair. Yet if Morthor had indeed gone ahead without MacEoin's knowledge his position as Force Commander would have been gravely compromised, and, indeed, he finally admitted in 1995 that he had known about Morthor from 2200 on 12 September.[8] He had made no attempt to stop the operation.

On the early afternoon of 12 September the commander of the 35th Battalion's Armoured Car Group, Comdt Pat Cahalane, summoned Capt. Art Magennis to receive orders that, with Lt Michael Considine, Magennis was to take three armoured cars and report immediately to the Indian 1st Dogra Battalion. They were to be prepared for at least two days attachment and were to take the attachment as 'a possible event, if not a probable event'.[9] As they were at immediate notice to move, Magennis, Considine and their crews were underway after Father Joe Clarke, the Battalion Chaplain, gave them general absolution and wished them 'God Speed'. Magennis knew his men were conscious of the deteriorating situation, but nobody said to him or them that ONUC was moving towards combat. Comdt Pat Quinlan, OC A-Company 35th Battalion, maintained that 'intelligence and information on operations in the Congo were disseminated by the army on a "need to know" basis, interpreted at Battalion HQ as "they don't need to know" which ended up as "tell them nothing".'[10]

Throughout the afternoon of 12 September Elisabethville was 'calm … no incidents'.[11] The officers commanding UN units reported for duty. Considine and Magennis arrived at Dogra Headquarters at 1700 and at 1830 Sgt Tom Carey arrived at Swedish Battalion Headquarters. Magennis reported to the Dogra commander, Col. Saqbal Singh, and only then did he learn definitely that a second ONUC operation against Katanga was imminent. As he waited with the Indian troops he wondered whether 35th Battalion Headquarters knew as much about the forthcoming operation as the Indians apparently did. Lt Tommy Ryan recalled that there was little warning of upcoming combat. Some of his C-Company colleagues who were in a Skiffle band were to play at a party hosted by Swedish troops on the night of 12–13 September and to maintain an air of normality the band went to the Swedish party.[12]

The final plans for Morthor were completed at a conference on the early evening of 12 September attended by Raja, Waern, Egge, McNamee, Singh and

1st Dogra Battalion (with under command one Company 3/1 Gurkha Rifles and three Irish armoured cars)	(a) Seize Post Office (D-Company) (b) Seize Radio Katanga Studio, Elisabethville (C-Company) (c) Arrest Minister for Information (M. Samalenge)[16] (d) Secure Airport (e) Keep arrested personnel in custody
35th Irish Battalion (with three armoured cars)	(a) Seize radio transmitter at College St François de Sales (Radio College) (C-Company – one platoon) (b) Hold railway tunnel at Chaussée de Kasenga and block if necessary (C-Company – two platoons) (c) Arrest Minister for Finance (M. Kibwe) at residence at Ave Droogmans 835 (d) Secure Refugee Camp at Factory and own lines (B-Company) (e) Guard Italian Hospital (one section each from HQ-Company and B-Company), Verfailles Garage (HQ-Company) and Battalion Headquarters (HQ Company and B-Company) (f) Platoon in reserve (B-Company) at Parc Albert to take into custody Minister for Foreign Affairs (M. Kimba)
12th Swedish Battalion (with under command one Company 3/1 Gurkha Rifles and two Irish armoured cars)	(a) Seize radio transmitter on Route de le Kilobelobe (b) Seize Minister for the Interior (M. Munongo) and European Sûreté officers (c) Secure refugee camp

Table 8. ONUC force objectives for Operation Morthor

Lt Col. Maitra (OC 3/1 Gurkha Rifles Battalion) and by staff officers from Sector-B and HQ Katanga Command. O'Brien also attended. An appreciation of the strengths of Gendarmerie and police facing ONUC forces was given and at 1800 Waern issued written operational orders to battalion commanders. The Indian, Swedish and Irish battalions each had specific objectives. The Indians would undertake the brunt of the assault, while the Irish and the Swedes would undertake security, arrest and holding operations. An Irish staff officer queried these plans asking that as 'we must be prepared to put our own lives and those of our troops on the line in the operation that is ahead … I propose that we in the sector staff and our battalion commanders learn directly from O'Brien the reasons why we should risk our lives'.[13] O'Brien explained that Morthor's goal

3 Cars	Capt. Magennis, Lt Considine, Sgt Morris	Under command 1 Dogra Battalion
2 Cars	Capt. Hennessy	Under command 12 Swedish Battalion
2 Cars	Lt Knightly	Under command 'A' Coy at Jadotville
1 Car	Capt. Lawless	Under command 'B' Coy 35th Battalion
1 Car	Capt. Carroll	Under command 'C' Coy 35th Battalion
1 Car	Cpl Holbrook	O/C 35th Irish Battalion command vehicle

From 13 to 16 September the ten armoured cars of the Armoured Car Group did not operate together. Magennis' and Considine's cars operated with the 1st Dogra Battalion. Two cars commanded by Capt. Seán Hennessey operated under the command of the 12th Swedish Battalion. Two commanded by Lt Kevin Knightly were with A-Company at Jadotville. The final three remained in Elisabethville. The car commanded by Capt. Frank Lawless was with B-Company, that by Capt. Mark Carroll with C-Company, and the vehicle commanded by Cpl P. Holbrook, was the 35th Battalion command vehicle.

Table 9. Dispersal of Irish Armoured Car Group from 13 to 21 September 1961[17]

Date	A-Company (Cmdt Quinlan)	B-Company (Cmdt McMahon)	C-Company (Cmdt O'Neill)
13 Sept.		Security duties for Operation Morthor; Force Kane I (attempted relief of Jadotville) 13-14 Sept.; Force Kane II (attempted relief of Jadotville) 16-17 Sept.	Seize and hold The Tunnel, guard Factory Camp and occupy Radio College, all in Elisabethville, during Operation Morthor
14 Sept.			
15 Sept.	Jadotville		
16 Sept.			
17 Sept.			
18 Sept.			
19 Sept.	Kolwezi (to 25 Oct) as POWs	Security duties at The Tunnel, Chaussée de Kasenga, Elisabethville	Leopold Farm, Elisabethville
20 Sept.			
21 Sept.			

Table 10. 35th Battalion infantry company positions 13–21 September 1961

was to prevent civil war in Katanga. Each commander was asked by Waern if they considered this was sufficient grounds for the operation and they all agreed that it was.

McNamee's operational orders to the 35th Battalion were issued at 2000. In the early hours of 13 September they would take part with ONUC forces in a 'simultaneous military operation' to maintain law and order in Elisabethville. ONUC would seize, hold and control the radio and telephone communications installations in the city and 'take into UN custody personnel who are responsible for disturbances of the peace in Katanga'.[14] Capt. Seamus Condon of B-Company 35th Battalion scribbled in his field notebook at a conference on 12 September as the clocked ticked down to Morthor that the operation's first objective was to 'Suspend Govt. Ministers' and only in second place was 'Comm[unications]s, seize'.[15] As the operation commenced O'Brien planned to explain to Tshombe that his best interests lay in co-operating with the UN and ending Katanga's secession. By keeping Tshombe visibly on side as Morthor proceeded ONUC hoped that there would be no disturbances among the local population that might lead to unrest. Munongo, Kibwe, Kimba and Lucas Samalenge (the Katangese Secretary of State for Information) were to be arrested. Muké would be informed that ONUC was taking action against Munongo and the Sûreté and not against Tshombe, the Gendarmerie or the police.

O'Brien's intelligence estimates in the days prior to Morthor suggested that 'discipline in Gendarmerie will not last long'.[18] They would either give up or not react to a UN attack and thus Morthor began with no expectation that the Gendarmerie would fight back. UN intelligence was categorical – 'advice to UN troops against Black – Don't hesitate. Be resolute and they will run.'[19] Morthor was based on the assumption that though apprehensive of ONUC, the Gendarmerie was loyal to Tshombe and would co-operate with the UN if Tshombe's status was assured. An Irish staff officer from Leopoldville who found himself in Elisabethville as the clock ticked down to Morthor learned that 'the job would start at 0400 on the Wednesday morning and would probably be over in an hour or two'.[20] This was a grave underestimation. Katangese forces had been planning their response to a UN attack in Elisabethville since at least March 1961.[21] Their capabilities and morale were higher than ONUC anticipated.

Plans for Morthor also took no account of the limited capabilities of UN forces in Elisabethville, or the strategic impact of the recent departure of the 35th Battalion's A-Company to Jadotville where they were now dangerously isolated from other ONUC forces. They should have done so. The isolation of these 156 men in Jadotville was a significant depletion in ONUC's military capability; it also created a remote outpost fit for capture and use as hostages. McNamee had sent A-Company to Jadotville under pressure and with great reluctance. He now faced into Morthor with a depleted battalion in Elisabethville and a dangerously situated unit 125 kilometres to the northwest. A-Company was in a trap that would spring once Morthor began.

'Victim of a stratagem':[22] A-Company in Jadotville

Before A-Company deployed to Jadotville a composite group of one Swedish company and one Irish company (B-Company, 35th Battalion) known as 'Force MIDE' had been stationed 'temporarily' in the town from 29 August as part of Operation Rumpunch.[23] It was to accept the surrender of mercenaries and 'guard against [an] uprising against [the] European population'.[24] MacEoin told Hammarskjöld that Force Mide was 'to ensure the maintenance of law and order and to prevent any trouble from the Gendarmerie.'[25] Its commander, Major Ulf Mide, was forcefully told by Jadotville's European population that he and his men were not wanted in the town. Assessing his precarious position and considering that his mission no longer had any objective Mide sensed his isolation and withdrew on 1–2 September.[26] When Spaak learned of Mide's return to Elisabethville he angrily told Hammarskjöld that the European population of Jadotville was now unprotected and consequently he intended to evacuate Belgian women and children.

The UN Secretariat had no idea where Force Mide was and in Hammarskjöld's absence queried Linner and MacEoin on Force Mide's whereabouts. In 'view of the panic aspect' of Spaak's proposed evacuation of Belgian civilians from Jadotville the Secretariat asked if UN troops would return to the town.[27] MacEoin had to act quickly. He had first to ascertain from Katanga Command 'whether UN troops [were] stationed at Jadotville and strength'.[28] This suggests that ONUC HQ was in the dark as to which of its forces were in Jadotville and whether or not they were still in the town. Katanga Command initially told MacEoin that Force Mide was still in Jadotville. MacEoin then explicitly instructed Katanga Command that Force Mide was not to be withdrawn from Jadotville without first notifying him.[29] He did not seem to know that Force Mide was no longer in Jadotville. Through 3 September, Katanga Command maintained that Force Mide was in Jadotville and New York received the comforting, if incorrect, information that they were in the town since 29 August.

However Force Mide was back in Elisabethville and a new force had to be assembled in a hurry to fill the gap left by Mide's withdrawal. As no one else was available, the duty fell on A-Company, 35th Battalion. Only on the afternoon of 3 September, after A-Company had departed for Jadotville, did Katanga Command change its message and, as cover was now in place, tell ONUC Headquarters that A-Company was in Jadotville replacing Force Mide.

The 35th Battalion received orders on the early afternoon of 3 September for A-Company to move to Jadotville to protect the white population in the town from an allegedly growing threat from the local population. Lt Noel Carey recalled OC A-Company Comdt Pat Quinlan returning from a Battalion Conference to announce that 'we were to pack up immediately and be ready to move to a town called Jadotville by 1300 hours … everything was rushed in order to make the deadline'.[30] As a result A-Company left their 81mm mortars and emergency pack rations in Elisabethville. Cpl Seán Foley of A-Company was suspicious of the move: 'there was this thing in the back of your mind … if [Force Mide] had come out of Jadotville they must have had a very good reason to come out.'[31] Pte John Gorman put it succinctly – 'Why would you send in 150 men less-equipped to replace a unit of 300 men?'[32] The answer was A-Company were sent to Jadotville as a scratch force after Mide's hasty return and in response to the UN Secretariat's reaction to Spaak's telegram.

Raja was against the deployment of A-Company to Jadotville, but ONUC HQ in Leopoldville acted 'against local military advice' and forced Raja to act.[33] Once A-Company was in Jadotville, ONUC Headquarters instructed Raja that UN troops should not be withdrawn 'without prior permission of this Headquarters'.[34] They hammered the message home – 'Do NOT repeat NOT withdraw UN troops from Jadotville without prior permission of this Headquarters.'[35] After Mide's withdrawal and Spaak's angry telegram to Hammarskjöld, A-Company was going to be kept in Jadotville to save the UN's face. The request to provide 'notification' to ONUC Headquarters should A-Company be withdrawn became instead a specific instruction to seek 'permission' from ONUC Headquarters if A-Company was to be withdrawn from Jadotville. O'Brien, in a private letter to an Irish officer, Capt. M.J. Masterson, who criticized Raja over the despatch of A-Company, explained that Raja 'was overruled by orders from ONUC Command Leopoldville, given by teleprinter in my presence. A different type of commander might well have ignored the risky instructions from on high, but this would not have been in Raja's character.'[36] Raja intended that A-Company would not remain long in Jadotville and would be removed as soon as possible. ONUC HQ had other ideas.

ONUC HQ was acting on orders from the Secretary General and Hammarskjöld told Spaak on 4 September that 'Le détachement de 150 hommes des forces de l'ONU qui se trouve a Jadotville n'a pas ete retire et ne sera pas'.[37] He told Linner on 5 September that 'protection in Jadotville should not be reduced below original strength', which suggests that Hammarskjöld was not aware of the difference in numbers between Force Mide and A-Company.[38] Indeed ONUC Headquarters had somewhat ambiguously told the UN Secretariat that 'our troops in Jadotville have not, repeat not been removed', so it would seem that Hammarskjöld did not know there were two different forces.[39] Hammarskjöld bears ultimate responsibility for the despatch of UN forces to Jadotville. However the decision as to which UN forces were sent to Jadotville rested with Raja at Katanga Command on instruction from MacEoin at ONUC HQ in Leopoldville, and the subsequent decision to keep A-Company there rested with Linner and MacEoin. To replace Force Mide with a group half its size was 'madness'; militarily, the decision to send A-Company to Jadotville was 'extraordinary'.[40]

A-Company brought with them a section of armoured cars commanded by Lt Kevin Knightly.[41] Due to the attachment of these vehicles Katanga Command told ONUC HQ in Leopoldville that Quinlan's deployment was a 'strong patrol'.[42] But some hours later they admitted that A-Company was 'weak', adding that there was 'considerable uneasiness' among the European population of Jadotville.[43] Views on the mood in Jadotville changed frequently and this suggests that Katanga Command had no accurate information on the mood in the town. On 4 September Jadotville was 'perfectly quiet' and Katanga Command described A-Company's role as being to 'allay anxiety'.[44] A later assessment suggested that up to five battalions of ONUC troops would be needed to hold Jadotville.[45] A-Company's dangerously isolated position was clear to Katanga Command. However they were expected to remain in Jadotville for only a few days and their deployment would be 'reviewed thereafter'.[46]

Quinlan's initial reports showed that A-Company was 'well received' and all was quiet.[47] The situation changed on the evening of 9 September when A-Company was surrounded by Gendarmerie who staged a mock attack and advanced up to Irish lines before being recalled.[48] A-Company was in a precarious situation as the white population they had been sent to Jadotville to protect now led the opposition to the UN presence in the town. Quinlan got a message through to Elisabethville that he was in a perilous position and recommended that A-Company be withdrawn at once or strongly reinforced. He was instructed to hold on as long as possible without resorting to force. To Capt. Liam Donnelly, who was in command of A-Company's Support Platoon and who had gone to great lengths to get Quinlan's message through to Elisabethville, 'the lack of direction, information and material support from higher authority was difficult to fathom'.[49] Quinlan ordered his men to dig in under cover of darkness and prepare defensive positions. His isolated force was set to become a political pawn in relations between the UN and Elisabethville.

A platoon of Irish troops accompanied by armoured cars left Elisabethville for Jadotville on 10 September carrying rations and medical supplies. Fifteen kilometres from Jadotville at Lufira Bridge they encountered a 'very apprehensive' 30-strong Gendarmerie force that feared the Irish would attack.[50] The vehicles carrying medical supplies and rations accompanied by a medical officer and a radio mechanic were let through. Lufira Bridge was the critical choke-point on the road between Elisabethville and Jadotville and it was Katangese strategy to hold it to isolate A-Company.

In Jadotville it was 'tense but not critical' as night fell on 11 September.[51] A-Company reported 'Alert on here. Situation very dangerous.'[52] The European population had attempted, unsuccessfully, to rouse locals against A-Company. Though food supplies had been cut, Quinlan's men had seven days emergency rations. A further re-supply patrol for Jadotville on 12 September was forced to return four miles out of Elisabethville. Sector-B now knew A-Company was stuck. In Dublin External Affairs had only press reports about Quinlan's 'uncertain fate' to rely on.[53] Irish diplomats urgently sought information on the 'action contemplated to relieve Irish troops' in Jadotville.[54] There was nothing to report. Rikhye had no information about 'any situation' at Jadotville and did not investigate further, instead leaving for Idlewild airport to see Hammarskjöld off to Leopoldville.[55] The Defence Forces Director of Plans and Operations cabled the Irish ONUC Liaison Officer in Leopoldville looking 'at once' for the locations of 35th Battalion units.[56] The following morning in New York it was the same story, and on 13 September as news of Morthor trickled through, the Irish permanent mission to the UN 'obtained some information regarding the situation in Elisabethville but no word of Jadotville.'[57] Bunche later cabled angrily to Linner that 'news of plight of Irish Company in Jadotville, received in Leopoldville 11 September was not relayed to New York until 14 September'.[58]

A-Company's position was not considered significant in New York, Leopoldville, or, most importantly, in Elisabethville as 'a positive indication of serious trouble but was considered … to be just another typical Congolese incident'.[59] Indeed the situation in Jadotville was reported 'improved' late on the afternoon of 12 September.[60] Egge felt that those planning Operation Morthor 'regarded the threat to the Irish company in Jadotville as a calculated risk'.[61] In fact Sector-B and Katanga Command had misjudged the implications of Jadotville for operations in Elisabethville. By keeping A-Company in Jadotville, essential troops for Morthor were cut off and tied down. Further assets required for Morthor had to be diverted to undertake two unsuccessful attempts to relieve A-Company. Hammarskjöld had fallen for 'a clever trick to disperse the UN forces'[62] and Jadotville became 'the great propaganda set-piece' of the September fighting.[63]

'It was the UN that started it. Everything was quiet until they came along with their armoured cars'[64]

At Dogra HQ Capt. Magennis and Lt Considine were introduced to the company commanders of the 1st Dogra Battalion. Before they entered into discussion Magennis asked for ten minutes to ensure that his armoured car crews were not neglected in his absence. The Battalion OC called in a senior NCO who assured Magennis that his crews would be looked after. Magennis briefed his crews on what was going on and told them to check over their vehicles. Magennis was then briefed by Maj. Sawan Singh, OC D-Company and Considine was briefed by Maj. Khahzan Singh, OC C-Company. Magennis only now learned that in the early hours of 13 September Dogra Battalion would take over, by force if necessary, Elisabethville Post Office and the Radio Katanga studios. The three Irish armoured cars, under Dogra command, would lead the assault troops at both locations. Magennis, commanding two armoured cars, was to cover the Dogra infantry in their assault on the Post Office at Place Albert. Considine's armoured car would at the same time be two kilometres away leading the Indian troops taking Radio Katanga on Place Delvaux. A complete reconnaissance of both locations was to be undertaken immediately. When that was completed, Maj. Singh said with a wide grin to Magennis, 'we will have a good meal ready for you … and after the meal: Orders.'[65]

Considine departed for Radio Katanga with Maj. Khahzan Singh and as night fell across Elisabethville Magennis left with a lieutenant, the second in command of D-Company, 1st Dogra Battalion, who would lead the assault on Elisabethville Post Office. As they drove through the city Magennis and the lieutenant discussed their route. The lieutenant had undertaken the reconnaissance run twice that day and Magennis assured him that he too was familiar with the route.

All that remained to be clarified was the location of the assault start line. As the lieutenant talked, Magennis began to apprehend what lay ahead. His mind 'was a tangled mess' as their car slowed along Avenue des Usines.[66] The lieutenant turned 'as we passed between Avenue Sankuru and Avenue Saio and said "This will be the start line".' Their target, the Post Office, was 200 yards away.

Magennis 'tried to concentrate on what lay ahead as the car moved closer' to the Post Office.[67] Passing the rear entrance of the Post Office a group of Gendarmerie para-commandos ordered the car to pull up. A lieutenant came forward and inquired where they were going. 'To the Irish camp', replied the Indian lieutenant. The Gendarmerie huddled together to discuss the reply and the car moved off. The Indian lieutenant turned to Magennis saying 'I'll remember that fucker's face at 4am tomorrow morning.' Moving slowly forward Magennis and the lieutenant carefully examined the Post Office. What worried Magennis was that the Indian lieutenant already knew the plan for the move against the Post Office and the location of the start line and had a detailed knowledge of the building. Magennis knew 'that we were heading into a combat situation and that this [Indian] Battalion was well prepared for it'. It was the first time he himself had become fully aware of ONUC's next planned move.

Magennis wondered how the Indians knew that the UN mandate in Katanga had been changed and how long had they known it. An operation like Morthor could not be planned in a matter of hours. Magennis had not been advised before he left the Irish camp that the UN was on the brink of an offensive operation. Had Comdt Cahalane even been informed? If so, why had he not passed on the information to Magennis and his men? His three armoured car crews, not one of which had fired a round of ammunition on anything other than a classification range during annual practices, were about to go into combat for the first time. Magennis wondered how he would react when he came under fire. How would his crews react? If he was scared at the very thought, how would they feel? Some of them were teenagers, not more than 17 or 18 years old, but he had the utmost faith in his men and he knew they were up to the task ahead.

On the way back to Dogra Headquarters Magennis saw no evidence of an approaching crisis. People passed on the sidewalks and the traffic seemed normal. When they reached the Dogra camp Magennis and the lieutenant were called into the operations room for a debriefing on the reconnaissance patrol. Then they joined Dogra officers as further orders were issued for the following morning's operation. The 'enemy' garrisons at Radio Katanga and Elisabethville Post Office were estimated to be of platoon strength – about 30 men each – and were commanded by mercenaries. ONUC casualties in the assault were expected to be in the region of ten per cent.

Across the city UN officers undertook similar covert reconnaissance. C-Company commander Comdt Tom O'Neill with Lt Tommy Ryan and other platoon commanders reconnoitred the Tunnel area and Radio College. The main component of C-Company was to close off The Tunnel, a railway bridge over the main road into Elisabethville that controlled access from the Irish and Swedish camps to the town, but the platoon commanded by Lt Ryan was to be dispersed. One section under Sgt Shannon would stay at The Factory, one section would go to The Tunnel with their C-Company colleagues and Ryan and an enhanced section would take over Radio College. Ryan was unimpressed by Radio College. It would be hard to defend because there was so much glass in the structure and his men inside would be visible. But it seemed the action required at Radio College would simply be 'flying the flag' and maintaining a visible presence once the operation was underway in case the UN required the facility. O'Neill and Ryan had been told that Morthor was a mopping-up operation and little opposition was expected. To Egge, Morthor 'from the very outset was looked upon with great optimism'.[68] When C-Company troops grouped up to commence Morthor there was a light-hearted atmosphere and men joked and laughed; this was to be a repeat of Rumpunch. Only when the Chaplain gave general absolution did the mood change and all went silent.

Just before midnight Magennis got his crews together for a final briefing. He outlined their orders, including a general outline of Morthor. Magennis left the expected ten per cent casualties to the very end as he felt this would emphasize the seriousness of what lay ahead. He did not take questions immediately, but gave the men thirty minutes to consider what he had told them. The men left and Considine and Magennis talked the situation over. Ten minutes later Sgt Ned Keogh arrived back. Magennis expected questions, but all Keogh said was 'We are all with you to a man. Will you come and join us at the saying of a decade of the Rosary?'[69] With that Keogh removed any tension Magennis was feeling. The crews said the Rosary and, as reveille was at 0315, Magennis urged them to rest and to use the time available to do a thorough check of their armoured cars. The next time Magennis and Keogh met was at 0315. The armoured cars and their crews were ready. Magennis now 'knew then that these young men would do all I asked of them'.[70] That night in Leopoldville Linner invited foreign diplomats and Congolese politicians to his villa for drinks. Operation Morthor would begin at 0400.

'The battle started promptly at 4 o'clock':[71] the assault on the Post Office

At 0330 Considine and Magennis parted company. Commanding one armoured car, Considine joined the Dogra infantry bound for Radio Katanga. Magennis brought his section to their lead position ahead of the Dogra vehicles proceeding to the Post Office. Two platoons from D-Company 1st Dogra Battalion, each supported by one Irish armoured car, would take the Post Office. It was a modern building housing important international telephone, telex and tele-printer circuits, and was on a crossroads at Place Albert in central Elisabethville 'in a commanding position near the centre of the city.'[72] Strongly defended by Katangese para-commandos armed with light machine-guns, anti-tank weapons and rocket launchers and with little cover in front it was a difficult position to assault.

Magennis' armoured car and No. 1 Platoon would assault along Avenue Sankuru. No. 2 Platoon with Sgt Dan Morris' armoured car would assault along

Avenue Royale. The armoured cars would 'lead the assault platoons and neutralise ALL located enemy fire'.[73] The platoons travelled in trucks immediately behind the armoured cars. With them was a jeep carrying Belfast-born interpreter Mike Nolan who had spent his adult life in Kivu province running a large agricultural plantation. The armoured cars and trucks reached their start line without incident and formed up. At 0350 Nolan, speaking through a loud-hailer, in French followed by Swahili, called on the Post Office garrison to surrender, leave their positions and place their arms on the road outside. If they did not the UN would open fire at 0400.

Other than Nolan's voice there was no sound. The first signs of dawn were in the cloudless African sky. There was absolute stillness and no reaction from the garrison. At 0355 Nolan again called on the garrison to surrender. Again there was no response. The entire city remained silent around the waiting United Nations forces. From the turret of his armoured car Magennis saw the Indian lieutenant, the assault platoon commander, about to lead his troops into the Post Office. In synchronization at 0400 Magennis opened fire with his armoured car's Vickers machine-gun on the rear door of the Post Office. The building was 'engaged for one minute by all Company S[up]p[ort] Weapons'.[74] The garrison was again called upon to surrender. There was no response.

Heavy firing began and the full assault on the Post Office commenced at 0403 in tandem with the entire UN action across Elisabethville. The two Irish armoured cars moved across the open ground in front of the Post Office and as the assault platoons went in 'the whole area was lit up with flashes from various weapons and searchlights'.[75] The *Chicago Daily News* described 'furious exchanges of rifle and machine-gun fire down the city's main streets' as Irish armoured cars 'rumbled towards the Elisabethville Post Office' in the darkness 'firing steadily at Katanga Gendarmerie and para-commandos entrenched inside'.[76] Watching the attack a local Belgian, Jacques Brassine, felt that though it was difficult to determine who fired first, 'the UN seemed to have done so after the refusal of the Katangese to surrender'.[77] The UN would quickly spin a different story.

The infantry moved into the Post Office and 'the assault went completely according to plan', though Katangese resistance was stronger than anticipated.[78] Fighting raged with exchanges of small arms and machine-gun fire. The first floor was lit up and the attacking Indians shouted orders to advance as they were engaged by Gendarmerie on the roof. The fighting lasted about an hour and a half, with heavy hand-to-hand combat. It was a 'bloody battle'[79] and, in the words of the Belgian Consul, 'perfectly organised'.[80] Even the official Katangese account agreed that 'the surprise tactics were successful. Forty paratroopers were taken prisoner.'[81]

The Irish armoured cars succeeded in 'neutralizing all enemy locations in the building'. Major Singh commended them for providing 'accurate and sustained fire ... that greatly helped Dogras to capture the Post Office'.[82] After the opening assault they saw very little of the fighting and were involved in 'offensive patrolling around [the] Post Office till the Company was firmly in a defensive position'.[83] The Indians fought their way through the building and 'systematically cleared and captured [their] objective'.[84] Katangese accounts portrayed a vicious assault in which the Indians beat and robbed civilian employees, a Katangese soldier was thrown off the roof by a Gurkha, and a civilian employee, Emmanuel Kasamba, was shot dead in cold blood after surrendering.[85]

Fighting died down about 0600 and Magennis' armoured car took up position at the main entrance to the Post Office while Morris' armoured car remained at a nearby roundabout. Firing was heard from the rear of the Post Office and Magennis saw three Katangese jeeps approach at speed supported by two Staghound armoured cars. The Indians quickly put the jeeps out of action as they crossed Place Albert. One Staghound moved towards the Post Office and took sustained fire from the Irish armoured cars and a Swedish armoured personnel carrier. As one of the Staghounds approached, Magennis shouted across the street to Morris to fire on the gunner's sight while he fired on the driver's sight.[86] In the Staghound Clement Kanza was hit in his right arm and chest and his vehicle turned back.[87] The second Staghound sped past without firing as Morris and Magennis fired bursts at its open hatch hoping that a ricochet might do some damage inside. Magennis knew that if the Katangese

> had the wit to stand back about 100 yards they could have demolished my two armoured cars and any soft-skinned vehicles the Dogras had with their 37mm cannons. The heaviest weapons I had were two .303" Vickers of First World War vintage. But the Katangese never fired a single shot during their so-called counter-attack. We used two belts of .303" ammunition and it was a miracle our machine-guns didn't seize because of overheating.[88]

The Indians then used a jeep-mounted recoilless gun to fire at the Staghounds. They missed, shattering a tree about 100 yards beyond the two Irish armoured cars. Magennis and Morris were lucky. 'Thank God it wasn't us', thought Magennis, if the round 'had been on the line of its target it could have hit either Sgt Morris' armoured car or mine.'[89]

The inadequacies in the design of the Ford armoured car were apparent early in Operation Morthor. It was essential that the commander occupied the turret as otherwise his view would be restricted to two small slots in the car hull.[90] As there was room for only one man in the turret the gunner had to give way to the car commander who then additionally became the gunner and became fully occupied swinging the heavy turret to lay the gun. The original gunner became number two on the gun, tasked with ensuring a constant feed of ammunition to the turret. There was no mechanism to catch the spent rounds ejected from the Ford's Vickers machine-gun. Red hot after firing, they were ejected at speed into the interior of the armoured car. The car crew often wore towels on their heads to protect against flying casings.

After Magennis learned that the Post Office had been captured he joined the Indian officers inside for coffee. The interior was a mess. The mail sorting room resembled a rubbish dump and the communications room was a mess of multi-coloured wiring. On the stairs to the second floor a Gendarmerie soldier lay dead. Casualties were estimated at one dead and eight wounded among the UN forces with 25 Gendarmerie dead, 41 taken prisoner and an unknown number wounded.

By 0800 the Post Office area was generally quiet. Later in the morning the UN reinforced the Post Office and by midday crowds were demonstrating nearby and armoured cars were used to keep them from getting too close to the building. By early evening a company of Gurkhas and a company of Dogras were dug in defending the Post Office. The Post Office remained a troublesome area for ONUC over the following days and the commander of Indian troops in the building often asked for Irish armoured cars 'to deal with snipers and other firing'.[91]

Magennis returned to his armoured car section at about 1000. He heard sirens as two ambulances moved fast straight across their field of fire. They sped past as the Irish held their fire, but Indian troops on the roof of the Post Office opened up. Their heavy machine-guns missed both ambulances and they continued at speed in the direction of Radio Katanga. A story circulated that the ambulances were carrying weapons and ammunition to re-supply the Gendarmerie at Radio Katanga and this was accepted in UN accounts. The UN assault on Radio Katanga had begun at 0400 and if the ambulances were on route there six hours later then it was more likely that they were trying to recover the dead.

'Short but revolting and murderous':[92] the assault on Radio Katanga

C-Company Dogra Battalion, under the command of Maj. Khahzan Singh, was ordered to take the Radio Katanga studio at Place Delvaux, which was being used to broadcast anti-UN propaganda. The station's transmitter was the most powerful in Katanga and controlling it was vitally important to both the UN and the Katangese. The attacking Dogra troops had no illusions that their job was anything other than a full-scale assault.

Lt Michael Considine's armoured car operated with the Dogras during the assault. The orders he received were almost identical to those issued for the action at Elisabethville Post Office. The armoured car and infantry were to be on their start line at 0345, an interpreter would call twice for the garrison to surrender; if there was no response the assault would begin at 0400. The armoured car 'would move in to within 20 yards of the building and lay down machine-gun fire on building and area'.[93] One infantry platoon would assault and one would be kept in reserve.

Dogra infantry and Considine's armoured car moved from their assembly area at 0330. At 0357 Considine was within twenty yards of the Radio Katanga studio. The interpreter called on the defending garrison to surrender. In the armoured car's searchlight beam Considine saw Gendarmerie crawling into position. Katangese sources estimated there were 9 policemen and 60 soldiers guarding the premises, more than the attacking UN force thought.[94] At 0400

Considine's armoured car opened fire on the radio station building. Its gunner, Sgt Jim Flynn, was 'told to fire so many belts of ammunition at the building'.[95] Armoured car driver Tpr Fred Sheedy remembered 'there was extensive fire from the Vickers machine-gun' and 'fire was returned to and from by both parties'.[96] With them in the armoured car was Tpr Mick Boyce, its radio operator. He recalled that he

> couldn't see the building from where I was ... but I could hear the infantry and all around outside ... and the next thing Jim Flynn opened up fire on the building ... Jim Flynn was firing for ages, hundreds and hundreds of rounds ... it seemed to take forever ... and the next thing he stopped.[97]

It was 0412 and as Flynn ceased firing the Indian assault troops moved in on foot. Boyce could hear 'the Indian [Major] shouting and roaring at the NCOs outside' as the troops ran from behind the Irish armoured car towards Radio Katanga. As they 'charged into the building firing their sub-machine-guns'[98] there was limited return of fire from the garrison. Sheedy recalled 'little resistance from Radio Katanga' to the assault. Amidst more shouting Considine's armoured car moved behind the infantry into an open space, Boyce recalled it was a yard or a car park, around the Radio Katanga building. Through his observation slot Sheedy saw 'small gun fire really, coming from Radio Katanga towards us and towards the flanks' where the Indian troops were entering the building.[99] It was not the 'strong and determined opposition' with a 'heavy exchange of fire' that was later reported.[1] The armoured car halted with its machine-gun trained on the studios. It was difficult to see where the rounds from the Vickers had hit the building but 'Radio Katanga was well hit from weaponry from ourselves and from the Indians'.[2]

By 0430 the assault was over. Initial reports to Dogra Battalion Headquarters were of 23 Katangese dead.[3] Considine reported approximately 20 Gendarmes and four or five police surrendering. They were disarmed and ordered out of the building. Boyce saw civilians among those surrendering. The Katangese account added that those who tried to escape via the rear of the building were shot by the Indians.[4] Radio Katanga was in UN hands. Considine covered the approaches to the station with his armoured car. Gendarmerie continued firing from the surrounding buildings, but by 0630 ONUC troops 'were well dug in.'[5]

Boyce saw the Indian Major go into the Radio Katanga building. Guessing it was now fairly safe he and Considine got out of their armoured car. They saw the Katangese who had surrendered being taken out and assembled by the Indians in three rows in the car park. Now they were prisoners and Boyce saw that their

> knees were knocking together with fear. I will never forget it as long as I live. I remarked to one of the crew, I don't know if it was Fred Sheedy or to Considine 'Jesus, says I, the fight is knocked out of them fellows anyway.' There was *fear* in them; I'd never seen so much fear in my life in a man.[6]

The prisoners were put back into the building and the doors were closed. The Irish armoured car turned around pointing its gun to the road. Boyce sat on the rear step and recollected his thoughts about what had happened. He was glad the armoured car crew had not suffered any casualties, though he knew an Indian sergeant had been killed. After about an hour Boyce saw the Indian Major with two Indian NCOs going across to the studio building and he 'thought there was something funny about the way he was carrying on.' The Major pointed to a window. Boyce turned to Considine saying, 'Jaysus, this fucking fellow's up to something ... I tell you he is up to something.'[7] The NCOs vanished. They came back, opened the window and each threw in a grenade; 'you could hear the fucking screaming and roaring inside in the room'.[8] Boyce saw each NCO throw in three grenades; he was 'shocked, the whole lot of us, we were fucking shocked. I'd say Mick Considine couldn't talk with shock, just couldn't talk.'[9] Sheedy remembered the same; the Katangese prisoners 'were put into a room and live grenades were thrown in on top of them.' The doors were unlocked and the survivors were shot as they crawled out. Sheedy continued

> those who didn't die from the blast some made it to the door and they were actually shot by a handgun, so there that were no survivors. It was a gruesome and terrible incident in my opinion. They were then carried from Radio Katanga carried out the hallway and buried in a very shallow grave. It was horrific.[10]

When they were exhumed many of the bodies were found to have point-blank range bullet wounds. Asked over forty years later about the Indian action Boyce simply replied 'pure murder'.[11] Sheedy said that even though he did not see the grenades being thrown into the room, the memory of the killings would 'stay with me forever'.[12]

After the grenades went off the interpreter, who they had not seen since the initial assault, came to the Irish armoured car crew and, gripped with fear, said to Considine 'don't say anything about this here or we won't get back alive.'[13] 'Fair enough' said Considine; Boyce agreed. They thought the Indian Major was insane:

> it seemed to me like as like he was losing his mind to me. He was strutting round the place shouting 'total war, that's the only way, total war, throw the bodies up on a truck bring them down to Elisabethville and throw them out on the fucking streets. That'll really demoralise them.'[14]

Boyce thought the Major had 'gone mad', ONUC was 'supposed to be a peacekeeping mission, we are a peacekeeping force, and here was this fellow strutting around, and this was the way he was behaving; you would think that we were at war with another nation, two nations fighting each other when everything goes'.[15] Boyce watched as the Major called 'a crowd of his own crowd down'. They went into the building. Boyce also saw Flynn go separately into the Radio Katanga building. When Flynn returned he was 'as pale as a ghost'. 'Says he to me', Boyce recalled, 'they're dragging the bodies out the back.' The Indian Major was nowhere to be seen, so Boyce took a chance and went into the building; he saw the bodies in the high grass outside the back door. Inside the building he picked up a fancy peaked cap and a 9mm revolver. As Boyce returned to the armoured car the Indian Major spotted him, called him over, and in front of Considine said 'put them back … there's no one to take fucking souvenirs out of here, make sure of that.'[16]

At 1630 the Indians withdrew and Raja informed MacEoin that Radio Katanga had been 'completely destroyed. It is of no use to anybody'.[17] The official Indian history makes no mention of the actions of C-Company, Dogra Battalion, or their commanding officer at Radio Katanga. Some days later Considine gave a vivid detailed account to Magennis of what he witnessed at Radio Katanga. The assault had started just like that at the Post Office, but some hours after the Katangese surrendered came the 'terribly sudden and savage attack' on the prisoners with grenades and weapons.[18] Magennis 'could see the horror' in Considine's face; Considine 'was still shocked and horrified at what he had witnessed'.[19] Magennis told him 'to take two days off duty and use the time to put his oral account in writing'.[20] Considine was to give Magennis the completed report, but when Magennis asked him for the account, Considine said that 'he had been instructed to give the account to Operations Section'.[21] Magennis never saw in writing what Considine told him but retained 'a very clear memory of his verbal account to me, and his obvious horror as he related it.' He knew that Considine's account was 'greatly at variance with what appears in the official history of 35th battalion'.[22]

In 2005, Magennis interviewed Boyce and Sheedy about what they had seen at Radio Katanga. He taped their conversation and the interviews are quoted from in the paragraphs above. Boyce and Sheedy knew that, though the incident was reported by Considine to his superiors, the UN covered up the killings. When Frank Aiken visited Elisabethville later in September 1961 Boyce, Sheedy and Flynn were prevented from meeting the minister. In the years that followed they used 'talk about it among ourselves, the troopers, but never heard anything official about it'.[23]

The Irish armoured car crew had not been involved in the killing of prisoners, but 'there were signs put up in that Radio Katanga saying that the Irish were murderers'.[24] Boyce believed the Irish were blamed because the Irish armoured car was prominently visible during the assault. It saddened him to think that 'the good name we had as Irish peacekeepers' was damaged 'by that Indian'.[25] Sheedy thought the Indians were 'excellent troops but had no regard for life whatsoever … very experienced and determined fighters, but had no regard for life'.[26] The 35th Battalion Unit History put it differently – 'our men too spoke of Indian planning, coolness and toughness in action'.[27]

O'Brien calmly told the press that at Radio Katanga 'sharp action followed with casualties on both sides … we profoundly regret the casualties and wish to pay tribute to the Katangan Gendarmerie for its valour'.[28] Responding to questions about the conduct of Indian troops he explained that 'any troops in the world are likely to get touchy under these circumstances, and while any unfortunate events are to be deeply regretted, it must be stressed that the troops are under the heaviest strain'.[29] However to others, including Rhodesian Federation Prime Minister Sir Roy Welensky, 'the brutality of the Indian troops is almost a by word among people here. There are so many eye-witnesses to the events that it is almost impossible to deny them.'[30]

The BBC carried a report on the 'brutality' of Indian troops in Katanga on 14 September and the following day the Indian press began heavily to criticize the British government. Relations between London and Delhi were reported to be at their worst since the Suez crisis as the Indian Ministry of External Affairs denied the allegations of atrocities in Katanga. Nehru denied the allegations levelled against the Indian military in Katanga and talk of a public inquiry in India was snuffed out. Macmillan attempted to calm matters by writing to Nehru that Britain was 'unwilling to believe anything which would reflect adversely on the fine record of the Indian Army'.[31] Though British Consul General Denzil Dunnett reported 'an Indian Major principally responsible for having 20 Katangese police shot (mostly in the back)', Foreign Office officials admitted they had no proper report on the conduct of the Indian Army in the Congo and London soft-pedalled the atrocity story.[32]

Irish journalist Raymond Smith reported that he had 'evidence to show that the Indians did not wish the Irish to see how they went about their work.'[33] Dunnett spoke guardedly of what had happened at Radio Katanga: 'The United Nations forces' behaviour I will leave for any comment that may be expressed by the international Red Cross'.[34] A note in Sir Roy Welensky's private papers dated 15 September 1961 included reference to 'a group of Katanga soldiers who had surrendered and actually had their hands up' being machine-gunned by Indian troops.[35] The French Consul General in Elisabethville reported to Paris 'evidence of the United Nations actions infringing the Geneva Conventions on the conduct of war'.[36] As news of the killings spread around Elisabethville, ONUC troops were seen as murderers. Some spoke of killing captured UN troops and an Italian officer explained that 'UN personnel should avoid being taken prisoner especially Indian'.[37] Rhodesian intelligence picked up that 'Katangese felt reasonably well-disposed towards Swedes and Irish but harboured very deep hate for the Indian troops'.[38]

Linner denied that there had been any UN atrocities in Elisabethville and O'Brien later wrote of the pressure in the UN to tone down, disguise and in some cases give 'plainly false' reports of 'controversial events'.[39] He explained that many of the atrocity stories he mentioned in *To Katanga and back* were 'fabricated' by pro-Katangese elements. However 'Irish officers whose word I have no hesitation in accepting' told him that 'on one occasion in September 1961, one contingent under United Nations command had killed Katangese paracommandos who had laid down their arms and sought to surrender.' O'Brien described 'a Colonel in the Indian brigade under UN command' who

1 Douglas C-124 Globemaster II No. 30045 of the United States Military Air Transport Service ferrying Irish soldiers, Leopoldville, 1961.

2 'Welcome to Free Katanga', Capt. Seamus Condon, Elisabethville, 1961 (both Col. Seamus Condon Collection, Military Archives).

3 Elisabethville from the air looking west, with 'The Tunnel' in the centre, 1961 (Col. Seamus Condon Collection, Military Archives).

4 Elisabethville airport, main terminal building, 1962 (Capt. Jack Browne Collection, in family possession).

5 Watching aircraft at Elisabethville airport, 1961.

6 Katangese Gendarmerie band at Elisabethville airport, 1961 (both Col. Seamus Condon Collection, Military Archives).

7 President of Katanga Moïse Tshombe and Godefroid Munongo (with glasses), Elisabethville airport, 1961 (Col. Seamus Condon Collection, Military Archives).

8 President of Katanga Moïse Tshombe, Elisabethville, 1962 (Capt. Jack Browne Collection, in family possession).

9 Soldiers from A-Company, 35th Battalion attend mass, Katanga, 1961 (Leo Quinlan, personal collection).

10 Comdt Pat Quinlan, OC A-Company, 35th Battalion, oversees training in anti-riot drill, Elisabethville, 1961 (Col. Seamus Condon Collection, Military Archives).

11 Refugee camp in Elisabethville, 1961.

12 Soldiers from the 35th Battalion on the move, Katanga, 1961 (both Leo Quinlan, personal collection).

13 A pair of Ford armoured cars, with a pair of Willys jeeps, on patrol in Elisabethville, 1961 (Comdt Art Magennis, personal collection).

14 Comdt Pat Quinlan (A-Company, 35th Battalion) prepares a message for transmission from a Willys jeep-mounted C12 radio set, Katanga, 1961 (Leo Quinlan, personal collection).

15 A Carl Gustav 84mm recoilless rifle in use by A-Company, 35th Battalion, Jadotville, September 1961.

16 A 60mm mortar about to fire, Jadotville, September 1961 (both Leo Quinlan, personal collection).

17 35th Battalion guard of honour (with 9mm Carl Gustav sub-machine guns), Elisabethville, 1961. (Comdt Art Magennis, personal collection).

18 35th Battalion personnel assembling at 'The Farm', Elisabethville, 1961 (the men are armed with the 9mm Carl Gustav sub-machine gun or the 7.62mm FN automatic rifle) (Col. Seamus Condon Collection, Military Archives).

19 Comdt Pat Quinlan with a group from A-Company, 35th Battalion, armed with 9mm Carl Gustav sub-machine guns, 7.62mm FN automatic rifles, a Bren light machine gun and a Vickers medium machine gun, Jadotville, September 1961.

20 Irish and Swedish ONUC personnel with Katangese Gendarmerie, 1961 (both Leo Quinlan, personal collection). In the centre wearing UN cap is Comdt Pat Quinlan.

21 Capt. Cyril McQuillan, Platoon Commander, Support Platoon B-Company, 35th Battalion with Indian troops who were co-located with B-Company in Nyunzu, north Katanga, November, 1961 (Col. Seamus Condon Collection, Military Archives).

22 Lt Col. Hugh McNamee, Col. Jonas Waern and Lt Col. S.S. Maitra, Elisabethville, 1961 (Comdt Art Magennis, personal collection).

23 A Bren gun crew digging in, Jadotville, September 1961.

24 Camouflaged A-Company position, Jadotville, September 1961 (both Leo Quinlan, personal collection).

25 A burned out bus, part of Comdt Pat Cahalane's ambushed patrol, outside Radio College, Elisabethville, September 1961. The graffiti reads 'Poor UN fools'.

26 Capt. Mark Carroll points to where a Katangese anti-tank projectile hit Comdt Pat Cahalane's Ford armoured car, Elisabethville, September 1961. The photograph includes Capt. Art Magennis (third from left) and Capts Mark Carroll (pointing) and Frank Lawless (extreme right) (both Comdt Art Magennis, personal collection).

27 Comdt Pat Quinlan, OC A-Company, 35th Battalion (Leo Quinlan, personal collection).

28 Lt Col. Hugh McNamee, unknown Gurkha captain, Lt Col. S.S. Maitra, Elisabethville, September 1961 (Col. Seamus Condon Collection, Military Archives).

29 Frank Aiken being briefed by Comdt John Keane (back to camera) while Lt Col. Hugh McNamee (facing camera) and a 35th Battalion Chaplin listen, Elisabethville, September 1961 (Col. Seamus Condon Collection, Military Archives).

30 Jack Conway, Conor Cruise O'Brien, Frank Aiken, Freddie Boland and Con Cremin, Idlewild Airport, New York, late 1950s (UCDA, P104/6021).

31 Irish Ford armoured cars and Willys jeeps at 35th Battalion Headquarters, Elisabethville, 1961.

32 Irish ONUC troops with a Swedish SKP m/42 Armoured Personnel Carrier, possibly during Operation Rumpunch, Elisabethville, August 1961 (both Comdt Art Magennis, personal collection). Comdt Pat Quinlan, OC A-Company, 35th Battalion, is first from the left.

told journalists that his men would take no prisoners.[40] The UN went through contortions to save its peace-loving image as it would have been awkward to accept the Indian's story. Any attempt to discipline him would have antagonized India, a major contributor to ONUC and led possibly to the withdrawal of the Indian contingent. It was the same with the killings at Radio Katanga – it was best not to hamper the UN in its pursuit of peace.

Taking The Tunnel and searching for Tshombe's men

At 0335 on 13 September, as the assaults on the Post Office and Radio Katanga took place, two platoons from C-Company accompanied by an armoured car commanded by Capt. Frank Lawless moved towards The Tunnel. They arrived at 0400, found the area unoccupied and set up a defensive position. Each had with them an anti-tank sub-section. Mortar and machine-gun sections arrived and were in position by 0530 having been engaged by Katangese forces en route. Throughout Morthor heavy machine-gun, mortar and sniper fire was directed at the Irish position at The Tunnel from the Gendarmerie Supply Depot, Camp Massart and the Railway Station. C-Company successfully held The Tunnel until 18 September when they were relieved by B-Company.

Lawless also assisted an infantry section commanded by C/S O'Sullivan in a fruitless attempt to arrest Katangese Minister for Information Lucas Samalenge. They searched the Ministry of Information and came under sniper fire. Returning fire they cleared the area, completed their search and moved on to check Samalenge's residence on Avenue des Chutes. He was nowhere to be found. Meanwhile across Elisabethville two Irish armoured cars operating with a Swedish platoon searched for Munongo at his residence off Boulevard La Reine. Capt. Seán Hennessey's armoured car pushed in the front gate and covered the attacking Swedish forces. As they took up position, Tpr Des Keegan, one of Hennessey's crew, saw

> Munongo's personal guard assembling by a building across the road. They were all heavily armed and were clearly getting ready for action. And that's when the fire started. I know some people say that the first shots that day were fired at Radio Katanga or the Elisabethville Post Office, but I reckon they were fired at Munongo's house.[41]

Sgt Hamill's armoured car covered the rear of the house. It was engaged by guards from the nearby Gendarmerie HQ. Hamill returned fire and 'neutralised [the] opposition'.[42] Munongo, like Samalenge, was nowhere to be found. After Rumpunch he lived in the expectation of arrest and was thought to be 'among his henchmen in the cité'.[43]

An infantry section from B-Company and a section of military police accompanied by an armoured car commanded by Capt. Mark Carroll had more success detaining Minister for Finance Jean Baptiste Kibwe. Arriving at Kibwe's residence on Avenue Droogmans they surrounded the house. Carroll's armoured car covered the front of the building with its searchlight and the military police disarmed the two policemen on duty. Kibwe was found in his bedroom and was led off under 'very heavy shooting all round' to the armoured car in which he was transported to custody at Dogra Battalion HQ.[44] Capt. P.L. Walsh of the Military Police reported that the mission was 'carried out one hundred per cent successfully'.[45] Walsh was strikingly honest in his report, saying that the Military Police section 'despite being generally inexperienced showed admirable restraint and courage when disarming the police guard' and detaining the minister. He concluded with a flourish that 'the MP section showed a firmness of purpose of which I was proud. They got a mission and were prepared to carry it out at any cost.'

Lieutenant Ryan's Platoon at Radio College[46]

Lt Tommy Ryan, commanding an enhanced section from his C-Company platoon, had a separate objective to his colleagues heading for The Tunnel.[47] Ryan's group was tasked to take and hold the radio station and transmitter at the College of St Francis de Salles known as 'Radio College'. Located on the corner of Avenue Wangermée and Avenue de Ruwe it was about fifteen minutes drive from The Tunnel and about three miles from 35th Battalion Headquarters.

Radio College was a school for radio technicians run by the White Fathers, Belgian priests who lived close to the station premises. Ryan reckoned his group had got the soft job on 13 September. There was no sign of life when they arrived at the station. Unsure of what awaited them in the darkness, Ryan had a number of his men fan out and give cover to the party entering the building. Lt Patrick Purcell from Signals broke down the glass entrance door and was first into the building. Ryan repositioned his men, inspected the interior and placed guards. Searching the studios he was again aware of the amount of glass in the building and how he and his men were vulnerable to attack. They were lightly armed, with one Carl Gustav sub-machine-gun, one Bren light machine-gun and the majority of the men with the recently introduced FN automatic rifle. Each man had fifty rounds for self-protection, scarcely adequate ammunition to defend the location.

Mounting a Bren gun inside the main door and riflemen at windows was all it was possible to do to defend Radio College. Ryan had been told to do as little damage as possible and was reluctant to smash windows to create proper fields of fire. Being Catholics, Ryan recalled that he and his men felt they should apologize for occupying the studios should one of the White Fathers come over to them. When one priest did come over he snarled at Ryan that he was a 'Communist Bastard'. The White Fathers were completely uncooperative and reluctantly tolerated the Irish at Radio College.

Their objective secured, Ryan's detachment was reduced as a section returned to The Tunnel shortly after 0500. Ryan had no radio communications with Battalion HQ or Sector-B Tactical HQ at Parc Albert. Nor had he a reporting schedule; Radio College was so near to Parc Albert that Ryan was to maintain communication by a foot messenger. He was only to be at Radio College until 1100 and communications were not expected to be problematic. Nor was food, as Ryan's section was told they would be fed from Parc Albert. These two points indicate the piecemeal way that Morthor was organized. No-one had thought of the contingencies that might arise should, and no-one expected it, there be a resolute Katangese response that would disrupt these arrangements.

Lt Purcell and Sgt O'Sullivan checked over the Radio College broadcasting equipment. The station was pencilled into UN plans to be used in a standby capacity for propaganda broadcasts against Tshombe and broadcasts to calm the local population. Their task came to a halt when the electricity supply was cut. Having no further orders and unsure if the power was gone permanently the Signals contingent remained at the Radio College until midday when they reported to Parc Albert. Ryan and his small group remained at Radio College. Through the morning they heard firing and occasionally saw UN armoured cars patrolling the street outside Radio College. One of the patrols was the Irish contingent tasked to arrest Munongo, which passed up Avenue Wangermée shooting out streetlights. The men were laughing and waving to each other. During the day two mortar rounds hit Radio College. Inside the defending Irish troops were edgy and would occasionally fire at suspected targets. Ryan was concerned that they would waste their meagre supply of ammunition and told them to conserve what they had. With a reduced force holding a strategically important position Ryan was very exposed and he had no idea how the fighting had gone on around the city.

'It looked as if the UN had finally mopped up'[48]

Despite the heavy fighting around the Post Office and Radio Katanga most ONUC objectives were taken shortly after 0400 on 13 September without resistance. Aware that Elisabethville was under attack, Tshombe phoned O'Brien in considerable anxiety seeking a ceasefire. O'Brien and Raja assured him of ONUC's intentions and sought his agreement that ONUC could complete its mission without Gendarmerie interference. O'Brien promised to guarantee Tshombe's safety and the Katangese president agreed to make a radio broadcast declaring Katanga's secession ended after which the Gendarmerie would cease fire. Tombelaine went to fetch Tshombe, returning empty-handed with the news that there was not a single UN soldier around the presidential palace.

No one had considered sealing off Tshombe's palace until three hours after Morthor was underway, giving him ample time to escape. O'Brien thought that he had stressed the importance of isolating Tshombe, but there were differing opinions on this between the Indians controlling Katanga Command and the Swedes at Sector-B headquarters. Raja blamed the Swedes, but there is no indication that they were ordered to apprehend Tshombe. ONUC lost contact with Tshombe. At about 0545 he arrived at the residence of British Consul Denzil Dunnett, telling him that the Gendarmerie refused to cease fire. Soldiers arrived with reports of the fighting and when Tshombe departed close to 0715 he was less inclined to halt the fighting: 'Morthor was beginning to go off the rails'.[49] The UN had 'assumed that a short sharp action would break the back of Gendarmerie resistance. They miscalculated sadly.'[50] The battle 'seemed to die out for a while and then start anew'.[51] The Katangese put up strong resistance. Under mercenary command the Gendarmerie regrouped to counterattack. O'Brien was to be guest of honour at a dinner at the 35th Battalion Officers Mess on the night of 13 September. The dinner did not take place. All was not going well for ONUC as news of the fighting in Elisabethville spread internationally. The UN had to move fast to put its spin on events that were fast moving beyond its control.

CHAPTER 9

Cover-up

The mythology of Morthor

A TELEPRINTER MESSAGE received in Leopoldville at 0620 local time on 13 September 1961 reporting heavy firing around Elisabethville Post Office and the capture of Radio Katanga told ONUC Headquarters that Morthor was underway.[1] Its language suggested that Linner and MacEoin already knew that Morthor was imminent – this message was merely confirmation. Two hours later Linner sent an urgent message to New York explaining the ongoing events in Elisabethville. It portrayed Tshombe as controlled by extremists and emphasized rising inter-tribal tension in Elisabethville; incidents organized by foreign personnel in the Sûreté; the burning of United Nations vehicles and arrests of United Nations staff. Linner explained that O'Brien's request for the removal of foreign personnel had been refused by Tshombe and, in a further escalation, Kimba had announced that Katangese forces were being reinforced from Rhodesia. Faced with these threats ONUC had been forced to act. Linner explained that the 'United Nations decided to apprehend for evacuation the remaining foreign military personnel and foreign officials of the Sûreté, after taking security precautions'.[2] Linner's account, based on early incomplete information, gave an incorrect version of the morning's events. It did not explain that ONUC had opened fire first. In what became the accepted UN version of Morthor, Linner maintained that ONUC troops met resistance executing their tasks. He endorsed Raja's account that the first shot had been fired from the Belgian Consulate, killing a Dogra soldier, and thereafter heavy fighting ensued. This incorrect assessment was New York's first inkling that Morthor was underway. That the UN assault across Elisabethville was simultaneous and co-ordinated shows that it was not a response to a local one-off incident as Linner suggested. Accounts from veterans show also that ONUC opened fire first.

Though Hammarskjöld had received a special situation report on Morthor from MacEoin at 1130Z on 13 September indicating that after heavy fighting Radio Katanga, the Post Office and the airport were in UN hands, though under Katangese counterattack, the Secretary General stuck to Linner's initial account that said the Katangese opened fire first.[3] Hammarskjöld knew that 'ground may be lost psychologically at the first shot from our side, if we can be accused of acting prematurely or in provocative way' and he was anxious to avoid this accusation.[4] Hammarskjöld continued to accept Linner's account and so 'allowed the world to be given an official version which was so phrased as to conceal the reality of what had happened, making what had been an active intervention by the UN look like a defensive action'.[5] The UN Secretariat maintained that Hammarskjöld did not know about Morthor in advance (despite his having given his authority for such an operation), that Morthor was Linner's sole responsibility (though he apparently did not know of the plans to arrest the senior Katangese cabinet members), and that UN troops had been fired on and were forced to respond.

Countering the suggestion that the Katangese had opened fire first, a telegram from the Irish permanent mission to the United Nations on the early afternoon of 13 September emphasized that ONUC had opened fire first as 'prior to [the] UN takeover UN troops mainly Indian engaged Belgian-led Katangese para-commandos and Gendarmerie with casualties'.[6] Showing how the Linner version of events took hold this was shortly after 'clarified' by an explanation that 'trouble began when a machine-gun opened fire on Indian troops from Belgian consulate killing one Indian'. It added 'O'Brien had authority to occupy post office and radio station to ensure communications'.[7] The telegram contains elements of actual events in Katanga and the developing UN cover story.

From New York Boland told Dublin that the United Nations Secretariat was circulating a 'rather weak and unconvincing' story about Morthor.[8] Boland tried to find out what had happened in Katanga, but news came in sporadically and was often contradictory. As international dismay rose over Morthor O'Brien became concerned that the UN was likely to deny that that Morthor's aim was to end Katanga's secession. In London Macmillan angrily exclaimed that the United Nations had exceeded its authority in Katanga and it was 'necessary to find some way of pulling Hammarskjöld up short'.[9] There was now a 'terrible responsibility' on Hammarskjöld 'to avoid disorder and chaos in the short term and the return of Soviet influence in the long run' in Congo and he came under pressure to draw the UN back from its action in Katanga.[10] UN sources now maintained that 'a wide measure of discretion had been left to the UN representative in Elisabethville.'[11] Hammarskjöld had 'not instructed' O'Brien and Raja 'to take over the Radio Station but had authorized them to do so "if it proved absolutely necessary".' Yet as they had Hammarskjöld's authority to act and it was 'hard to believe that all the blame can be put on O'Brien for misrepresenting [the] United Nations objective'.[12]

In To Katanga and back O'Brien absolved himself from dealing with the fighting caused by Morthor by explaining that 'I am not qualified to do so, being a total civilian'.[13] The Observer concluded that O'Brien was 'certainly not a man of violence – though he may well be a man who has badly misjudged a military situation'.[14] O'Brien had no military training and believed Raja's optimistic assessment of Morthor's likelihood of success. O'Brien was 'temperamentally an adventurer'. To him, 'outwitting Tshombe and his Gendarmerie was a matter for action, not agonized debate.'[15] Lt Col. S.K. Dhar of the Indian Army raised a separate but equally important point – 'O'Brien was a strong, and in some respects ruthless man, and would have produced results had he had the proper backing. The greatest strength of Dag Hammarskjöld lay in his being basically and essentially a man of peace, but herein also lay his bigger weakness.'[16] Conditioned to instinctively move back from drastic solutions Hammarskjöld maintained that he first heard of Morthor when his plane touched down to refuel in Nigeria on 13 September en route to Leopoldville. He arrived in Leopoldville later on 13 September and was again apparently taken by surprise to hear that Radio Katanga had been taken over by the United Nations.[17] Hammarskjöld chose to follow Linner's account and later wrote to Bunche that 'our action which was a duty under A-2 had become a necessity under our right of self-defence as first reports amply show.'[18] Boland reckoned that Hammarskjöld had authorized Morthor before 10 September, had kept this to himself and 'fully expected the operation to go off with the same degree of smoothness as characterised the arrest of foreign military personnel in Katanga on the 28 August'.[19] Archival sources bear this out. Hammarskjöld made 'two grave miscalculations, one political and the other military'.[20] Politically, he misjudged the active resistance of Tshombe's government; militarily, he miscalculated the relative strengths and abilities of the opposing forces on the ground. He failed to realize that Katangese troops would resist the UN and he did not realize 'the unsuitability for heavy fighting of UN troops equipped for purely police operations'.[21]

The Gendarmerie counter-attack

After Morthor began Adoula declared a state of emergency in Katanga and confirmed the despatch of a special commissioner to the province with instructions to arrest Munongo and Kibwe. He said that the situation in Katanga was a Congolese internal affair and that foreign states should not get involved. Adoula also announced the end of Katanga's secession. At a mid-morning press conference O'Brien, with bursts of machine-gun fire echoing behind him, declared that Morthor was undertaken at the request of the central Congolese government and explained the objectives of the operation. He then uttered the fateful phrase ... 'the secession of Katanga is ended'. To Bunche, O'Brien's former statement was 'most unfortunate and damaging' because it suggested that the UN had acted at the request of the Leopoldville government to end the secession of Katanga, whereas the UN had been anxious to publicly keep its distance from Adoula's government over Morthor and portray it as a local security operation.[22] Hammarskjöld later told Lord Lansdowne that Morthor 'was undertaken at the initiative of the UN in continuation of the action of August 28, and definitely not at the request of the Central Government'. Lansdowne countered that 'O'Brien gave a precisely contrary impression'.[23]

By mid-morning on 13 September ONUC controlled most of Elisabethville. The Rhodesian Federal Intelligence Service Bureau 'accepted that the Katanga Government has fallen'.[24] As the day unfolded Katanga Command learned what was happening across the city. There had been 'heavy hand to hand fighting' at Radio Katanga and the Post Office and casualties were suffered by the Indian and Swedish forces.[25] A roving patrol of Irish armoured cars was used 'to deal with snipers and other firing coming mainly from Gendarmerie HQ' and Indian forces mortared Gendarmerie Headquarters.[26] At the Post Office the crowds, mostly Europeans, began to disperse amid occasional bursts of machine-gun fire from the Indians on the roof. Kibwe had been apprehended and Muké was at large.

Gendarmerie reinforcements were heading for Elisabethville and as midday approached the Gendarmerie regrouped. Col. Muké ordered a counterattack that was well co-ordinated except for the poor use of armoured cars. The counterattack took a 'critical turn' as Samalenge encouraged Gendarmerie 'to open fire with heavy weapons' on ONUC-held buildings.[27] O'Brien tried to get Tshombe to make a radio appeal for calm and contact the UN before the Congolese Commissionaires arrived. Tshombe was meant to call on O'Brien at 1300. He did not show, but Kibwe, in ONUC custody, was anxious to co-operate and appeal for calm. O'Brien hoped that suitable statements by Kibwe would bring calm and an acceptance of the 'new situation'.[28]

The fighting and loss of life continued. Two ONUC trucks which had been escorted by a patrol commanded by Sgt George Shaughnessy of C-Company were burning at the junction of Avenue Churchill and Avenue Leplac having been ambushed by a Katangese armoured car. Driver Tpr Edward Gaffney lay dead in the cab of one truck having been shot as the patrol took cover. Shaughnessy took his men into the bush and regrouped. Pte French had been badly wounded and two men were missing. Shaughnessy distracted the Katangese armoured car, attempting to allow the missing men to emerge from the bush. They could not be found and Shaughnessy then used his local knowledge to get the remaining men to the nearby UN Officers' Mess. At the mess Lt Col. Cullen 'heard shouting from the avenue and saw a party of our men running to the Mess'.[29] It was Shaughnessy's patrol, including the wounded Pte French. The missing soldiers stayed under cover until nightfall and made their way to Irish lines. Cullen wrote to the Chief of Staff of the Defence Forces, Maj. Gen. Collins Powell, that Shaughnessy deserved 'the highest commendation' for his action.[30] He 'had accepted a heavy responsibility' in carrying on with his men and leaving two behind and 'showed up as a real man when the crisis came'. Shaughnessy was awarded the Distinguished Service Medal with distinction for his actions.

By the afternoon of 13 September MacEoin was worried by the lack of information coming from Elisabethville and reprimanded Raja that he had 'received no sitrep from you since this morning except two personal messages'.[31] Raja was now to submit situation reports every two hours and ensure that 'this order is strictly complied with'. Katanga Command responded that Raja and O'Brien were in conference, but that 'Radio Station, Post Office and Airport held by us. Gendarmerie appears to be retaliating … Refugees becoming scared. Stray firing and sniping continues. Situation generally fluid.'[32] Strangely, this report concluded that 'all seems to be normal'. Further reports emphasized that 'firing in town still continuous. Militarily situation under control but troops not enough to cover whole town or to carry out effective patrolling. Politically situation uncertain. All UN troops action gallant.'[33] Raja was concerned that the European officers leading the Gendarmerie were manning heavy weapons and trying to retake Radio Katanga. Word came from Linner and MacEoin that it was 'essential you aim at foreigners leading troops against UN or capture some'.[34]

United Nations forces were stretched to their limit. Katanga Command moved ammunition to Elisabethville and asked ONUC Leopoldville to send light machine-guns, grenades and ammunition immediately. In Elisabethville tension mounted and 'the possibility of widespread attacks on United Nations (but *not* on European civilians) is very real when darkness falls'.[35] Summing up the military problems Waern reported that Sector-B lacked transport and troops and was having difficulty meeting its commitments due to ongoing heavy duties. High on his list was the 'Jadotville problem'.[36]

A-Company under attack

On the morning of 13 September McNamee discussed the situation in Jadotville with Raja. 35th Battalion Headquarters considered Quinlan to be 'in a tight spot – but we are not perturbed'.[37] A-Company remained under siege but had adequate rations and morale was high. However mid-morning Elisabethville learned that after receiving brief but sustained Gendarmerie mortar and machine-gun fire around 0730 A-Company 'returned [fire] with success' scattering the attackers into the bush.[38] They were now surrounded by an estimated 300 Gendarmerie. It was A-Company's first time in combat and they did not know that Morthor was underway until just before they were attacked. Quinlan had asked McNamee the previous evening if further operations were planned in Elisabethville and McNamee told him there was no news.

A second assault on A-Company began mid-morning and 'all hell broke loose.'[39] With 'rounds impacting off the buildings and rounds impacting off the trenches'[40] the attack lasted for over an hour and A-Company 'fought gallantly', repulsing the attack.[41] Quinlan was, Linner reported, 'quite confident that he will be able to hold out.'[42] In fact Quinlan knew he was 'greatly outnumbered, by perhaps 20 to 1, and that the enemy had heavy mortars with which they could reduce my position from outside the range of my weapons.'[43]

Jadotville had become 'very unpleasant' by early afternoon on 13 September and Quinlan radioed Elisabethville seeking urgent reinforcement.[44] MacEoin ordered that A-Company be reinforced. He 'was NOT willing to withdraw the Company' as to do so would 'have [a] bad psychological effect'.[45] Preparations began to send to Jadotville a force made up of a reduced strength B-Company, commanded by Comdt John Kane, now second-in-command of the 35th Battalion. This force would comprise two Rifle Platoons from B-Company and B-Company Support Platoon, a Cavalry detachment and a medical unit. It is not clear why this force was not commanded by B-Company commander Comdt McMahon. Neither was it totally clear if, despite MacEoin's instructions, 'Force Kane' was to relieve or reinforce A-Company. Force Kane left Elisabethville at 1615 on 13 September in five trucks and a minibus protected by two Irish armoured cars and two Swedish APCs.[46] Hastily organized it had received no formal orders for the tasks ahead, the most difficult of which was to attack and cross the defended road bridge over the deep, wide and fast-flowing Lufira River eighteen miles from Jadotville. Lufira Bridge was of critical strategic importance as the forces that controlled it controlled overland communications between Elisabethville and Jadotville. Force Kane received no intelligence assessment of what forces, defences and terrain lay ahead, and lacked 120mm heavy mortars and engineering equipment, but the troops making up Force Kane had no reason to feel they would not reach A-Company.

On the evening of 13 September British diplomats in Salisbury reported that the possibility of A-Company holding out 'seems small'.[47] Force Kane was expected to be 'fighting their way through' to Jadotville.[48] Force Kane arrived at Lufira Bridge at dusk when visibility was poor. An Irish armoured car and a Swedish APC pressed forward through the initial bridge barricades before coming under small arms fire. They returned intense fire on the Katangese positions from the twin machine-guns on the Swedish APC. Kane's plan was to burst through the bridge with his armoured assets, but some of the obstacles on the bridge were too big to move or roll over. The column halted as a truck following the armoured units got stuck. Kane ordered the column to retire south of the bridge. Reversing and turning under fire was difficult and it took the lead Irish armoured car 45 minutes to extract itself, all the time under fire and returning fire on the Katangese. Kane instructed the column to 'move back and re-organize and prepare for further action at daylight'.[49]

Morthor 'had gone very wrong'

Early on 14 September Raja conceded that Morthor 'had gone very wrong'.[50] Muké had proclaimed that he now would 'fight on until he gets back what they have lost'.[51] By contrast UN forces lacked a clear mission. They had been ordered to bring Katanga's secession to an end, but once this goal was denied them by Hammarskjöld's anxiety for a ceasefire they moved by default to self-defence. Ground could still be gained to strengthen relative positions, casualties inflicted and prisoners taken. Overnight, fire had been directed by 'Europeans' at the refugee camp and the Gendarmerie regrouped under mercenary command. Gendarmerie counter-attacks on the Post Office were unsuccessful and cost 'vast amounts of ammunition' to the Katangese.[52]

ONUC forces had brought only their first-line ammunition to Elisabethville and the supply position facing them after the first day of Morthor caused Raja concern. He informed MacEoin that there had been heavy ammunition expenditure. Indian forces at the Post Office were using captured Katangese weapons and ammunition. The Swedes immediately required 700,000 rounds of ammunition as well as ten 84mm anti-tank guns and 1,300 hand grenades. The 35th Battalion requested 400 81mm Mortar rounds and 500 hand grenades. MacEoin contacted the Department of Defence in Dublin explaining that as the 'time element [was] vital' the ammunition should be flown in directly from Ireland.[53] The despatch of ammunition took until 19 September, some being sent under the cover of food supplies because the mood in Ireland had turned against the UN action in Congo. These ammunition requirements show how ill-prepared ONUC had been for Morthor. The projected orders for anti-tank and mortar rounds show what ONUC expected to lie ahead in Katanga.

Raja also lacked sufficient troops to undertake further large-scale operations in Elisabethville. He contacted MacEoin seeking the urgent airlift of a Swedish Battalion to the city. Anticipating that operations against the Gendarmerie throughout Katanga might be required, MacEoin refused as a further thinning out of ONUC forces would 'render position chaotic and uncontrollable [in the] whole [of] Katanga.'[54] Raja instead sought two companies of Jats with 'full scale first line and second line ammunition', as 'any delay in this WILL have adverse effect present ops here'.[55]

It was clear too that ONUC was insufficiently supplied with armour. The HQ of Swedish forces in Elisabethville asked MacEoin to immediately obtain from Sweden five SKP Armoured Personnel Carriers 'as this type of car has proved excellent for transport of troops and supplies and has been essential to the whole support of situation in Elisabethville'.[56] The arrival in Elisabethville of Malayan Special Forces with four Ferret armoured cars was also anxiously awaited. The Swedes also looked urgently for radio batteries 'as [the] Swedish battalion is supplying radio sets for the whole Brigade [and] the same will be out of communication completely by tomorrow if these batteries are not immediately supplied. Please realise that situation in Elisabethville for the moment is on the limit of a break down.'[57] The same could be said for the entire ONUC operation in Elisabethville immediately after Morthor.

International criticism of the ONUC operation was rising. London approached Washington to find out if the United States, which remained supportive of Hammarskjöld, had any advance notice of Morthor. Britain expressed its 'deep concern' and asked Hammarskjöld to explain under what authority operations in Katanga were undertaken. In Leopoldville the British ambassador, Derek Riches, explained to Hammarskjöld that Britain would consider removing all support from ONUC unless the Secretary General could provide an acceptable explanation for what had happened in Katanga and also an assurance that the fighting would end. MacEoin, Khiari and Fabry favoured a strong line, reinforcing Elisabethville and continuing Morthor. MacEoin felt that another two days of UN action would be enough to complete the operation. Faced with the British démarche, Hammarskjöld was forced to overrule them. He had already lost French and Soviet support on the Security Council for ONUC and now faced the loss of British support. Faced with such opposition Hammarskjöld was under increasing pressure. He had to make it look as if ONUC had acted in self-defence after a locally devised plan had failed. Morthor had gone awry and so the UN story covering up the events of 13 September was drawn up.[58]

The United States hoped that order would be restored and that Katanga would play a constructive role in Congo's future. Washington adopted a muted public position on Katanga, not wanting to overtly criticize the UN. Privately,

United States Secretary of State Dean Rusk spoke in strong terms to Bunche, asking that President Kennedy's concerns be transmitted to Hammarskjöld. Bunche thought both men 'excited' and 'badly informed', but nonetheless 'extremely upset' about events in Katanga, particularly because the UN had undertaken 'extreme action' without prior consultation with Washington.[59] Hammarskjöld was angered by Rusk's 'extraordinary demarche', cabling to Bunche

> what a page in UN history … Who are they defending and do they suppose that implementation of a resolution approved by them should be conditioned on whether or not we may meet resistance or on whether or not the final outcome may be one which does not suit their political taste?
>
> However the key question is this one: what have our critics done to bring Mr Tshombe to his senses?[60]

Like the United States Britain forcefully conveyed its deep concerns to Hammarskjöld. On Macmillan's instructions Lord Lansdowne travelled to Leopoldville to find out from Hammarskjöld why military action was taken in Katanga. Britain opposed the use of force in Katanga and was 'gravely concerned about the consequences' of the United Nations action.[61] The British attitude was 'that there is no point in instituting an inquest on how it began, though there is a tendency here to put the whole blame on Dr Conor Cruise O'Brien'.[62]

The Department of External Affairs was acutely aware of how international opinion on O'Brien was changing. His nationality was beginning to exert an influence on perceptions of Ireland overseas. On 14 September the Irish ambassador's residence in Brussels was 'daubed in red paint … the slogan read "O'Brien a lacheté - M[erd] à l'ONU - Vive le Katanga" and there were also a fair supply of red crosses'.[63] Ambassador Frank Biggar, who was a relation of O'Brien's, added that the 'undoubted holder of the title best-hated man in Belgium was Conor Cruise O'Brien' and explained that Belgian press criticism of the UN had reached fever pitch. Biggar sought to separate himself from the situation, explaining that 'Dr Cruise O'Brien and the Irish troops in the Congo are under the orders of the UN and that the Irish Government has no responsibility for their actions.' Dublin had consistently sought to keep its distance from UN operations on principled grounds, now it was also necessary on political grounds. But as news from Jadotville arrived in Dublin, that distance became a real problem.

Jadotville

A-Company's isolated position in Jadotville was of minor importance to the UN Secretariat as it remained unsure if there was any basis for reports of an incident in the town. However A-Company was in grave danger; there had been rumours of a ceasefire, but they came to nothing and Quinlan refused all Katangese requests to surrender. Surrounded by Gendarmerie at nightfall on 13 September

A-Company expected a further assault. It came at dawn on 14 September. Katangese mortar units came up so close to A-Company that, as Cpl Tadhg Quinn recalled, 'we were able to take them out'.[64] During further Gendarmerie attacks that morning, A-Company found their Bren guns and 60mm mortars particularly useful repulsing the Katangese. From their trenches A-Company could also hear the sound of mortar fire from Lufira Bridge.

Overnight Force Kane made unsuccessful attempts to discover the extent of obstacles on Lufira Bridge and destroy them with 84mm anti-tank rounds. Early on 14 September Force Kane again attacked the bridge with 81mm mortars, hitting Gendarmerie positions and destroying transport parked nearby. No attempt was made to follow up with an infantry advance and Force Kane made no headway against what was estimated to be a well dug-in company-sized contingent.[65] Kane informed his headquarters that he was launching a 'final attack. Must return to Elisabethville if not successful.'[66] He was instructed to 'inflict as many casualties and do as much damage as possible. Stay trying as long as possible.'[67] Armoured cars and mortars again engaged Katangese positions. The assault was unsuccessful and by 1100, reporting 'ammunition, food and men almost exhausted', Kane was ordered back to Elisabethville by 35th Battalion Headquarters.[68] Force Kane radioed at 1313 that they had 'failed to take Lufira Bridge' and were returning to Elisabethville.[69]

As Force Kane returned, A-Company was strafed and bombed by the Katangese Air Force's Fouga jet. Lt Noel Carey recalled that mortaring was bad, as was machine-gun fire, but the jet was particularly shocking as it was unclear where it would arrive from and A-Company had no weapons capable of countering air attack.[70] Raja telexed MacEoin of his 'horror' at the Fouga attack; adding that A-Company were 'holding out gallantly'.[71] Quinlan asked McNamee for further strong reinforcements, adding 'we are holding out to the last man'.[72] It was rumoured in Dublin that there were 57 Irish dead at Jadotville, with the remainder of A-Company taken prisoner. This was 'war propaganda of unbridled mendacity'.[73]

Quinlan remained resolute and refused to negotiate. He reported to Elisabethville that he was 'quite secure in his present position but was still under fire'.[74] Dunnett speculated that isolated and worn down A-Company 'might now suffer a worse tragedy at the hands of the Katangese and if this happened the UN would not hesitate to proceed to more extreme measures including the disarming of the Gendarmerie and the introduction of the ANC'.[75] O'Brien had told Tshombe that there would be 'serious consequences' for the Katangese if the attacks continued against A-Company.[76] But O'Brien was bluffing; ONUC did not have the means to undertake this option, even if it was being seriously considered.

After the failure of Force Kane further plans were suggested to relieve A-Company. McNamee considered that Lufira Bridge 'cannot be got around without bridging equipment', but none was available. MacEoin speculated about landing troops by air at Jadotville. He also proposed using rafts to cross the Lufira River and most spectacularly, and implausibly, was 'considering [a] move by road from Kamina to Jadotville but the distance is over 200 miles and the road is bad and easily obstructed.'[77] He proposed using Malayan Ferret armoured cars and a battalion of Swedish infantry. A more realistic plan emerged on the evening of 14 September to send a helicopter with water and ammunition to A-Company to enable them to hold out while a stronger Force Kane II assembled.

The military outlook in Elisabethville

Across Elisabethville in the aftermath of Operation Morthor the mercenaries who had gone into hiding after Rumpunch reappeared leading Gendarmerie forces. ONUC established roadblocks to 'check any entry of whites from Rhodesia into Elisabethville'.[78] Katanga Command informed ONUC HQ in Leopoldville that 'military action [was] being pursued vigorously'.[79] ONUC tried to work out its next move. In political terms the situation remained 'uncertain',[80] while militarily Raja and O'Brien told Linner that the 'situation [was] well under control'.[81] This was an optimistic assessment. An anti-aircraft gun at the Gendarmerie base depot opened fire on Elisabethville airport on the morning of 14 September. ONUC held that 'we should be able to stop this interference with air safety by last light today'.[82] Orders were given to destroy the depot. By 1200 it was on fire, targeted by an Irish mortar battery commanded by Capt. Roger McCorley. ONUC had to keep the airport open, but were struggling and night landing was not possible. The situation at the Post Office remained volatile and armoured cars and APCs brought 'urgent and essential' ammunition and rations to the troops holding the location.[83] ONUC was 'on the defensive and is subject to repeated assaults in the town.'[84]

MacEoin asked Raja for a concise report on the situation in Elisabethville and Jadotville in order to brief Hammarskjöld. The Secretary General was in the most delicate situation facing him since the Congo crisis began. Waiting to be briefed he inquired whether there had there been 'any firing and have you made contact with Tshombe?'[85] O'Brien had been trying to contact Tshombe and had gone with Egge and Kibwe to see Dunnett. They hoped the British Consul could put Kibwe in touch with Tshombe to arrange a ceasefire. Dunnett had no idea where Tshombe was, though Egge maintained that Tshombe was at Dunnett's home. Tshombe was in fact now in Northern Rhodesia with Munongo. Dunnett had been instructed by the Foreign Office to do everything possible to bring about a ceasefire, but O'Brien felt that he instead encouraged Tshombe to resist.

Because of the need to contact Tshombe, O'Brien 'took [the] risk of liberating Kibwe' in the hope that he might make contact.[86] He told Kibwe that any discussions on negotiations with the Katangese president would 'be on basis of ending Katanga secession'.[87] Kibwe was expected to return to make a recording of a radio message calling on Katangese troops to cease fire. Not surprisingly he took the opportunity to escape. At 1700 the BBC reported that the situation had worsened and bodies of dead Gendarmerie lay in deserted streets as casualties mounted. Irish journalist in Elisabethville Ray Moloney reported that 'bitterness' was 'growing rapidly on both sides'.[88] Kibwe's statement was broadcast over his name on Radio Katanga on the evening of 14 September. It asked the citizens of Elisabethville to remain calm and ordered the Gendarmerie to cease fire, adding that persons 'continuing fire after 2000 tonight will be guilty of treason and shot'.[89] The broadcast worried Katangese forces, in particular the mercenaries. They sought UN hostages to counter the threat.

Radio broadcasts across Elisabethville remained critical to UN attempts to influence the local population. HQ Katanga Command instructed Sector-B that the transmitter station outside the town on Route de la Kilobelobe was 'the most vital point and must be protected from all types of attacks. Ensure it is garrisoned in strength. Report completion immediately. Also ensure it is NOT put out of action by hostile fire.'[90] The Radio Katanga studios in the city centre were unusable and the UN instead used the smaller Radio College station held by Lt Ryan. Sector-B refused to reinforce Ryan's detachment early on 14 September. Katanga Command often confused which station required reinforcement. On the afternoon of 14 September Raja ordered Waern to 'send immediate reinforcement to transmitting station at ~~College St FRANCOIS~~ route de le KILOBELOBE. This is necessary as attack on this likely after commencement broadcast'.[91] A later 'flash request' from Raja to Waern on 15 September made the same point in more stringent terms: 'Radio transmitting station is still being guarded by 20 men only. This strength is considered totally inadequate and must be increased to at least two platoon strength. This may please be done now straightaway without delay. Please acknowledge and confirm completion immediately.'[92] If there was any thought given at this stage to reinforce Radio College, then it was too little too late.

Ambush at Radio College

As evening had approached on 13 September an APC carrying Michel Tombelaine and Swedish UN interpreter Lt Stig von Bayer approached Ryan's position at Radio College. Tombelaine intended to broadcast from Radio College and asked Ryan if he could get the station operational. Ryan contacted the White Fathers who grudgingly assisted. As Tombelaine went on air Ryan let the White Fathers see that the studios were undamaged. Unfortunately, this allowed them to see how exposed Ryan's position was and they passed this information to the Gendarmerie.[93]

Ryan asked Tombelaine if he would take a message to McNamee explaining that he needed to rest the soldiers guarding Radio College; they had no food, their ammunition was depleted and they needed reinforcements. Ryan recalled that Tombelaine 'got nasty', snarling, 'Am I a messenger boy?' Von Bayer said he would try to contact McNamee and asked Ryan what communications he had. Ryan replied that he 'hadn't a bloody flag to wave', but that was no problem because he could easily communicate by foot with the nearby UN Tactical HQ at Parc Albert. Von Bayer explained that the Tactical HQ had departed after Katangese mortar rounds had fallen on Parc Albert. 'You are on your own', von Bayer told Ryan, and as the UN party left and night fell Ryan and his men knew they were now completely isolated. Ryan later learned from Capt. Paddy Barry that in their urge to depart Parc Albert they had simply forgotten about the Irish section at Radio College. Later in the evening von Bayer returned in an APC. He threw two ration packs to Ryan's guards and shouted he had no ammunition and also there would be no reinforcements for Radio College as all 35th Battalion resources were needed for Force Kane.

A formal request was sent at 0100 to Sector-B by 35th Battalion Headquarters to reinforce Radio College. Permission to put the Radio College transmitter out of action and withdraw Lt Ryan's depleted force was refused as the station and transmitter were required for United Nations broadcasting until Radio Katanga was again operational. After a day of fighting and with their focus on Force Kane I 35th Battalion HQ only remembered late on 14 September that they had not heard from Ryan for 24 hours. Unknown to ONUC, Katangese forces had taken Radio College on the afternoon of 14 September in what was their only concrete success counterattacking ONUC. A UN report explained that 'Irish guard at College Radio Station was taken prisoner after severe fighting as they were outnumbered'.[94] They were outnumbered because Sector-B had refused their reinforcement. The report is incorrect in one aspect – there had been no fighting at Radio College. In an interview over fifty years later Ryan explained why this was so and how he was taken prisoner.

On the morning of 14 September the White Fathers had brought provisions to Ryan and his men. That afternoon two civilians had also arrived with tea and food. When they returned for their cups and plates a third man was with them. Ryan recalled a small man with blonde hair who reminded him of Illya Kuryakin from the 1960s television espionage series 'The Man from U.N.C.L.E.' The newcomer introduced himself as Lt St. Paul and said he was a mercenary officer. Ryan told St. Paul that he should arrest him, but as he had enough trouble could St. Paul not just move off? St. Paul replied that he would like to bring another mercenary to talk to Ryan. A tall dark-haired French man calling himself Capt. Pierre approached and told Ryan that Radio College was surrounded. Ryan thought the mercenary was bluffing, but Pierre gave a signal and Gendarmerie and mercenaries appeared out of the bushes and a jeep carrying a heavy machine-gun came into view. Ryan realized he and his men were in trouble. 'We have nothing against the Irish', Pierre insisted, 'but we need hostages.' Ryan knew his ammunition was low, his men exhausted and his outpost was vulnerable; he could not alert ONUC or Battalion HQ to his situation. Pierre gave Ryan five minutes to decide what to do. Ryan recalled that it was 'the hardest five minutes of my life'.

Ryan explained the position to his men. Two 'young die-hards' proposed to fight it out. The others wanted to follow Ryan's decision. He concluded it simply 'wasn't our day' and his men agreed to lay down their weapons. In retrospect Ryan assessed whether they could have fought their way out and thought it unlikely given the forces surrounding them and their lack of ammunition. He put it simply and forcefully: 'I could have taken ten young lives and what would I have achieved?' If Ryan had stood his ground the Gendarmerie could have obliterated his position with their heavy machine-gun. It was 'an impossible situation' facing the isolated Irish unit and so they surrendered. Ryan and his men were brought to a farm house close to the Northern Rhodesian border. He recalled that he did not sleep that first night of his captivity – he had too much on his mind.

A message from the Gurkhas to Waern at 2010 on 14 September indicated something was wrong at Radio College. Eye-witnesses reported UN soldiers being taken prisoner there by Gendarmerie at 1700.[95] Because of the commitment involved with Force Kane the 35th Battalion lacked suitable armour and transport to organize a dedicated patrol to investigate and instructions were instead given to a routine resupply patrol commanded by Comdt Pat Cahalane, OC Armoured Car Group, to try to make contact with Ryan. Though commanding the Armoured Car Group, Cahalane normally delegated operations to his second-in-command, Capt. Magennis, but Magennis had been assigned to the Dogras and Cahalane took personal command of the patrol. The patrol comprised two Ford armoured cars – one turretless –, a jeep carrying an 84mm anti-tank gun, and a bus carrying dismountable troops. Cahalane's armoured car led, with Sgt Tim Carey driving, Tpr Patrick Mullins gunner and Cpl Michael Nolan radio operator. Carey had just returned from patrolling but he volunteered to drive as he knew the Elisabethville road network. Mullins, who had also been on patrol, volunteered because the assigned gunner, his friend Tpr John O'Mahony, had a broken hand and could not operate the Ford's machine-gun. The intensity of operations in Elisabethville meant that such scratch crews were regularly put together to mount patrols made up of whatever equipment, vehicles and personnel were at hand. The rear armoured car was commanded by Capt. Frank Whyte, who was Assistant Quartermaster and did not have armoured car experience. Cpl Paddy Holbrook, Whyte's driver, though trained as a gunner/driver had to stay behind the wheel, leaving the armoured car's main weapon, a Browning .300" machine-gun, unmanned because the remaining crew member Sgt Peter Dignam had to man the radio.

Carey explained how it happened that they were sent to Radio College, 'as we were pulling out of Battalion Headquarters, Captain Parker, Assistant Brigade Intelligence Officer, jumped on the armoured car and ordered us to stop'. He told Cahalane, who was sitting beside Carey, that 'he had just come from Katanga Headquarters where he had heard a rumour that the party of Irish troops holding Radio College had been captured. He asked us to call there and check on the accuracy of this rumour.'[96] Cahalane's patrol left 35th Battalion Headquarters at 2045 for Radio College. All being well at Radio College the patrol it would collect there a tape required by Katanga Command, undertake supply and recovery tasks at various positions, and continue to the Factory Camp. It was all to be routine.

As the patrol approached Radio College all was quiet. Carey observed a civilian ambulance opposite the building. The patrol stopped and discussed its options by radio with headquarters. There was no sign of Ryan. As Cahalane moved to get out and investigate, his armoured car was hit by an anti-tank round or rocket-propelled grenade fired at close range from nearby bushes.[97] Cahalane was dazed; Carey was 'shocked'; and Mullins, in the turret, and Nolan who, at the radio took the full impact of the blast, were knocked unconscious. Carey climbed over Mullins and Nolan and helped Cahalane out the rear door. He returned to get Mullins but Mullins was stuck in the vehicle. With a full-scale ambush in place and heavy machine-gun fire hitting the armoured car and shells hitting the pavement, Carey made a break for Radio College but was hit and badly wounded by shrapnel. Whyte and Holbrook, unable to get the rear armoured car started, arrived on foot to assist the lead vehicle. Cahalane ordered Whyte to get everyone to cover. Machine-gun fire hampered the infantry dismounting the bus and they left their ammunition reserves onboard. As the patrol was under fire it was impossible to assist Mullins or Nolan. The last time these men were 'seen alive by [their] own troops' was 2115 on the evening of 14 September.[98]

Under heavy fire the patrol took up defensive positions in a nearby ground floor flat, the residence of Elisabethville Chief of Police, Gerard Soete. Facing a heavy Gendarmerie attack Cpl Dan Sullivan and Pte Patrick Crowley inflicted heavy casualties with fire from an 84mm anti-tank gun. During a lull in the fighting a local priest tried to persuade the Irish troops to surrender before being killed. He explained that local anger was rising after the heavy casualties suffered by the Gendarmerie and they were intent on revenge.

Did Cahalane's patrol realize, or had it been briefed, that it was heading into a likely ambush? It most likely did not, given the ad hoc nature of its departure to Radio College. Yet Ryan's silence, the anti-UN feeling in the city and the continued sporadic fighting should have been warning signs; so too should the presence of the ambulance. Ambulances were often used for clandestine and undercover operations during the September fighting.

Cahalane asked for volunteers to report to Battalion HQ that the patrol had been ambushed. With their radio out of action there was no other way to get their predicament known. Whyte and Dignam volunteered and made a break back to 35th Battalion camp. Overnight Cahalane planned an escape but in the morning the priest reappeared with a message from a Gendarmerie commander – the Irish were surrounded and had ten minutes to get out. Seeing Carey's barely conscious condition the priest undertook to get him hospital treatment. None of the patrol wanted to surrender but a French officer in civilian clothes came to the house and explained that he had taken prisoners the day before and no harm would come to Cahalane or his men. This was presumably the officer who had also captured Ryan's unit at Radio College.

Shortly after midnight on 15 September an unidentified UN station queried the situation at Radio College.[99] At 0300 Waern informed Katanga Command that the 'Irish patrol ... has not yet returned or reported'.[1] The detachment at Radio College was missing, now too was the patrol sent to investigate. Whyte and Dignam reached 35th Battalion Headquarters at 0500 and reported that there was no sign of Ryan at Radio College, that their rescue patrol had been attacked, that Mullins and Nolan were dead and at least two men were wounded. The

Gendarmerie force attacking Cahalane and his men in Soete's house was estimated to be of platoon strength, equipped with personal weapons and at least two light-machine-guns. At first light on 15 September a strong mobile patrol was organized by 35th Battalion Headquarters to search for Cahalane's beleaguered unit. It returned to report that it had seen and found nothing. It is possible that the patrol had mistakenly gone to Radio Katanga instead of Radio College. So dangerous were conditions that a foot patrol sent out to search for Cahalane by C-Company units at The Tunnel could only undertake a limited local search.

On the morning of 15 September Cahalane's patrol was captured. Having not been located by their colleagues and being surrounded by Gendarmerie they were called upon to surrender or be killed. With Cahalane deafened and with Carey badly wounded they were in an impossible position, and like Ryan before them they had 'no other outlet' but to surrender.[2]

In a garbled message to New York at 0700Z on 15 September Linner reported that 'yesterday evening an Irish vehicle carrying troops was shot at. Men escaped and the vehicle was destroyed. We had one Irish soldier wounded.'[3] He added 'we had a small detachment of Irish soldiers looking after Radio College. Apparently post was attacked yesterday evening and we are waiting for detailed information.'[4] Where this information came from is unclear and it makes no reference to Mullins and Nolan. The assumption in Elisabethville was that Mullins and Nolan were dead at the scene of the ambush because at 0950 35th Battalion requested a Swedish armoured car for 'collecting two killed in the town.'[5] Though Lt Col. A.G. Cullen 'tried to get evidence to establish the death of Nolan and Mullins' in the days after they went missing, there was no immediate 35th Battalion investigation into Ryan's capture, the loss of Cahalane's patrol, or Mullins' and Nolan's disappearance.[6] Responsibility for investigating these events was given to the 35th Battalion Intelligence Section but little immediate action was taken. Two men were missing presumed dead, and the recovery of their bodies would be undertaken when resources allowed.

Morthor had disintegrated in less than twenty-four hours and ONUC was becoming dangerously stretched. The fate of Ryan's outpost and the subsequent ambush of Cahalane's patrol show both how ill-prepared ONUC was to carry out combat operations and how Morthor had been based on the false premise that the Katangese would not fight back. The operation failed in its major objectives. Tshombe had gone into hiding, Katanga still stood intact politically and militarily, and was fighting back. There had been casualties, ONUC troops had been taken hostage and A-Company's position in Jadotville had gone from bad to worse. The UN now had a major international incident on its hands in Katanga and like ONUC it was ill prepared to deal with the consequences as its largest peace-keeping mission to date became an urban war. The potential loss of United States and British support for ONUC would be fatal to the operation and Hammarskjöld was now in an impossible situation. He could not admit the truth that Morthor had been undertaken with his authorization. With the General Assembly about to open, Hammarskjold had somehow to draw the UN back from its military adventure in Elisabethville and preserve his own and the UN's position.

CHAPTER 10

'"Little" Katanga had checked the "big" United Nations'

FORTY-EIGHT HOURS into Operation Morthor, ONUC controlled Elisabethville city centre and airport and there were 'signs of Gendarmerie soldiers getting tired and fed up with fighting'.[1] O'Brien thought the military position 'obscure', and 'less favourable to the UN than communiqués claim'.[2] ONUC lacked transport, Raja explaining that 'we cannot move reinforcements from one place to another. APCs are in urgent necessity because of sniping.'[3] ONUC Leopoldville told Raja to compile a list of the vehicles he required and O'Brien thanked them for this offer, adding 'your news of reinforcements and support greatly encourage us'.[4] Raja did not get these reinforcements; they were diverted to defend Kamina Base where a Gendarmerie attack was expected. It was feared that Kamina might become another, larger, Jadotville.

The Katangese Fouga bombed Elisabethville airport on 15 September and dropped bombs at the Gurkha camp and The Tunnel. Attempting to get anti-aircraft guns from Sector-A for airfield defence, a Sector-B message, which was seen by MacEoin, set out the position starkly: 'We have no anti-aircraft resources except for light automatics'.[5] Sector-A had no spare anti-aircraft weapons and suggested Katanga Command 'explore [the] possibility of fighter aircraft'.[6] ONUC was unsure how many Fougas the Katangese had; some reports said six, but Egge reported that only one was operational out of three purchased. UN civilian air staff argued that unless jet fighters were deployed with ONUC they would not fly as civilian aircraft faced too great a risk from the Fouga. The UN air commander in Elisabethville considered evacuating his men and aircraft if the Katangese jet continued to attack. He angrily told ONUC Leopoldville that 'UN detached aircraft are now requested to fly war mission[s]. In a short time we do not have any serviceable aircraft or helicopters. Request more personnel, except DC3 pilots, and instruction for fighting this war.'[7] War was what Elisabethville had descended into.

Reports of Irish casualties reach Dublin

Late on 14 September O'Brien announced that A-Company had suffered heavy casualties at Jadotville. Rumours also spread around Dublin newspaper offices of large Irish losses in Jadotville. Katangese propaganda spoke of massacres of Irish soldiers in the town with those remaining held as hostages, ten being shot for every Katangese killed. The Department of Defence could not verify these reports. It leaked that the Defence Forces were 'in short-wave radio communication with Leopoldville, but apparently this effort at linking up collapsed some months ago.'[8] The absence of news in Dublin about A-Company angered relatives and resentment grew at the inability of the military to keep up with events in Congo. Army Headquarters insisted that no Irish soldiers had been killed and that five were wounded. Through the night of 14 September Army Headquarters tried to contact Leopoldville but telex lines to the city were closed. Close to midnight Lt Col. Lee made contact with Rikhye's office in New York explaining that Dublin urgently needed news of casualties from Jadotville. Rikhye only said that there had been further fighting in Jadotville, Irish positions were intact and Force Kane was halted at Lufira Bridge. MacEoin was to provide details of casualties, but all that was known was that four unnamed Irish soldiers were wounded. Lee explained that Irish media reports were 'most disturbing' and families needed information.[9]

On the morning of 15 September Lee finally made contact with ONUC in Leopoldville. He was told that reports of air attacks on A-Company were exaggerated. A contemporary handwritten note on a teletype message to Raja reads 'one wounded in leg – many minor injuries – names later – radio communication with Company very difficult'.[10] Casualty reports from Elisabethville suggested five wounded; there were 'no reports of any Irish killed'.[11] A note by Cabinet Secretary Nicholas Nolan stressed that Dublin had received no 'official reports of any fatal casualties'.[12] The use of the word 'official' by Nolan suggests that news of the deaths of Gaffney, Mullins and Nolan had leaked. MacEoin angrily telexed Raja and McNamee: 'Get names and numbers of Irish dead at once ... Irish government [is] appealing for information'.[13] Raja replied that three Irish personnel were 'missing believed dead. No. 806566 CPL NOLAN MICHAEL. No. 810552 TPR MULLINS PATRICK. No. 80899 PTE GAFFNEY EDWARD'.[14]

Acting Chief of Staff of ONUC Col. James Quinn sent these details to the Plans and Operations Section at Army HQ in Dublin who received them at 1930 Dublin time on 15 September. A handwritten note on the file was more explicit: 'Two killed last night. One killed earlier. Names later. One Section believed captured last night by Gendarmerie. Details later.'[15] Further communication would follow after Katanga Command Staff Officers met McNamee. Mention of three dead also appeared in a cable from MacEoin to Bunche on the evening of 15 September. Covering the capture of Ryan's section it continued, 'Three Irish vehicles fired upon from an ambulance car with a red cross. Vehicles damaged. Three other ranks missing believed killed.'[16] O'Brien told the same story to Dunnett on 15 September. However O'Brien's version contained the truth that Nolan's note in Dublin only hinted at 'UN casualties which they have not announced include, at least one Swedish major killed and the crew of an armoured car killed'.[17] Finally an official UN Security Council document released on 15 September explained that in Elisabethville 'a small detachment of UN troops was surprised by a sudden attack in overwhelming force and suffered serious losses, including three missing presumed dead'.[18] No nationalities were given. What is noteworthy from these reports is the mention of three vehicles destroyed. The convoy investigating Radio College comprised four vehicles; no one noticed that one armoured car was missing. This would later prove significant in the search for the missing Irish soldiers.

'They have the right man out there':[19] Aiken goes to Congo

Minister for Defence Kevin Boland spent 15 September at Army Headquarters reading reports trickling in from Congo. It was little better for External Affairs as the department relied on Irish and foreign press reports for its Congo news. External Affairs did learn that the UN Secretariat was 'obviously taken unawares and [was] disconcerted by developments in Katanga ... they are bothered by conflicting reports and bad communications'.[20] The lack of information from Congo was causing problems on the domestic front in Ireland. Col. Quinn telexed Dublin that it was 'not feasible' to get any details of the incidents in Elisabethville and Jadotville or of casualties, though he realized 'the anxieties at home which are shared here'.[21] Senator Patrick Quinlan called for O'Brien to be withdrawn as the 'Black and Tan methods of the UN under his leadership are fast putting Katanga – the Catholic part of the Congo – under the heel of the pink regime in Leopoldville'.[22] Quinlan added that 'all Irishmen are shocked and saddened that Irish blood should be recklessly spilled in the diabolical task of spreading communism in the Congo'.[23] The *Evening Herald* of 15 September carried the headline 'Grim News from Katanga. Irish at Jadotville said to have surrendered. Katanga Radio claims 57 killed.'

The news of the three dead in Elisabethville was not included in Lemass' evening statement on 15 September. He instead expressed 'profound shock and sorrow' at the 'tragic events' in Congo 'involving serious casualties to an extent not yet ascertained amongst Irish soldiers'. Lemass announced that he had asked Aiken 'to proceed as soon as possible to the Congo for discussions with UN officials on the spot'.[24] He had taken this unprecedented step and personally ordered Aiken to Congo because 'the position in Katanga is so fluid and liable to sudden change' and the reports coming in 'were so alarming' that Aiken's presence was required 'to secure reliable information on the situation'.[25]

Aiken was about to leave for one of the strangest missions of his long political career. His nine-day visit to Congo was an unusually hands-on approach to UN operations for a minister who preferred the General Assembly to frontline peacekeeping. British diplomats concluded that Aiken and Secretary of the Department of External Affairs Con Cremin were not 'very closely in touch with the changes in the political situation' in Congo.[26] The British ambassador in Dublin, Sir Ian Maclennan, felt that before Morthor, Aiken and Cremin were 'content to think of MacEoin and Cruise O'Brien as UN representatives who happened only incidentally to be from the Irish Republic'.[27] After meeting Cremin, Maclennan added that Dublin had 'never been closely in touch with the political situation in the Congo'.[28] It was a harsh judgment, but fair. It was Aiken's policy that once Irish soldiers and diplomats were seconded to UN service they were of no concern to their donor country.

'Grim-faced and determined', Aiken flew unaccompanied from Dublin airport on 16 September telling journalists that there would be no Irish withdrawal from Congo. Asked about O'Brien's position he cryptically responded 'all UN officials from the beginning have acted in good faith but, as you know, they did not get co-operation from a lot of people they should have got it from'.[29] Aiken's immediate departure indicated 'the government's deep anxiety at the grave turn of events in the Congo'.[30] Without his Iveagh House advisors, Aiken now had single-handedly to find out what was happening in Katanga and 'confront UN officials on command decisions committing Irish [troops] to battle'.[31]

With a general election only weeks away Aiken's sudden departure to Congo could be seen as electioneering to show that the government in Dublin was in command. However Aiken's trip was no stunt. Lemass was seriously worried. A sign of Lemass' concern was his cancellation of election meetings in Galway and Athlone, the main towns in the Defence Forces' Western Command, the command from which A-Company was drawn. News reports explained that many Irish politicians were waiting for Aiken's return before raising the Katanga fighting as an election issue. The Washington *Evening Star* reported that 'word of the bloodshed came as a general election campaign began. Feelings ran high in the capital, but few voices were raised to demand the recall of Irish troops from the United Nations forces.'[32] Discussing Aiken's departure with Hammarskjöld, Cordier put it bluntly: 'purpose is to get direct report developments Katanga. Election will take place Ireland in a few weeks.'[33]

'A most courageous intervention'[34]

In Elisabethville, O'Brien and Tshombe remained out of contact as fighting continued. They were to meet to discuss a ceasefire, but Tshombe failed to show. O'Brien had guaranteed his safety, but Tshombe thought the meeting a trap. Hammarskjöld felt that Tshombe remained 'under the influence of Munongo and foreign officers'.[35] Tshombe wanted a cease fire but would hold out and Kibwe boasted that if the UN continued in its actions 'the Katangans would wear them out, and none of them would get home'.[36] While waiting for Tshombe, O'Brien told Dunnett that he had 'not received authority from Leopoldville to order or accept an unconditional 48-hour ceasefire. The attitude there was very firm and amounted to insistence on pursuing the action to achieve its original objectives.'[37] This suggests Hammarskjöld, Khiari and MacEoin were still holding firm to Morthor.

O'Brien also told Dunnett that a German journalist, Hans Gomani, had arrived in Elisabethville from Northern Rhodesia with worrying information about Cahalane, Ryan and their men. Gomani had spoken to a French mercenary officer who said he had captured the Irish detachment at Radio College and subsequently ambushed an Irish patrol outside the building, killing two soldiers. The mercenary said he had been in contact with Munongo who had given him a message for O'Brien that Cahalane and Ryan would be court-martialled and would be executed unless two Belgians, Paucheun and van der Wegen (named in some sources as Redivo and Maurras), held prisoner in Jadotville were released. O'Brien's was to reply to Munongo by the night of 15 September. Munongo added that 28 Irish troops were being held prisoner in a villa two kilometres from the Rhodesian border. He threatened that if the terms of Tombelaine's statement on Radio Katanga that all whites and Africans caught carrying arms would be shot was carried out all the Irish prisoners would be executed. Munongo wanted an Irish or a Swedish officer to accompany Gomani to the Rhodesian border to hand over O'Brien's reply. As O'Brien and Dunnett spoke, Capt. Art Magennis was heading to meet Munongo with O'Brien's response.

In his memoirs Magennis wrote how on 15 September he was on duty at Elisabethville Post Office when he was summoned to the commanding officer of the Dogra unit he was attached to during Operation Morthor. The Indian greeted Magennis with a quizzical smile:

> This time you have a personal problem. No it isn't a family affair. There is a German journalist at the Italian hospital and he wants to see you urgently. He has asked for you personally. The NCO in charge of the Irish group securing the hospital brought the message here and is waiting to talk to you.[38]

Magennis was 'thunderstruck' and had no idea what this could mean. The messenger, a corporal from Headquarters Company, 35th Battalion, explained that

> There is a guy there who met your brother, Tim, a couple of days ago, when he was passing through Nyasaland en-route to Katanga. Says his name is Dr Hans Gomani, a German national. He is leading a television crew en-route to Katanga. Tim told him you were in Elisabethville with the Irish Battalion serving there with the UN, and suggested he should call on you as you might be of some assistance. He says he has been in touch with the Katangese military and has an important message from Munongo to pass on to O'Brien. He needs your assistance. He is waiting for you in the Hospital.[39]

The Dogra commander agreed that Magennis meet Gomani to pick up the message for O'Brien, adding 'call on me when you get back, it all sounds very interesting. Information has just been received that an Irish patrol was ambushed in the city last night, but there are no details. Perhaps the two are connected?' Magennis found Gomani at the Italian hospital and learned what had happened at Radio College and the fate that according to Munongo awaited Cahalane, Ryan and their men. Magennis now knew that this was really a serious war situation. I only knew that a detachment from C-Company commanded by Lieutenant Ryan had been sent to hold Radio College. I had no idea that Ryan's position had been overrun; that an Irish patrol had been captured and that two soldiers had been killed. And to learn that the remaining officers and men of the detachment and the relief patrol were now held prisoner by the Gendarmerie? It was an awful shock.

Magennis had to get Gomani's message to O'Brien at ONUC Headquarters at Dogra Castle and hope that O'Brien would respond. Gomani waited at the hospital while Magennis returned to the Post Office to speak to Dogra company commander. Travel to Dogra Castle would require a substantial armoured escort, but thankfully the phone network was partially in operation and the Indian commander picked up the telephone: 'Tell Dr O'Brien this is Dogra Battalion from the Post Office. I have an urgent message.' With that he handed the phone to Magennis. O'Brien reacted immediately and asked Magennis for the message. He listened while Magennis explained and replied: 'I'll call you in ten minutes … I will have a written reply shortly for Munongo. Will you volunteer to go with this Dr Gomani and deliver it to Munongo?' 'Yes', Magennis replied, 'but you must first get the approval of the OC 35th Battalion. If he says yes, I'll do it.' 'Good', O'Brien replied, 'I'll have the letter delivered to you as soon as possible.' He hung up. A call soon came in that McNamee approved Magennis delivering the message. Magennis returned to the hospital and told Gomani that he would accompany him with a response for Munongo. They arranged to meet later at the Hotel Leopold and Magennis would have with him O'Brien's reply.

Back at the Post Office and with daylight fading Magennis saw an Irish armoured car pulling up. Its commander, Cpl Mickey Rowland, had O'Brien's letter for Munongo. Rowland had been delayed getting to Magennis dodging two Gendarmerie Staghound armoured cars. Each armed with a .5" Browning machine-gun, a more powerful weapon than the obsolete .303" Vickers on the Irish Ford, Rowland used the one-way road system in Elisabethville to avoid the Katangese vehicles until finally he had to confront one head-on and opened fire. The more powerfully armed Staghound did not return fire. Magennis thought of his own requirements for making that trip – two armoured cars and infantry in a jeep. He was 'gobsmacked'. Rowland had made the trip with one armoured car and no dismountable troops. For this action Rowland was promoted to Sergeant and later awarded the Distinguished Service Medal with distinction.

At dusk Magennis made his way with two armoured cars to the Hotel Leopold to meet Gomani. On seeing Gomani Magennis had Sgt Ned Keogh take command and bring the armoured cars back to the Post Office. Keogh called out 'Good luck and God bless' and Magennis turned to face the unknown. He was uneasy but knew he was hardly in as dangerous a position as Cahalane or Ryan and felt that nothing serious could happen to him if he was with Gomani. Gomani told Magennis that he was to go to Munongo blindfolded and unarmed travelling with Gomani in his Citroen 2CV. On reaching a specific location

Gomani would leave Magennis in the car and walk ahead calling out a prearranged signal until he was contacted by the Gendarmerie. At this point Magennis was again to be checked for weapons. Magennis would then transfer to a jeep to be driven to a final destination.

Magennis put his wallet and pistol in the hotel safe, recording the pistol's serial number and counting out his ammunition. Gomani also recorded the details, saw that the safe was locked and they set off. Neither spoke. Then Magennis, now blindfolded, noticed a strong metallic smell; the clutch of the 2CV was burning out. They were stranded in the middle of a hostile city. They were close to the Reine Elizabeth Hospital in western Elisabethville. Gomani drove there to borrow a car and Magennis took cover in a roadside drainage trench. Gomani returned with a car borrowed from a Belgian doctor.

Five minutes later they stopped and Gomani went forward on foot to contact the Gendarmerie. Magennis 'was alone again, and more uneasy than ever'. He listened to Gomani calling out into the distance. There was silence, then chattering conversation. Magennis was ordered out of the car and was politely searched for arms. He was directed to the rear seat of a jeep, accompanied by three Gendarmerie soldiers, a white officer and a black officer, and their driver.

The jeep set off. The Katangese talked about what the Indian troops were doing to their fellow Gendarmerie soldiers. Magennis knew that most of what he heard was propaganda. He was in no mood to debate the subject. Being again blindfolded and moving at speed made for an unpleasant journey.

At about 2130 they arrived at a substantial farmhouse. Magennis was led inside and seated on a comfortable armchair. His blindfold was removed. He found himself in a decent room lit by three paraffin oil lamps. A middle-aged white officer, a French mercenary, sat opposite him on a reversed wooden chair, his arms lolling over the back. Two other men, one black, one white, one in battle dress and one in civilian clothes, sat nearby. The officer, speaking fluent English, politely asked for O'Brien's letter. Equally politely Magennis told him that he could not hand over the letter; his instructions from O'Brien were to hand the letter to Munongo in person. Magennis learned he could not see Munongo.[40]

'Have you the letter on your person?', the officer inquired. Magennis said it was in his trouser pocket. 'May I see it?', the officer continued. 'Yes', said Magennis, 'but do not open it. That I must not do until I am with Mr Munongo.' Magennis had all along suspected that Munongo was not involved in the episode. He wondered what he was to do and what would happen if the Gendarmerie or the mercenaries court-martialled and shot Cahalane and Ryan.

The three men huddled together, speaking fast in French and Swahili. Magennis could not make out a single word. He decided that if there was an impasse he would take any opportunity to hand over the letter for delivery to Munongo. The senior officer suggested to Magennis that the African in civilian clothes was Munongo's adjutant. He undertook to deliver the letter to Munongo by dawn. The senior officer gave Magennis his word that no harm would come to any Irish prisoner. Then Magennis had a brainwave and asked him 'Will you repeat that assurance in the presence of Dr Gomani?' 'Bring in the doctor', he told the man in military fatigues. In Gomani's presence he repeated the assurance. They shook hands on it and Magennis handed over the letter. O'Brien had given Magennis an outline of the letter. In terms which were the very opposite to peacekeeping and contrary to what might be considered the spirit of the UN it contained a threat that ONUC would kill Gendarmerie prisoners in its custody if the two Irish officers were executed. An internal UN code telegram sent as Magennis was with the mercenaries gave the details:

> Comdt Cahalane should be treated as an officer in accordance with the Geneva Conventions. If Munongo shoots Comdt Cahalane both persons held by us will be shot. Mr Tombelaine has been wrongly quoted. The correct version of the broadcast is that those white persons who shoot at the UN persons will be shot at. There is no mention of shooting black or white persons just carrying arms.[41]

During the conversation in the farmhouse the attack on Cahalane's patrol had come up. Magennis said the Irish 'were fired on from an ambulance'. The mercenary officer denied this, he had earlier said that the Katangese 'were firing according to law of war', and continued that he 'would not have fired on our armoured cars if he knew Irish troops were crews' and explained that 'he tried to rescue any survivors from the hit car, but that the doors were locked from the inside.' His explanation for the Gendarmerie presence at Radio College was 'to evacuate their wounded from Radio College after action taken to oust the holding party in the Radio Station'. He continued that Indian troops had carried out atrocities on civilians; they had fired on a civilian car flying a Red Cross flag and that 'everybody who moved on Avenue Etoile was shot upon by the Indians'. The officer continued that 'the native population of the Cité had threatened to kill any Irish troops, Swedish or Italians they catch'. In a chilling insight into the possible fate of Mullins and Nolan, who were by now missing presumed dead, the officer continued that 'two Irish officers who escaped from Comdt. Cahalane's patrol were dragged through the streets of Cité by civilians and killed'.[42]

The following morning Magennis was blindfolded and driven back to Elisabethville by the French officer. Gomani did not appear; Magennis never saw or heard from him again. In reality Gomani was not the white knight he might appear from this tale. Earlier on 15 September Ryan had seen Gomani organizing a group of Irish prisoners and their Katangese guard in a choreographed photoshoot that presented the Irish troops as the downcast charges of a tough Katangese soldier. The photograph appeared in the London Times of 20 September 1961.[43] Gomani was a man of many agendas and of varying loyalties and was a journalist looking for a story. The Federal Rhodesian intelligence service believed he had been 'brought especially to interview Irish captives and then sent away again'.[44] Who was the senior officer? No names were exchanged on either side, but Magennis believed, having seen press photographs of dissident

French officers who later became famous mercenaries, that the Frenchman was Col. Bob Denard.[45]

After about a thirty-minutes drive Magennis' blindfold was removed. He saw they were a short distance from the White Fathers' monastery in Elisabethville. As if awaiting their arrival four priests appeared from the building. The French officer excused himself. He hurried towards the clergymen who greeted him warmly. After some animated conversation with the clergy he came back to the car and said 'Now I'll bring you back to the hotel'. 'Wait a minute', Magennis replied, 'I have something to say to the priests.' 'Angrier than I ever was in my life' he walked over to the fathers. They made no attempt to greet him. Magennis 'reminded them that I had two teenage Irish soldiers dead somewhere in Elisabethville – their city – and two Irish officers under threat of death. I told them, and I really meant it at the time, that if anything happened to Pat Cahalane and Tom Ryan I would hold them responsible and I would personally destroy their monastery by burning it to the ground. There was no word of excuse from them and I returned to the car.' Later Magennis regretted what he called 'that angry stupidity' when he heard from Tim Carey about the risks the White Fathers took to get him medical attention after the ambush at Radio College. Magennis knew that 'more than likely they saved Carey's life'.[46]

Magennis collected his belongings at Hotel Leopold and walked back to the Post Office. If it was safe for the French officer to travel in his own car then he could cross two streets on foot. At the Post Office Magennis 'was very glad to see Sgt Keogh's head coming out of the turret of one of the Fords' positioned near the main entrance. The Indian company commander welcomed Magennis back, O'Brien was sent a message to notify the 35th Battalion of Magennis' safe return, 'and in no time I was in front of a fine meal from Irish pack rations and hot strong Indian tea'.[47]

That night ONUC Katanga Command reported that across Elisabethville the situation was 'improving'.[48] Stray shots were heard at the airport and there was intermittent firing at the Post Office. O'Brien hoped that a statement by the Central Government's Commissaries d'Etat on Radio Katanga, coupled with the closure of clandestine Katangese radio stations, would help restore peace. UN reinforcements finally arrived in Elisabethville on 16 and 17 September, including one company of Jats, a 3"-mortar platoon and a medium machine-gun section. With MacEoin's consent they brought two jeep-mounted anti-tank guns and two ferret armoured cars.

Gendarmerie forces attacked C-Company at The Tunnel on the afternoon of 16 September, 'advancing along Avenue Luxembourg with [an] armoured car … tunnel under mortar fire all morning and many civilians passing'.[49] That evening HQ Katanga Command came under sustained mortar and machine-gun fire. Reports to Leopoldville caught the tension of this surprise attack: 'This HQ presently under mortar fire. We have no lights.'[50] The messages continued, 'It is hard to tell what is happening. NO casualties so far no casualties in the HQ building so far. This is urgent. Having trouble with transmitter.'[51] The attack was repulsed, though one Indian soldier was killed and seven wounded. Firing continued through the night. There was stalemate and in the coming days Elisabethville remained volatile as moves towards a ceasefire began.

Force Kane II

The position facing A-Company in Jadotville remained difficult. Quinlan remained in touch with Elisabethville, though contact was difficult, and sought immediate reinforcements. By early on 15 September he was bordering on despair signalling 'in the name of God send reinforcements now. Promises of such are NOT sufficient'.[52] Another Fouga attack followed and after McNamee regained contact with Quinlan he reported to MacEoin that A-Company was 'bombed and strafed this AM. Few casualties … No reinforcements yet. Plans to co-ordinate breakout in hand.'[53]

MacEoin sent an urgent message to Elisabethville that 'must be got to Quinlan': 'We all here admire and commend you and your men on your gallant stand. The whole UN force, our own people and in fact the world are watching the outcome of your brave efforts. Inform all under your command that help is near and that in the meantime you have already earned for yourselves the name of heroes.'[54] Quinlan did not receive this until 0645 on 16 September and immediately replied 'Many thanks for encouragement. We will stay to the last man.'[55] This has been variously recorded as 'fight to last man'[56] and 'hold till last man', but the point was clearly made.[57] Later the OC of Western Command signalled Quinlan he was 'Proud of your gallant stand. You are constantly in our prayers.'[58]

On the evening of 15 September MacEoin informed New York, who relayed the message to Dublin, that A-Company was under fire and still holding out, though the relief force was delayed by a road block. This was a considerable understatement of what had happened at Lufira Bridge the previous day. Linner told New York that A-Company 'received [an] ultimatum twice yesterday to surrender, one at 1730 and second at 2130 hours. This was refused, boys are still holding on to their post gallantly.'[59] However the simple truth was that after the failure of Force Kane it was now 'not clear' how UN reinforcements would get to Jadotville.[60] Yet at the same time O'Brien told McNamee to tell A-Company 'to hold and not capitulate'.[61]

Through 15 September Lt Col. Maitra and Comdt Seán Barrett developed a proposal to send a combined Irish and Gurkha force 'to pull the Coy out from Jadotville'.[62] There was no obvious agreement as to the task facing any new relief force bound for Jadotville. Was A-Company to be reinforced, as MacEoin seemed to favour, or be withdrawn from Jadotville as Katanga Command now favoured? A-Company did not have much ammunition or food left and could not hold on much longer. Waern knew there were two DC3s at Elisabethville airport 'ready for air dropping or any other mission' and he considered using them for a supply drop to Jadotville.[63] Through 15 September he worked out a plan for the relief of Jadotville by air. Waern explained that the Gendarmerie were capable of pitting more troops against Company in Jadotville than against all the forces in Elisabethville. Resupply of Company by means available is not guaranteed. If they are not resupplied or relieved they may be wiped out. This risk must be considered against possible losses in Elisabethville with reduced strength. Possible reinforcements to Elisabethville could offset depletion in strength. *Success of this operation would be a great boost to UN operations. Failure to relieve this company would be a crippling blow to UN.* Reinforcements, more ammunition supplies transport armoured cars from outside Sector-B are a must if we are to succeed.[64]

Waern's rationale was correct, as was his understanding that Jadotville was the pivot point for what happened in Elisabethville and that control of Lufira Bridge was the key to success in both locations.

Waern sought permission from Raja to resupply A-Company by air while simultaneously despatching a relief force by road from Elisabethville to Jadotville. This force needed to be 'strong and self-sufficient'.[65] One Irish company and one Gurkha company with engineers and medics, protected by armoured cars and APCs would advance to Jadotville. At Lufira Bridge they would assault the defending Gendarmerie, crossing the river upstream and outflanking them, remove the barriers on the bridge and advance to Jadotville to assist A-Company's breakout. This was the plan. It turned out very differently.

The plan to pull A-Company out of Jadotville with a combined Irish–Gurkha force known as Force Kane II received approval at 0020 on 16 September. 'An air of tension descended' on Dogra Castle as Force Kane II set off at 0650.[66] It comprised four armoured cars and Swedish APCs protecting sixteen commandeered single-decker buses carrying troops. The Irish contingent was B-Company, 35th Battalion under the command of Comdt Alo McMahon, and the Indian contingent B-Company of the 3/1 Gurkha Rifles under the command of Major Mangla. While in theory under the overall command of Comdt Kane, the Irish and Indian contingents worked independently of each other. Force Kane II received no distinct orders from its commander as to the tasks individual components were to undertake. Progress was very slow and six kilometres outside Elisabethville the convoy was strafed and bombed by the Fouga. It was again attacked by the Fouga fifteen miles and seven miles from Lufira Bridge. Advancing in stops and starts as the absence of the Fouga allowed, Force Kane II arrived nine kilometres south of Lufira Bridge at 1000, having already lost the element of surprise due to the strafing and, they later found out, their advance and strength having been reported on the BBC World Service. Now they were ambushed by Gendarmerie concealed in the bush on either side of the road.

At almost the same time the promised helicopter-load of water and ammunition arrived at Jadotville. The water was tainted, having been transported in jerry cans that had previously carried oil. The Swedish helicopter pilot, Lt Hovden, had flown 'under enemy air superiority whereby his helicopter was attacked several times' and had undertaken an 'act of bravery in flying in ammunition and supplies to [the] encircled Irish company at Jadotville'.[67] There was heavy fighting at A-Company's position after Hovden's helicopter arrived. A-Company also came under heavy attack by Gendarmerie 'endeavouring to pass through' A-Company lines to Lufira Bridge.[68]

Because of the heavy casualties inflicted on the Gendarmerie at Lufira Bridge by Force Kane I the bridge had been heavily reinforced by about 1,200 well dug-in Katangese troops. Force Kane II remained well south of Lufira Bridge, coming under fire from the Katangese Fouga and from small arms fire from the surrounding bush. The Gurkhas deployed into the bush and the Irish infantry remained on the roadside. The Gurkhas tried unsuccessfully to outflank the Katangese and cross the river downstream across the nearby railway bridge which the Katangese promptly blew up. Force Kane II was in trouble. Armoured contingents undertook some forward reconnaissance, but the infantry contingent never got near to the bridge.

At Jadotville Quinlan was worried that he could not hear firing from Lufira Bridge and asked Elisabethville what was happening. Elisabethville replied that 'the reinforcements were hit from the air. They are heading in your direction now. They are not across the bridge yet.'[69] With the possibility of a ceasefire in Jadotville, Quinlan asked whether Force Kane II had managed to break through. They had not; they had withdrawn. Without air support they could not press forward without heavy casualties given the strength of the defending Katangese force. Katanga Command sent the sober message to ONUC HQ in Leopoldville that 'we have lost the battle of the bridge roadblock on way to Jadotville after very heavy fighting ... we have issued orders for the withdrawal of reinforcement Companies.'[70] Quinlan was only told that Force Kane II had been instructed to 'consolidate present position'.[71] He did not know that it was withdrawing. MacEoin, in a teletype conversation with Elisabethville unemotionally said he was 'very sorry to hear the attack failed. We will be glad to get anything ... any news of Jadotville.'[72] Elisabethville could only respond 'thank you very much. We have nothing for you at present.'

Force Kane II withdrew in disorganization. It was bombed, strafed and ambushed on its return trip and found its route mined. The Gurkhas suffered 5 killed and 12 wounded, the Irish 4 wounded. The failure of Force Kane II to cross Lufira Bridge was unknown in Dublin and on the evening of 16 September the Government Information Bureau announced that A-Company was holding out and

> putting up [an] excellent fight. Elisabethville has been in touch by radio recently; supplies of ammunition and food got in by helicopter this morning; a further relieving force has been sent. The relieving column which was held up yesterday [is] still trying to fight a crossing at the broken bridge near Jadotville.[73]

The two attempts to reach Jadotville were a failure. Force Kane I and Force Kane II suffered from a lack of intelligence, poor command and imprecise and uncoordinated orders. Were they to 'relieve' or 'reinforce' A-Company? In both operations the planning and weaponry of ONUC forces were inadequate to the task facing them. By comparison in a later operation in 1963 it took an Indian brigade supported by Irish 120mm mortars, engineers and air power to take Lufira Bridge.[74] The impact of the attempts to reach Jadotville and the fighting in Elisabethville on the Irish troops was noticeable to Lt Col. Cullen who thought 'they were bearing up well though the strain was apparent, especially in those who had made the attempt to reach Jadotville'.[75]

Then suddenly all seemed to be working out at Jadotville. Quinlan radioed Elisabethville that he had negotiated a ceasefire and the resupply of his men with food and water. He added 'we have NOT, repeat NOT surrendered'.[76] The Gendarmerie had thrown out their mercenary commanders and were fraternizing with A-Company. The Mayor of Jadotville sought a truce and Quinlan accepted. Quinlan and the Jadotville Chief of Police were jointly touring the town announcing a ceasefire. O'Brien told MacEoin that it was 'the best possible news that could happen in Katanga'.[77]

It was not good news for Quinlan when Elisabethville told him that Force Kane II had withdrawn. Having successfully negotiated a ceasefire Quinlan knew that if the Katangese realized that Force Kane II had withdrawn and Lufira Bridge was secure in Katangese hands the ceasefire would crumble. Quinlan told his officers that Force Kane II had withdrawn and was not consolidated at Lufira Bridge observing the ceasefire. They were shocked and immediately increased their vigilance. It was as if the ground had been pulled from under them and they did not tell their men what had happened.[78] As Lt Noel Carey recalled, 'the outlook did not look good'.[79]

Ceasefire attempts

Meanwhile Hammarskjöld, with Leopoldville's agreement, instructed O'Brien to propose to Tshombe a ceasefire followed by a meeting. The British embassy in Leopoldville ordered Dunnett to put O'Brien in touch with Tshombe. O'Brien argued that ONUC was already observing a ceasefire across Katanga, except in Jadotville, and was willing to commence talks. Yet before making any commitments, O'Brien wanted Tshombe to accept Congolese unity and the authority of the federal government. Dunnett suggested O'Brien and Tshombe meet at Bancroft in Northern Rhodesia. Tshombe was only willing to meet O'Brien following a written guarantee from Britain concerning his and his ministers' security. On the evening of 16 September Hammarskjöld instructed O'Brien to establish a ceasefire first and then commence discussions with Tshombe. O'Brien had to be 'persuaded to relax his present rigid attitude' regarding the ceasefire terms.[80] Dunnett informed O'Brien that Tshombe, who was at Kipushi with his ministers, would meet him at Bancroft at 1130 on 17 September.

Hammarskjöld instead proposed meeting Tshombe at Ndola at midday on 17 September. Tshombe agreed and told the Secretary General that he also agreed to an immediate ceasefire, but requested that UN troops at Elisabethville airport be sent to their camps and the UN cease the despatch of reinforcements to Elisabethville. Hammarskjöld refused; an unconditional ceasefire was a precondition to talks. Tshombe later agreed to these terms. Hammarskjöld left for Ndola without O'Brien, telling him that he would 'understand my reasons to desire the present phase to be outside ONUC framework and in my own hands'.[81]

Aiken's first days in Congo

Irish diplomats in New York were unsuccessful in getting regular updates from the UN Secretariat on what was happening in Katanga. Boland felt that the UN had available in New York and Leopoldville 'information which they failed to pass on to us'.[82] The UN operations room in New York 'proved entirely unequal to the task' of countering 'alarmist and erroneous reports, owing to the extreme paucity of the information reaching them from the Congo'.[83] The *Sunday Express* of 17 September, under the headline 'Premier briefs Aiken to fly on find-the-truth mission', explained that Lemass was on the verge of withdrawing Ireland from ONUC unless Aiken got satisfactory answers as to why A-Company was left in Jadotville and whether Irish troops in Katanga had been deployed in accordance with the February resolution.

Aiken arrived in Leopoldville early on 17 September. Journalists in London wishing to talk to him as he passed through were told that an unusually reticent Aiken 'would not encourage interviews'.[84] In Leopoldville he planned discussions with UN officials to get reliable information about what was happening in Katanga. The UN authorities saw his task as being 'to investigate stories of severe Irish losses in Katanga and to confer with UN leaders on the Katanga operation'.[85] Dublin remained worried. Sir Ian Maclennan informed London that 'the Government must indeed be exceedingly anxious that there should be a ceasefire in Katanga and that the Irish prisoners should be restored to a place of safety, because if any further misfortunes should befall the Irish contingent the reactions on the electoral prospects of the Fianna Fáil Government are likely to be serious'.[86]

In a telex message for the Taoiseach and the Minister for Defence, Aiken explained from Leopoldville that he 'found morale very high'.[87] As he arrived the 35th Battalion informed ONUC HQ 'Three other ranks killed. Some wounded. Morale tip-top.'[88] Aiken was silent on these casualties when reporting to Dublin. He was due to meet Hammarskjöld on 18 September and told a journalist that he had 'no immediate plans – I shall not rush out of here tonight, not to Dublin anyway'.[89] He had long meetings with Adoula and Congolese Foreign Minister Justin Bomboko, finding them 'extremely cordial'. They asked Aiken to 'convey to [the Irish] Government their gratitude for Irish help and admiration for gallantry of Irish troops and sorrow for casualties'.[90] The minister's main message for Dublin was about the proposed ceasefire in Katanga and after speaking with O'Brien and Irish officers at UN Headquarters he telexed Dublin 'that early reports of Irish casualties in Katanga had been grossly exaggerated'.[91]

Obtaining this information was an important achievement because Defence Forces Plans and Operations Section in Dublin now began to disregard reports of casualties from Katangese sources as they knew 'how unreliable such attributions are.'[92] Aiken's soothing messages were soon reported across the Irish media. The situation in Katanga was not rosy, but it 'had never been as desperate as was reported.'[93] From what Aiken had 'seen and heard' reports were 'deliberately written for the purpose of deceiving people' and he was sorry for the trauma this caused families in Ireland.[94] Aiken had achieved a major success.

A-Company downs arms in Jadotville

Aiken's arrival in Leopoldville and Hammarskjöld's departure for Ndola occurred as A-Company's position worsened in Jadotville. The ceasefire had collapsed; some suspected it had always been a trick. After midday on 17 September Sector-B received a message that the men of A-Company were now 'more or less hostages' and Quinlan asked Elisabethville whether any force could 'break through to me, if necessary'.[95] Isolated, A-Company was surrounded by 2,000 Gendarmerie and was 'offered accommodation in [a] hotel. This is of course as hostages.'[96] As Katangese hostages A-Company became valuable leverage in the ceasefire negotiations that were soon to commence in Katanga.

Quinlan and McNamee now exchanged a difficult series of radio messages that showed the lack of understanding in Elisabethville of A-Company's position and Quinlan's frustration at this in Jadotville. McNamee asked Quinlan 'are you prisoners'?[97] Quinlan explained that he had sought a written ceasefire and feared that if he was attacked there would be a massacre. A-Company had fought hard for four days against a stronger enemy. They had requested a ceasefire and it was broken because the Katangese knew that with Lufira Bridge in Gendarmerie hands A-Company was isolated. On receiving this message McNamee instructed, A-Company to stand its ground because another relief force would soon be underway. Quinlan tersely replied 'help is too late now ... I am trying to save my men'.[98] He sought orders from MacEoin, but none were forthcoming. With no other option and with the welfare of his men in mind, Quinlan signed ceasefire terms with Munongo on 17 September. McNamee responded to this news at 1800 and radioed Quinlan: 'Are you deserting the men?'[99] Quinlan sent a hurt reply:

> the last sentence of your message was not nice of you. We were surrounded for eight days with fierce fighting for four days. There was no food for two days, nor sleep for four days. There was no water. Is it worth your while to kill the men without cause? I frequently requested instructions today but I did not get them. I have surrendered honourably to Munongo. We keep our arms in hotel. Regret this was necessary.[1]

Interpretations of McNamee's message have varied. Was it confused in translation between Irish and English? Some suspected a more personal angle.

MacEoin's response to Quinlan's surrender was downbeat; A-Company had been 'overwhelmed by vastly superior numbers' and were 'hopelessly outnumbered'.[2] Chief of ONUC Military Operations Lt Col. G.S. Paul reported to MacEoin that A-Company had made an 'heroic stand', adding that 'the fact that casualties are slight is a consolation. The Company has acquitted itself well during the week in a difficult situation.'[3] Opinion in ONUC on Quinlan's defence of his position was much more positive than MacEoin's: 'Company did very well – they fought for 4 days with NO food, water, ammunition, or hoped-for reinforcement'.[4] Aiken told a reporter in Leopoldville that Quinlan and A-Company had 'held an "open camp" post under siege for almost a week.'[5] He felt 'their bearing under bombardment was exemplary'. From Elisabethville came a final positive message: 'You did well. You have earned every military honour. Every blessing on you all.'[6] UN delegations in New York considered that A-Company had 'got a raw deal and acquitted themselves very creditably.'[7] It would nevertheless take many years for Quinlan's achievements and those of A-Company to be recognized and honoured by the Irish Defence Forces.

Late on the night of 17 September Lemass instructed Nicholas Nolan to inform the leaders of the main opposition parties in the Dáil 'that the latest news we had – from General MacEoin … about the situation in Jadotville was bad, that the recent truce there was merely a ruse and that resistance by the Irish Company there had come to an end but that there was nothing to suggest that there had been very heavy casualties'.[8] Conscious of public opinion, Lemass instructed Aiken that 'anxiety about [the] Jadotville prisoners' was rising in Ireland and he was to 'get all possible information including additional casualties if any, treatment and intentions regarding them'.[9] Dublin soon learned that Quinlan and his men were being well treated, 'but many of the men show signs of the strain that they have been through since they went to Jadotville'.[10] The message arrived in Dublin at 1320 on 18 September and was circulated to opposition party leaders by 1500. This was quite a change in the speed of communication with Congo, a change of speed that showed the value of Aiken's mission.

Aiken visited wounded Irish troops in Leopoldville and 'found all well'.[11] He also had 'a full and satisfactory talk' with Linner.[12] There was, he thought, 'a general easement in the situation and there seems to be a fair prospect of a truce.' What Aiken was now planning was unclear to the Irish diplomatic service. The permanent mission to the United Nations inquired of Dublin 'is Minister still in Congo?'[13] The British ambassador to Ireland concluded after meeting with Cremin that 'even now with Aiken in Leopoldville the Government here are as much in the dark as anyone, both about what is going on and about how the existing situation in Katanga was brought about'.[14]

Having spent five days in Leopoldville Aiken next set off for Elisabethville hoping to visit Irish prisoners and casualties. He had been trying to arrange transport to the Katangese capital since his arrival in Leopoldville. The UN was anxious that he would not undertake the journey. Commercial air services to Elisabethville were suspended and Lemass cautioned Aiken that he 'should not proceed … if any considerable risk although in the event of a reliable truce would like you to do so'.[15] External Affairs knew from contacts with the Belgian embassy in Dublin that all Irish prisoners were 'in good health and well taken care of by Katangese authorities'.[16] The Department of Defence was in contact with the International Red Cross to ensure their welfare. When Red Cross representatives visited Irish prisoners they confirmed that they were in good health. In Elisabethville 35th Battalion chaplains were in touch with the British Consulate and liaising to provide supplies to the prisoners.

Elisabethville, 18 September 1961

Early on 17 September, MacEoin reached Elisabethville. O'Brien was grateful for his arrival; he was the only senior ONUC figure to go to Elisabethville during the fighting. His 'eyes were swollen and red-rimmed'; he had been up until 0400 every night since Hammarskjöld's arrival examining and re-examining the situation in Katanga.[17] MacEoin visited the 35th Battalion Armoured Car Group, but its units were busy undertaking escorts and patrolling The Tunnel and the refugee camp. That afternoon Elisabethville airport was again bombed by the Fouga, destroying a UN civilian aircraft; however there were no casualties. Through the night of 17–18 September Gendarmerie mortared ONUC HQ, Dogra Battalion HQ and the Post Office. Witnessing the attack Lt Col. Cullen saw an Indian mortar section go 'immediately into action' and take out the Katangese mortars, 'and the Gurkhas then went out with bayonet. After that, except for sporadic machine-gun fire there was silence.'[18]

    That night Hammarskjöld's plane failed to arrive at Ndola and through the following morning concerned UN officials sent and received frantic messages querying the Secretary General's whereabouts. O'Brien continually phoned Dunnett for news and by midday had heard nothing. Throughout the day news trickled in that Hammarskjöld's aircraft had crashed on approach to Ndola and the Secretary General was dead.

    As ONUC began to take in the reality of Hammarskjöld's death they continued to deal with daily life in Elisabethville. Inspecting troops across the city MacEoin found morale high. Waern reported that 'we are in good condition and have been able to rest most of us last night'.[19] The area around The Tunnel and the radio station remained quiet, though heavy firing was heard across the city during the afternoon and mortaring of the Post Office continued. The Fouga returned and bombed Katanga Command Headquarters and Elisabethville airport. Two platoons of Dogras were sent to the airport 'to thicken up defence' as Gendarmerie were rumoured to be digging in near the perimeter.[20] The Dogras looked for Irish mortar support, but it was not given as 'fire control or direction could not be guaranteed'.[21] Under direct orders from MacEoin, Irish mortars later shelled the Gendarmerie Base Depot as Dogra units at the airport thought they were being attacked from that location. Irish armoured cars escorted infantry from B-Company and C-Company during rotations of men to and from The Tunnel. There was often 'considerable enemy activity during rotation' and this was 'answered by armoured cars'.[22]

The condition of existing ONUC armoured cars and APCs in Elisabethville was 'critical' and the Gendarmerie now had the 'upper hand with their armoured vehicles'.[23] In a revealing evaluation Katanga Command explained:

> general population hostile to UN it is NOT possible to move men or material without armour escort. Soft vehicles cannot operate under present circumstances. [The] few armoured cars and armoured personnel carriers held by IRISH and SWEDISH Battalions have run considerably during these days and cannot be depended upon. GORKHAS [sic] and DOGRAS have NO (NO) armoured vehicles.[24]

It was thus 'imperative' that a full squadron of Malayan armoured cars be sent to Elisabethville for day-to-day operations.[25] None were immediately available and an improvement in the air transport situation was needed before any could be sent to Elisabethville. A sign of what Katanga Command thought might be in the offing was a final request making 'a strong case'[26] for 'one squadron AMX light tanks' which was required 'urgently for offensive action wherever to be taken'.[27]

Mullins and Nolan

The 35th Battalion spent from 13 to 17 September in combat in Elisabethville and Jadotville and mounted two unsuccessful attempts to relieve A-Company. It had two officers and over two dozen men held prisoner and had lost three men – Gaffney, Mullins and Nolan. Only Gaffney was confirmed dead and his body had been recovered. An armoured car was missing and no-one had made a serious effort to locate it. More strangely, no-one had tried to locate Mullins or Nolan. A Swedish intelligence officer, Lt Stig von Bayer, reported that on 15 or 16 September he had seen an Irish armoured car in a trench some distance from Radio College and thought it had been abandoned. Due to intelligence communication problems within Katanga Command and Sector-B he did not know that an Irish armoured car was missing and that two of its crew were presumed dead. Not until 21 September did the 35th Battalion investigate the whereabouts of the armoured car and its missing crew members.

Even though reports to Dublin and New York already listed them killed in action, on the morning of 17 September Katanga Command reported Nolan, Mullins and Gaffney as 'missing believed killed'.[28] No one could say for certain whether Mullins or Nolan was alive or dead. 35th Battalion reported '3 dead (?)' on the afternoon of 17 September.[29] On 19 September McNamee informed ONUC HQ in Leopoldville that 35th Battalion HQ was 'at great pain ... not to use expression presumed dead or killed as long as there was doubt. We said "3 O/Ranks were missing". We now understand that Cpl Nolan and Tpr Mullins are in an unknown civilian hospital in Elisabethville condition unknown.'[30] Passing this message to Dublin, Capt. Basil Greer cautioned that he did not want to raise 'false hopes', urging Army HQ to 'go easy on this information until we can check it firmly'.[31]

There was much hearsay about casualties circulating around Elisabethville as the fighting ended. The Gendarmerie were, MacEoin remarked, 'well-led, particularly by people trained in psychological warfare'.[32] A report from a local informer to the British Consulate contained an unwelcome rumour: 'Many Irish and some Indians have been captured in civilian houses here and their bodies seriously mutilated by local people. One Irish had his body cut to pieces by pulling legs and arms apart.'[33] Another version of this story appears in the official Indian history of the Congo operation: 'two Irish officers who had escaped from Comdt. Cahalane's patrol, were dragged through the streets of the city by civilians and killed.'[34] The same story was told to Magennis by a Gendarmerie officer on the night of 15 September. It was impossible to say with any certainty what had happened to Mullins and Nolan. Dunnett heard from a doctor attached to the Gendarmerie that 'at least 5 Irish were killed in the attack on Radio College and 7 European civilians shot dead.'[35] This was untrue, but if it was untrue, so too might be rumours that Mullins and Nolan were dead. McNamee informed ONUC HQ in Leopoldville that 'there are none missing, 1 killed and 2 in civilian hospital.'[36] But this was hoping against hope. At 0845 on the morning of 18 September Capt. Parker made contact with Dunnett concerning what the British Consul General described only as 'bodies'.[37] McNamee still hoped for the best, informing ONUC in Leopoldville, without foundation, that Nolan and Mullins 'must now be regarded as prisoners'.[38] Greer had already reported to Dublin that 'hopes are receding that the two missing Irish may be still alive but every effort is being made to check the report that they are in hospital somewhere in Elisabethville.'[39] However these optimistic reports concealed a general recognition that Mullins and Nolan were missing in action, presumed dead. Unlike Gaffney, their bodies had not been recovered and no one could say how they died.[40]

Ceasefire

By the afternoon of 19 September an 'uneasy calm' prevailed in Elisabethville.[41] The lull was an 'apparent reaction to tragic death of [the] Secretary General.'[42] MacEoin held a battalion commanders' conference at Katanga Command HQ to reallocate operational tasks across Elisabethville as Raja redeployed Indian forces to key strategic sites in the city.[43]

ONUC still faced considerable threats in Elisabethville and continued to bring in ammunition and reinforcements where possible. There were four Gendarmerie armoured cars and three Gendarmerie scout cars operational and approximately 2,000 Gendarmerie across Elisabethville and the surrounding countryside. The sole piece of good news was that fighter jets were flying in from Sweden, Ethiopia and India to aid ONUC. The danger of Gendarmerie reinforcement of Elisabethville from Jadotville and Northern Rhodesia remained. Dogra troops maintained roadblocks on the Jadotville Road, but due to a lack of troops the road from the Rhodesian border was not blocked. Anticipating further ONUC operations, MacEoin hoped to move the remainder

Indian:
1. 1 Dogra Battalion (less one Company): defence of airfield.
2. 1 Company Dogra Battalion: defence of Post Office.
3. 3/1 Gurkhas (less two Companies): defence of Jadotville Road.
4. 1 Coy 3/1 Gurkhas: Manono.
5. 1 weak Company Group 3/1 Gurkhas: defence of Post Office.
Swedish:
1. Infantry: security of refugee camp and security of radio station.
2. APCs: patrolling town and protection of supply columns.
Irish:
1. Infantry: security of Tunnel area and protection of refugee camp.
2. Armoured Car Group: patrolling of Post Office and Tunnel areas.
Malayan Armoured Car Group (under Dogra command)
1. Airfield defence and patrolling of Elisabethville to Jadotville Road.

Table 11. ONUC redeployment in Elisabethville, 19 September 1961

of the Indian Jats and an Ethiopian battalion to Elisabethville. MacEoin told Waern and Barrett that he was 'very pleased with our actions'.[44] He congratulated Raja and the troops under his command for their 'spirit, restraint and patience shown in the most difficult situation. You have maintained the very highest tradition of the UN Force and have consistently refused to be provoked into offensive action by repeated mortar shelling and sniping, both by day and night'.[45]

After questioning a captured Gendarmerie officer in Elisabethville MacEoin believed that Belgian officers in civilian attire who had taken refuge in the Belgian consulate were commanding the Gendarmerie and that no planning or directing of operations was being conducted from Gendarmerie HQ. MacEoin sought permission to take 'military action against [the] consulate but [this was] not given by Secretariat who asked him to think of other means of eliminating the Belgian officers so as not to prejudice ceasefire talks'.[46] Late on 19 September, Waern informed Katanga Command that 'mortar fire from Irish Companies or HQ Katanga (Dogra Castle) only may take place after permission from HQ Sector-B'.[47] This order arose after these units had fired on Elisabethville railway station at the request of the Dogra commander at the Post Office. MacEoin had already instructed that limits should be placed on retaliatory action. Such action 'should be specifically against military targets and we should be careful of women and children – warning should be issued if possible.'[48] Military action was now only to be taken if the ceasefire talks and all other means failed and after consultation with the permanent missions of contributing countries in New York. There would be no solo runs in Elisabethville – 'actions from now until further notice must avoid jeopardy of talks which are pending.'[49]

Efforts to secure a ceasefire in Katanga continued as Khiari prepared to go to Ndola to continue the mission that cost Hammarskjöld his life. Linner wished Khiari to conduct his meetings with Tshombe 'in his own way ,... to see Tshombe alone, preferably without other Katangese'.[50] Bunche thought the plan 'splendidly conceived and we pray that it will work.'[51] Khiari left for Ndola early on 19 September. Tshombe was willing to meet UN officials, but not Khiari as he was 'one of the principal persons responsible for the sad events in the Katanga.'[52] Tshombe accused the UN of breaking the ceasefire, adding that he required written acceptance from O'Brien of the ceasefire conditions. He was bullish and out to cause offense, telling British diplomats that Katanga had beaten the UN. Dunnett digested these remarks and felt that the United Nations' position was 'much graver ... than they yet admit'.[53] He added that among the Katangese government there was 'a general determination to pursue the struggle until, in words frequently used, the last representative of the United Nations in Katanga has been finished off'. A ceasefire was possible, but only if the UN gave some concession to Tshombe such as withdrawing ONUC troops from Elisabethville Post Office.

Seemingly oblivious to the military balance, O'Brien thought it regrettable that Tshombe was laying down preconditions. He understood that there was to be an unconditional ceasefire as a preliminary to negotiations and that Tshombe and Hammarskjöld had agreed on this point. This remained the UN position. Tshombe played hard to get but he eventually met Khiari on the afternoon of 19 September at Ndola Airport. There was 'reasonable hope that the talks will go alright but it may take a long time for them to end'.[54] Tshombe was under 'very heavy pressure' from Union Minière to agree ceasefire terms and from intercepted Gendarmerie messages ONUC thought the Katangese 'were very tired of the fighting'.[55]

Khiari and Tshombe hoped to agree a series of ceasefire statements that would be played on Radio Katanga, Tshombe's own stations and the Congolese federal network. Tshombe would not proclaim a ceasefire on UN radio as 'nobody would listen and nobody would believe that it was I.'[56] His only condition remained that UN troops in Elisabethville withdraw to their camps. Knowing that the text of the ceasefire announcement would be read to O'Brien, Tshombe said he was going to 'dedicate this ceasefire to the memory of the late Mr Hammarskjöld' and sincerely hoped 'that Mr O'Brien will respect in turn the memory of his chief'.[57] Khiari told ONUC in Leopoldville that the ceasefire negotiations were difficult but no efforts were being spared to find a satisfactory solution. In New York Rikhye thought the Katangese were preparing to recommence fighting and tentatively asked Dublin to consider sending 'mortars, machine-guns, mobile light artillery like bazookas and anti-tank guns' to Elisabethville.[58] O'Brien and Raja felt the Katangese had 'recovered much confidence in face of our relative immobility and apparent powerlessness' and sought the speedy arrival of jet fighters and more armoured cars.[59]

Khiari and Tshombe concluded a provisional ceasefire to become effective at midnight on 21 September. O'Brien sarcastically wrote that it ended 'the operation which [Khiari's] instructions of September 11 had begun'.[60] All commanders were to ensure that the ceasefire was enforced immediately. A Joint Commission would supervise the position of troops.[61] Reinforcement was prohibited but resupply was allowed and an exchange of prisoners was planned. Elisabethville was quiet but tense as the ceasefire came into effect. There were complaints of violations and firing on the Post Office continued as did sniping at the refugee camp. In response 'sniper hunter teams', of Swedes and Irish 'silenced many snipers'.[62]

A day before the ceasefire O'Brien wrote to his family in Dublin that 'things are quiet here at present and there's nothing to worry about'.[63] To his External Affairs colleague Máire MacEntee he explained 'we now have difficulties but we will win of course. I am not in danger as long as I don't spend my holidays in Belgium.'[64] O'Brien was now a spent force in Katanga and his departure was only a matter of time. Before he died, Hammarskjöld had told Linner he was going to dismiss O'Brien due to what Linner called 'bad judgment, bad tact'.[65] Dublin anticipated O'Brien's immediate recall to New York and knew confidentially that he would take over the duties of Heinrich Wieschoff in the Department of Political and Security Council Affairs.[66] Unwilling to facilitate O'Brien's removal, Dublin felt that it was up to the Secretariat to sanction O'Brien's transfer from Elisabethville. Lemass minuted that O'Brien would 'need all the moral support he can get' and personally redrafted a press statement held in readiness for O'Brien's move to show that Dublin supported him and that his transfer did not imply that 'during the difficult and confused situation in Katanga, he acted otherwise than in strict accordance with his instructions from his superiors in the United Nations service'.[67] Dublin would 'take a serious view' of any attempt to make O'Brien personally responsible for UN policy in Katanga. The Secretariat argued that 'blame for many of the mistakes in Katanga lay with the UN staff on the ground', but knew that 'Hammarskjöld "could not disavow his own people"'.[68] Yet this was what the Secretariat and its pro-Hammarskjöld elements would move to do.

The United Nations achieved little between 13 and 21 September; officially it had not even tried to end Katanga's secession. Militarily, Morthor had failed as it lacked air cover, artillery and sufficient armour, but, 'the real reason for the failure of the operation, in spite of the fact that most of its objectives were achieved, was political rather than military'.[69] UN forces in Katanga were destabilized by politically inspired actions such as sending A-Company to Jadotville. While conflict between the political and military sides of ONUC was not uncommon, the political side had buckled under pressure from the permanent members of the Security Council. Hammarskjöld pulled the plug on Morthor under British pressure. Tshombe emphatically told the Rhodesian

Federation Minister for Home Affairs Sir Malcolm Barrow that 'Khiari had admitted that U.N.O. was furious that "little" Katanga had checked the "big" United Nations'.[70] O'Brien later wrote to Khiari that Morthor was 'un échèc' ('a failure'), but the problem was more serious than this.[71] The Foreign Office concluded that 'if (as Khiari is reported to have expected) the United Nations had toppled Tshombe's government in two hours, this would have grossly simplified the Congo problem. It is now at least as complicated as before'.[72]

CHAPTER II

'Continual and violent flux'[1]

THE CEASEFIRE IN Katanga held, though both sides alleged breaches. ONUC maintained a visible presence across Elisabethville, holding pre-ceasefire positions so as to be seen to have prevailed over Tshombe. Khiari planned to use the return of these locations, particularly the Post Office, to Katangese control as bargaining chips when negotiating with Tshombe on implementing the February resolution. However Khiari's immediate priority, and with this UN Secretariat agreed, was a prisoner exchange and recommencing the evacuation of foreign personnel from Katanga.

Meanwhile 35th Battalion alternated between guard duties at The Tunnel, the Refugee Camp and O'Brien's official residence at Les Roches, while Irish and the newly arrived Malayan armoured cars patrolled the city. Otherwise the battalion was 'back to normal routine including siesta and swim at Lido', and there was 'NTR' – Nothing To Report.[2] Battalion personnel remained 'in good spirits but [were] anxious about [their] comrades in JADOT'.[3] Jadotville and the fighting in Elisabethville impacted on the 35th Battalion and there was 'growing sympathy for Katanga among UN soldiers ... particularly among the Irish, there are many who express extremely bitter feelings against the European population of Elisabethville and who freely express their intention to kill a great many more "next time".'[4]

Raja was already thinking about 'the next time' and sent a top secret instruction 'to be destroyed when read' to Waern outlining his intentions should hostilities recommence. In such a scenario ONUC would destroy the Gendarmerie 'wherever possible' and apprehend, by force if required, foreigners operating with them. Sector-B would hold its strong-points across Elisabethville, raid mercenary camps, destroy Gendarmerie ammunition dumps, and organize company-strength mobile columns supported by armour 'for offensive action against all possible hostile elements'.[5] Raja was on a war footing, a very different posture to that which existed before Morthor and one which culminated in a further round of fighting in Operation Unokat in December 1961. Waern doubted he had the capacity to put Raja's plan into effect without reinforcements and Sector-B knew that due to the extent of its security duties 'the bulk of our forces in [the] Elisabethville area would NOT be available for any form of offensive action'.[6]

Tshombe returned to Elisabethville the day after the ceasefire. He and his cabinet had played little part in the fighting, which had been mainly directed by the mercenaries. But this was forgotten and, in the words of a British diplomat, they 'convinced themselves that they had been responsible for victory and made remarks to the effect that it was the Bantu spirit that had won through against the cosmopolitan efforts of the United Nations.'[7] In such an atmosphere a Katangese accommodation with Leopoldville remained unlikely. Leopoldville still spoke openly of ending Katanga's secession by force and Khiari put pressure on Tshombe by telling him to reach an accommodation with Adoula because otherwise the Katangese leader would be seen as 'a supporter of colonialism and a traitor to [the] African cause.'[8] Khiari, Linner and O'Brien thought Tshombe could thus 'be intimidated into resigning Katanga's independence.'[9] Their policy had so far failed and many in Elisabethville thought Tshombe had 'grown considerably in confidence and subtlety'; some said that he had learned a lot from the UN.[10] Now politically stronger he saw the ceasefire with ONUC as a Katangese victory.

The main problem in Elisabethville was unrest at the refugee camp where numbers had reached 35,000. The camp was explosive because of a lack of faith in the ability of the UN to secure the area and the likelihood of a humanitarian disaster should an epidemic break out. The Gendarmerie continued sniping at the camp and the Baluba Jeunesse endeavoured to break out to attack the Gendarmerie, Europeans and unfriendly tribes. The Jeunesse dominated the camp and mixed groups of UN and Katangese police patrolled, trying to maintain order, break up Jeunesse groups and apprehend their leaders. Irish troops undertook regular patrols in the camp 'to break up meetings and disarm the more aggressive elements'.[11] Conflict between the Jeunesse and the Katangese police led to deaths on both sides. In response the Katangese threatened to 'clean out' the camp, but the UN calmed them down, pointing out that this would break the ceasefire.[12] The camp continued to grow, remaining a hub for anti-Tshombe opposition. Capt. Magennis recalled a particularly violent episode at the camp on 22 September when he was instructed by Comdt Kane to investigate reports of trouble –

> I took a jeep up to the location and found troops of Headquarters Company drawn up in lines and confronted by a line of very aggressive looking Baluba Jeunesse. Some carried sticks and the occasional ones had panga knives which they were brandishing in the air. Our troops were of course armed with weapons at the ready. I walked along our lines and stopped to talk to occasional NCOs to get a feeling of the situation. All the NCOs were of the opinion that the Jeunesse were full of dope and hyped up. Our troops were under orders not to fire unless physically threatened. Along the line I caught sight of C/S Mick O'Sullivan, a man I knew very well and knew also as a very competent NCO as we had served together at home in the Cavalry School. I knew he would give me a good briefing on the situation.
>
> I was talking at that time to a Sergeant from Headquarters Company who advised me that a particularly aggressive Baluba Jeunesse wielding a panga knife looked likely to break the line. The Baluba immediately did

this and ran directly at me, panga at the ready. I thought my last day had come. There were about twenty paces between the UN and Baluba lines. I was armed with a pistol but knew I could never draw it in time. Just in time I heard a burst of Gustaf fire from quite close on my left and the aggressor crumpled up on the ground. There also was Mick O'Sullivan saying 'I had to fire or he would have got you.' 'Thank God you did', I said, 'I thought I was finished.' O'Sullivan saved me from serious injury or possibly saved my life. In addition to that, the Jeunesse aggression quickly dispersed and the situation returned to normal.[13]

British ambassador to Congo Derek Riches saw the camp in mid-November and thought it 'appalling'.[14] He reported that violence was 'just beneath the surface' across Elisabethville. The camp remained a major source of unrest and it became difficult to see how it could be removed 'without genuine collaboration between the UN and Katanga authorities – and there is still a complete lack of trust on both sides'.[15] Katangese anti-UN propaganda recommenced. Katangese ministers alleged that ONUC was 'reinforcing their position with a view to an anticipated second round'.[16] This was denied, but Tshombe used the UN's delay appointing delegates to the ceasefire monitoring commission as evidence of ONUC's negative intentions. At the same time Gendarmerie messages intercepted by ONUC showed that Katanga was bringing weapons and ammunition into Elisabethville. Neither side trusted the other, Khiari declaring 'that any statement by Tshombe was worthless.'[17]

O'Brien wanted a stronger visible UN presence across Elisabethville but Linner and MacEoin refused. MacEoin exerted much stronger control over Katanga Command after the ceasefire. Lt Col. G.S. Paul was sent to Elisabethville as Chief of Staff and MacEoin looked for frequent situation reports from Raja. Linner carefully instructed O'Brien and Raja on the line to follow with Tshombe and preparations were underway for Khiari to go to Elisabethville as part of the joint ceasefire commission. O'Brien's enemies wondered what he would do next. Prime Minister of the Federation of Rhodesia and Nyasaland Sir Roy Welensky, a strong supporter of Tshombe, reckoned that O'Brien 'has decided that he might as well be hung for a sheep as for a lamb and that he will stake all on a further bid to subdue the Katanga government by force. If he is successful his past failures will be forgotten.'[18] O'Brien's days were numbered, but until prisoners were exchanged in Katanga he would not be moved.

Searching for Mullins and Nolan

As these agendas played out the 35th Battalion Armoured Car Group returned to full Irish command. The section operating with the Dogras packed up and their Indian commander thanked them for their assistance and talked to them informally to congratulate them on their performance. At 35th Battalion HQ Magennis also thanked his men; he 'was really proud of them'.[19] His next stop was Operations Section to report on their period under Dogra command and get briefed on fate of Cahalane's patrol to Radio College. Cmdt Kane was more interested in hearing how Magennis had fared with the Katangese mercenaries than providing information about the missing patrol. Magennis realized there had been no formal investigation into the capture of Cahalane's patrol or the related disappearance of Mullins and Nolan. Finding it difficult to understand how an armoured car could have been destroyed and two crew members killed without the vehicle being located over a week later, Magennis got Kane's agreement to take a reconnaissance patrol to retrace Cahalane's route to investigate where Cahalane's armoured car could be and what had become of Mullins and Nolan.

Early on 22 September Magennis' patrol set off in two Land Rovers. Magennis and Capt. Mark Carroll led with Capt. Frank Lawless and Coy Sgt Dan Carroll following. They took Cahalane's route and about a hundred yards south of Radio College on Avenue Wangermée they found three of the Cahalane's vehicles. The rear armoured car had its Browning machine-gun facing away from Radio College at maximum elevation, suggesting that it had not placed fire on those who had disabled Cahalane's vehicle. An attempt had been made to burn the vehicle, but it was still driveable. Further ahead were the jeep and the bus, both burned out. There was no sign of Cahalane's armoured car. A substantial amount of spent ammunition casings lay where Cahalane's vehicle had been hit, indicating an intense fire-fight. Magennis photographed the scene and reported back to Kane. Kane was puzzled about the failure of the patrols sent out on 15 September to find these vehicles and Magennis left Kane to make further enquiries. That afternoon, while the three vehicles were being recovered, Magennis and his colleagues searched Elisabethville unsuccessfully for the remaining missing armoured car.

Unknown to Magennis Capt. Basil Greer was also investigating the whereabouts of the missing soldiers and reported to Dublin that 'no trace has yet been found of CPL NOLAN or TPR MULLINS previously reported missing presumed killed. They are not in any Civilian Hosp., as far as can be ascertained.'[20] Reports and rumours still maintained that both men were alive and McNamee concurrently reported to the Irish Liaison Officer in Leopoldville that 'in [an] unknown hospital [in] Elisabethville Corporal Nolan and Private Mullins [are] both believed to be doing well'.[21] At the same time O'Brien received a detailed letter from one of his informants, Solomon Mulabaka, a Northern Rhodesian African 'who has supplied us with reliable information previously',[22] that Mullins and Nolan had been shot by the Gendarmerie after surrendering. Locals had disposed of one of the bodies nearby and brought the other body to the African townships on the southern outskirts of Elisabethville.[23] This information could not be acted upon because, as O'Brien told MacEoin, 'without even a single intelligence officer we are not in a position to check adequately on the numerous reports we receive'.[24] As ONUC lacked an integrated intelligence-processing system there was no process available to gather facts together from the mass of information circulating around Elisabethville and consolidate the picture regarding the two missing men. A further example of this was that no one alerted the Irish that the Swedes possessed tracker dogs that could assist in the search for the missing men.

On 23 September an anonymous message arrived at 35th Battalion Headquarters that an abandoned Irish armoured car was lodged in a drainage trench one block up from Gendarmerie Headquarters at the west end of Avenue Droogmans, adjacent to Boulevard Reine Elizabeth.[25] Magennis with Dan Carroll, Frank Lawless and a team of fitters set off with recovery equipment and located the missing vehicle. It was at an angle across the road with its front end lodged in the trench. These drainage trenches, on both sides of the road, were about three feet deep to carry off water during the rainy season. The armoured car appeared to have attempted a U-turn with the driver misjudging the distance to the trench and toppling over the edge in the process. Lawless and Magennis were discussing this possibility when Dan Carroll said, almost to himself, '"Maybe the two boys weren't dead. Maybe one or both of them was just unconscious". If so, they had survived the Radio College ambush and attempted to use the armoured car to return to Battalion Headquarters. If Carroll was right, where were they now?'[26] Information later received from Cpl Dan Sullivan, who was a member of Cahalane's captured patrol, adds a further piece to the story. In the early hours of 15 September, as Sullivan and his colleagues took cover in Soete's house, they heard the distinctive sound of an Irish armoured car's Ford V8 engine starting. Sullivan thought it was about 0200 as the armoured car rumbled into the distance.

The drainage trench was littered with spent 9mm casings, suggesting a prolonged period of combat. The car lay at an angle that ruled out use of the turret gun. All other equipment appeared to have been stripped as had any personal possessions other than a set of keys that was later identified as belonging to Mullins. The recovery patrol got the armoured car back on the road and combed the area thoroughly but nothing else was found. How had the armoured car got from Radio College to Avenue Droogmans? The more they discussed this, the more likely Carroll's solution seemed. The spent ammunition casings suggested that the two men had been killed in a fire fight as they attempted to return to 35th Battalion Headquarters. The issue now was to find their bodies.

The patrol towed the armoured car back to the 35th Battalion camp. Lawless and Magennis reported their findings to Kane and McNamee. They again discussed what might have brought the armoured car to its final location. As the Gendarmerie was unlikely to have moved it, one of the crew must have recovered sufficiently to drive the vehicle. About two hundred yards from where the armoured car had been hit there was a crossroads. The right turn led to the 35th Battalion Camp. Here a confused driver might have made a fatal error and instead turned left towards Gendarmerie Headquarters. Recognizing his error the driver might have tried a U-turn and ended up in the trench. Abandoning the vehicle the occupants of the armoured car sought cover in the roadside trench. Clearly there had been a fire fight, and in it, or subsequently, both Mullins and Nolan were killed. The conclusion of these discussions at Battalion HQ was that the matter could be left to the Intelligence Officer and the Armoured Car Group could resume its normal duties.

There was no cause for optimism. McNamee signalled to the Irish Liaison Officer in Leopoldville that 'we are not so hopeful of the two missing but we are still trying'.[27] Their comrades in Elisabethville were 'convinced they are dead'. Greer had 'no hope regarding NOLAN and MULLINS'.[28] Searches for the men reported 'no trace found' and Greer concluded 'I do not think we can even expect to find bodies.' Greer must have picked up the rumours circulating in Elisabethville, but he did not send explicit details to Dublin. By 5 October there was still no definite news and McNamee expressed the now inevitable conclusion: 'Nolan and Mullins may be presumed dead. No trace of bodies, but we are still trying.'[29]

Interrogation in Leopoldville

Frank Aiken arrived in Elisabethville late on 22 September 1961. He met O'Brien, visited Irish troops and saw where fighting had occurred. He wanted to continue to Jadotville to see A-Company but was unable to do so. Others in the 35th Battalion were not to meet Aiken. As the minister arrived Magennis and Considine learned from 35th Battalion HQ that they were to take leave in Leopoldville. Magennis was astonished; he had not requested leave. He protested that his place was with the Armoured Car Group, particularly as Cahalane and Knightly were prisoners. He was overruled by Kane and told to follow orders.

As Aiken toured Elisabethville Magennis and Considine were the only passengers on a DC6 bound for Leopoldville. There they were put up with a contingent of Irish officers serving at ONUC Headquarters and left to their own devices. Magennis 'began again to question myself as to why we had been sent on the so-called "rest-break".'[30] Then Lt Col. Art Cullen, Curragh Command Legal Officer, now posted to ONUC Headquarters, informed Magennis and Considine that they were to be interviewed by senior UN officials. The reason for the enforced leave then became clear: Magennis and Considine were the only 35th Battalion officers who had been in combat under Indian command in Katanga. Both knew there were vastly differing accounts circulating of the fighting in Elisabethville and they discussed their position as they prepared to meet the officials. Magennis advised Considine 'that if this did in fact turn out to be the reason for our presence, then he should tell it how it was with no attached embellishments'. They agreed this and Magennis hoped they would be interviewed together. It was not to be so.

Magennis was called first. He felt uneasy entering the interview room but that passed as he was greeted by name and invited to sit in a comfortable chair by two men dressed informally in open-necked shirts and dark slacks. They introduced themselves. One said his name was Khiari and he was acting in place of the Secretary General.[31] Coffee and water were offered. Initially there was small talk about Ireland, the climate in Africa and comparisons between Leopoldville and Elisabethville. That was 'by way of a "loosener up" to get the talking going' and, as Magennis had guessed, 'the real subject switched to the recent fighting and in particular that involving my experience with the Indian Dogra Battalion'.

Khiari asked about the assault on the Post Office during Operation Morthor. Magennis explained his orders, adding that 'no mention of force was given to me when I was instructed to go under the command of Dogra Battalion'. Khiari's associate interjected that the use of force was allowed under ONUC's mandate. Magennis agreed but countered that 'it would have been nice if I had been so advised before leaving my own battalion'. 'Why?', the official asked. 'Well', Magennis continued, tongue in cheek, 'I could have so advised my men and as we are all Roman Catholic we might have wished to have had our pot scraped by the Chaplain before leaving.' 'Your pot! What's that?', said the confused official. Khiari and his colleague laughed as Magennis explained to them his 'old school expression for going to confession'. This broke the ice. After a cup of coffee the questions started. What time did you reach the start line? What happened at the start line? How often was the Post Office garrison called on to surrender? Were you fired on from the Post Office when you were on the start line? Were you fired on from the Belgium Consulate? Magennis gave the times and denied that fire had been directed against the UN troops when they were on the start line. He was then asked to describe the assault on the Post Office and the Gendarmerie counterattack. Again they asked 'Did you hear any firing at all prior to your leaving the start line?' 'No', replied Magennis, 'my two cars led the assault accompanied by the platoon commander who was wounded. I opened fire at the objective precisely at 04.00 hours as ordered.' 'How did the Gendarmerie in the Post Office behave?' they asked. 'I have no personal knowledge', Magennis explained, 'I wasn't in the building during the fighting which lasted, I think, about forty-five minutes. But I was told later by the Dogra Company Commander that they resisted strongly until their white leaders disappeared and then they gave in rapidly.' 'Thank you Captain, that is as we thought', said Khiari and the interview ended. Outside Magennis outlined to Considine what awaited him.[32]

When Magennis got back to Elisabethville, Aiken had gone. He had spent less than twenty-four hours in the city; long enough to get the public relations results required for Lemass but not so long as to see anything the UN did not want him to see. Magennis learned that during Aiken's visit the crew of Considine's armoured car had been ordered to report to 35th Battalion Headquarters but after arriving and waiting for an hour they were told their presence was no longer required and they were dismissed without catching a glimpse of Aiken. Aiken left Elisabethville late on 23 September; Khiari arrived in Elisabethville on 26 September to commence his duties with the Katanga Joint Ceasefire Commission.

Aiken arrived back in Dublin on 26 September. Lemass had instructed that if he were giving press interviews he should 'avoid comment on UN purpose in Congo' and was 'to take on this subject the line "no comment pending report to my government".'[33] Aiken sent a general message to Dublin that he had found all Irish troops in good health and spirits, the wounded were out of danger and he had ascertained that Irish prisoners were well treated. If he saw or heard anything untoward about the actions of UN forces he did not hint at it.

The prisoner exchange

There was deadlock in Elisabethville over the release of ONUC and Katangese prisoners and Boland felt that 'anything might set off another conflagration at any moment'.[34] UN defences were strengthened and Khiari broke off relations with Tshombe. Kjellgren was angered by Katangese prevarication, telling MacEoin and Khiari that the Katangese were 'NOT repeat NOT honest. They have NO repeat NO wish to fulfil their part of the agreement. They are cheating us and trying to delay.'[35] Tshombe was playing for time and strengthening his military capacity aware that the imminent arrival of the rainy season would prevent further ONUC operations.

ONUC monitored the arrival of mercenaries and weapons from Northern Rhodesia and Capt. Michael Purfield and Capt. Terence McKeever of the 35th Battalion crossed clandestinely into Northern Rhodesia on 8 and 9 October on what ONUC called a 'special patrol' to gather intelligence. They travelled with two Irishmen living in Katanga to Bancroft and Ndola by bush road. There they saw Katangese aircraft, but no Fougas (and were told there never had been any Fougas at Ndola) and got into conversation with mercenaries and pilots. After arranging with an Irishman living in Ndola to pass on information about movements at the airport they returned to Elisabethville by a 'route used by mercenaries coming from Rhodesia'.[36] Purfield reported Katangese aircraft operating from an airstrip on a main road and Gendarmerie converting bulldozers into armoured vehicles. These details, along with the patrol's first-hand account of mercenaries operating from Northern Rhodesia, showed that Katanga was rearming.[37] Katanga Command expected 'to have a military showdown with Tshombe and force a decision by military strength' and submitted to MacEoin a plan to capture Elisabethville and seal the Northern Rhodesian border using existing ONUC forces plus two squadrons of armoured cars and newly arrived UN air cover.[38] They still needed a further brigade of troops, artillery and engineers to carry out this plan and required a month's preparation before it could be put into effect.

After a difficult meeting on 13 October Khiari and Tshombe agreed to exchange prisoners at the old aerodrome in Elisabethville at 1600 on 16 October. ONUC would simultaneously hand over or re-open strategic locations including the Post Office, The Tunnel and the airport. It was a climb-down for ONUC and Khiari looked grim-faced after it was signed, but Tshombe emerged smiling from his presidential palace. He had got nearly all he wanted. At the UN Secretariat the agreement was met without joy as 'the concessions made to Mr Tshombe tend to bolster his prestige to some extent and must, therefore, make him hard to handle'.[39] However there was 'no practical alternative'.

ONUC brought its prisoners to the old airfield for the exchange but 1600 on 16 October came and went and no Katangese prisoners appeared. They had been returned to Jadotville on Munongo's orders as Tshombe accused the UN of breaking the ceasefire protocol. Angry meetings followed and Tshombe refused to deal with O'Brien, whose presence in Katanga he considered to be a 'menace permanente pour paix Katanga et Afrique'.[40] Kjellgren took offense and walked out. The situation was 'unpredictable and might turn nasty' and the UN were 'very worried' about the prisoners.[41] Boland was 'very worried' about A-Company and on UN and Irish requests Sir Patrick Dean asked that Dunnett 'take appropriate action immediately'. A revised release schedule was drawn up and the British, French and American consuls in Elisabethville acted as intermediaries.

Khiari now managed, partly by disassociating himself from O'Brien, to gain Tshombe's confidence. He developed his relationship with Tshombe to such an extent that Katangan emissaries were preparing to proceed to Leopoldville for negotiations. The 185 prisoners held by the Katangese finally arrived at Camp Massart on the morning of 17 October. Khiari's return to Elisabethville was delayed to 23 October so he could accompany Tshombe's emissaries back from Leopoldville. He gave Tshombe the UN's approval of the 13 October agreement and at 1600 on 25 October the prisoners, including A-Company, were released at the old airstrip. The transmitter station and the Post Office were handed back to the Katangese and ONUC withdrew from positions around Elisabethville. Elisabethville airport reopened under UN technical control.

Corporal Nolan's grave

In the days before the prisoner exchange McNamee wrote to Dublin that 'despite enquiries in many directions we have failed to locate' Nolan or Mullins.[42] Reports received on their fate were all 'at variance with each other'. However McNamee could 'glean' that Mullins and Nolan had recovered after the attack on their armoured car and got the vehicle going. It was then attacked by Gendarmerie in the Commune Albert area in the south of Elisabethville, both men were killed and their bodies burned.[43] One body was mutilated and dismembered and McNamee stated that, in the opinion of one source, cannibalism was likely. None of this was then, or has since, been proven outright, but it seemed to McNamee the best assumption on the evidence available.

An Elisabethville nun reported that she had had the body of a six-foot soldier buried in the Union Minière Cemetery. Although Mullins and Nolan were 5' 5" McNamee sought permission to have the body exhumed. He wished to know from Dublin if next of kin had been informed that both men were missing presumed dead, as he wanted to write to their relatives. Both men's relatives were receiving letters from the 35th Battalion 'which gave rise to the hope that they are still alive' and McNamee felt that in view of the information received 'I can NO longer share that belief'.[44]

Magennis, now acting OC of the Armoured Car Group in Cahalane's absence, was told by 35th Battalion Headquarters that information received indicated that a burial had taken place in a local cemetery of what could be one or two white United Nations soldiers. 35th Battalion's Engineer Section was to undertake an exhumation at which Engineer Officer Capt. Sean Donlon and Legal Officer Comdt Tadhg O'Shea would attend. Magennis was given permission to attend also. En route he learned that if the bodies were buried in wooden coffins they were definitely Europeans as at African funerals the deceased was wrapped in a shroud. The party made for the Union Minière Hospital Cemetery in the Lubumbashi Commune. For Magennis

> the cemetery was a desolate place with one fairly wide unmetalled track running down the centre and foot tracks running left and right. The rainy season had begun some days earlier and the red clay was sticky and greasy. There were no headstones and the surface of some graves was strewn with bits and pieces of household equipment. It was a most depressing sight and the heavy rain did not help.[45]

The information the 35th Battalion had received was precise – grave number 3225. The party followed the central track and halted along a side track leading to the right. The engineers started digging. It 'was very difficult work; the clay was saturated, heavy and sticky and rain soon filled the excavation. Then came the sound of metal on wood and with it the dread at what was to come'.[46] The body in the coffin was identified by identity discs as Cpl Michael Nolan. There was only one coffin.

Back at 35th Battalion Headquarters Comdt O'Shea made the necessary reports. Magennis 'stretched out on his bed and listened to the rain'. The heat and humidity were intense and the rain was 'preceded by an electric storm the like of which most of us had never experienced'. Frank Lawless and Mark Carroll arrived and Magennis told them about the exhumation. The three chatted about what could now be done about Mullins and how to brief the Armoured Car Group. They decided on an informal huddle in one of the Group's billets and an open discussion. There was little they could otherwise do except to keep their eyes and ears open for information. Responsibility for gathering information on Mullins' burial place remained with the Battalion Intelligence Section and further information might still come in.

With the situation worsening in Elisabethville and the rainy season in full swing it would be hard to make further progress finding Mullins' body. Magennis decided to get in touch with Bill Williams. Through the good offices of Stan Zurakovsky Magennis contacted Williams and arranged a meeting on 24 October. Williams undertook to ferret out information from his employees but explained that this could take weeks. Magennis later received a message from Zurakovsky that Williams had information. They met at Zurakovsky's house and from the look on Williams' face Magennis guessed that the news was bad. Williams told him that before daybreak on 15 September a UN armoured car had slowly come down Avenue Drogmans and turned left. It tried to do a U-turn but ended up in the roadside trench. A soldier got out by the rear door helping another soldier and they got into the trench. Gendarmerie arrived and shooting started. One of the soldiers was hit, the other soldier continued to shoot until he ran out of ammunition and he too was killed. The Gendarmerie stripped the armoured car and put the body of the second soldier to be killed into a truck and drove off towards the ethnic city. They left the body of the other soldier in the trench. The body lay there for two days and was buried in an ethnic cemetery. Williams 'added that there was a long-standing practice, among African tribes to cannibalize the bodies of enemies who had shown outstanding bravery in combat. Some of the dead warriors' courage and bravery would then pass on to the victors. It was most likely that this was what happened. There was a rumour to this effect in the ethnic city.'[47] Williams had no further information; tension was high in Elisabethville and he felt it wise to postpone further enquiries until the city became quieter. It was Magennis' last contact with Williams.

The events leading to the deaths of Mullins and Nolan remain unclear. The 35th Battalion's unit history explains that, following the ambush on Cahalane's patrol, Nolan recovered and attempted to drive the armoured car back to camp. Magennis' investigation, accompanied by Capts Lawless and Carroll and Sqdn Sgt. Carroll, led to a different conclusion – Mullins had recovered first and he, and not Nolan, attempted to return to the Armoured Car Group camp when he made a wrong turn. They agreed with Sgt Tim Carey's account, which put the two crewmen on the floor of the car with Mullins lying on top of Nolan. In this scenario Nolan, the co-driver of the armoured car, was blown by the blast of the explosion towards the rear door. Mullins, standing in the turret fell on top of Nolan. In those circumstances Mullins, not Nolan, would have recovered first. As a trooper, Mullins was less familiar with the layout of Elisabethville than Nolan and so took a wrong turn at the crossroads. Nolan was familiar with the city layout and would have more than likely turned right at the crossroads knowing that the UN camp lay in that direction. Nolan also would have been well aware of the drainage trenches on either side of the roads and the hazard they presented. On these assumptions it was Mullins who, in Williams' account of events, brought Nolan from the armoured car into the drainage trench and continued to fight until killed. Such bravery resonated with the story of the removal of a soldier's body after the incident.

In 1964 Boland's successor as Irish ambassador to the United Nations, Con Cremin, wrote to Hammarskjöld's successor Secretary General U Thant about Mullins that 'despite the most exhaustive inquiries undertaken by the Irish contingents in the area at the time and later his remains were not located or recovered.'[48] Cremin inquired if there was any information from inquiries made by the UN that might assist the Irish authorities or 'which might indicate that further investigation at this stage would be likely to lead to a successful conclusion'. This was merely a precautionary move; it was 'the opinion of the [Irish] military authorities that further inquiries in the matter at this stage would not yield the desired result'.[49] What the punctilious and exact Cremin meant by the use of the word 'desired' is unclear.[50]

The November Resolution: 'a critical moment for Katanga'[51]

In early November, 1961 stories circulated that the UN was planning a final initiative to end Katanga's secession. Katanga Command had drawn up plans for further military action but nothing was imminent. At a meeting of the UN Congo Advisory Committee on 17 November U Thant indicated that the round-up of mercenaries in Katanga remained the 'primary objective' of ONUC.[52] Force could be used and the Acting Secretary General said that the UN would soon have sufficient forces in Katanga for that purpose. This indicated to Boland 'the adoption of a new and more active role in the Congo for ONUC'.[53] On learning this Aiken travelled to New York to consult with military and diplomatic figures including Sir Patrick Dean, deputy US ambassador to the UN Charles Yost, MacEoin and Rikhye. Their opinion was that the contemplated round-up of mercenaries 'would involve the risk of renewed large-scale fighting' in Katanga.[54] Aiken met U Thant on 20 November. He counselled caution and suggested peaceful ways of increasing international pressure on Tshombe as 'recourse to force should be avoided to the utmost extent possible'.[55] U Thant let slip that ONUC still 'did not have sufficient forces at its disposal to deal with any widespread fighting' in Katanga.[56]

A draft resolution on Congo tabled by Liberia, Ceylon and the UAR was before the Security Council and, after amendment to strengthen its provisions, became resolution 169, which authorized the Secretary General to take vigorous action, including the use of force, if necessary, for the immediate apprehension of all foreign military and paramilitary personnel and political advisers not under United Nations command in Katanga.[57] The resolution condemned external support for Katanga and its secession and enabled the UN to increase its support for the Leopoldville government to end the secession. It fitted growing international opinion that Katangese independence was no longer at issue; the question was how to integrate Katanga back into the Congo and when and, though the resolution gave the UN no mandate to end the secession by force, how the UN would strike again against Tshombe. With the resolution passed, U Thant told the Security Council that the UN would implement the new resolution 'with determination and vigour'.[58]

The new resolution shook Tshombe's administration in Elisabethville. On 26 November, seemingly inspired by reports that ONUC was planning an immediate attack on Elisabethville, he made a flamboyant speech to prepare Katanga for war, telling the population that they would be given weapons for self-defence. The speech and associated Gendarmerie movements caused tension and ONUC went on alert in Elisabethville as the atmosphere was 'explosive'.[59] ONUC remained determined to implement the new resolution. 'Katanga is sick, perhaps mortally', wrote Douglas Brown in the *Daily Telegraph*, the 'persistent sabotage by the United Nations is at last having its effect'.[60]

O'Brien and MacEoin assessed the implementation of the new resolution and concluded that 'the earlier this job is tackled the better'.[61] Military advisors at the Secretariat concluded that 'the combat effectiveness of the ONUC Forces should ... be highest in January/February 1962'.[62] Passing through Dublin, MacEoin told the press that though the new resolution had come down against the secession of Katanga, it did not direct that force be used to end Katanga's secession. The Force Commander reiterated that its objective was the removal of foreign mercenaries. MacEoin was playing down one fundamental factor in the resolution that Irish diplomats at the UN emphasized to Dublin. That was that 'much depends on [the] Secretary General's use of the powers conferred on him' by the resolution.[63]

Raja was conscious of the possibility of military action being taken by ONUC and stressed that it was 'imperative' to maintain the strength of ONUC troops in Elisabethville.[64] The upcoming rotation in December of Swedish and Irish forces left Raja 'in no position to take any particular initiative here in the immediate future'.[65] Reports from Elisabethville suggested that the Katangese would adopt a scorched-earth policy and 'meet force with force'.[66] The incoming 36th Irish Battalion was supposed to deploy to northern Katanga. On 30 November Raja learned that the United States were 'prepared if the situation in Elisabethville deteriorates and your need for troops is vital to fly replacement direct to Elisabethville'.[67] Raja agreed, citing the 'serious situation and continuing tension' in the city as justifying the deployment of the 36th Battalion direct to Elisabethville.[68]

'A chronic irritant':[69] *O'Brien's resignation*

After the September ceasefire Adoula refused to accept O'Brien's removal and the latter's transfer to New York was 'in a state of suspense' by early October.[70] A strong anti-O'Brien feeling existed in the British media and at Westminster and there was 'a great deal of anxiety' about the Katanga situation among the UN delegations Boland met in New York.[71] Since Morthor, O'Brien maintained that in commencing the operation he had acted under authorization from Hammarskjöld. Dublin still supported O'Brien and Boland acted in a paternal manner towards his former colleague, explaining to Dublin the UN Secretariat's question of 'whether it is wise for Conor O'Brien, *in his own interest*, to remain in the Congo'.[72] By mid-October Boland's outlook changed as the international mood turned further against O'Brien. Boland's Swedish counterpart Ambassador Agda Rössel let him know that while there was no suggestion that O'Brien had 'acted at any time without proper authority', the feeling was that the authority given by Hammarskjöld to Linner to act in Elisabethville 'was based on assessments and value judgments by Conor which turned out not to be sound.' Was there a way, Rössel wondered, 'of passing on the hint to Conor?'

Boland thought a way around Congolese opposition to O'Brien's removal was for O'Brien to request to return to New York. The stumbling block was Aiken's sense of obligation to O'Brien; he did not want him to be transferred in circumstances that might look like a slight. Boland began working behind Aiken's and O'Brien's backs, suggesting to Sir Patrick Dean that the Foreign Office get Sir Ian Maclennan, the British ambassador in Dublin, to have a word with Lemass to find a means to remove O'Brien. Dean reported that the Irish United Nations delegation told him that

> the best way to get rid of O'Brien (whom incidentally they all hate) is somehow to get beyond the Irish Foreign Minister, Aiken, and to see that Lemass knows about the trouble. Apparently Aiken has taken a personal stand on the matter, but Lemass might think differently, particularly if he knew how unpopular O'Brien was among delegations here, specially those of the Common Market Countries.[73]

While Maclennan moved to 'outflank Aiken and have a direct word with Lemass' and MacEoin was urged to 'do what he can discreetly to have O'Brien removed.'[74]

One possibility was that Dublin would ask the United Nations to end O'Brien's secondment. London was interested in this as it would leave the next step to Dublin and required no further British action. But O'Brien had told Aiken that Boland was co-operating with the British in orchestrating his removal. Writing in Irish, he told Aiken that 'is eagla liom nach bhfuil Seán Buí ró-sásta leat-sa ach oiread' (I am afraid that 'Britain' is not too satisfied with you either).[75] He explained that the British 'had been out for my head' ever since he began applying Security Council resolutions to Katanga. O'Brien found Boland's attitude 'considerably harder to take', but understood that 'if he is trying to sacrifice me at present I am sure it is entirely without malice and in the interests of expediency alone'. He also knew that 'Bunche took it – and still takes it – from Boland that I no longer have the confidence of my own government.'[76] On the contrary, O'Brien still had Aiken's confidence.

What no one realized was that O'Brien felt that he 'should leave his assignment in Elisabethville so as not to jeopardize the possibilities of reconciliation'.[77] He would move to Leopoldville as Linner's Senior Political Advisor so his ultimate departure from Congo to New York would not be seen as a failure. O'Brien feared that an immediate move to New York would lead to his being sidelined rather than taking over a high-profile UN position, such as he maintained he had been offered by Hammarskjöld.

Stories circulated that senior Secretariat official Brian Urquhart would take over from O'Brien in Katanga in mid-November and O'Brien would leave for New York. Criticizing O'Brien at the Security Council Spaak exclaimed that he had pursued 'a personal policy' and 'grossly exceeded instructions' over Katanga.[78] This ruined planning in New York, London and Dublin for O'Brien's recall. U Thant now had no alternative but to send O'Brien back to Congo to save face. Dean planned to approach Adlai Stevenson, US ambassador to the UN, to use his influence with U Thant to prevent O'Brien's return. Lord Home planned to meet the Irish ambassador to the United Kingdom, Hugh McCann, to convince him that O'Brien's return 'could do nothing but harm' to Congo.[79]

U Thant responded to Spaak that he would discharge his responsibilities under the November resolution with determination. Towards the end of his statement he agreed 'that mistakes had been made in the past in the Congo operation'.[80] O'Brien took this badly. He knew the line had been included by Bunche and told Bunche that it referred to him personally and would 'be taken as tacitly admitting the truth of that case', in particular by Britain and Belgium. O'Brien maintained that he had acted 'fully in accordance with the instructions' received from Hammarskjöld and expected that in responding to Spaak, U Thant would explain 'that my action did not exceed or deviate from instruction'.[81]

O'Brien wrote to Aiken that due to events in Katanga 'it was falsely asserted … that I was pursuing a policy of my own rather than that of the UN'.[82] Realizing the need for 'conciliation and negotiation' he had 'reluctantly come to the conclusion that I can no longer usefully represent the UN in Katanga. Should you request me to resume service in the Irish Department of External Affairs, I shall be happy to do so.' Anticipating the media reaction and the likely fallout, O'Brien told his External Affairs colleague Máire MacEntee, to whom he was now engaged and who was on leave in Elisabethville, staying at his official residence, to return to Dublin immediately.[83] MacEntee received this message on 28 November.

Aiken did not reply immediately to O'Brien's letter. Three days after it was sent O'Brien's situation 'assumed very unfortunate aspects.'[84] The news reached New York on the evening of 29 November as Bunche, Rikhye, O'Brien and others were in a meeting. Narasimhan arrived with a telex, saying that 'this is very bad news'.[85] Bunche read the document and 'obviously stricken' passed it to O'Brien.[86]

The bad news was that on 28 November there had been an attack on a UN car heading for a dinner to honour the arrival in Elisabethville of Senator Thomas Dodd 'the self-appointed American patron of Tshombe'.[87] In the car was George Ivan Smith, acting UN representative in Katanga, the newly arrived Brian Urquhart, as well as Fitzhugh Greene (US embassy, Leopoldville), and Máire MacEntee. Close to its destination the car came to the attention of the para-commando guard at General Muké's nearby residence. The guard surrounded the vehicle though its occupants got to safety after the dinner party guests intervened. Shortly afterwards a group of paracommandos burst in to the dinner and MacEntee endeavoured to prevent them rounding up Urquhart and those who had arrived with him. Ivan Smith's driver, Pte Patrick Wall, sought immediate UN support from the nearby Officers' Mess, finding Lt Kevin Knightly of the 35th Battalion Armoured Car Group who, with machine-gun readied, drove to the party to intervene. When MacEntee opened the door to them she was never 'so glad to see anyone' in her life.[88] Dodd's party had arrived as a badly beaten Ivan Smith and Urquhart were about to be taken away by the Gendarmerie. Ivan Smith was released, but Urquhart was taken prisoner and released only after the UN told the Katangese to do so or face full-scale military action.

UN and international opinion was incensed at the attack. In Ireland news focussed on why Máire MacEntee was involved and what an official from the Department of External Affairs was doing in Elisabethville. That she was the daughter of the Tánaiste and Minister for Health Seán MacEntee, a senior member of Lemass' cabinet, gave the story added importance. External Affairs unofficially explained that she was on annual leave and her visit was 'purely a private one'.[89] A spokesman added that 'we did not know she was in the Congo'.[90] It was common knowledge in Iveagh House that O'Brien and MacEntee were in a relationship and that O'Brien, while separated from his wife, was not yet divorced. Amidst a growing media storm MacEntee returned to Dublin and resigned. In her memoirs she wrote that she 'did not fully appreciate how pivotal my Katanga visit was in inducing the outcome that, hitherto, all the badmouthing of Conor by his unfriends ... had been unable to achieve, namely Conor's resignation'.[91]

On 30 November Aiken, still in New York, with the MacEntee story being telexed from Dublin and the Secretary General upset, was forced to act on O'Brien's letter of five days earlier. O'Brien was called to meet Aiken and learned that Bunche had, on U Thant's instructions, asked Aiken about MacEntee's presence in Elisabethville and asked him to recall O'Brien to the Department of External Affairs. If Aiken did not do so, U Thant would call for O'Brien's resignation as he had shown himself 'to be so indiscreet as to be unsuitable for further service with the United Nations'.[92] O'Brien told an upset Aiken that if he agreed he 'had better ask for me back'.[93] Aiken used the excuse of shortages in top-level personnel at External Affairs to request O'Brien's release.

U Thant replied immediately, praising O'Brien for his 'devotion and courage'.[94] Aiken said no more publicly than that O'Brien sought to return to External Affairs and he subsequently expressed this to the Secretary General 'a couple of days after that'.[95] Twisting the story O'Brien placed his 25 November letter to Aiken seeking to return to External Affairs after Aiken's letter to U Thant asking for his recall, though press coverage mentioned that Aiken had received a letter from O'Brien in advance of Thant's request.[96]

There was serious discontent between Dublin and the Irish permanent mission to the UN over how O'Brien's departure was being spun by the UN and reported internationally. Aiken's public statement had gone down badly in Dublin. Before it was issued Cremin spoke 'rather strongly' to Boland conveying Lemass' instruction that in statements issued in New York about O'Brien's resignation 'the maximum responsibility for the charge should be placed elsewhere – and not here, where it does not belong'.[97] Lemass was not having Ireland's international reputation damaged by making it look as if Aiken was responsible for O'Brien's recall due to a human resources issue at Iveagh House. O'Brien's removal was a UN responsibility.

Yet Aiken had been truthful in his press release. O'Brien had written to him seeking to leave UN service and Aiken had supported this in his letter to U Thant. But it was the UN that moved first and pressurized Aiken into acting. Critically, Aiken did not act on O'Brien's letter until the Secretary General forced his hand after the revelations surfaced about MacEntee's presence in Elisabethville. The public were instead told that UN sources had 'disclosed' that O'Brien had been relieved of his post 'at the request of the Irish government'.[98] O'Brien's letter to Aiken of 25 November was leaked to support Aiken's letter and appear as nothing more than a personal confession of guilt than a prior request to Aiken to be recalled. U Thant of course 'felt bound to accede to Mr Aiken's request', but this was duplicitous to say the least. Aiken remained personally loyal to O'Brien to the last. He did not see though, that the UN had made him appear responsible for recalling O'Brien. He was carrying out their wishes, neatly deflecting criticism away from the Secretariat. It also deflected attention from London. Boland, who had supported all moves to get O'Brien out of Congo, was nowhere to be seen.

O'Brien maintained that he had offered to leave UN service in advance of Aiken's letter to U Thant as he knew his presence in Katanga was hampering attempts at reconciliation. Determined to tell his story he also resigned from External Affairs on 1 December 1961.[99] Subject to mounting international criticism he wished to speak freely and 'to be more explicit about the quarters which had come to regard me as an "obstacle to conciliation in Katanga".'[1] At a hurriedly called crowded press conference in New York, O'Brien accused the British press and the Katanga lobby in Westminster of influencing the British government in its Congo policy and argued that they and Welensky were attempting to bring the UN operation in Congo into disrepute, thus buying time for Katanga to solidify as an independent state. O'Brien felt that the United Nations could 'only gain by having a spotlight brought to bear on the forces that have been frustrating our efforts in Katanga'.[2]

At the same time O'Brien announced that he was getting divorced and he and MacEntee would shortly marry. The Department of External Affairs and the Department of the Taoiseach went into crisis mode as news of O'Brien's and MacEntee's resignations broke. The resignation of a top diplomat with an international reputation and the concurrent resignation of one of Ireland's few female diplomats, who was Irish representative to the Council of Europe and the Tánaiste's daughter, was unprecedented; not to mention that O'Brien and MacEntee were in a relationship. External Affairs eschewed the limelight. This was not the way Aiken's department liked to appear in public.

O'Brien received some unexpected support. MacEoin's term as Force Commander was up in late December and he told reporters that he did not wish to remain in UN service.[3] He then unexpectedly explained that he shared O'Brien's view that Britain, France and the Rhodesian Federation were interfering in Katanga. Cremin reported confidentially to Aiken that 'the Taoiseach and everybody else are very surprised and concerned with General McKeown's statements – both their content and the fact that he should have made them at all.'[4] Lemass was 'concerned' that MacEoin had given him no indication when they had met recently that he would make this statement.

Lemass told the British ambassador in Dublin that he regretted that the Force Commander had 'lent himself to statements of this kind'.[5] Increasingly worried at what O'Brien and MacEoin were saying, Lemass disassociated the Irish government from their statements. On receiving this 'very gratifying' news, Macmillan's private secretary minuted to the British prime minister 'Mr Lemass is very sensible', to which Macmillan replied simply 'Yes'.[6] Lemass was anxious to dampen down any potential rift in British–Irish relations over Katanga. With Irish entry into the Common Market in mind Lemass told Aiken that 'it must be [our] primary objective at present to avoid indisposing Britain, Belgium [and] France'.[7] Reinforcing the point, Lemass used the opportunity of a speech in Dublin on 7 December to restate Irish support for ONUC and the territorial unity of Congo. Macmillan told Lemass that he was 'very glad to know' that O'Brien's views 'in no way represent the views of your Government' and that MacEoin 'should not be regarded in any sense as speaking with Governmental authority'.[8] Maclennan wondered if MacEoin had been trapped by a reporter and on Lemass' suggestion Boland asked Bunche to have a word with MacEoin about his public statements. However MacEoin was not the only one to support O'Brien; on 8 December Col. Bjorn Egge, returned from ONUC service, explained that 'certains pays pratiquent le double jeu' in Katanga.[9]

The *Irish Times* hinted that there were international political pressures on Dublin behind O'Brien's recall and resignation. The paper suggested that if 'the Government has put the interests – promoted perhaps by heavy pressure – of any one of the Great Powers ahead of the demands of the United Nations, ex-colonial members of the Organisation are hardly likely to miss the point' and hinted at the Anglo–Irish intrigue surrounding O'Brien's fate.[10] Describing O'Brien as 'the chief architect of modern Irish foreign policy and its principal exponent in the UN and the Congo', the paper could not understand how Dublin had supported him for so long and suddenly changed tack. The British embassy in Dublin 'had the feeling that the whole story was eluding us'.[11] What both missed was the pressure placed on Aiken by the UN, the institution the minister was devoted to, and which was the centrepiece of Irish foreign policy. It was not the Great Powers that had forced Aiken to recall O'Brien, but the UN itself under pressure of its membership, including the Great Powers.

O'Brien's departure was in reality a side-story. The November resolution, which saw power in Katanga move towards the UN, was the most significant event regarding Katanga in the immediate run-up to renewed fighting in Elisabethville in December 1961. Tshombe did not accept this, and on the face of it remained strong with his military power replenished by new mercenaries who, under the control of René Falques, remained in command of the Gendarmerie. Internationally Tshombe was less secure. His supporters were growing weary of him, though he retained the support of international business concerns. He had also lost his tactical cards with the release of his UN prisoners. The UN was now regrouping behind a new team. U Thant was more open to strong action in Katanga than Hammarskjöld had been. Raja, despite the failings of Morthor, had replenished his forces and now had air superiority. He had also removed most non-Indian forces from Elisabethville and was determined that the next round of fighting would be a largely Indian affair. After the Security Council vote in November, the UN would act again in Katanga and it would act vigorously. The Katangese would have been well advised to behave circumspectly, but instead they caused the United Nations to act with an uncharacteristic aggression.

CHAPTER 12

The point of no return

B Y DECEMBER 1961 Katanga faced a further round of ONUC military operations. U Thant had little time for Tshombe, calling the Katangese president 'a very unstable man' and intimating that the UN would soon act in Katanga.[1] Linner also let Tshombe know that the UN intended to implement the November resolution and remove the mercenaries. Tshombe's response to this would set the direction of future events. As the Kennedy administration swung behind the UN's policy in Katanga, Tshombe's international isolation increased. In Elisabethville, out-of-control mercenaries incited the Gendarmerie to hostilities against ONUC. The city was tense and events were 'moving to a new climax'.[2] Yet Tshombe departed on 1 December on an overseas visit. The mercenaries commanding the Gendarmerie planned to use Tshombe's absence and ONUC's weakness during the forthcoming rotation of Irish and Swedish battalions to provoke a trial of strength with the UN. Raja, worried that hostilities might erupt before the new battalions arrived, told ONUC HQ that he could 'NOT accept responsibility if [the] situation deteriorates for lack of troops'.[3] UN forces were on alert with 'all troops on short notice for action'.[4]

'Provoke ONUC to a trial of military strength'[5]

On the afternoon of 2 December at Elisabethville airport, a scuffle broke out between Katangese soldiers, two Baluba airport workers, and a local woman. The Indian ONUC guard intervened and after a skirmish they arrested 36 Gendarmerie and 15 policemen. Those arrested were later released but as news of the incident spread Gendarmerie began to patrol Elisabethville in strength, interpreting the scuffle as the beginning of a new UN campaign against Katanga. Gendarmerie paracommandos established roadblocks in the east of the city at The Tunnel, 'the vital communications link for ONUC freedom of movement' across Elizabethville, and were hampering UN operations; the following day eleven UN personnel were abducted.[6] The Katangese hoped their roadblocks would divide Elisabethville, isolating ONUC forces and preventing them from seizing strategic points. On 3 December at The Tunnel a Swedish UN jeep was attacked, killing the driver and wounding three passengers. The UN warned Munongo and Kimba to lift the roadblocks or ONUC would take action and the Katangese would be held responsible. Kimba took it as an ultimatum and the British and United States consuls mediated, urging 'the avoidance of anything likely to touch off further disorder'.[7]

U Thant now gave ONUC commanders authority 'to act vigorously to establish law and order and protect life and property' in Katanga.[8] As Raja feared, the situation was deteriorating. He urgently requested a further infantry battalion and an armoured car squadron. They were 'imperative if stern action [is] required and success [is] to be assured'.[9] Katanga Command warned that due to the Gendarmerie action in Elisabethville 'a general drive' against the Gendarmerie was possible.[10] Raja and Ivan Smith briefed commanders and visited ONUC positions 'to persuade the troops to hold steady'.[11] ONUC faced continued Katangese provocation with 'firmness and restraint' in the 'almost hysterical atmosphere of fear and panic caused by ministerial propaganda and exploited by mercenaries'.[12] Ivan Smith's cool-headedness became 'a sensible moderating influence particularly with the United Nations Military Commanders'[13]

On 4 December, in a further escalation, Gendarmerie blocked the main roads from Elisabethville north to the airport, including the junction on Avenue Saio controlling the road to Jadotville. A strong Swedish patrol failed to remove them. Kimba, who was in charge in Tshombe's absence, said the roadblocks would be removed but they remained. Tshombe admitted 'he had no real control of what was going on' and 'it would be suicide for him' to ask for the removal of the roadblocks.[14]

On U Thant's instructions ONUC battalions due to be repatriated remained in Elisabethville until their replacements had deployed. The Secretary General feared that a reduction in ONUC strength 'may precipitate further bloodshed' and stressed that his instruction was 'solely to meet defensive needs'.[15] His instructions had implications for the remaining elements of the 35th Irish Battalion.[16] The rainy season had arrived in Elisabethville and 'rain was falling in an almost solid vertical sheet'.[17] The 35th Battalion's base at Leopold Farm was 'a mud bath [and] the slit trenches we had dug for camp defence were full of water. It was pretty miserable all round but despite it all, morale was high.' The men expected that they 'would go ahead, pack our kits, and be ready to do all we could to help the relieving 36th Battalion adapt to difficult conditions and we would be home for Christmas'.[18]

The 36th Battalion: 'Good luck and the best I can wish you is peace'[19]

Meanwhile in Dublin the 650 officers and men of the 36th Battalion assembled at McKee Barracks under the command of Lt Col. Michael Hogan. The request to send a battalion to succeed the 35th had arrived in Dublin in October and saw Lemass take a strong line with Aiken. Lemass told Aiken that Ireland could not take any course 'which could be represented as implying a change of mind, or lessening of enthusiasm on our part, about the UN's Congo operation'.[20] But since the fighting in September Irish public opinion had become 'very sensitive about this whole Congo business, and any further fighting there would certainly lead to more vocal demands for our withdrawal, which would be very damaging to national prestige and morale'. It was an unusually strong line for Lemass on a foreign policy issue and indicated his input into United Nations policy-making at critical moments. It also showed a greater-than-usual concern for the impact of public opinion on foreign policy. Lemass' suggested alternatives ranged from replacing the 35th Battalion without making comment; sending a further battalion plus specialist contingents; limiting future ONUC contributions to specialist personnel only; or sending a further battalion and telling the UN that it would not be replaced. Lemass asked Aiken to give these options 'very careful consideration' and left the Minister for External Affairs in no doubt that his preferred option was 'to continue to show our full support by contributing to the UN force but not sending a full battalion of line troops to replace the 35th'.

The cabinet decision on the 36th Battalion was surprising. Lemass did not get his way. The cabinet agreed to send a full replacement battalion, make immediately available eight light anti-aircraft guns plus crews and ammunition and, and here the real surprise lay, the replacement battalion 'should be equipped with such support weapons as the Supreme Commander of the United Nations' Force might consider necessary for their own defence'.[21] MacEoin was, by cabinet decision, being given control over the armament of the 36th Battalion. Aiken felt it would be best not to tell the UN that Ireland was willing to deploy a further battalion until the release of the men captured during the September fighting. Only on their release would Dublin inform New York that the 36th Battalion would be available to ONUC.

36th Irish Battalion – ONUC
Battalion OC: Lt Col. Michael Hogan
Second-in-Command: Comdt Timothy Ryan
Operations Officer: Comdt James Griffin
Adjutant: Comdt James Beary
Quartermaster: Comdt Cornelius Donovan
Intelligence Officer: Comdt Michael Harrison
Legal Officer: Comdt Seamus Connolly
Air Liaison Officer: Comdt Desmond Knowles Johnson
Assistant Operations Officer: Capt. James Fagan
O/C Headquarters Company: Comdt John Foran
O/C A-Company: Comdt Joseph Fitzpatrick
O/C B-Company: Comdt William Callaghan
O/C C-Company: Comdt Dermot Hurley
O/C Armoured Car Group: Comdt John Larkin

Table 12. 36th Battalion – key post holders

ONUC initially proposed sending the 36th Battalion to north Katanga and its armoured car group to Elisabethville. The battalion's advance party of 19 officers and 31 men left Dublin on 18 November commanded by 36th Battalion second-in-command, Comdt Timothy Ryan. Ryan had served with the 32nd Battalion and like many of the 36th Battalion was an ONUC veteran. The 36th took more jeeps with them than their predecessors and were issued with recoilless rifles. They were also issued with tropical uniforms in advance of departure and, in a sign of what was to await them in Katanga, with steel helmets. Only on 6 December did the advance party learn that the entire battalion was to deploy to Elisabethville. By then no one doubted that further hostilities in Katanga were imminent.

Brigadier Raja takes control

Late on 4 December Raja took a critical decision. Sensing an imminent Katangese attack he signalled to Linner, MacEoin and the commander of UN air assets in Katanga that ONUC 'may have to strike early 5 Dec. if situation continues to deteriorate ... request fighters stand by to strike Kolwezi and also local targets if practicable'.[22] After three days of provocation Raja was poised to take action to restore ONUC freedom of movement across Elisabethville, regarding Katanga as having broken the September ceasefire. 35th Battalion soldiers in Elisabethville 'knew that a combined effort by UN forces in the city would clear the main road to the airport. It would involve more fighting but we knew at this stage that we could fight if fighting became necessary. We knew we could fight as well as the Swedes and the Indians and, combined with them, we could hammer the Gendarmerie.'[23]

At midday on 5 December Urquhart announced that the position of ONUC troops could not be further eroded by Katangese actions. The roadblocks would be cleared by military means and Urquhart handed control to Raja. Raja explained that 'I shall do what I am here to do. I have come to maintain peace as far as it is possible, but if I am ordered by the United Nations to take action I shall do so to the best of my ability'.[24] He would swiftly put his words into action. Backing Raja, Nehru emphasized that Tshombe was 'a rebel who should speedily be brought to book', 'swift and effective action' was needed to end the secession of Katanga for the good of Congo.[25]

In New York there was 'great concern about the deteriorating situation ... any incident might spark off a serious conflict'.[26] Linner was 'determined to carry out an operation by force designed to put an end to resistance in Katanga and avenge Hammarskjöld's death.'[27] ONUC did not intend to launch a general offensive against Katanga; U Thant explained that he conveyed 'authority to the United Nations Military to use within their own sphere all necessary force to attain their objectives i.e. to defend themselves and restore their freedom of communication'; adding that the UN 'must retaliate for reasons of self-defence'.[28] Despite U Thant's spin, it was clear that Raja had been 'given a free hand' by the Secretary General and 'the idea of a second round following their humiliation in September' had never been far from the minds of ONUC commanders.[29]

Raja had his plan ready. On the morning of 5 December, Capt. Art Magennis received orders from 35th Battalion Operations Officer Comdt Kane to take a section of armoured cars and report immediately to Sector-B Headquarters to join

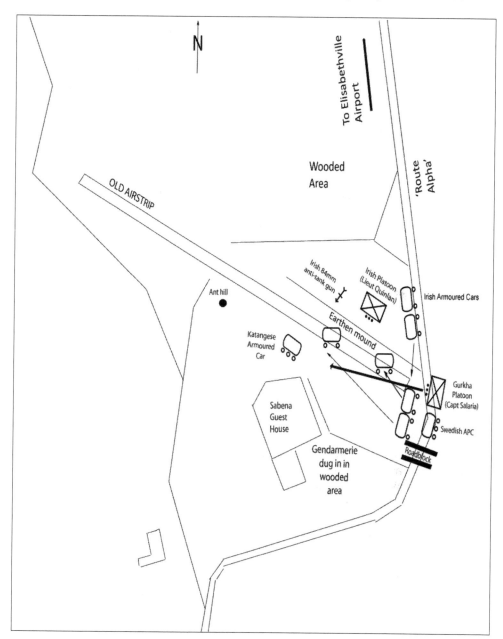

5 Roadblock battle, 5 December 1961

an Indian detachment. Kane added 'you will learn what the task is at Sector-B'.[30] He had no advice about the type or quantity of ammunition required for what lay ahead. Leaving Kane, Magennis met Lt Tom Quinlan, a platoon commander in A-Company. Quinlan's platoon was to join Magennis' section and was waiting assembled in four jeeps. Indicating what they felt lay ahead, they carried two 84mm anti-tank guns with high-explosive and armour-piercing ammunition.

On arrival at Sector-B Headquarters Quinlan and Magennis met Comdt Sean Barrett, Sector-B Operations Officer, who introduced a young Gurkha officer, Capt. Gurbachan Singh Salaria, and outlined their mission. Raja had ordered that the road between the city and the airport be opened. A company of Gurkhas would attack the Avenue Saio roadblock from the south while a smaller Irish–Indian force under Salaria's command attacked from the north. Barrett took Magennis aside and explained that Salaria had been placed in command by Raja against Sector-B's wishes. Sector-B had wanted Magennis, who was senior to Salaria, to lead the combined force, but Raja said no, 'it will be commanded by Salaria because it will be a Gurkha operation'.[31] Salaria's column would report to Dogra Headquarters at Elisabethville airport before midday and prepare to advance along the airport road to support the Gurkha attack to the south. Salaria's orders to move came shortly before midday, just as Urquhart was preparing to hand over to Raja.

Salaria's orders from Dogra HQ were brief: 'move towards Avenue Saio Roundabout to link up with the 3/1 Gurkha Battalion. There is a troop of 4.2-inch mortars based here and available to you.'[32] At midday Salaria's column left the Dogra Camp with Salaria leading in a Swedish APC with his Gurkhas on board, followed by a Swedish-crewed Jeep with an anti-tank gun, Quinlan's platoon and Magennis' Ford armoured cars brought up the rear. It was two miles to the Gendarmerie roadblock. At 1230, one mile into the trip, the column halted at a second roadblock near the old airstrip and came under heavy anti-tank and small arms fire from a concealed Katangese position on the right flank in a wooded area by the Sabena Guest House. The Gurkhas took cover in roadside drainage ditches and alongside them Magennis conferred with Salaria about the next move. Salaria was awaiting orders and Magennis used the hiatus to deploy Quinlan's platoon along the roadside, sections to the right, left and rear.[33] A private from the section to the right sighted a camouflaged Gendarmerie armoured car hidden in the bush on the perimeter of the old airstrip. Magennis instructed that an 84mm anti-tank gun be readied to engage the vehicle. As he was relaying the armoured car's location to Salaria it opened fire, missing the Swedish APC leading the UN column. An Irish 84mm opened fire and two hits were observed on the Katangese vehicle.[34] Heavy automatic fire followed from Gendarmerie positions on both sides of the road. Quinlan and his men cleared isolated Gendarmerie positions on the left side of the roadblock, but Sgt Walter Hegarty reported a strong Gendarmerie machine-gun position on the right flank.

Meanwhile to the south the second, larger, Gurkha force 'stormed the Katangese road-blocks on the road to the city and the airport and destroyed the main Katangese position in 45 minutes'.[35] There was heavy fighting; 'the Katangese fought well at first and died where they stood ... but later others were shot whilst fleeing'.[36] By 1430 UN troops had 'infiltrated round the road blocks' and small-scale firing and mortar shelling began. The UN 'quickly secured control of [the] roundabout and removed [the] road-blocks'.[37] That was the official version. In fact Salaria's column had run into an unexpectedly strong Katangese position. What happened next was more chaotic than the official UN report suggested.

At 1400 Salaria ordered the two Irish armoured cars to replace the Swedish APC at the head of the column as the Swedish vehicle's guns were faulty. He planned to soften up the Gendarmerie with a bombardment from Indian mortars and the Irish anti-tank guns. Then, supported by covering fire from the two Irish armoured cars and Quinlan's platoon, he would lead his troops forward on foot to attack the dug-in Gendarmerie. Magennis suggested that Salaria use the Swedish APC to transport his Gurkhas across the exposed ground between the roadblock and the Gendarmerie position. A head-on attack on foot against a well dug-in enemy would lead to many casualties, but Salaria disagreed, replying 'no, I have to exercise these men'.[38] It was a fatal decision.

At 1430 the Indian mortars commenced firing, and at 1500 Salaria brought his Gurkhas across the open ground towards the Gendarmerie. Moving in line but bunched too closely, they covered about 400m, halted and went to ground. The Gendarmerie were resisting strongly. Trying to work out what had happened, Magennis moved up the roadside trench to the assault start line. He learned from a Gurkha corporal that Salaria and his men had been enfiladed by Gendarmerie fire. With bayonets, khukris and grenades they had charged the Katangese position, which was occupied by over 100 paracommandos and the Katangese had scattered. Ivan Smith described Salaria's assault as 'one of the most gallant actions yet undertaken in the Congo'.[39] Gallant perhaps, but Salaria was dead and seven of his sixteen men were wounded.[40] Covered by Irish armoured cars Magennis moved forward to Salaria's position. Shooting had stopped except for cover fire from the Irish vehicles and desultory Katangese bursts. Aware he was now in command, Magennis called for medical teams to assist the wounded. There were none. Using first aid kits from the Irish armoured cars and the Swedish APC, three seriously wounded were tended to where they lay. Irish armoured car crews removed the dead and injured. Magennis realized that the remaining Gurkhas had little or no English and he had also lost contact with the Indian group moving north from Avenue Saio. Attempts to obtain mortar fire from the Indians failed due to the lack of a common language.

It was close to 1600, with only two hours of daylight remaining. The arrival of Lt Quinlan brought significant support to Magennis. Quinlan had fought at Jadotville with A-Company and had considerable combat experience; Magennis was glad to have him close by. They got in touch by radio with 35th Battalion Headquarters who replied that Sector-B radio intercepts indicated that they faced a 150-strong Katangese force, which was exaggerating the strength of the UN attack and was seeking reinforcements. Magennis decided to have another go at the Katangese before night fell and planned a further mortaring of their position followed by an infantry assault by Quinlan's platoon with the Gurkhas and the Irish armoured cars providing supporting fire. When ordered to relocate, the Gurkhas refused to fight without their captain and Magennis had them removed. The operation moved on without them. Sgt Hegarty reported that he had cleared the remaining problematic Gendarmerie machine-gun position and 'thanks to Tom Quinlan and Sgt Hegarty', Magennis later wrote, 'I was getting things organized'.[41] At 1730 the UN force prepared to attack. The situation quickly changed as Capt. Seán Hennessey arrived and explained that the airport road was opened from the south. This was confirmed when Raja's liaison officer, Capt. Pandit, arrived with orders that all offensive action cease. The Gurkhas advancing from the south had almost reached the old airstrip and the area held by Magennis' column was to be evacuated at 1900. A second assault was unnecessary and Raja planned to insert Indian troops into the area at daylight. By removing the roadblock Raja had shown that ONUC was prepared to act vigorously against Katangese provocation.

The build up to Operation Unokat

Reacting to the fighting on the airport road Kimba promised that he and his ministers would die at their posts. Mercenary-led Katangese forces attacked UN Headquarters in Elisabethville and began sniping at Irish forces at Leopold Farm and the nearby Swedish Camp, engaging the UN 'with considerable determination'.[42] ONUC admitted that the Katangese were tenaciously holding their own. Their morale was good and about 600 Gendarmerie led by European officers bore the brunt of the fighting. Arriving back in Katanga on 7 December, Tshombe declared that 'as long as the UN continues to attack us, we will fight back. The battle goes on.'[43]

ONUC could now easily suppress any Katangese attack and was prepared to do so. After a Katangese aircraft bombed Elisabethville airport, United Nations aircraft made their first strikes against the airfields at Kolwezi and Jadotville and attacked Lufira Bridge. Swedish forces fired on Radio Katanga in an attempt to silence Katangese propaganda broadcasts. ONUC felt they had 'consolidated their positions in the main parts of the city'.[44] The mercenaries, still convinced that they could beat the UN, had miscalculated and enabled a better-armed UN force legitimately to take extensive action in self-defence under existing UN resolutions. Had the mercenaries held off it would have been difficult for the UN to engage them so forcefully.[45]

Further increasing the UN's military capability in Elisabethville, Raja flew Irish, Indian, Swedish and Ethiopian reinforcements directly to the city. Leading elements of the 36th Battalion arrived on 7 December having flown for twenty-two hours 'in the full knowledge that hostilities were inevitable'.[46] An aircraft carrying two officers and forty-four men from A-Company approached Elisabethville airport in broad daylight in torrential rain and 'what a reception that aircraft got! As it entered the south city airspace at very low altitude rifle fire commenced and continued as the aircraft decreased altitude and airspeed. The plane landed without casualties despite a number of hits.'[47] It took forty hits and landed with a trail of petrol vapour streaming behind. The crew considered it 'miraculous that the aircraft did not take fire in the air'.[48] They added that 'landing in Eville airport "wasn't just war but suicide".'

MacEoin reacted by issuing strict instructions that ONUC troops fly into Elisabethville under fighter cover and Katanga Command was to vigorously defend the approach paths of incoming aircraft. He chastized Raja that the 'complete reinforcement plan [was] being jeopardized by your inability to neutralize approach of transport aircraft' and instructed that 'strong patrols must be sent out along direction of fly-in. Mortars must also be used to neutralize likely areas from which fire may come. Cutting tight around airfield not sufficient.' The Indian defence of Elisabethville airport was not watertight and might 'prejudice the whole reinforcement programme and may in fact cause the USAF to withdraw from the operation.'[49] The message was seen in Elisabethville; handwritten on it is 'no reply'. Despite the attack the United States Air Force continued, after a short hiatus, to airlift the 36th Battalion into Elisabethville.

After deploying under fire in combat formation at Elisabethville airport, the 36th Battalion was harassed by snipers on its way to its base at Leopold Farm. Advance units, including Battalion OC Lt Col. Hogan, arrived at the Farm as a noisy fire fight broke out. The attack was repulsed by Irish troops in forward trenches, their positions thick with mud and filled waist-deep with water as the rainy season continued.

As further reinforcements arrived in Elisabethville, ONUC became stronger and continued 'their defensive action to secure freedom of movement and to restore law and order'.[50] They aimed to hold their positions in the city and open communication routes between them. Some probing operations were carried out in eastern Elisabethville as mixed Swedish and Irish units pushed the ONUC perimeter closer to The Tunnel under barrage and counter-barrage of mortar fire. Katangese forces east of The Tunnel tried to reach the refugee camp between the Irish and Swedish Camps to provoke an uprising by attacking the refugees. There was an estimated 45,000 Balubas in the camp and it was 'a stiff battle to keep Katangese snipers and bands armed with sub-machine-guns from committing [a] massacre' of the refugees.[51]

On 8 December, Adoula and Linner issued a communiqué reiterating that neither the central government nor the UN wanted to conquer Katanga or to destroy its economy. Strong pressure would be needed to induce Tshombe to negotiate with the UN and Adoula. Washington feared the consequences of Adoula's downfall and was 'prepared to countenance any action to reduce Katanga' as they regarded it 'essential to preserve a moderate government in Leopoldville and to maintain the prestige of the United Nations'.[52] This gave U Thant the American backing ONUC required to exert greater military pressure on Tshombe. In New York there was agreement that the ongoing ONUC operation in Elisabethville 'should now be turned into an action to end once and for all the reign of the mercenaries in Katanga'.[53] While ONUC publicly planned 'to "seal off" Elisabethville' and remove the mercenaries, UN forces saw their action in more robust terms.[54] Waern's 'Operational Instruction No. 7' described their mission as an 'offensive action to destroy Gend resistance in [the] Elisabethville area'.[55]

ONUC had just under eight infantry battalions, twenty armoured car sections, a heavy mortar battery, supporting arms and air power in Elisabethville. Raja planned to use these troops to '"clean up" Elisabethville, i.e. establish complete control'.[56] In preparation he divided his force into a two-brigade division, creating an Irish–Swedish brigade and an Indo–Ethiopian brigade. Journalists in Elisabethville expected the military situation 'to develop swiftly and favourably' for the UN and the early days of the coming week 'will probably be decisive'.[57] This time there would be no stalemate or ceasefire. Boland was worried that 'as happened before, UN Headquarters and the UN military and civil representatives in the Congo may not be completely ad idem as regards the future development of the Congo operation', though he hoped that the presence of Bunche in Leopoldville would help 'eliminate any divergence of policy, or the interpretation of policy, which may exist'.[58] On the contrary, telexes from UN civilian representatives in Elisabethville to Linner in Leopoldville show that they were as determined as Raja to bring matters to a conclusion. MacEoin expected that the UN could 'restore law and order "in a matter of days".'[59]

Commander: Brigadier K.A.S. Raja	
1 Brigade (Col. Waern) East Elisabethville (excluding the Airport)	**2 Brigade (Lt Col. Hazari)** West Elisabethville
35th Irish (minus)	1 Dogra
36th Irish	3/1 Gurkha Rifles
12th Swedish	35th Ethiopian
14th Swedish	8th Ethiopian
Irish armoured cars and six Swedish APCs	Malayan armoured cars, six Swedish APCs

Table 13. ONUC forces in Elisabethville for Operation Unokat

Indian UN aircraft attacked Elisabethville Post Office and Swedish UN aircraft knocked out Radio Katanga. Outside the city UN aircraft strafed Katangese convoys moving towards Elisabethville. Elisabethville had become 'a witches' cauldron of rival charges, counter charges and suspicions' as mortar rounds from each side hit hospitals, schools and houses, and civilians were killed.[60] The UN wished to stop the 'reckless mercenaries' who 'decided to pull the house in while there was still a desperate chance'.[61] Ivan Smith reported that Katangese forces, once driven out of strong military positions, moved into 'red cross centres, schools, or other locations likely to be useful for subsequent propaganda purposes. Therefore take with many grains of salt [word missing?] you may hear about attacks on such seemingly innocent locations.' He added, but not for publication, that he and Raja in the first convoy along the newly opened airport road were ambushed by troops 'signalled into action by a car carrying a Red Cross flag'.[62] MacEoin hit out at the 'foreigners who were waging a "dirty war" and appeared to have political leadership' over Tshombe who had lost control of his troops.[63]

ONUC intercepts suggested a major Katangese attack on the Irish and Swedish camps in eastern Elisabethville on 9 December. Linner told U Thant that Raja was 'absolutely confident about our defences but he warns that losses of attackers will be very heavy'.[64] Swedish and Irish mortars continued attacking Katangese locations around The Tunnel. This weakened Gendarmerie resolve and the expected attack did not materialize. But the night of 9–10 December was 'a nightmare for everybody in 35th and 36th Battalion HQ' as through heavy rain Gendarmerie mortars and machine-guns kept continuous fire on the Irish Camp.[65] Eye-witnesses described it as the heaviest shelling the city had yet seen.

Sector-B now ordered the remaining sections of the 35th Battalion to relocate to Rousseau Farm, three miles northeast of Elisabethville, to ensure that the six-mile-long Route Charlie was clear of Katangese road blocks. It was a muddy bush track but was often the only route between the Swedish and Irish camps and the airport. At Rousseau Farm the battalion found 'complete isolation from everything – no light, only candles, no drinking water except what could be bought from the shop located at the eastern end of Route Charlie; a limited supply of buckets to collect water from roofs for washing. Nothing in plenty except rain that continued to fall in waterfall dimensions, only tentage for cover from the rain – wet, wet, wet everywhere'.[66] The only noise was from rain and 'the distant thump of mortar fire and airplanes attacking enemy positions in Elisabethville. The quietness made everything comfortable, no matter how uncomfortable it was'.[67] Some were said to have slept for over thirty hours during their first days at Rousseau Farm.

Meanwhile, on the afternoon of 10 December in an assault preceded by an air strike on Camp Massart to neutralize mortar fire, an Irish–Swedish force advanced further towards The Tunnel. To clarify the purpose of the UN action in Elisabethville U Thant made, with United States support, what the Department of External Affairs called 'a most important statement'.[68] He explained that the UN operation did not aim to force a political solution on Tshombe by smashing the Gendarmerie, nor had UN officials on the ground been given a free hand. The UN reacted 'only when it became obvious that there was no use in continued negotiations'. The purpose of the ongoing operation was 'to regain and to assure our freedom of movement, to restore law and order … and meanwhile to react vigorously in self-defence … by all means available to us'. ONUC would pursue its operations until these ends were achieved and then the UN would implement the November resolution 'without let or hindrance from any source'. Discussing this with Aiken and Boland, U Thant added that it had been said that he was inclined to favour force as a means of rebutting the charge that, as a Buddhist, he would not be a sufficiently firm Secretary-General. The suggestion was wrong, of course. The UN position in Katanga would have to be sustained by force, if necessary, within the terms of the Security Council resolutions. It was his personal conviction, however, that only negotiation and conciliation could provide a final solution.[69]

Aiken was similarly 'convinced that force was no solution for the Katanga problem'.[70] He pressed U Thant for 'vigorous conciliatory efforts and for negotiations to prevent major fighting in Katanga'.[71]

From Elisabethville an exasperated Ivan Smith explained that the 'very simple way to end the bloodshed … is for the white population to stop sniping and round up the mercenaries who started all this'.[72] He thought the main body of mercenaries 'could scarcely be called the brains behind operation'; they represented a 'pathetic group of psychotics who exploit one point of human misery after another'. Leading them was a small group of French ex-OAS personnel, a well-trained 'highly organized band of fanatics' who had 'almost certainly encouraged' several of members of Tshombe's government to 'provoke a trial of strength at this time before it is too late to avoid implementation of SECCO resolution'.[73] They could only be countered militarily.

ONUC was still operating around the fringes of the city. Gurkhas were beginning to counter mortar units who had attacked Katanga Command Headquarters and were 'mopping up many houses on [the] main route to [the] airport where mercenaries are directing groups of snipers and bazookas against ONUC convoys'.[74] The Ethiopians consolidated around the old airstrip and Sabena Guest House, this latter being a 'well known mercenary gathering point'.[75] They also took the New Hospital, the tallest building in Elisabethville and an observation point for the Gendarmerie, as it dominated the airport road. Mobile Katangese mortar units moved on to the stadium area close to where refugees were gathered. It was, Ivan Smith reported to Linner, 'yet another example of Katangese use of civilians as [a] shield',[76] On the eastern side of the city Irish and Swedish forces remained in contact with Katangese forces attacking the Refugee Camp. To the northeast under the command of Comdt Pat Quinlan A-Company, 35th Battalion advanced on a roadblock set up by Katangese forces in an attempt to cut off Sector-B from Katanga Command HQ. In a commando raid A-Company destroyed two of the three Socopetrol oil tanks on Avenue Usoke used by the Katangese as a fuel dump.

Operation Unokat

Washington's support for ONUC caused a rift in Anglo-American relations over when to call a ceasefire in Katanga. Britain wanted an immediate ceasefire and the United States a ceasefire only once a Tshombe–Adoula meeting was arranged. London and Washington agreed that France would put pressure on Tshombe to

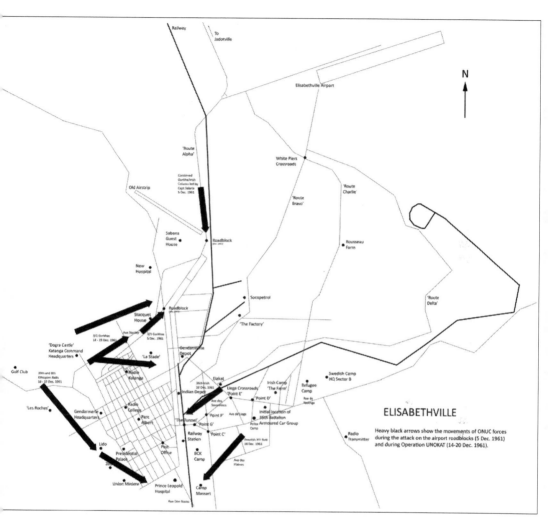

6 Operation Unokat, 14–20 December 1961

meet Adoula. President Kennedy called the American ambassador in Leopoldville, Edmund Gullion, on 13 December to impress on Adoula the importance of early discussions with Tshombe and at the same time to ensure that Bunche understood that the UN having achieved its minimum objectives in Elisabethville should conclude its military operations once Adoula and Tshombe entered talks.

Tshombe realized by mid-December that the Gendarmerie could not defeat a strengthened ONUC in Elisabethville and that Katangese propaganda no longer could sway world opinion behind his government. Dunnett told Munongo that 'Katanga had not convinced the outside world that it was only fighting in self-defence – the various incidents leading up to the recent events, and finally the road block on the United Nations vital lines of communication to the airport, led many people to think that Katanga had been provocative'.[77] Tshombe called on President Kennedy to intervene in Congo, to act as an intermediary and 'as a friendly man and as a Christian to designate a suitable negotiator and to stop at once useless bloodshed'.[78] Washington saw Tshombe as '"an essential part" of any Congo settlement. Now that he was ready to negotiate they had no wish to see him put out of business.'[79] They planned to arrange a meeting between Adoula and Tshombe at the ONUC base at Kitona in Leopoldville province.

While these complex diplomatic moves were taking place, Dunnett saw 'growing evidence' that the UN civilian representatives in Elisabethville had 'little influence on General Raja'.[80] The Indian had his own agenda and Ivan Smith portentously told Linner that, having restored its freedom of movement, the UN would in the coming days 'assist in restoring law and order'.[81] Ivan Smith asked Linner to inform New York that 'our controlled hold operation has been successful and from now on we move more actively to ensure our freedom of movement and clear areas of any continuing offensive against UN forces'.[82] Journalists reported that the UN build-up would be completed in forty-eight hours 'in preparation for a major strike' against the Katangese.[83] By the afternoon of 14 December, ONUC had cleared 'vital lines of communication of Katangese snipers, machine-gunners and mortar detachments' and had ensured 'protection of [the] airport and communication lines to protect reinforcements' arriving in Elisabethville.[84] It had also completed its airlift of reinforcements. MacEoin arrived in Elisabethville for a conference as ONUC prepared to 'take a more active role in securing freedom of movement'.[85] UN intercepts indicated that Gendarmerie morale was flagging and 'there would be little fight left in them if it were not for about a hundred mercenaries'.[86] An all-out military initiative by ONUC against Katanga appeared imminent. It was 'impossible to make a frontal attack on the town' to dislodge the Gendarmerie because it would cause heavy damage to property and loss of civilian lives.[87] Instead Raja decided to move around Elisabethville, eliminating Katangese positions on the edges and establishing control around the perimeter. With a division of infantry, heavy mortars and armoured cars at its disposal and with air superiority, ONUC could easily engage the estimated Katangese force of just over three battalions plus a mobile mortar group.

At 1700 on 14 December Katanga Command issued 'UNOKAT OP ORDER No 1', outlining a two-phase operation to lock down Elisabethville. It was to implement the 'overall Katanga Command plan for [the] destruction of Gendarmerie in [the] Elisabethville area'.[88] In phase one the Indians and Ethiopians would surround Elisabethville in the north and west, and in phase two the Irish and Swedish would assault the east of the city.

Phase one would begin at 2000 local time on 14 December as the 3/1 Gurkha Rifles secured positions east from Katanga Command Headquarters to the Avenue Saio roundabout. They would drive an estimated three companies of Gendarmerie plus one mobile group out of the surrounding areas. Concurrently Irish and Swedish forces would keep constant pressure on the Tunnel area, engaging an estimated Gendarmerie force of two companies plus. The first phase of UNOKAT would give the UN control of northern Elisabethville and maintain free communications between Katanga Command HQ and Elisabethville airport while pinning down Gendarmerie in the east of the city.

Phase two would commence on the morning of 16 December at 0400 with the Ethiopian 35th Battalion taking the Lido area to the west of the city close to Tshombe's palace, cutting off the road to Kipushi and the Rhodesian border. Meanwhile, Irish and Swedish forces would simultaneously attack Camp Massart and The Tunnel, and isolate the approaches into Elisabethville from the Kenya and Katuba townships. The Irish would capture the Tunnel area and the Swedish Rue Don Bosco and Katuba Road 'in order to assist in sealing off Elisabethville City preparatory to the destruction of enemy resistance'.[89]

UNOKAT would be nothing like the badly planned Operation Morthor. This time the UN would use its strength of numbers to isolate Elisabethville and cut off the Gendarmerie. There would be no next round, as Linner explained to U Thant, 'the UN did not start this battle and [it] cannot finish it only to find another attack upon ONUC being prepared'.[90] ONUC expected to be in control of Elisabethville within twenty-four hours. Others were not so positive. Dunnett reported that Tshombe had left the city and the mercenaries were preparing for the long-term harassment of ONUC. He feared that both ONUC and the Katangese would lose control of the city to the mercenaries. Linner told U Thant that Elisabethville was in an 'an anarchical state inflamed by fear, mercenaries and misguided infuriated European population'.[91]

UNOKAT began on the night of 14 December as 'after bitter fighting' the Gurkhas, supported by heavy mortars and Indian armoured cars, cleared Katangese forces in the north of the city from Avenue Stanley, Avenue Leplac and Avenue Churchill to the Stadium and Theatre areas.[92] UN forces also took without opposition the high ground of the golf course area west of UN Headquarters from where mortar fire had been directed at UN Headquarters. Across Elisabethville there was 'much Katangese military movement and haphazard firing in [the] town which caused some casualties'.[93] A message from MacEoin broadcast in Swahili, Lingala and French explained that the UN wished only to restore law and order and regain freedom of movement.

At 0400 on 16 December phase two of UNOKAT began as Ethiopian, Swedish and Irish battalions moved against three strategic points in Elisabethville that had been the origins of Katangese attacks on ONUC or which had been used to impede ONUC movement in the city. These were the Lido area in the west of the city, The Tunnel in the east and the Gendarmerie base to the south of The Tunnel at Camp Massart.

The Ethiopian 35th Battalion moved through the night into the bushlands on the western outskirts of Elisabethville and captured the Lido Hotel, before moving south to take the road leading to Kipushi and the Rhodesian frontier. They came under heavy continuous fire and were engaged by Katangese mortars from the Union Minière site south of the Lido. The Ethiopians suffered 6 killed and 4 wounded. The following day UN Sabre and Canberra aircraft attacked with cannon and rockets Katangese positions around the Lido and Union Minière.

Wishing to expand UN control in eastern Elisabethville Raja ordered the Swedes and Irish to move west as the second phase of UNOKAT began. Lt Col. Hogan received orders on the afternoon of 15 December that at 0400 on 16 December, with Indian mortar support, the 36th Battalion would attack The Tunnel. Simultaneously the Swedish 14th Battalion would attack Camp Massart. At 2100 on 15 December Hogan issued his orders to the 36th Battalion for the assault on The Tunnel, codenamed Operation Sarsfield.[94] A-Company and B-Company, with C-Company in reserve, faced three Katangese companies at The Tunnel. The main arterial link between east and west Elisabethville and between Sector-B and Katanga Command, it had 'long been regarded as one of the most difficult places to assault ... a traffic underpass surrounded by high buildings all of which occupied by Katangese could bring devastating fire upon any opposing force.'[95] Operation Sarsfield was made more difficult because the maps provided gave no indication of the terrain or buildings nearby, nor were aerial photographs provided. As a result company and platoon commanders were 'completely in the dark re the surroundings of the objective area'.[96]

Operation Sarsfield is of great significance as it remains the only time in the history of the Defence Forces that they placed a full battalion in attack. The operation began in trying conditions as before dawn on 16 December the 36th Battalion moved towards The Tunnel in a 'solid downpour of tropical rain'.[97] Transport for the operation was poor. A-Company and B-Company and the battalion Tactical HQ were transported in eleven vehicles, six of which were 'so unroadworthy that if a Transport Officer allowed them on the road in Ireland he would be charged on the spot'.[98] There was no reserve transport to bring C-Company quickly from Leopold Farm to The Tunnel and they had a 2km march ahead of them if they were required.

The 36th Battalion approached The Tunnel from several directions. One group crawled along nearby railway track to a point crossing The Tunnel, another group came by foot along Avenue des Savonniers to provide covering fire about 300 yards from the tunnel. B-Company was to secure a triangle of land in front of the eastern side of The Tunnel as A-Company moved along the railway to the north to seize and hold the track over The Tunnel. Both companies had Irish and Indian mortar support. B-Company with a section of armoured cars moved forward at 0400 and despite coming under Katangese mortar fire secured its objective by 0500. The final assault on The Tunnel by A-Company commenced at 0525 on Hogan's instruction from 36th Battalion TAC HQ. At 0545 A-Company was pinned down by Katangese mortar fire, which was ultimately neutralized by A-Company in conjunction with support from Indian 120mm heavy mortars. A-Company made its final assault at 0600 hours local time, during which Lt Patrick Riordan was killed along with his radio operator Pte Andy

Wickham. Though held up by two strong points, which were destroyed by 84mm recoilless rifle fire, The Tunnel was in A-Company hands by 0630.[99] It had been a difficult operation. Platoon commanders found it hard to get men moving after they had been fired on at close range, as they tended to remain in cover to return fire, and men tended to bunch together rather than disperse when moving. The 36th Battalion's Unit History put the success of the operation on 'the initiative, energy and determination of junior leaders in applying the Company Commander's plan'.[1]

As The Tunnel was cleared there was a sharp engagement to the south between the Swedes and Gendarmerie at Camp Massart. The Swedish 14th Battalion – two companies in attack and one in reserve – moved at first light to assault the Gendarmerie base, a location roughly a mile by half a mile in area. They came under heavy machine-gun fire from the camp and its approaches and from local civilian buildings belonging to BCK, the Katangese Railway Company. The ground they crossed was so thick with mud from the torrential rain that they abandoned their vehicles at the River Kampemba about 1,000 yards from Camp Massart and went forward on foot under their own covering fire. The Swedes entered Camp Massart at 1030 through a direct assault and came under a strong counterattack by mercenary-led Gendarmerie. Early afternoon saw hand-to-hand fighting with the Swedes facing at least three Katangese Companies. But by dusk Camp Massart was in UN hands, the Swedes having suffered five wounded.

Meanwhile the Gurkhas moved further down Avenue Churchill to reach the Athenée School and the Ethiopians had moved south east from the Lido to the Zoo and towards Camp Massart to close the ring around the city. During the night of 16–17 December the Gurkhas strengthened their hold across the north of Elisabethville, the 8th Ethiopian Battalion held the northwest and west of the city and the 35th Ethiopian Battalion were consolidating their hold in the southwest, though it would take them two more days to take the Union Minière district. The Swedish 14th Battalion held the railway station and the BCK camp and planned to move west from Camp Massart to link with the Ethiopians to the west at Union Minière. Most of these UN units were spread thinly and only the 36th Irish Battalion was concentrated 'with the task of dominating their immediate area' – at The Tunnel itself and in an area to the east of The Tunnel where they linked with the Swedes to the south.[2] On paper this looked like the complete UN encirclement of Elisabethville, but in reality it 'was not completely successful and [the] enemy continued to have routes to and from the City'.[3]

'Militarily Katanga is run by the Indians', wrote British ambassador Riches, and under their command the 'United Nations force is out to win and will do eventually, in [the] town of Elisabethville. I get the clear impression that this operation has passed from internal security to virtually total war and that this is the wish of most of the troops involved.'[4] It had not been a completely trouble-free and smoothly run operation and there were problems of command and control between the forces making up ONUC. In a strongly worded memorandum to MacEoin, Major Mide requested the 'movement of the

Swedish contingent from this theatre to Kamina Base' because of 'too great [a] difference in fighting spirit, military education and conception between participating units'.[5] He explained what he saw as the 'complete lack of co-ordination of different units' operations aiming for the same targets', illustrating this with how the Irish–Swedish brigade attempting to surround central Elisabethville on 16 December had not initially been successful in its task and had fought without assistance from the Indians and Ethiopians for ten hours. The upcoming repatriation of the main body of the 12th Swedish Battalion would leave it at insufficient strength to defend Camp Massart, the Refugee Camp and its own camp area in addition to 'expected demands for offensive activity'. In addition the 14th Swedish Battalion was 'not organized and equipped for expected mobile operations which require sufficient vehicle-equipment and heavy support weapons such as tanks, heavy mortars, mines, tents, etc..' Mide's memorandum concluded that the Swedish battalion was 'ready to participate in any operations which are within its ability and strength but so far a proper assessment of our limitation has not been made by the higher command'. UNOKAT had succeeded less by strategic and tactical outcomes than by sheer weight of numbers and power of equipment against a less well-armed and numerically smaller and more poorly trained adversary.

The Kitona talks

By 17 December, ONUC controlled Elisabethville. The Swedes held Camp Massart and the Irish held The Tunnel. The 36th Battalion found that while the Gendarmerie were better armed than previously, two factors that assisted the battalion in its operations were 'that the enemy did not stand and fight to the last round and that, although he could have dug in extensively with great facility he did not do so as a matter of course'.[6] The battalion's Unit History added that 'the Gendarmerie while they may be organized to attack have never yet pushed an attack to the assault stage'. Katangese resistance had been tougher than expected. There had been fierce fighting at UN Headquarters in the west of the city and Andrew Wilson from the Observer saw how 'White-painted UN lorries lay upturned on the road. Jeeps and landrovers and in one place a UN helicopter were smashed and twisted by mortar fire.'[7] It was, he felt, 'a testament to the ferocity of the Katangese attack' and was not the work of Tshombe's troops but 'bore the stamp of a European directorate more organized and fanatical than even the UN itself can ever have suspected'. Some fighting continued in the west of the city where the UN attack had not attained all its objectives and Ethiopian forces near the Lido remained under attack from Union Minière.

U Thant met representatives of the countries contributing to ONUC to tell them that 'all UN objectives in Elisabethville would be achieved' by 18 December.[8] He was awaiting a cable from MacEoin confirming this and on its receipt, and with confirmation of Tshombe's departure to meet Adoula, UN forces in Elisabethville would hold fire except in self-defence. The Ethiopian and Nigerian representatives were dubious, but Boland, the Indian and Tunisian representatives agreed with this as they realised that rather than take over Elisabethville the UN wished to use UNOKAT as a way to edge Tshombe into negotiations. If ONUC captured Elisabethville the chances were that Tshombe and his cabinet would retreat to Rhodesia. Thus the threat of a UN takeover was judged to have more power than a takeover to persuade Tshombe to negotiate. Hoskyns made the valid point that

> the insistence that negotiations should be carried on between Tshombe and Adoula rather than between Tshombe and the Organisation, together with the threat (which was surely implicit) that if Tshombe refused to agree to Adoula's terms, the fighting would continue, obviously came close to an imposition of a political solution by force.[9]

Washington favoured a de facto ceasefire under the guise of rest and regrouping and the UN accepted this. Hoskyns added that this attitude underlined that U Thant was less concerned than Hammarskjöld with legal principles, and more concerned with getting political results. There were political results to report. Tshombe met with Gullion and agreed to meet Adoula at Kitona, but he insisted on a ceasefire first. The UN Congo Advisory Committee and Adoula were both opposed to any ceasefire being called prior to negotiations. U Thant was prepared, and the United States and Britain agreed, that provided all UN objectives in Elisabethville were attained and Tshombe had left for Kitona, UN troops would hold fire for the duration of the Kitona talks. Tshombe departed for Kitona on 18 December. MacEoin hoped 'to finish off and clean up the town within three days' and planned to move to Jadotville and Kolwezi as he believed the Katangese would leave Elisabethville and make their last stand these towns.[10]

MacEoin was 'fully satisfied with the results achieved by the Elisabethville operation thus far' and, though he did not expect prolonged continued Katangese resistance to continue, he was unable to forecast when 'actual hostilities' would end.[11] The main bulk of active Katangese forces remained grouped around the Lido and Union Minière. Early on 20 December the Ethiopian 35th Battalion took the final sections of Union Minière. Elsewhere across Elisabethville scattered Katangese units harassed ONUC by sniping from civilian houses. Each side continued to make accusations of breaches of the order to hold fire. MacEoin stressed in a 19 December press release that ONUC operations had 'been carried on with great restraint in order to protect to the fullest extent possible the innocent civilian population', yet despite this 'there had been some unavoidable suffering brought about largely as the result of the enemy's tactics of using civilian premises as a shield for their offensive operations'.[12]

Katangese and Central government delegations met at Kitona on 20 December. Bunche and Gullion were present, though they were not in the room where the discussions took place and got involved only when the meeting became heated. On 21 December Tshombe signed an eight-point declaration recognizing the indissolubility of Congo. He effectively renounced Katanga's secession and agreed to the application of the Loi Fondamentale throughout the Congo. Tshombe met the British, American and French Consuls on his return to Elisabethville. Uncommunicative about the Kitona talks, he said only that 'we have accepted in principle and it will have to be discussed'.[13] In order to gain time Tshombe planned to refer the Kitona agreement to the Katangese assembly. He expected its rejection and was 'in a bitter and depressed frame of mind'.[14] Tshombe felt the talks had been anything but free negotiations. Adoula, he surmised, was under American instructions to be inflexible as Washington had only Katanga's complete capitulation in mind. Commenting on the aftermath of the Kitona agreement the 36th Battalion Unit History emphasized that 'the main victory for the UN has been the capture, in great part, of world opinion as expressed in the world press. People of influence are now coming to realize Katangese irresponsibility and to accept that the UN is the only stable element here.'[15] As the fighting ended over 200 Katangese military personnel, an unknown number of civilians and 25 ONUC soldiers lay dead.

The situation across Katanga and its capital remained unsettled and, Ivan Smith ruefully reported to New York, 'sadly, it looks like an Eville Christmas in all senses'.[16] At least one third of the European population had departed, there were rising crime levels and civil order was breaking down across the city. ONUC tried to restore order in Elisabethville and troops drove slowly through the city to maintain law and order, distributing leaflets explaining the recent operations. Ivan Smith reported that 'many of the Congolese who read it began to wave'.[17] The 36th Battalion was engaged at refugee camp trying to keep order. Groups of Baluba regularly tried to leave the camp to loot and pillage in residential districts. Irish guards would fire warning shots to dissuade them and ONUC-strengthened patrols by Irish and Swedish units at the Refugee Camp. Unrest in the African communes remained high. Union Minière had ceased operation and 30 per cent of Katanga's copper production was suspended indefinitely. The December fighting deeply affected Dunnett. In a more-than-usually frank and personal despatch he explained that 'It is difficult to convey the sense of tragedy now hanging over Elisabethville. Though I have been here only eight months, six of my circle of friends have been killed in the last ten days, and another is missing. Most of the Europeans living here have had similar or worse experiences. But clearly much worse may still happen.'[18] The UN maintained that its mission in Katanga would 'continue to be dominated by a desire to maintain tranquillity, order and legality',[19] but ONUC soldiers were reported to be 'frankly apprehensive' and feared that 'the whole of the Katanga game is in danger of slipping back to "square one".'[20] Munongo said simply that 'no-one understood what was happening.'[21] It was 'a watchful Xmas' as joint ONUC and local police patrols were increased to discourage looting.[22]

Direct contact between Urquhart and Tshombe was restored and arrangements to send a delegation of nine Katangese senators and deputies to Leopoldville to press for a federal government across Congo proceeded satisfactorily after the UN guaranteed their safety.[23] Some wondered how much

Tshombe knew about what was actually going on, and Dunnett, on meeting the delegation, wondered whether they were aware of the importance of their mission. In Elisabethville, senior ONUC officers were meeting regularly with their Katangese counterparts and the British, French and US consuls acted as couriers between the UN and the Katangese. UN troops managed to keep the refugee camp under control. Within urban Elisabethville the water and electricity supplies were restored, and efforts continued to restore daily life to normal. Outbreaks of violent inter-tribal warfare continued on the outskirts of the city. UN armoured cars patrolled African communes attempting to maintain order, but their patrols seemed to cause general panic. Tshombe and his ministers were 'frightened men' prone to 'exaggerate every topic' and they reflected the attitude of the population of Elisabethville.[24]

Tshombe had capitulated at the Kitona talks, and on 15 February 1962 the Katanga Assembly adopted the Kitona agreement and authorized the government of Katanga to enter into discussions with Leopoldville. On 14 January 1963 Tshombe ended Katanga's secession. It had taken almost a year of negotiations and another round of fighting before Leopoldville had complete control over Katanga, nevertheless from December 1961 this outcome was never in any doubt.

'Deliver us from E-ville'

IN SUMMER 1960, there was optimism that ONUC would become newly independent Congo's guardian and mentor. This optimism had disintegrated by December 1961, demolished by realpolitik and international intrigue. The bitter slog of urban warfare in Elisabethville had shown the blunt realities of peacekeeping. Hammarskjöld's confident step into the unknown in Congo in the cause of peace had been principled and brave. But it was taken without regard for the possible negative consequences for the UN or Congo. Each had been dealt a hard blow. Alongside Congolese civilians and UN peacekeepers Hammarskjöld lay dead. National and international forces with dark desires and malevolent intent triumphed in Congo in a lethal clash between high-minded idealism and the brutal realities of international politics.

In December 1961, the future did not look promising. Congo was in the hands of a weak government, which, in 1965 would give way to the Western-backed dictatorial rule of Mobutu. During his three decades in power Congo would be pillaged much as it had been under Belgian rule. Tshombe's hopes for Katangese independence were also dashed. The province's wealth too would be squandered during Mobutu's rule. If ONUC had given Congo a chance, it had not followed through on the hopes of its idealistic founders. The mission remained in Congo until 1964 but the country was not successfully stabilized. Perhaps ONUC bought Congo time, but if so, this was subsequently squandered.

The only certainty for the newly-independent Congo was that the international powers still circled and coveted its territory and resources according to their strategic interests. Cold War divisions, the plans of newly independent states in Africa (such as Ghana) for regional cohesion, India's desires for hegemony in Africa, and the schemes of the great powers and their allies ensured that Congo remained the scene of a multidimensional international power-struggle. The events of July 1960 to December 1961 did nothing to disentangle that struggle. The powers and colonial interests would return, often by proxy, and remain within the Congolese milieu.

In New York, Hammarskjöld and his colleagues were never fully in command of the situation facing them in Congo. It was one thing to issue an order to ONUC from New York; it was an altogether different matter to put those instructions into operation locally. All the creative skill of preventative diplomacy that Hammarskjöld could muster was incapable of teasing apart the web of Congolese independence and Katangese secession. In Congo and its provinces, the paradigms of international relations did not conform to the complex reality on the ground. Such complexities bred confusion, as was seen in northern Katanga where ONUC, caught between Katangese, Baluba and local Belgian interests, was often unable to accommodate their conflicting agendas. The permanent missions of UN members in New York, the Secretariat, and even states with a diplomatic presence in Leopoldville or Elisabethville, often remained unclear about current events in Congo and Katanga. The day-to-day realities of Congolese and Katangese affairs were often only visible to the ONUC troops on the ground. They saw the realities but were unable to fit them into a larger strategic picture as this was often not available to them. Whatever ONUC forces and their immediate commanders or political masters experienced and anticipated, Congo turned up the unexpected. The Niemba ambush brought home to Irish troops the realities of peacekeeping through the deaths of their comrades.

Hammarskjöld believed he could solve the crises facing Congo. He had succeeded against the odds before and surely the famous 'leave it to Dag' philosophy would bring peace to Congo. His belief in his capabilities seemed infinite, yet Hammarskjöld's papers and internal UN Secretariat documents show a more uncertain Secretary General than that suggested by the internationally accepted picture of Hammarskjöld. They also show an increasing tendency during 1961 for Hammarskjöld to pass the initiative over to his senior officials in Congo and Katanga. This was to prove highly significant in the events leading to Operation Morthor.

Uncertainty, inexperience and prevarication became the defining ethos of ONUC through 1960 and 1961. The UN underestimated the lethal internal politics of the young and failing Congolese state. The UN and ONUC were never close to mastery of the situation facing them in Congo. As long as ONUC did not have to do anything other than maintain a notional thin blue line, it could undertake its vague mandate. But once that mandate was redefined by the February 1961 resolution, and that revised mandate had to be implemented, all changed. The resolution opened the way to allowing ONUC to undertake military action unprecedented for UN peacekeepers. Recourse to force in Katanga was in the air in the Secretariat and in ONUC after February 1961. Hammarskjöld's actions between February and September 1961 show him developing a more belligerent outlook towards Katanga, though he was never completely comfortable with the use of force by ONUC. His authorization of Morthor also shows his devious and calculating side, and his difficulties in coming to terms with putting the revised ONUC mandate into operation. Hammarskjöld's outlook on Congo was based on the views of Linner, Khiari and O'Brien as much as his own views. This small group had long-term aims, but in reality found it difficult to get beyond short-term policies in attempting to obtain a united Congo under a strong central government. As the run-up to Operation Morthor indicated, disjointed confusion, sometimes one suspects the confusion was deliberate, was the reality behind the scenes in New York, Leopoldville and Elisabethville. Hammarskjöld's senior Congo team was divided by differing aims and objectives. The clinical academic thinking of the Secretary General and the brutal realities necessitating ad hoc diplomacy by ONUC officials on the streets of Elisabethville were poles apart. By September 1961 UN thinking on Katanga was fatally disconnected. As a result, senior ONUC officials launched into Morthor a divided body; the mission's strategic leaders had no unity of purpose as to what was to be achieved.

The next steps, vague and murky negotiations and sleight of hand within ONUC and between ONUC and Hammarskjold, brought ONUC to war in Katanga. There is no point in trying to disguise Morthor, and later Unokat, under the misleading term of 'peace enforcement'. 'Peace enforcement' is simply another word for 'war'. ONUC moved onto a war footing in Katanga in the second half of 1961, as those running the operation became overly sure of the political and military strength of their position and failed to estimate the true relative strength of their Katangese adversaries. The result, as the failure of Morthor and the subsequent substantial rearmament of ONUC showed, was that during Morthor, ONUC was ill-prepared to undertake offensive operations with the weapons at its disposal. ONUC had not been envisaged or deployed with offensive operations in mind. After the February 1961 resolution no attempts were made to re-equip the mission with the weapons needed to implement its revised stronger mandate. Only belatedly, after the failure of Morthor, did such an increase in capability, in particular the provision of air power, take place.

That it is more accurate to describe ONUC's experience in September and December 1961 in Katanga as 'war' than 'peacekeeping' has been ignored or played down in many accounts, though recent accounts of A-Company's action at Jadotville place Quinlan and his men fighting a conventional small-unit operation.[1] The actions of the 34th, 35th and 36th Battalions show how ONUC's stance in Elisabethville, from the initial deployment of the 34th Battalion at Elizabethville airport, became increasingly aggressive. The plans developed by Kjellgren, O'Neill and others show they were prepared to take the offensive. Their political counter-parts were working in parallel as Linner's and O'Brien's accounts from July 1961 show. The development of an offensive capacity in Elisabethville was enhanced across ONUC in Katanga by the arrival of the Indian brigade. Raja, believing that he had a job to do in Katanga, amplified this stance. Raja's political colleagues O'Brien, Khiari and Linner agreed with him; at times even Hammarskjold agreed. Here Linner's 3 July 1961 communication to Hammarskjöld that ONUC take over Katanga by force was a significant pointer in the direction ONUC was about to take. ONUC policy, particularly in Elisabethville, had turned to increasingly favour the use of force. Force was permitted by the February resolution and, after the success of Rumpunch, ONUC mistakenly believed that it had the military strength to use this option successfully.

Despite the short-term success of Rumpunch, ONUC, in fact, remained fundamentally incapable of mounting robust action in Katanga. Senior UN military and political figures in New York, Leopoldville and Elisabethville nevertheless maintained a naive and foolhardy belief in their own abilities, and were convinced that Katanga was incapable of fighting back. Operation Rumpunch was a dangerous initiation to ONUC's use of force in Katanga. It had given a false impression of ONUC's abilities and Katanga's likely reactions. Morthor showed that Katanga could, and would, fight back.

ONUC policy from June to September 1961 in Katanga culminating in Morthor was an outright failure. The bleak hurtful truth for Hammarskjöld's supporters was that Hammarskjöld had authorized the operation that led to his death. The exact nature of what he thought he had actually authorized still remains unclear, but it is clear that he authorized ONUC to act. The Secretary General's subsequent careful distancing of himself from Morthor was transformed to become part of the myth of Hammarskjöld after his death. The inconvenient realities of history were neatly covered up. It was the same for many episodes during Operation Morthor. The UN sought to manipulate events to show that, as Morthor began, the Katangese had opened fired first. Interviews with ONUC veterans show that this was not so and that ONUC opened fire first during a synchronized assault across Elisabethville. Indian actions at Radio Katanga in the aftermath of the assault were hardly in the tradition of conventional warfare, let alone the high-minded principles of UN peacekeeping. No reference to the murder of prisoners emerges from UN files, though such material may exist in still-classified papers. Nevertheless, there is solid evidence in British and Rhodesian state papers and in international newspapers to back up the eye-witness accounts of the Irish soldiers who were present at Radio Katanga. The UN Secretariat also soft-pedalled the critical point that the Katangese Gendarmerie had fought ONUC to a stalemate and that Tshombe emerged substantially strengthened from Morthor. O'Brien's assertions in To Katanga and back that there was a UN cover-up after Morthor have been queried, but they are backed up by the contents of the UN's own archives.

O'Brien and Raja were crucial, with Linner and Khiari, in the events leading to Morthor. O'Brien's role was much greater than he allowed for in To Katanga and back. His personal correspondence shows that he placed the need for another swipe at Katanga after Rumpunch into the minds of Khiari and Linner. When initiating Morthor, O'Brien and Raja came to believe that they held the upper hand in a situation far more volatile than they ever imagined. O'Brien's letters on the politics of Katanga and the calibre of its government and administration, and Raja's military evaluation of the Katangese Gendarmerie, show both adopting an attitude not dissimilar to Congo's former Belgian overlords, or even to Ireland's and India's former colonial rulers in Britain. They had 'gone local' in Elisabethville, a development Hammarskjold never fully took on board. Not only had O'Brien 'gone local' but the stress and confusion of late August and early September appeared to have left him incapable of responding effectively to the military and political crisis resulting from his actions in Elisabethville. Like Linner he was taking risks. His letter to Munongo that ONUC was prepared to execute prisoners was not an action expected of an international civil servant during a peacekeeping mission. It suggests instead that O'Brien was being sucked deep into the lethal realities of Katangese vendetta politics.

ONUC's experience in Katanga was remote from the view of UN operations held by the Secretariat in New York or even of ONUC HQ in Leopoldville. No operational blueprint could prepare ONUC for what it undertook in Katanga. Policy was made on the hoof to fulfil the terms of a vague, yet over-strong, mandate given by the Security Council without an awareness of its ultimate possibilities. O'Brien, Raja, Linner, Khiari and MacEoin were too close to events, and Hammarskjöld too remote for them to see eye to eye. Hammarskjold was too academic to fully appreciate the cruel street-politics and poisonous local rivalries of Elisabethville. The UN archives press home the often-forgotten point that the UN is not an homogenous organization; there were many fatal differences of understanding, opinion and outlook over Katanga in the Secretariat.

While the UN's diplomats and bureaucrats made policy, their military counterparts in ONUC remained under their political control, and often appear as pawns in the Congo game. This was exemplified by the deployment of A-Company, 35th Battalion, to Jadotville, despite Raja's objections, by MacEoin on Hammarskjöld's orders. The overview available in New York could never convey effectively what was happening on the ground in Congo because New York never obtained the necessary degree of information to make informed decisions. Battalions deployed at the decision of the Secretary General and his advisers and even by the decision of the Force Commander, had to operate in a local environment that was never visible to those in ultimate command of ONUC. Communication problems and the sheer size of Congo meant that local realities were never translated effectively into the overall strategic picture. The essential intrinsic detail that was needed to form effective policy at strategic level was lost in the provision of the generalized accounts required up the line. General summary accounts prepared for the UN Secretariat or Hammarskjöld show none of the essential gritty low-level close-up details seen by units on the streets of Elizabethville and on the highways and tracks of Katanga. So diluted are UN Secretariat documents on Congo that without examining the operation of battalions, their sub-units and local UN representatives on the ground it is impossible to understand how ONUC really operated and what it was facing.

Individual soldiers were rarely given the big picture about the operation they were involved in, or informed about the political and societal landscape of their area of operations. The intricacies of Katangese politics remained a mystery to many. They did not realise that they were present at a potential Cold War flashpoint or a defining moment in the history of modern Africa. To some Irish soldiers the name Congo meant nothing, one private is said to have told his wife he was going to 'Cong' and would be back soon from that small Galway village. Others thought they were going on six months holidays to look at monkeys, lions and giraffes. Most had never been overseas before. Some Irish troops gravitated towards Belgian mercenaries or local Belgians when socializing. Their common white European background proved more significant where one might have expected the personnel of a 'post-colonial' state to steer clear of a colonizer. Others however saw the Katangese point of view, equating Ireland's struggle for independence from the United Kingdom with that of Katanga from Congo. It is impossible to generalize about the expectations and experiences of Irish ONUC soldiers; except that is, that they did not expect to see active combat under the UN flag.

Committed to the UN, Ireland became a pawn in Hammarskjöld's and the UN's plans for Congo. Aiken made a virtue of loyalty to the United Nations and his naive belief in the organization was a fundamental reason for Ireland's inability to deal in a realistic manner with involvement in ONUC. A less idealistic minister might have ensured that by back-channel contact with MacEoin, O'Brien and other senior officials and officers, Ireland could have obtained a greater flow of information on Congolese and Katangese affairs. Had Aiken acted in this manner, Dublin could have ensured that Boland was working from a more informed position. Instead Aiken took all the steps possible to ensure that Ireland maintained its distance from ONUC and kept itself studiously in the dark when its citizens, whether in military green or in diplomatic grey, put their lives at risk under the UN flag. He was ultimately forced to revise this attitude amid the crisis over Jadotville during the September fighting and go to Katanga himself to investigate ONUC activities.

In 1923, when the Irish civil war ended it would have been unthinkable that the next time Irish soldiers would see combat was in central Africa. The Defence Forces had never deployed outside the national territory. They had not seen combat for almost forty years. It was unprecedented that in Katanga they suffered fatalities and serious casualties, had men taken hostage and missing in action. Consequently MacEoin's seemingly-unquestioning agreement to send the men of the 32nd and subsequent battalions to Congo is worth questioning. His own views on sending these men overseas initially appear almost flippant. He seemed to be taking a wild chance. Yet his response was rational given the low and worsening morale his forces were experiencing stuck in barracks in Ireland. Irish participation in peacekeeping missions is now taken for granted, but Hammarskjöld's request to participate in ONUC appeared to be a once-in-a-lifetime chance for a largely garrison army. Here was the opportunity to undertake operations in the field. Such an opportunity might not occur again, particularly if Ireland turned participation down. MacEoin's instinct was correct, subsequent operational difficulties notwithstanding.

It would be foolish to suggest that Irish troops did not at times show imperfect operational awareness in Congo. For example, the Niemba ambush, Force Kane I and Force Kane II all display problems from which lessons were eventually learned, and new tactics implemented. There were problems with training, tactics, communications and overall outlook. However these issues were solved over time and the ONUC deployment enhanced the overall capabilities of the Irish Defence Forces to a level that would otherwise not have been achieved. O'Neill's plans to defend Elisabethville airport, the patrolling and reconnaissance skills developed in Elisabethville by the 35th Battalion and, without a doubt, the realities of active operations in combat by the 35th and 36th Battalions, in particular the actions at Jadotville and the capture of The Tunnel, support this view. Deficiencies remained, as was seen in the Defence Force's lacklustre response to the outbreak of the Troubles in Northern Ireland in 1969, but overseas service with the UN provided training and experience that would never otherwise have been achieved. Participation in ONUC enabled Ireland to situate itself as one of the initial contributors to what would become a major UN activity. Subsequent Irish peacekeeping deployments to Cyprus and Lebanon grew from the 'tradition' established in Congo.

The manner in which the UN strayed increasingly out of its depth in Congo caused what became in 1961 Ireland's most significant foreign policy crisis since the end of the Second World War. Ireland's involvement in ONUC has generally been viewed by historians as a disconnected series of military and political episodes. These run from deployment in July 1960, through the Niemba ambush, MacEoin's and O'Brien's appointments, on to Jadotville and finally O'Brien's resignation in December 1961. This disconnected narrative includes to a lesser extent the fighting in Elisabethville in September and December 1961.

This jigsaw puzzle view is misleading. Placing these events together in their national and international diplomatic, political and military contexts shows that over eighteen months they formed a foreign policy challenge of unprecedented proportions for the Lemass government. The challenge turned into a major foreign policy crisis by the time of the October 1961 general election. It had its denouement in December 1961 with the resignations of two senior diplomats and with renewed fighting in Elisabethville. Never before had an Irish government faced a situation where Irish troops were missing, killed and taken prisoner overseas in an international mission under the command of a senior Irish officer and a senior Irish diplomat.

The significance of this situation becomes clearer when it is incorporated into Ireland's wider United Nations experience of the Congo crisis. From July 1960 to December 1961 Ireland was involved, in New York and on the ground in Katanga, in an international crisis the intensity of which Dublin had never previously experienced. Ireland had, until this point, never participated in multilateral crisis management and had no experience of having its diplomats and military personnel acting in a large international military force or holding senior roles as decision makers in such forces. In Congo Ireland had for the first time to shoulder the burden of major international political and military obligations and responsibilities. Irish experiences concerning Congo from July 1960 to December 1961 touched integral aspects at the core of Irish foreign policy. Support for the UN was intrinsically connected with all that happened in Congo and so too were other core concerns of foreign policy including relations with Britain, the EEC, of which Ireland applied for membership in August 1961, and post-colonial Africa, with which Ireland felt a special relationship.

MacEoin and O'Brien, and to a lesser extent Boland and Aiken, bore responsibility for the implementation of Hammarskjöld's great experiment in international intervention in Congo, and for its execution and outcome. Boland and Aiken were household names in 1960s Ireland, a position as unusual for an Irish diplomat, as it was normal for an Irish politician. They were soon joined by O'Brien and MacEoin. It was a sign of Ireland's growing role in the UN in the early 1960s, but it was involvement in a crisis that the government in Dublin could not control. On Hammarskjöld's death Ireland had become involved in the highest levels of UN decision-making as Boland grappled with the question of Hammarskjöld's successor and Aiken, who had appeared out of touch with the realities of Congolese affairs, was forced to place personal loyalty to O'Brien against the wishes of the UN itself. The drama of British–Irish relations in the weeks before O'Brien's departure was unprecedented. Boland directly sought to bypass his minister by intriguing with a British counterpart to fashion a direct channel to the Taoiseach to have O'Brien removed.

In the foreign policy crisis of 1960–1 caused by Irish participation in ONUC Taoiseach Seán Lemass took control of the direction of Irish United Nations policy. Aiken, previously Ireland's voice in the General Assembly, became Lemass' loyal lieutenant – being often over-ruled at cabinet and flying off in haste on his leader's instructions to Congo. Lemass took control in cabinet and his view directed the final collective cabinet opinion. He successfully limited the fallout of events in Congo into domestic politics and, following the 1961 general election, limited the spill-over of ONUC and Congo into other aspects of Irish foreign policy.

Cabinet and civil service contact over Congo was ad hoc. There was no Congo sub-committee of the cabinet, no process to streamline the distribution of what little information on Congo came into Dublin. In fact, the picture that emerges is of a struggling permanent mission to the United Nations conveying snippets of information to a noticeably disconnected Iveagh House, which stood aloof on the instructions of the minister. In economic matters the 1960s saw the pre-eminence of the 'Committee of Secretaries' led by Ken Whitaker at Finance, there was no such body co-ordinating Irish civilian and military policies toward ONUC and Congo or Katanga. Minister for Defence Kevin Boland was reduced to a bystander. External Affairs traditionally looked down on the Department of Defence and the Defence Forces. There was neither streamlined thinking nor co-operation between the departments that should have been at the helm of Ireland's involvement in the Congo crisis.

Irish involvement in Rumpunch, Morthor and Unokat was the centrepiece of Defence Forces involvement in ONUC in 1960 and 1961. These small-unit operations in built-up areas were the key UN military operations in Katanga in ONUC's first eighteen months but they have been almost completely crowded out of Irish military history by a concentration on the Niemba ambush and A-Company's defence of its position at Jadotville. It might not suit the narrative of the Irish peacekeeping tradition to incorporate two offensive operations and a police raid into the early years of a lengthy tradition of peacekeeping, but doing so creates a more all-encompassing perspective. This perspective situates the participation of Irish ONUC battalions in actual operations within the experience of the military forces of fellow troop-contributing states as well as within the hierarchy of ONUC as an international force. It also recalibrates it as international rather than a national action.

Soldiers of all ranks learned how to operate in this new environment, as they evolved methods to face conditions in Congo. Training was put into practice, chances were taken and UN instructions followed, and it is remarkable that there was only one Niemba ambush. Compared to overall UN fatalities, Irish casualties were light, and were light given the episodes Irish troops found themselves fighting in during 1961. During Morthor both Ryan and Quinlan got all their men back alive. The deaths of Mullins and Nolan were due to a highly unexpected turn of events. Gaffney's death in Morthor and the deaths of Fallon, Mulcahy, Riordan and Wickham in Unokat were combat-related in the normal sense. In its own right, and as an action in the history of the Defence Forces, A-Company's performance in Jadotville was quite remarkable. A-Company could easily have been wiped out had the Gendarmerie wished to destroy them. Quinlan's under-equipped and ill-situated unit faced up in an exceptional manner to a numerically superior force with an advantage in terms of weapons and supplies. Perhaps the greatest contrast, one which shows what had been learned between July 1960 and December 1961, is the manner in which the 36th Battalion deployed under fire at Elisabethville airport and the manner in which Hogan successfully placed the full battalion in attack so soon after its arrival. This can be contrasted to the 32nd Battalion arriving in piecemeal form in Kivu with weapons and ammunition on separate aircraft and no units loaded in tactical formation. One can see a rising level of Defence Forces professionalism as a result of active service with ONUC. However, on examining case studies, a slow reaction to events, or in cases the lack of any reaction at all, is evident. The provision of FN rifles and 84mm anti-tank guns was too little to really call modernization. It is perhaps better to look at the personal operational experience gained from involvement in ONUC by a large proportion of the early 1960s Defence Forces. This was later put to use in UNFICYP and UNIFIL. By the late 1960s, as a result of ONUC and UNFICYP, the Defence Forces knew how to deploy as part of a wider international force. Nevertheless they remained vastly under-strength and under-equipped and were incapable of mounting an expeditionary force in their own right.

A product of Hammarskjöld's supreme faith in himself and in the abilities of the United Nations, ONUC showed the limits of UN independence and interventionism. It showed the limits of great power tolerance of a motivated international organization seeking an independent role in the international system. Looking back from the age of 'responsibility to protect' ONUC was an operation before its time; an operation for which the UN was not yet ready. ONUC showed that the UN always remained interdependent of the great powers and reliant on the support of membership of the General Assembly and the permanent members of the Security Council. The lofty ideals of the air-conditioned UN Secretariat in New York were far away from the heat of Leopoldville and the tension of Katanga where those ideals had to be implemented. This account has merged these perspectives to show ONUC at its various levels and as a result to show how, when 'peacekeeping' becomes what some call 'peace enforcement', it has in fact become 'war'. Operations Morthor and Unokat were nothing less than war between the United Nations and Katanga. The actions at The Tunnel, at Elisabethville Post Office, Radio Katanga and in Jadotville are each significant parts of the Irish military tradition. The 35th and 36th Battalions ended up fighting a small conventional war as part of an international force in urban Elisabethville and Jadotville. It was as unexpected for them and for the United Nations, as it was for the Irish government, military and diplomatic service.

Notes

Introduction: 'There is nothing like the Congo. You will thank God for that'

1   UN official Gustavo Duran to Conor Cruise O'Brien before O'Brien's departure for Katanga. Quoted in Conor Cruise O'Brien, *To Katanga and back: a UN case history* (London, 1962), p. 66.
2   Conor Cruise O'Brien, *Murderous angels* (Boston, 1968), p. 147. Brian Urquhart's *Hammarskjöld* (London, 1972) remains the standard account of Hammarskjöld's life. Roger Lipsey's *Hammarskjöld: a life* (Ann Arbor, 2013) was published as this book went to press.
3   NLS L179/141, Hammarskjöld to Abbas, 30 Aug. 1961.
4   Michael Ignatieff, 'The faith of a Hero', *New York Review of Books*, 7 Nov. 2013, p. 38. Thank you to Dr Kevin O'Sullivan for bringing this review to our attention.
5   See for example David O'Donoghue's oral history, *The Irish army in the Congo, 1960–1964* (Dublin, 2005), Declan Power, *Siege at Jadotville* (Dunshaughlin, 2005), and two earlier accounts: Conor Cruise O'Brien, *To Katanga and back* (London, 1962) and Tom McCaughren, *The peacemakers of Niemba* (Dublin, 1966). The only book coming close to a full-scale study of the Defence Forces in Congo is Raymond Smith, *Under the Blue Flag* (Dublin, 1980). While Irish forces were deployed with ONUC *An Cosantóir*, the Defence Forces' journal, carried regular articles on the deployment.
6   Madeline G. Kalb's *The Congo cables: the cold war in Africa from Eisenhower to Kennedy* (New York, 1982) and volume 20 of the *Foreign relations of the United States, 1961–1963* cover the Congo crisis from a Cold War perspective.
7   NAI DFA 305/384/31/II, Boland to Cremin, 30 Oct. 1961.
8   NAI DFA 305/384/2/II, Boland to Cremin, 6 Sept. 1960.
9   MA 33rd Battalion Unit History, foreword.
10 William J. Durch, *The evolution of UN peacekeeping* (London, 1993), p. 316.
11 Alan James, *Britain and the Congo crisis, 1960–63* (London, 1996), p. 25.
12 Durch, *Evolution*, p. 345.

Chapter 1. Intervention

1   Conor Cruise O'Brien, *United Nations: sacred drama* (London, 1968), p. 60.
2   NAI DFA 305/384/2 Pt 1, Kasavubu and Lumumba to Hammarskjöld, 12 July 1960.
3   TNA FO 371/146769, Dixon to Foreign Office, 13 July 1960.
4   Article 99: 'The Secretary-General may bring to the attention of the Security Council any matter which in his opinion may threaten the maintenance of international peace and security'.
5   Hernane Tavares de Sá, *The play within the play* (New York, 1966), p. 135.
6   Arthur L. Gavshon, *The last days of Dag Hammarskjöld* (London, 1963), p. 85.
7   Dublin's initial concern was how ONUC deployment would affect Irish officers serving with UNTSO and UNOGIL, particularly as it was reported that Col. Justin McCarthy, Deputy Chief of Staff of UNOGIL, would be appointed acting chief of staff of UNTSO on von Horn's departure.
8   NAI DFA 305/384/2 Pt1, No. 65, Uneireann to Estero, 12.30pm, 14 July 1960.
9   Ibid., note on file by Edward Brennan, 14 July 1960.
10 NLS L179/161, 837, Hammarskjöld to Gyani, 17 July 1961.
11 NAI DFA 305/384/2 Pt1, Hammarskjöld to Boland, 16 July 1960.
12 TNA FO 371/154957, Maclennan to Chadwick, 19 Sept. 1961.
13 Lecture by Lt Gen. MacEoin, United Nations Training School, Curragh Camp, July 1995.
14 UNA S/209/9/10, memorandum of conversation with Mr Kennedy of Ireland, 19 July 1960.
15 NAI DFA 305/384/2 Pt1, note of conversation with Eamonn Kennedy, 11pm, 18 July 1960.
16 UNA S/209/9/10, memorandum of conversation with Mr Kennedy of Ireland, 19 July 1960.
17 NAI DFA 305/384/2 Pt1, note of conversation with Eamonn Kennedy, 11pm, 18 July 1960.
18 UNA S/209/9/10, memorandum of conversation with Mr Kennedy of Ireland, 19 July 1960.

19   NAI DFA 305/384/2 Pt 1, Request for Irish assistance for UN military force in the Congo, 18 July 1960.
20   Ibid., phone message, O'Brien to Kennedy, 19 July 1960.
21   *Dáil Debates*, 183: 1882, 20 July 1960.   22   Ibid., 183: 1881, 20 July 1960.
23   *Evening Mail*, 20 July 1960.   24   *Times*, 12 July 1960.
25   *Dáil Debates*, 183: 1878, 20 July 1960.
26   Lecture by Lt Gen. MacEoin, United Nations Training School, Curragh Camp, July 1995. Recording in Dr
     Kennedy's possession.

Chapter 2. The learning curve

1   TNA FO 371/146775, Dixon to Foreign Office, 7 Aug. 1960.
2   UNA S/213/3/3, Bunche to Hammarskjöld, 7 Aug. 1960.
3   NLS L179/140, B375, Bunche to Hammarskjöld, 6 Aug. 1960.
4   NAI DFA 305/384/2 Pt1, No. 110, Estero to Uneireann, 11 Aug. 1960.
5   TNA FO 371/146642, British Ambassador, Accra to CRO, 18 Aug. 1960.
6   NAI DFA 305/384/2 Pt1, extract from report of 1 Aug. 1960.
7   Ibid., Fay to Cremin, 2 Aug. 1960.
8   The battalion arrived with weapons but without ammunition; its main weapon became its pipe band which
     was 'received with wild enthusiasm' (MA 32nd Battalion Unit History, p. 19).
9   UNA S/788/4/2, special report by O'Brien, 2 Aug. 1960.
10   MA 32nd Battalion Unit History, p. 29.
11   TNA CO 822/2075, Commissioner of Police, Kampala, to Permanent Secretary for Security and External
     Relations, Entebbe, 23 Aug. 1960.
12   TNA FO 371/146650, Comments on the Congo by an Observer, undated, but Nov. 1960.
13   MA 32nd Battalion Unit History, p. 29.
14   NAI DFA 305/384/2 Pt1, Department of External Affairs memorandum to cabinet, 3 Aug. 1960.
15   Ibid., No. 99, Estero to PMUN, 5 Aug. 1960.
16   In contrast to later Swedish and Indian dominated commands in Katanga, HQ SCOMEP was a largely Irish
     operation.
17   NLS L179/140, B480, Bunche to Hammarskjöld, 16 Aug. 1961.
18   NAI DFA 305/384/2 Pt1, No. 101, Estero to PMUN, 5 Aug. 1960.
19   Ibid., No. 100, Estero to PMUN, 5 August 1960.
20   MA 33rd Battalion History, p. 1.
21   ÙNA S/788/4/2, Lee to Director Plans and Operations, Army HQ, Dublin, 5 Aug. 1960.
22   R.A. Hinchy, 'Early days in Kamina', *An Cosantóir*, 21: 1 (1961), 1–10 at 10.
23   Ibid., p. 9.   24   MA 33rd Battalion Unit History, p. 6.   25   Ibid.
26   UNA S/787/3/4, Operation 'Neutral Zone', ONUC Operation Order No. 9, 21 Oct. 1960. McCarthy had
     served with UNTSO and UNOGIL before transferring to ONUC. He was killed in a car crash in Leopoldville
     on 28 October 1960.
27   MA 33rd Battalion Unit History, p. 8.
28   TNA FO 371/146779, Scott to Home, 31 Aug. 1960.
29   UNA S/791/43/2, SCOMEP to Irish battalion, Goma, 30 Aug. 1960.
30   NAI DFA 305/384/2/II, Boland to Cremin, 6 Sept. 1960.
31   TNA FO 371/146645, The Prime Minister's meeting with Mr Hammarskjöld, 26 Sept. 1960.
32   TNA FO 371/154959, Dixon to Beeley, 7 Sept. 1960.
33   UNA S/772/1/1, Desta to UNMOGE, Elisabethville, 5 Oct. 1960.
34   McCaughren, *Peacemakers*, p. 50.
35   Smith, *Blue flag*, p. 66.
36   MA 33rd Battalion Unit History, p. 38. Perhaps because of the Niemba ambush the 33rd Battalion Unit History
     portrays the Baluba negatively whereas the Katangese Gendarmerie is rarely shown in such a light.
37   Ibid.
38   McCaughren, *Peacemakers*, p. 95. The Balubakat was the Baluba political party led by Jason Sendwe.
39   UNA S/213/1/13, EV 102, von Horn and Dayal to Byrne and Berendsen, 24 Oct. 1960.
40   TNA FCO 371/146650, Scott to Home, 26 Oct. 1960. Scott added that Irish troops were 'doing little to stop
     them'.
41   MA 33rd Battalion Unit History, p. 72.

42 Ibid., p. 77.   43 Ibid., p. 76.   44 Ibid., p. 73.
45 Ibid., p. 73. The 'Gustav man' refers to the Carl Gustav 9mm sub-machine gun carried by some battalion personnel.
46 Ibid., p. 68. Manioc, also known as cassava, is an edible starchy root high in carbohydrates.
47 Thank you to Lt Col. Pat Power for identifying the area. While serving with the UN's MONUC mission in Congo Lt Col. Power visited the area in March 2007.
48 The patrol was in radio contact with Albertville.
49 Gleeson's patrol had taken the only two vehicles available to the Irish in Niemba.
50 For a detailed account of the Niemba ambush in the context of 33rd Battalion operations see Edward Burke, 'Ireland's contribution to the United Nations mission in the Congo (ONUC): keeping the peace in Katanga' in Michael Kennedy and Deirdre McMahon (eds), *Obligations and responsibilities: Ireland and the United Nations, 1955–2005* (Dublin, 2005), pp 117–53. The most detailed near-contemporary account is Tom McCaughren, *The peacemakers of Niemba* (Dublin, 1966).
51 UNA S/791/43/4, OPS 415, SCOMEP, Elisabethville to ONUC HQ, Leopoldville, 1000Z, 11 Nov. 1960.
52 NLS L179/156, B1386, Rikhye to Hammarskjöld, 1925Z, and 3289, Hammarskjöld to Rikhye, 9 Nov. 1960.
53 UNA S/772/1/2, ELLEO 120, Berendsen to Rikhye, 1535Z, 14 Nov. 1960.
54 UNA S/791/43/4, OPS 381, SCOMEP Elisabethville to ONUC Leopoldville, 10 Nov. 1960.
55 UNA S/787/13/8, Tribunal de Première Instance d'Elisabethville, séant en matire pénale, 13 Nov. 1961. The phrase translating as 'either the Irish soldiers turn back or it's war, and you will win or you will die'.
56 The remains of Tpr Anthony Browne, the final missing member of the patrol, were located in 1962. The initial search for Browne was called off on 13 November 1960.
57 MA 33rd Battalion Unit History, p. 99.
58 Burke, 'Katanga', p. 149.
59 UNA S/772/1/1, Byrne to Berendsen, 1800Z, 9 Nov. 1960.
60 NLS L179/156, 3325, Hammarskjöld to Rikhye, 10 Nov. 1960.
61 NLS L179/162, Rikhye to Hammarskjöld, 15 Nov. 1960.
62 Burke, 'Katanga', p. 151.
63 UNA S/803/1/7, Directive No. 4, Nov. 1960.
64 NLS L179/156, B1396, Rikhye to Hammarskjöld, 10 Nov. 1960.
65 Ibid., B1421, Rikhye to Hammarskjöld, 10 Nov. 1960 and Rikhye to Hammarskjöld, 14 Nov. 1960.
66 Ibid., unnumbered cable, Rikhye to Hammarskjöld, 14 Nov. 1960.
67 Ibid., B1444, Rikhye to Hammarskjöld, 17 Nov. 1960.
68 NAI DFA 305/384/2/II, Cremin to Aiken, 28 Nov. 1960.
69 NAI DFA 305/384/2/III, Estero to PMUN for Aiken, 10 Dec. 1960.
70 MA 33rd Battalion Unit History, p. 48.
71 NAI DFA 305/384/2/II, Ronan to Coffey, 12 Sept. 1960.
72 MA 33rd Battalion Unit History, p. 4.
73 Patrick MacDonald, 'Intelligence in United Nations operations', *An Cosantóir*, 27:11 (1967), 592–4 at 594.
74 NAI DFA 305/384/2/II, Irish embassy Ottawa to Dublin, 7 Sept. 1960.
75 The Landswerks were too heavy to transport by air to Congo.
76 MA 35th Battalion Unit History, p. 50.   77 Ibid.   78 Ibid., p. 51.
79 NAI DFA 305/384/2/II, Request from UN for Irish battalion for Congo Force to replace present contingent when withdrawn, 22 Nov. 1960.

Chapter 3. Deepening crisis

1   TNA FO 371/146784, Scott to Foreign Office, 1 Dec. 1960.
2   TNA FO 371/146786, Foreign Office to UKMIS, New York, 1 Dec. 1960.
3   TNA FO 371/146784, minute, Hoyer-Millar to Home, 3 Dec. 1960.
4   NLS L179/162, Hammarskjöld to Dayal, 3 Dec. 1960.
5   Ibid., Hammarskjöld to Dayal, 4 Dec. 1960.
6   TNA FO 371/146785, Dean to Foreign Office, 6 Dec. 1960.
7   TNA FO 371/146723, British embassy Dublin to Commonwealth Relations Office, London, 8 Dec. 1960.
8   TNA FO 371/146784, draft of telegram No. 3040 from Foreign Office to New York, 9 Dec. 1960.
9   TNA FO 371/146723, British embassy Dublin to Commonwealth Relations Office, London, 8 Dec. 1960.
10 TNA FO 371/146784, draft of telegram No. 3040, Home to Dean, 9 Dec. 1960.

11 Ibid. 12 NAI DFA 305/384/2/III, Lemass to Dillon, 19 Dec. 1961.

13 *Irish Times*, 19 Dec. 1960. 14 Ibid., 21 Dec. 1960.

15 NAI DFA PMUN 444 (M13/6/4 ptı), quote from Pierre J. Huss, undated newspaper clipping.

16 *Irish Independent*, 22 Dec. 1960. 17 TNA FO 371/146723, Scott to Foreign Office, 24 Dec. 1960.

18 Irish Press, 22 Dec. 1960. 19 UNA S/791/43/4, MacEoin to Dayal, 23 Dec. 1960.

20 TNA FO 371/154982, minute by Stevens, 4 Jan. 1961.

21 Ibid., Congo: The Irish General, minute by Boothby, 9 Jan. 1961. 22 Ibid.

23 Ibid., minute by Home on Congo: The Irish General, minute by Boothby, Jan. 1961.

24 TNA FO 371/154981, Foreign Office to Scott, 17 Jan. 1961.

25 Ibid., Scott to Foreign Office, 22 Jan. 1961. 26 Ibid.

27 TNA FO 371/154982, Boothby to Dean, 24 Jan. 1961.

28 TNA FO 371/155094, Scott to Foreign Office, 16 Feb. 1961.

29 TNA FO 371/155004, Scott to Foreign Office, 8 Apr. 1961. 30 O'Brien, Katanga, p. 74.

31 TNA FO 371/155009, Congolese armed intervention in Katanga, 18 Sept. 1961.

32 Remark by Bunche in Nov. 1961, quoted in James, *Congo crisis*, p. 24.

33 NAI DFA 305/384/31, Kiernan to Cremin, 28 Sept. 1961, quoting *Washington Post*, 26 Sept. 1961.

34 TNA FO 371/155009, Irish Interests in the Congo, 30 Nov. 1961. 35 Ibid.

36 RH RW 258/4, Macmillan to Welensky, 31 Jan. 1961.

37 John Terence O'Neill, 'The Irish Company at Jadotville, Congo, 1961: soldiers or symbols?', *International Peacekeeping*, 9:4 (2002), 127–44 at 131–2 and 134.

38 NAI DFA PMUN 387, McCann to Cremin, 10 Jan. 1961.

39 Ibid., Cremin to McCann, 16 Jan. 1961.

40 NAI DFA 305/384/III, minute, Keating to O'Brien, 19 Jan. 1961.

41 Ibid., minute, Keating to Ronan, 14 Jan. 1961. 42 Ibid.

43 Ibid., minute, Ronan to O'Brien, 16 Jan. 1961. O'Brien also minuted that Col. Justin McCarthy, when Chief of Staff of UNTSO and UNOGIL, reported regularly to the Chief of Staff and on occasion to External Affairs.

44 Ibid., minute, Ronan to O'Brien, 17 Feb. 1961. Ronan added that only the civilian side of the Department of Defence had been consulted.

45 Ibid., minute, O'Brien to Cremin, 2 Mar. 1961.

46 Ibid., minute, Cremin to Ronan, 16 Mar 1961.

47 UCDA P104/7069, speech by Aiken, Curragh Camp, 7 Jan. 1961.

48 Dáil Deb., 186:1019-21, 1 Mar. 1961.

49 Michael Considine, 'Cavalry in the Congo', *An Cosantóir*, 22:10 (1962), 525–9 at 526.

50 Rajeshwar Dayal, Mission for Hammarskjöld (Princeton, 1976), p. 172.

51 NAI DFA 305/384/III, minute from Keating to O'Brien (shown to Aiken), 18 Jan. 1961.

52 NAI DFA 305/384/2/III, Notes on the situation in the Congo, 1 Feb. 1961. 53 Ibid.

54 NAI DFA PMUN 387, Cremin to Boland, 2 Feb. 1961. 55 Ibid.

56 Ibid., Cremin to Boland, 2 Feb. 1961.

57 NAI DFA 305/384/2/III, Estero to Uneireann, 31 Jan. 1961.

58 Ibid., Boland to Cremin, 2 Feb. 1961.

59 NAI DFA 305/384/III, confidential note by Cremin, 7 Feb. 1961.

60 Ibid., Boland to Cremin, 14 Feb. 1961. 61 Ibid., Boland to Cremin, 9 Feb. 1961.

62 Ibid. 63 Ibid., Boland to Cremin, 10 Feb. 1961.

64 Dayal, Mission, p. 189.

65 NAI DFA 305/384/III, Lemass to Khrushchev, 14 Apr. 1961.

66 Ibid., No. 39, Boland to Cremin, 14 Feb. 1961.

67 Ibid., Boland to Cremin, 14 Feb. 1961. 68 Dayal, Mission, pp 199–200.

69 NAI DFA 305/384/III, confidential note by Cremin, 17 Feb. 1961.

70 Ibid. 71 TNA FO 371/154952, Nehru to Macmillan, 17 Feb. 1961.

72 TNA FO 371/155101, James to Chadwick, quoting Nehru, 18 Feb. 1961.

73 NAI DFA 305/384/III, Biggar to Cremins, 22 Feb. 1961.

74 TNA FO 371/154878, Evans to Foreign Office, 16 Feb. 1961.

75 NLS L179/140, D414, Dayal to Hammarskjöld, 15 Feb. 1961.

76 Anthony Parsons, *From cold war to hot peace: UN interventions, 1947–1994* (London, 1995), p. 87.

77 Parsons, *UN interventions*, p. 87.

78 NAI DFA 305/384/III, No. 73, Uneireann to Estero, 24 Feb. 1961.

Chapter 4. Conflict in Katanga

1 TNA FO 371/154953, High Commissioner, Delhi, to Commonwealth Relations Office, London, 28 Feb. 1961.
2 TNA FO 371/154953, Indian contingent for the United Nations force, 2 Mar. 1961.
3 Ibid., Record of a discussion at Chequers at 9.35pm on Sunday, March 12, 1961.
4 Ibid., James to CRO, 25 Mar. 1961.
5 Ibid., High Commission, New Delhi to CRO, 31 Mar. 1961.
6 NLS L179/158, 1795, Hammarskjöld to Abbas and MacEoin, 14 Mar. 1961.
7 Col. John Terence O'Neill, private papers, Egge to O'Neill, 22 Apr. 1998.
8 *Irish Press*, 21 Mar. 1961. Moloney's article is incorrectly titled 'Phantom battalion of Luena base'.
9 UNA S/805/19/2, Int report for the period ending 31 Jan. 61, 2 Feb. 1961.
10 *Irish Press*, 21 Mar. 1961.
11 UNA S/805/19/2, Int report for the period ending 31 Jan. 61, 2 Feb. 1961.
12 Ibid., Periodic Information Report, 34th Batt HQ to HQ ONUC, 24 Feb. 1961.
13 NAI DFA PMUN 387, aide memoire, Boland to Hammarskjöld, 20 Feb. 1961.
14 *Irish Times*, 24 Mar. 1961.
15 TNA FO 371/154987, Despatch of an Indian Infantry Brigade to the Congo, 24 Apr. 1961.
16 UNA S/805/19/2, Periodic Information Report, 34th Batt HQ to HQ ONUC, Leopoldville, 23 Mar. 1961.
17 TNA FO 371/154880, The Katanga: April – mid-June 1961, report attached to Dunnett to Riches, 17 June 1961.
18 NAI DT S16137/I61, Report on 34th Battalion moves – April 1961.
19 Ibid., noted seen by Lemass.
20 UNA S/213/1/13, ONUC 1622, Abbas and MacEoin to Hammarskjöld, 28 Mar. 1961.
21 Ibid., 2136, Hammarskjöld to Abbas, 29 Mar. 1961.
22 Ibid., Hammarskjöld to Abbas and MacEoin, 31 Mar. 1961.
23 Ibid., 2389, Hammarskjöld to Abbas and MacEoin, 8 Apr. 1961.   24 Ibid.
25 NLS L179/158, 2278, Hammarskjöld to Abbas, 3 Apr. 1961.
26 UNA S/805/15/2, memo to Maitra, 10 Apr. 1961. Whyte is incorrectly named 'Wright' in this document.
27 NAI DT S16137/I61, Report on 34th Battalion moves – April 1961.
28 TNA FO 371/154879, Evans to Foreign Office, 4 Apr. 1961.
29 NLS L179/158, 2303, Hammarskjöld to Abbas, 4 Apr. 1961.
30 NAI DT S16137/I61, Report on 34th Battalion moves – April 1961.   31 Ibid.
32 *Irish Times*, 27 June 1961.
33 NAI DT S16137/I61, Report on 34th Battalion moves – April 1961.
34 Ibid. The battalion pipe band also played at Elisabethville airport on Sunday afternoons to large crowds.
35 Abbas was a Sudanese administrator who had been a Rhodes Scholar and would become the first Executive Secretary of the United Nations Economic Commission for Africa. He was Hammarskjöld's acting Special Representative in Congo.
36 NLS L179/140, A887, Abbas to Hammarskjöld, 4 Apr. 1961.
37 UNA S/213/1/13, ONUC 1776, Abbas and MacEoin to Hammarskjöld, 5 Apr. 1961.
38 *Irish Press*, 6 Apr. 1961.
39 UNA S/788/4/1, Conference – Force Commander's Office, 21 July 1961.
40 NLS L179/157, ONUC 1777, Abbas and MacEoin to Hammarskjöld, 6 Apr. 1961.
41 NLS L179/140, Rikhye to Hammarskjöld, 10 Apr. 1961.
42 NAI DT S16137/I61, Report on 34th Battalion moves – April 1961.
43 TNA FO 371/154879, Dunnett to Foreign Office, 17 Apr. 1961.
44 NAI DFA 305/384/2/IV, O'Brádaigh to Cremin, 13 Apr. 1961. The weapons arrived in Kamina on 18 May.
45 MA, 32nd Battalion Unit History, p. 64.
46 For example see *Evening Mail*, 11 May 1961.
47 MA 35th Battalion Unit History, p. 51. The consignment was 254 FN rifles plus ammunition and 13 84mm anti-tank guns.
48 NAI DT S16137/I61, Report on 34th Battalion moves – April 1961. Subsequent quotes in this paragraph from this source.
49 UNA S/788/3/5, Report on visit to 34 Irish Battalion, Eville, 15 Apr. 1961.
50 UNA S/791/43/4, OPS 118, South Katanga Cmd to ONUC HQ Leopoldville, 15 May 1961.
51 NAI DT S16137/I61, Report on 34th Battalion moves – April 1961.
52 Ibid.
53 In the initial deployment three of the eight armoured cars with the 34th Battalion were sent to Elisabethville.

54 NAI DT S16137/I61, Report on 34th Battalion moves – April 1961.
55 Ibid.   56 C-Company did not arrive in Elisabethville until 20 Apr. 1961.
57 UNA S/213/1/13, Operational Order, 20 Apr. 1961.
58 UNA S/788/3/5, Operational Instruction for Defence of Elisabethville Airport (undated).
59 NAI DT S16137/I61, Report on 34th Battalion moves – April 1961.
60 UNA S/788/3/5, Operational Instruction for Defence of Elisabethville Airport (undated).
61 Ibid.   62 Ibid.
63 NAI DFA 305/384/IV, O'Brien to Cremin, 18 Apr. 1961.
64 UNA S/213/1/13, 2627, Hammarskjöld to Abbas and MacEoin, 17 Apr. 1961.
65 NLS L179/162, Abbas and MacEoin to Hammarskjöld, 30 Apr. 1961.
66 TNA FO 371/154879, Scott to Foreign Office, 17 Apr. 1961.
67 TNA FO 371/154880, The Katanga: April – mid-June 1961, attached to Dunnett to Riches, 17 June 1961.
68 TNA FO 371/154879, Scott to Foreign Office, 23 Mar. 1961.
69 Ibid., Evans to Home, 27 Mar. 1961.   70 Hoskyns, *Congo*, p. 395.
71 TNA FO 371/154956, minute by Byatt, 6 June 1961.
72 MA 33rd Battalion Unit History, p. 16.
73 NAI DT S16137I/61, Notes on the situation in the Congo, 1 June 1961.
74 TNA FO 371/154880, Foreign Office to Elisabethville, 7 June 1961.
75 UNA S/604/1/1, Linner to Hammarskjöld, 25 May 1961.
76 UNA S/840/2/5, Force Commander's Meeting at Kamina, 4 June 1961.
77 TNA FO 371/154956, Home to Welensky, 2 June 1961.
78 TNA FO 371/154880, Dunnett to Scott, 17 June 1961.
79 Ibid., The Katanga: April–mid-June 1961, confidential report by Dunnett attached to Dunnett to Riches, 17 June 1961.
80 Gavshon, *Hammarskjöld*, p. 92.   81 *Observer*, 17 Sept. 1961.
82 NLS L179/157, 1332, Cordier to Dayal, 24 Feb. 1961.
83 Hoskyns, *Congo*, p. 395.
84 NLS L179/162, 3934, Cordier to Abbas and Linner, 17 May 1961.
85 James, *Congo crisis*, p. 99.
86 TNA FO 371/154957, Maclennan to Chadwick, 19 Sept. 1961.
87 *Times*, 15 July 1961.   88 O'Brien, *Katanga*, p. 49.
89 UNA S/767/1/1, O'Brien to Linner, 27 July 1961.
90 Ibid., O'Brien to Linner, 5 July 1961.   91 Ibid., O'Brien to MacEoin, 5 July 1961.
92 UNA S/805/15/2, 35th Irish Bn – Int Report No. 1 to 10 July 61, undated.
93 TNA FO 371/154881, Dunnett to Foreign Office, 10 July 1961.
94 TNA FO 371/154956, Browne to Allan, 11 July 1961.
95 NLS L179/162, A1605, Linner to Hammarskjöld, 3 July 1961.
96 Ibid., Hammarskjöld to Linner and MacEoin, 3 July 1961.
97 TNA FO 371/154881, Dunnett to Foreign Office, 13 July 1961.
98 UNA S/767/1/1, O'Brien to Linner, 9 July 1961.
99 Ibid., O'Brien to 'Eileen', 2 Aug. 1961.   1 Ibid., O'Brien to Henson, 2 Aug. 1961.
2 Ibid.   3 Ibid., O'Brien to Munongo, 20 July 1961.

Chapter 5. The 35th Irish Battalion

1 NAI DFA 305/384/IV, press release copy of Aiken's speech, 28 Mar. 1961.
2 UNA S/213/1/13, 2446, Hammarskjöld to Abbas and MacEoin, 11 Apr. 1961.
3 NAI DT S16137/H61, Department of External Affairs memorandum for government, 20 Apr. 1961.
4 The 1st Infantry Group were based first in South Kasai and then at Kamina from May to November 1961. They are often seen as the forgotten Irish Congo deployment as they received little publicity.
5 NAI DT S16137/H61, Draft Press Release, 21 Apr. 1961.   6 Magennis Memoir.
7 MA G2/E/55/IV, Kane to Director of Military Intelligence, Dublin, 11 July 1961.
8 Rose Doyle (with Leo Quinlan), *Heroes of Jadotville* (Dublin, 2006), p. 192.
9 From 12 Sept. 1961 Chief of Military Operations, Sector-B HQ, Elisabethville.
10 Appointed to Sector-B HQ, Elisabethville.
11 Appointed Chief of Military Information, Sector-B HQ, Elisabethville, 12 Sept.–12 Nov. 1961.

12 Appointed to Sector-B HQ, Elisabethville.
13 Each Platoon was divided into three Sections. Each Section had four riflemen (FN) and two LMG (Bren).
14 60mm mortar, 84mm anti-tank gun, medium machine-gun.
15 NAI DT S16137/161, Report on 34th Battalion moves – April 1961.
16 Ibid. The tanks were not deployed.   17 Taken over from the 34th Battalion.
18 Kept in reserve.   19 MA 35th Battalion Unit History, p. 59.
20 MA 32nd Battalion Unit History, p. 67.   21 MA 35th Battalion Unit History, p. 60.
22 MA 36th Battalion Unit History, p. 76.   23 UNA S/593/4/3, 2 Aug. 1961.
24 MA G2/E/55/IV, Kane to Director of Intelligence, Dublin, 2 Aug. 1961.
25 UNA S/840/2/4, Quinn to HQ South Katanga Cmd, 9 Aug. 1961.
26 NAI DT S16137/161, Report on 34th Battalion moves – April, 1961.
27 UNA S/787/6/1, O'Neill to Director, Plans and Operations, Army HQ, Dublin, 13 May 1961.
28 Magennis Memoir.   29 Ibid.
30 TNA FO 371/154890, Riches to Home, 17 Nov. 1961.
31 Magennis Memoir.   32 Ibid., all quotes in this paragraph from this source.
33 UCDA P104/7071, speech by Lemass, 19 June 1961.
34 Ibid.   35 Doyle, *Jadotville*, p. 158.   36 Verrier, *Peacekeeping*, p. 41.
37 The first 200 troops were delayed 24 hours as their aircraft had not obtained incoming clearance over France.
38 'Minus' being used to designate a unit of less than full strength.
39 A-Company was based at The Factory from 26 June to 1 August, they then moved to Sabena Villas.
40 UNA S/767/1/1, unsigned letter to Grindall and Brackenbury, 6 June 1961.
41 Note by Quinlan in his journal, 28 June 1961, quoted in Doyle, *Jadotville*, p. 173.
42 UNA S/767/3/5, MacNeill to MacEoin (Confidential), 4 July 1961.   43 Ibid.
44 MA G2/E/55/IV, Perint Report No. 1. to 4 July, 4 July 1961.   45 Ibid.   46 Ibid.
47 The Armoured Car Group had initially been temporarily located separately in a bungalow on Avenue des Savonniers which had one acre of grounds to accommodate their vehicles. This location later became a refugee camp.
48 MA G2/E/55/IV, Perint Report No. 1. to 4 July, 4 July 1961, p. 6.
49 UNA S/209/9/10, Hammarskjöld to Supreme Commander ONUC (undated, but July 1960).
50 UNA S/822/2/3, Headquarters Katanga Cmd. Operational Directive Number 1, 11 Aug. 1961.
51 *Times*, 8 Dec. 1961.
52 Brian Urquhart, *A life in peace and war* (New York, 1987), p. 186.
53 The Dogra Regiment is an infantry regiment of the Indian Army.
54 UNA S/822/2/3, Headquarters Katanga Cmd. Operational Directive Number 1, 11 Aug. 1961.
55 Ibid.   56 O'Brien, *Katanga*, p. 53.
57 UNA S/840/2/5, ELLEO 0550, Egge to Linner, MacEoin and Raja, 14 July 1961.
58 UNA S/840/2/7, FC 369, MacEoin to Raja, 15 July 1961.
59 TNA FO 371/154882, Dunnett to Foreign Office, 19 July 1961.
60 Magennis Memoir.   61 Parsons, *Interventions*, p. 93.   62 Magennis Memoir.
63 Ibid.   64 NAI DFA PMUN 387, O'Brádaigh to Cremin, 20 June 1961.
65 Ibid., Nolan to Keating, 24 July 1961.
66 NAI DFA 305/384/2 Pt V, Cullen to Collins Powell, 17 Oct. 1961.
67 MA G2/E/55/IV/A, Irish Liaison Officer to Director, Plans and Operations, Army HQ, Dublin, 5 July 1961.
68 MA 35th Battalion Collection, box 8, file HQ 30, Cloth Model Ex Instrs, undated.
69 MA G2/E/55/IV, Perint Report No. 1. to 4 July, 4 July 1961.
70 Ibid., Kane to Director of Military Intelligence, Dublin, 11 July 1961.
71 *Times*, 15 July 1961.   72 MA G2/E/55/IV, Perint Report No. 2, 2 to 17 July, 18 July 1961.
73 UNA S/805/15/2, 35th Irish Bn - Int Report No. 1 to 10 Jul 61, undated.
74 UNA S/805/19/2, PerintRep No. 4 to 2 Aug 61, 2 Aug. 1961.
75 UNA S/805/15/2, 35th Irish Bn – Int Report No. 1 to 10 July 61, undated.   76 Ibid.
77 Lt Noel Carey, quoted in Doyle, *Jadotville*, p. 178.   78 Quoted in Doyle, *Jadotville*, p. 187.
79 Magennis Memoir.   80 Ibid.
81 MA 35th Battalion Collection, box 8, file HQ 30, Kane to all company commanders, 1 Sept. 1961.
82 Ibid.   83 NAI DFA 305/384/2 Pt V, Cullen to Collins Powell, 17 Oct. 1961.
84 UNA S/788/4/1, Conference – Force Commander's Office, 21 July 1961.   85 Ibid.
86 TNA FO 371/155008, Scott to Foreign Office, 22 July 1961.
87 Ibid., Dunnett to Foreign Office, 24 July 1961.

88 TNA FO 371/154955, Welensky to Home, 22 July 1961.　　　89 Magennis Memoir.
90 Ibid.　91 Ibid.
92 MA 35th Battalion Collection, box 8, file HQ 30, Kane to all company commanders, 31 July 1961.

Chapter 6. Rumpunch

1 UNA S/767/1/1, O'Brien to 'Eileen', 2 Aug. 1961.
2 MA G2/E/55/IV, Kane to Director of Intelligence, Dublin, quoting O'Brien, 31 July 1961.
3 NLS L179/160, A1867, Linner to Hammarskjöld, 2 Aug. 1961.
4 RH RW 258/6, Welensky to Robinson, 26 Aug. 1961.
5 UNA S/805/19/2, Perintrep No. 5 1961, 5 Aug. 1961.　　　6 Magennis Memoir.
7 UNA S/805/19/2, Perintrep No. 5 1961, 6 Aug. 1961.　　　8 Ibid.
9 UNA S/803/1/7, Operation instructions for the employment of UN forces in Elisabethville area, 4 Aug. 1961.
10 TNA FO 371/154882, Dunnett to Foreign Office, 20 Aug. 1961.
11 UNA S/840/2/4, ELLEO 722, ONUC Elisabethville to ONUC Leopoldville, 17 Aug. 1961.
12 UNA S/788/4/5, A1981 and A1982, MacEoin and Khiari to Hammarskjöld, 22 Aug. 1961.
13 Ibid.　　　14 Ibid.　　　15 *Daily Telegraph*, 29 Aug. 1961.
16 UNA S/788/4/5, A1981 and A1982, MacEoin and Khiari to Hammarskjöld, 22 Aug. 1961, which contains a transcript of Adoula's letter to Khiari.
17 NLS L179/160, A1952, Khiari to Hammarskjöld, 16 Aug. 1961. 'Our representatives in Elisabethville are eager to use military force.'
18 UNA S/767/1/1, O'Brien to Williams, 23 Aug. 1961.　　　19 Magennis Memoir.
20 MA 35th Battalion Collection, box 8, file HQ 30, Int Report w.e. 26 Aug. 1961, 26 Aug. 1961.
21 UNA S/766/9/10, 5933, Hammarskjöld to Linner, 25 Aug. 1961.
22 Hoskyns, *Congo*, pp 402–3.
23 RH RW 258/6, Welensky to Robinson, 26 Aug. 1961.
24 UNA S/840/2/4, ELLEO 735, O'Brien to MacEoin and Khiari, 23 Aug. 1961.
25 UNA S/766/9/10, Hammarskjöld to Linner, 26 Aug. 1961.
26 *Foreign relations of the United States*, 20: 101, Godley to State Dept., Washington, 31 Aug. 1961.
27 Ibid.　　　28 TNA FO 371/154883, Powell Jones to Foreign Office, 27 Aug. 1961.
29 Ibid., Powell Jones to Foreign Office, 28 Aug. 1961.
30 UNA S/840/2/4, ELLEO 743, O'Brien, Egge and Waern to Linner, Khiari and MacEoin, 26 Aug. 1961.
31 Ibid., ELLEO 744, Cruise O'Brien to Linner, Khiari and MacEoin, 26 Aug. 1961.
32 TNA FO 371/154883, Smith to Foreign Office, 26 Aug. 1961.
33 UNA S/840/2/4, ELLEO 745, O'Brien and Egge to Linner, Khiari and MacEoin, 26 Aug. 1961.
34 TNA FO 371/154883, Powell Jones to Foreign Office, 28 Aug. 1961.
35 UNA S/840/2/4, ELLEO 745, O'Brien and Egge to Linner, Khiari and MacEoin, 26 Aug. 1961.
36 Ibid.　　　37 Ibid.
38 Ibid., O 1625, O'Brien and Raja for MacEoin and Linner, 27 Aug. 1961.
39 MA 35th Battalion Collection, box 8, file HQ 30, Int Report w.e. 26 Aug. 1961, 26 Aug. 1961.
40 MA 35th Battalion Unit History, p. 13.
41 UNA S/840/2/4, OPS 1369, Quinn to McNeill, 25 Aug. 1961. In early October he was appointed Military Controller of Refugees by MacEoin, in charge of the reception and dispersal of evacuees from Katanga.
42 Quote from Conor Cruise O'Brien, *Sunday Independent*, 12 Nov. 1962.
43 Interview with Comdt Art Magennis.　　　44 MA 35th Battalion Unit History, p. 13.
45 UNA S/840/2/4, O 1625, O'Brien and Raja for MacEoin and Linner, 27 Aug. 1961.
46 Linner sent Hammarskjöld a top secret unnumbered cable at 1904Z on 27 August and a further cable at 1022Z on 28 August that the operation was being brought forward to 28 August, but gave the time as 1000 but after discussion with local ONUC commanders in Elisabethville the time was brought forward to 0500 (NLS L179/162 and L179/160).
47 UNA S/840/2/4, ELLEO 748, O'Brien to Linner, Khiari and MacEoin, 2000Z, 27 Aug. 1961.
48 UNA S/822/3/14, 3/1 Gurkha Rifles to HQ Katanga Cmd, 0830Z, 28 Aug. 1961.
49 Magennis Memoir.　　　50 Ibid.　　　51 Doyle, *Jadotville*, p. 207.
52 Noel Carey, 'The siege at Jadotville', unpublished memoir in author's possession.　　　53 Ibid.
54 Quinlan, letter of 29 Aug. 1961, quoted in Doyle, Jadotville, p. 210.　　　55 Carey, 'Siege at Jadotville'.
56 Magennis Memoir.　　　57 Doyle, *Jadotville*, p. 210-11, quoting Quinlan to his wife, 29 Aug. 1961.

58 UNA S/735/16/4, Disase to Munongo, 28 Aug. 1961.

59 UNA S/822/3/14, Barrett to Dhar, 0620, 28 Aug. 1961.

60 UNA S/840/3/4, ELLEO 0750, O'Brien and Raja to Khiari and MacEoin, 0810Z, 28 Aug. 1961.

61 Ibid., ELLEO 0751, O'Brien to Linner, Khiari and MacEoin, 0925Z, 28 Aug. 1961.

62 NAI DT S16137I/61, report from Linner to Hammarskjöld, 14 Sept. 1961, annex 2.

63 Ibid., ELLEO 0751, O'Brien to Linner, Khiari and MacEoin, 0925Z 29 Aug. 1961.

64 UNA S/840/3/4, OPS 180, HQ Sector-B to ONUC HQ Leopoldville for Military Information Section and Military Operations Section, 1700Z, 28 Aug. 1961.

65 A group of former French officers with OAS leanings also remained in Elisabethville.

66 UNA S/772/1/6, FC 438, ONUC HQ Leopoldville to ONUC HQ Elisabethville, 1708Z, 28 Aug. 1961.

67 UNA S/840/2/4, ELLEO 760, O'Brien to Linner, 1102Z, 29 Aug. 1961.

68 UNA S/822/3/14, O1621, to all commanders from O'Brien and Raja, 0930B, 29 Aug. 1961.

69 Ibid., EV 380, Linner to O'Brien, 1100Z, 29 Aug. 1961. The 'Congo Club' was the colloquial name given to Hammarskjöld's advisors on Congo affairs at the UN Secretariat.

70 NLS L179/141, Hammarskjöld to Abbas, 30 Aug. 1961.

71 NAI DT S16137I/61, No. 302, Uneireann to Estero, 31 Aug. 1961.

72 UNA S/840/2/4, O 1626, Raja to MacEoin, 0950Z, 29 Aug. 1961.

73 The movement order was cancelled on 30 August.

74 UNA S/840/2/4, ELLEO 764, O'Brien and Raja to Linner and MacEoin, 1620Z, 29 Aug. 1961.

75 NLS L179/160, 5992, Hammarskjöld to Linner, 29 Aug. 1961.

76 UNA S/772/1/6, EV 387, Linner to O'Brien, quoting Hammarskjöld, 30 Aug. 1961. 'A clear and indisputable legal basis'.

77 TNA FO 371/155008, Dunnett to Foreign Office, 30 Aug. 1961.

78 UNA S/840/2/4, ELLEO 773, O'Brien and Raja to Linner and MacEoin, 1147Z, 30 Aug. 1961.

79 UNA S/772/1/6, Faura to O'Brien, 1515Z, 31 Aug. 1961.

80 UNA S/840/2/3, ELLEO 787, O'Brien and Raja to Linner and MacEoin, 2045Z, 31 Aug. 1961.

81 Ibid., A2036, Linner to Hammarskjöld, 0309Z, 31 Aug. 1961.

82 NLS L179/160, 6050, Hammarskjöld to Linner, 31 Aug. 1961.   83 Smith, *Blue flag*, p. 87.

84 NAI DFA 305/384/31/II, Boland to Cremin, 30 Oct. 1961.

85 TNA FO 371/155001, Dunnett to Foreign Office, 31 Aug. 1961.

86 TNA FO 371/154883, Dunnett to Foreign Office, 31 Aug. 1961.

Chapter 7. From Rumpunch to Morthor

1 UNA S/840/2/4, ELLEO 793, O'Brien to Linner and MacEoin, 1000Z, 1 Sept. 1961.

2 UNA S/772/2/3, ELLEO 794, O'Brien to Linner and MacEoin, 1 Sept. 1961.

3 UNA S/840/2/4, ELLEO 803, O'Brien and Raja to Linner and MacEoin, 2210Z, 1 Sept. 1961.

4 UNA S/767/1/1, O'Brien to Linner, 3 Sept. 1961.

5 UNA S/840/2/4, ELLEO 793, O'Brien to Linner and MacEoin, 1000Z, 1 Sept. 1961.

6 Ibid., ELLEO 781, O'Brien and Raja to Linner and MacEoin, 0430Z, 1 Sept 1961.

7 Ibid., O1601, Raja to MacEoin, 2 Sept. 1961.   8 Ibid.

9 O'Brien, *Katanga*, p. 242.

10 UNA S/840/2/4, ELLEO 811, O'Brien and Raja to Linner and MacEoin, 1835Z, 2 Sept. 1961.

11 Ibid., ELLEO 781, O'Brien and Raja to Linner and MacEoin, 0430Z, 1 Sept 1961.

12 Ibid., ELLEO 811, O'Brien and Raja to Linner and MacEoin, 1835Z, 2 Sept. 1961.

13 O'Brien, *Katanga*, p. 242.   14 Ibid.

15 UNA S/767/1/1, O'Brien to Linner, 3 Sept. 1961.

16 UNA S/840/2/4, O1632, O'Brien and Raja to MacEoin, 2240Z, 3 Sept. 1961.

17 NLS L179/160, A2076, Linner to Hammarskjöld, 1855Z, 3 Sept. 1961.

18 UNA S/767/1/1, O'Brien to Khiari, 3 Sept. 1961.   19 O'Brien, *Katanga*, p. 305.

20 Brian Urquhart, *Hammarskjöld* (New York, 1994 edition), p. 558.

21 UNA S/766/9/10, A2081, Linner and Khiari to Hammarskjöld, 5 Sept. 1961.

22 Ibid.   23 Urquhart, *Hammarskjöld*, p. 559.

24 UNA S/766/9/10, A2081, Linner and Khiari to Hammarskjöld, 5 Sept. 1961.

25 James, *Congo crisis*, p. 102.   26 Urquhart, *Hammarskjöld*, p. 557.

27 NLS L179/160, 6148, Hammarskjöld to Linner, 5 Sept. 1961.

28 Ibid., 6158, Hammarskjöld to Linner, 6 Sept. 1961.
29 UNA S/788/4/5, EV 410, Linner to O'Brien (quoting Hammarskjöld's 6149), 6 Sept. 1961.
30 UNA S/820/2/4, OPS 190, HQ Sector-B to ONUC Leopoldville, 1815, 4 Sept. 1961.
31 NLS L179/160, 6181, Hammarskjöld to Linner, 6 Sept. 1961.
32 On 6 September Raja also met with Gurkha commanders Harazi and Maitra in Elisabethville.
33 NLS L179/160, ONUC 5222, MacEoin to Bunche, 1502Z, 9 Sept. 1961.
34 UNA S/840/3/4, OPS 191, HQ Sector-B to HQ ONUC, Leopoldville, 6 Sept. 1961.
35 UNA S/788/4/5, 6210, Hammarskjöld to Linner, MacEoin, 7 Sept. 1961.
36 NAI DFA PMUN 387, Estero to Uneireann, 4 Sept. 1961.
37 NAI DFA 305/384/31, No. 223, Estero to Uneireann, 6 Sept. 1961.   38 O'Brien, Katanga, p. 243.
39 TNA FO 371/146720, Barrett to Home, 6 Sept. 1961.
40 Ibid., No. 3664, Foreign Office to UKMIS, New York, 8 Sept. 1961.
41 TNA FO 371/154884, No. 2290, Caccia to Foreign Office (Confidential), 6 Sept, 1961.
42 TNA FO 371/146720, Macmillan to Welensky, 6 Sept. 1961.
43 UNA S/767/1/1, O'Brien to Tshombe, 5 Sept. 1961.   44 Ibid.
45 NLS L179/162, Hammarskjöld to Linner, 7 Sept. 1961.
46 NLS L179/160, ONUC 5180, MacEoin to Hammarskjöld, 7 Sept. 1961.
47 UNA S/840/2/4, ELLEO 825, ONUC Elisabethville to ONUC Leopoldville, 0935Z, 5 Sept. 1961.
48 UNA S/822/3/14, I1021, Raja to MacEoin, 2050, 5 Sept. 1961.
49 TNA FO 371/154887, Dunnett to Powell-Jones, 6 Sept. 1961.
50 UNA S/772/2/3, Unnumbered, O'Brien to Linner, 7 Sept. 1961.
51 NLS L179/160, A2096, Linner to Hammarskjöld, 7 Sept. 1961.
52 UNA S/772/2/3, ELLEO 853, O'Brien to Linner, 8 Sept. 1961.
53 UNA S/840/2/4, ELLEO 845, O'Brien to Linner and Khiari, 1310Z 8 Sept. 1961.
54 O'Brien, Katanga, p. 245, letter of 10 Sept. 1961 to Máire MacEntee.
55 UCDA P104/6409, Aiken to Boland, 9 Sept. 1961.
56 UNA S/840/3/4, Sitrep, HQ Sector-B to HQ ONUC, Leopoldville, 10 Sept. 1961.
57 UNA S/840/2/4, O1604, HQ ONUC Elisabethville, HQ ONUC Leopoldville, 9 Sept. 1961.
58 Ibid., ELLEO 865, O'Brien and Raja to Linner and MacEoin, 9 Sept. 1961.   59 Ibid.
60 UNA S/788/4/5, 6189, Hammarskjöld to Linner, 7 Sept. 1961.
61 TNA FO 371/154959, 1363, Dean to Foreign Office, 8 Sept. 1961.
62 A cable from Linner to O'Brien in UN archives (S/766/9/10) suggests the text is from Hammarskjöld, but Hammarskjöld's papers show that the document is a memo from the UN's legal section 'Observations on the legal aspects of the present situation' (NLS L179/176). Emphasis in original.
63 Urquhart, Hammarskjöld, p. 562.
64 NLS L179/162, Linner to Hammarskjöld, 1414Z, 8 Sept. 1961.
65 NLS L179/160, A2107, Khiari to Hammarskjöld, 2050Z, 9 Sept. 1961.   66 Ibid.
67 Ibid., Hammarskjöld to Khiari, 9 Sept. 1961. 68 Ibid., 6270, Hammarskjöld to Linner, 10 Sept. 1961.
69 Ibid.   70 UCDA P104/6410, Boland to Cremin, 18 Sept. 1961.
71 NAI DFA PMUN 387, Boland to Cremin, 18 Sept. 1961.
72 NLS L179/160, 6272, Hammarskjöld to Linner, 10 Sept. 1961.
73 Quoted in Ludo de Witte, The assassination of Lumumba (2001, London), p. 20.
74 UNA S/767/1/1, O'Brien to Tshombe, 10 Sept. 1961.
75 NLS L179/160, A2123, Linner to Hammarskjöld, 11 Sept. 1961.
76 MA 35th Battalion Unit History, p. 15.
77 NLS L179/160, A2122, Linner to Hammarskjöld, 1916Z, 11 Sept. 1961.
78 UNA S/219/7/15, O'Brien to Bunche, 18 Nov. 1961.   79 O'Brien, Katanga, p. 246.
80 NLS L179/160, A2100, Linner to Hammarskjöld, 8 Sept. 1961.
81 UNA S/219/7/15, O'Brien to Bunche, 18 Nov. 1961.
82 NAI DFA 305/384/III, O'Brien to Cremin, 7 Feb. 1961.
83 According to Hammarskjöld's desk diary it was Boland's first formal meeting by appointment with the Secretary General since 27 June 1961 (NLS L179/175).
84 NAI DFA 305/384/31, Boland to Cremin, 12 Sept. 1961.
85 NAI PMUN 387, Boland to Cremin, 18 Sept. 1961.
86 TNA FO 371/154959, 'Expanded instructions', 14 Sept. 1961.
87 TNA FO 371/154957, No. 2150, FO to Leopoldville, 12 Sept. 1961.
88 TNA FO 371/154885, No. 2149, FO to Leopoldville, 12 Sept. 1961.

89 UNA S/772/2/3, EV439, Linner to O'Brien, 12 Sept. 1961.   90 Urquhart, *Hammarskjöld*, p. 564.
91 O'Brien, *Katanga*, p. 251.   92 UNA S/213/3/4, A2131, Linner to Narasimhan, 13 Sept. 1961.
93 TNA FO 371/154899, 'Memorandum of events in Katanga, September 1961'.
94 TNA FO 371/154888, Riches to Home, 28 Sept. 1961.
95 NLS L179/160, A2099, Linner and MacEoin to Hammarskjöld, 7 Sept. 1961.
96 TNA FO 371/154888, Riches to Home, 28 Sept. 1961.   97 *Irish Times*, 5 Oct. 1961.
98 Diarmuid Whelan, *Conor Cruise O'Brien: violent notions* (Dublin, 2009), p. 109.
99 O'Brien, Katanga, p. 328.
1   TNA FO 371/154885, No. 2149, Foreign Office to Leopoldville, 9.45pm, 12 Sept. 1961.
2   O'Brien, Katanga, p. 246. 'above all no half-measures'.   3 Ibid.

Chapter 8. Morthor

1   *Livre blanc*, p. 49.
2   UNA S/822/7/3, 'Katanga War Diary', p. 3. My emphasis.
3   TNA FO 371/154889, 'Memorandum of events in Katanga, September 1961'.
4   UNA S/840/2/4, ELLEO 876, O'Brien and Raja to Linner, Khiari and MacEoin, 1440Z 12 Sept. 1961.
5   Ibid., EV-442, Linner and MacEoin to Raja, 12 Sept. 1961.
6   UNA S/209/10/2, Linner to Bunche (Strictly Confidential), 6 Nov. 1961.
7   Letter written by Purcell, 12 Sept. 1961. Our thanks to Brig. Gen. Purcell for a copy of this letter.
8   Interview with Brig. Gen. Purcell, Dublin, Feb. 2011 and information from Col. J.T. O'Neill.
9   Magennis Memoir.   10 Doyle, *Jadotville*, p. 223.
11 UNA S/840/3/4, Daily Sitrep from 111600Z to 121600Z, 2100Z, 12 Sept. 1961.
12 Interview with Capt Ryan, Newbridge, Co. Kildare, Feb. 2012.
13 Nils Skold, *Mid FN i Kongo: Sveriges medverkan i den fredsbevarande operationen, 1960–1964* (Stockholm, 1994) p. 123.
14 UNA S/788/4/5, Operation Order No. 6 Operation Morthor, 12 Sept. 1961.
15 MA, Col. S. Condon papers, notes taken at 'Conf C/O SO, AO', 12 Sept. 1961.
16 According to Frank Lawless' report, this action was carried out by 'C' Coy of the 35th Battalion.
17 Magennis papers, Operations report for period 13/9/61 to 20/9/61 inclusive.
18 UNA S/816/16/2, memorandum for Chief of Staff and O'Brien by Liarommatis, 11 Sept. 1961.
19 UNA S/805/19/2, Perintrep No. 5 1961, 6 Aug. 1961.
20 NAI DFA 305/384/2 Pt V, Lt Col. A.G. Cullen to Maj. Gen. Collins Powell, 17 Oct. 1961.
21 UNA S/746/4/10, Directives (Très Secret), Quartier General de la Force Terrestre, Etat-Major – Section G2, signed by Tshombe, Elisabethville, 1 Mar. 1961.
22 NAI DFA 305/384/31 Pt 1, confidential note by Cremin of conversation with Boland, 20 Sept. 1961.
23 UNA S/840/2/4, HQ Katanga Cmd to ONUC HQ Leopoldville, 1205Z, 3 Sept. 1961.
24 Ibid., HQ Katanga Cmd to ONUC HQ Leopoldville, 1616Z, 3 Sept. 1961.
25 NLS L179/160, ONUC 5034, MacEoin to Hammarskjöld, 30 Aug. 1961.
26 It is unclear if Mide withdrew on his own initiative or was recalled by Raja. Archival and interview sources suggest both and which is correct is unclear.
27 NLS L179/160, 6111, Narasimhan and Rikhye to MacEoin, 2 Sept. 1961.
28 UNA S/822/1/4, OPS 1402, HQ ONUC Leopoldville to HQ Katanga Cmd, 0724Z, 3 Sept. 1961.
29 UNA S/840/2/4, FC 503, MacEoin to ONUC Elisabethville, 1645Z, 3 Sept. 1961. FC 503 is in response to a signal (O1621) which refers only to Force Mide.
30 Capt. Noel Carey, 'The siege at Jadotville', unpublished memoir.
31 Interviewed in *War stories: the Congo: Jadotville* (RTÉ, 2007).   32 Quoted in Power, *Siege*, p. 145.
33 NAI DFA 305/384/31/II, Boland to Cremin, 30 Oct. 1961.
34 NLS L179/160, A-2074, Linner and MacEoin to Narasimhan and Rikhye, 3 Sept. 1961 (Incorrectly dated as 3 Aug. 1961), and NLS L179/160, ONUC 5117, Linner and MacEoin to Narasimhan and Rikhye, 4 Sept. 1961.
35 UNA S/822/1/4, ONUC HQ Leopoldville to HQ Katanga Cmd, 1926Z, 3 Sept. 1961.
36 UCDA P82/540, O'Brien to Capt M. J. Masterson, Athlone, 19 Mar. 1963.
37 UNA S/772/2/3, EV-409, Linner to O'Brien, draft of Hammarskjöld's reply to Spaak, 4 Sept. 1961.
38 Ibid., 6152, Hammarskjöld to Linner, 5 Sept. 1961.
39 NLS L179/160, A2074, Linner and MacEoin to Narasimhan and Rikhye, 3 Sept. 1961.
40 John Terence O'Neill, 'The Irish Company at Jadotville, Congo, 1961: soldiers or symbols?', *International Peacekeeping*, 9:4 (2002), 27–44 at 131–2.

41 Knightly later became Director of Cavalry. He served in Lebanon and organized and commanded the first Irish 'Force Mobile' to serve with UNIFIL.

42 UNA S/840/2/4, HQ Katanga Cmd to ONUC HQ Leopoldville, 1616Z, 3 Sept. 1961.

43 Ibid., HQ Katanga Cmd to ONUC HQ Leopoldville, 2235Z, 3 Sept. 1961.

44 Ibid., ELLE0822, HQ Katanga Cmd to ONUC UN HQ Leopoldville, 1815Z, 4 Sept. 1961.

45 UNA S/219/7/15, relative strengths, no date.

46 UNA S/822/1/4, HQ Katanga Cmd to ONUC HQ Leopoldville, 1740Z, 3 Sept. 1961.

47 UNA S/840/3/4, OPS 191, (Secret), HQ Sector-B to ONUC HQ Leopoldville. 2010Z, 6 Sept. 1961.

48 Information from Capt. Noel Carey, Oct. 2012.

49 Congo – 1961: submission to the Chief of Staff (1996). Copy provided by Comdt Donnelly.

50 UNA S/840/3/4, unnumbered Sitrep for 10 to 11 September 1961, 12 Sept. 1961.

51 Ibid., secret Sitrep 1, 12 Sept. 1961.   52 MA 35th Battalion Unit History, p. 15.

53 NAI DFA PMUN 387, No. 232, Estero to Uneireann, 12 Sept. 1961.   54 Ibid.

55 NAI DFA 305/384/31, Report by Brendan Nolan, Sequence of events at Jadotville.

56 UNA S/791/43/4, teleprinter message, 12 Sept. 1961.

57 NAI DFA 305/384/31, Report by Brendan Nolan, Sequence of events at Jadotville.

58 NLS L179/160, 6338, Bunche to Linner, 17 Sept. 1961.

59 NAI DFA 305/384/31, Report by Brendan Nolan, Sequence of events at Jadotville.

60 UNA S/840/3/4, Sitrep 11-12 September 1961.

61 Colonel J. T. O'Neill private papers, Egge to O'Neill, 22 Apr. 1998.

62 B. Chakravorty, and S.N. Prasad (eds), *Armed forces of the Indian Union: the Congo operation, 1963–63* (Delhi, 1976), p. 70, footnote 2.

63 Máire Cruise O'Brien, *The same age as the state* (Dublin, 2003), p. 242.

64 TNA FO 371/154889, Memorandum of events in Katanga, September 1961. Annexed account of phone conversation between Rigby and Dunnett, 0415, 13 Sept. 1961.

65 Magennis Memoir.   66 Ibid.

67 Ibid., all quotations in this paragraph from this source.

68 Colonel J.T. O'Neill private papers, Egge to O'Neill, 22 Apr. 1998.   69 Magennis Memoir.

70 Ibid.   71 NAI DFA 305/384/2 Pt V, Lt Col. A.G. Cullen to Maj. Gen. Collins Powell, 17 Oct. 1961.

72 *Irish Press*, 14 Sept. 1961.   73 Magennis papers, Operations Report – 13/9/61 to 16/9/61.

74 Ibid.   75 RH RW 261/2, statement by Daniel Rouben contained in Evans to Welensky, 23 May 1962.

76 *Chicago Daily News*, 13 Sept. 1961.   77 TNA FO 371/154889, Attaque de la Poste, 0830, 13 Sept. 1961.

78 Magennis papers, Operations Report – 13/9/61 to 16/9/61.

79 UNA S/822/4/4, Aide Memoire – Op Morthor, undated.

80 TNA FO 371/154889, Attaque de la Poste, 0830, 13 Sept. 1961.   81 *Livre blanc*, p. 48.

82 Magennis Papers, confidential report by Major Singh.   83 Ibid.

84 Sitrep from 1 Dogra Batt to Sector-B, 0030, 14 Sept. 1961, quoted p. 7 appendix a 35th Battalion Unit History.

85 *Livre blanc*, pp 7–9.

86 The Staghound's hull and turret were much lower than the Irish Ford. Its turret mounted a 37mm cannon and the Irish Fords, their Vickers machine-guns firing only non-armour-piercing .303" ball ammunition, were of little use against the higher calibre modern weapons of these Katangese vehicles.

87 *Livre blanc*, p. 48.   88 Magennis Memoir.   89 Ibid.

90 The crew was made up of car commander, gunner, driver, radio operator and reserve gunner/driver.

91 UNA S/822/4/2, OPS/B/27, Sector-B to HQ Katanga Cmd, 1240, 13 Sept. 1961.

92 *Livre blanc*, p. 50.

93 Magennis Papers, Report of Lt Considine, Armoured Car Group 35th Irish Battalion, undated.

94 *Livre blanc*, p. 10.

95 Magennis papers, Boyce and Sheedy taped joint interview by Comdt Magennis and Col. Heaslip, Kilbeheny, Sept. 2005.

96 Ibid.   97 Ibid.   98 Ibid.   99 Ibid.

1 Sitrep from 1 Dogra Batt to HQ Sector-B, 0030, 14 Sept. 1961, quoted p. 7 appendix a 35th Battalion Unit History.

2 Magennis papers, Boyce and Sheedy taped joint interview by Comdt Magennis and Col. Heaslip, Kilbeheny, Sept. 2005.

3 UNA S/822/4/2, OPS/B/15, telex message Sector-B to HQ Katanga Cmd, 0800, 13 Sept. 1961. The Katangese *Livre blanc* gives a similar figure: 16 gendarmes, 7 policemen and 2 soldiers.

4 *Livre blanc*, p. 10.

5   UNA S/822/4/4, Aide Memoire – Op Morthor, undated.
6   Magennis papers, Boyce and Sheedy taped joint interview by Comdt Magennis and Col. Heaslip, Kilbeheny, Sept. 2005.
7   Ibid. In this passage of his interview Boyce's uncharacteristic use of expletives together with his raised voice suggests a traumatic recollection of the actions of the Indian troops.
8   Ibid.   9 Ibid.   10 Ibid.   11 Ibid.   12 Ibid.   13 Ibid.   14 Ibid.   15 Ibid.   16 Ibid.
17 UNA S/840/3/4, Raja to MacEoin, sitrep (unnumbered), 13 Sept. 1961.
18 Livre blanc, p. 51.   19 Magennis Memoir.   20 Ibid.   21 Ibid.   22 Ibid.
23 Magennis papers, Boyce and Sheedy taped joint interview by Comdt Magennis and Col. Heaslip, Kilbeheny, Sept. 2005.
24 Ibid.   25 Ibid.   26 Ibid.   27 MA 35th Battalion Unit History, p. 25.
28 UCDA P104/7042, O'Brien quoted in the *Irish Independent*.
29 *Irish Press*, 16 Sept. 1961.   30 RH RW 261/4, Welensky to Ferraz, 25 Sept. 1961.
31 TNA FO 371/155009, Macmillan to Nehru, 27 Sept. 1961.
32 RH RW 258/3, List of documents contained in this file for the Prime Minister's personal use and eventual return to the archives, no date.
33 Smith, *Blue flag*, p. 94.
34 TNA FO 371/154889, Memorandum on events in Katanga, September 1961.
35 RH RW 263/2, note to Welensky's Principal Private Secretary, 15 Sept. 1961.
36 TNA FO 371/154890, Pedler to Harvey, 7 Nov. 1961.
37 UNA S/766/9/10, Statement by Lt Valerio, Italian Red Cross, 17 Oct. 1961.
38 RH RW 260/6, Report of conversation with friend from Kolwezi, 21 Sept. 1961.
39 Ibid., Colyton to Salisbury, 12 Feb. 1962 and O'Brien, *Sacred drama*, p. 135.
40 O'Brien, *Sacred drama*, pp 135–6.
41 Quoted in Ralph Riegel and John O'Mahony, *Missing in action* (Cork, 2010), p. 109.
42 Magennis Papers, Report of Capt Hennessey, Armoured Car Group 35th Irish Battalion, undated.
43 O'Brien, *Katanga*, p. 249.
44 MA 35th Battalion Collection, box 8, file HQ 30, Arrest of Minister for Finance, 13-9-61, 8 Oct. 1961.
45 Ibid.
46 The information in this section, except where footnoted, is from an interview with Capt Ryan, Newbridge, Co. Kildare, Feb. 2012.
47 Described in the 35th Battalion Unit History as 'No. 1 Platoon less 1 Section' (appendix d. p. 1).
48 *Chicago Daily News*, 13 Sept. 1961.
49 Radio message from Rosen to Waern at 0640 local time, quoted in appendix a to 35th Battalion History p, 1.
50 TNA FO 371/154889, 'Report by Mr Neil Ritchie', undated.
51 NAI DFA 305/384/2 Pt V, Lt Col. A.G. Cullen to Maj. Gen. Collins Powell, 17 Oct. 1961.

Chapter 9. Cover-up

1   UNA S/840/3/4, O1601, O'Brien and Raja to Linner and MacEoin, 13 Sept. 1961.
2   UNA S/213/3/4, A2131, Linner to Narasimhan, 13 Sept. 1961.
3   NLS L179/160, ONUC 5278, MacEoin to Hammarskjöld, 1130Z, received 1147Z, 13 Sept. 1961. It is unclear when Hammarskjöld received this message. The mention of a counter-attack suggests MacEoin knew that the UN attacked first.
4   NLS L179/162, Hammarskjöld to Khiari, 9 Sept. 1961.
5   O'Brien, *Katanga*, p. 264.
6   NAI DT S16137/61, No. 316, Uneireann to Estero, 13 Sept. 1961.
7   Ibid., No. 317, Uneireann to Estero, 13 Sept. 1961.
8   NAI DFA PMUN 387, Boland to Cremin, 18 Sept. 1961.
9   TNA FO 371/154884, Foreign Office to New York, No. 3741, (Immediate, Secret), 11.20pm 13 Sept. 1961. At this point Sir Basil Boothby, head of the African section of the Foreign Office was by contrast 'relieved that the Katanga problem appears now settled' and Foreign Secretary Lord Home was prepared to accept the UN version of events in Elisabethville that morning (NLS L179/160, Kelly to Linner, 15 Sept. 1961).
10 Ibid.   11 NAI DFA PMUN 387, Boland to Cremin, 18 Sept. 1961.
12 TNA FO 371/154887, Dunnett to Foreign Office, 26 Sept. 1961.
13 O'Brien, *Katanga*, p. 258.   14 *Observer*, 17 Sept. 1961.
15 Verrier, *Peacekeeping*, p. 68.   16 Chakravorty and Prasad, *Congo operation*, p. 83.

17 NAI DFA PMUN 387, Boland to Cremin, 18 Sept. 1961.
18 NLS L179/160, A2155, Hammarskjöld to Bunche, 16 Sept. 1961.
19 NAI DFA PMUN 387, Boland to Cremin, 18 Sept. 1961.   20 Ibid.   21 Ibid.
22 NLS L179/160, 6387, Bunche to Hammarskjöld, 15 Sept. 1961.
23 TNA FO 371/154892, confidential note from Lansdowne to Hammarskjöld, 17 Sept. 1961.
24 RH RW 261/5, Katanga situation, Serial 9, 13 Sept. 1961.
25 UNA S/840/3/4, O1605, O'Brien and Raja to Linner and MacEoin, 13 Sept. 1961.
26 UNA S/822/4/2, OPS/B/27, Sector-B to Katanga Cmd, 1240, 13 Sept. 1961.
27 UNA S/840/2/5, ELLEO 879, O'Brien and Raja to Linner and MacEoin, 1240Z, 13 Sept. 1961.
28 Ibid., priority telex message from O'Brien to Linner, 13 Sept. 1961. Time stamp not clear.
29 NAI DFA 305/384/2 Pt V, Lt Col. A.G. Cullen to Maj. Gen. Collins Powell, 17 Oct. 1961.   30 Ibid.
31 UNA S/840/2/7, OPS 1456, MacEoin to Raja, 1700, 13 Sept. 1961.
32 UNA S/840/2/5, unnumbered and undated telex message in blue ink.
33 Ibid., unnumbered and undated telex message with number 4991 in top right-hand corner.
34 UNA S/840/2/7, unnumbered top secret telegram, Linner and MacEoin to O'Brien and Raja, 13 Sept. 1961.
35 TNA FO 371/154886, No. 1321, Salisbury to London, 1925, 13 Sept. 1961.
36 UNA S/840/3/4, OPS199, Waern to Irish and Swedish Liaison Officers, Leopoldville, 15 Sept. 1961.
37 *Irish Independent*, 13 Sept 1961.
38 UNA S/822/4/2, OPS/B/30, Sector-B to Katanga Cmd, 1350, 13 Sept. 1961.
39 Tadhg Quinn, *War stories: Congo: Jadotville* (RTÉ, 2007).
40 Sean Foley, *War stories: Congo: Jadotville* (RTÉ, 2007).
41 UNA S/213/3/4, A2143, Linner to Narasimhan, 1218Z, 14 Sept. 1961.   42 Ibid.
43 Doyle, *Jadotville*, quoting Quinlan, p. 28.   44 RH RW 261/5, Katanga situation, Serial 9, 13 Sept. 1961.
45 UNA S/822/4/4, Aide Memoire – Op Morthor, undated.
46 Thanks to Brig. Gen. James Farrell and Col. Michael Shannon, who were platoon commanders on Force Kane I and Force Kane II, for their comments on this and the following sections on operations at Lufira Bridge.
47 TNA FO 371/154886, No. 1321, Salisbury to London, 1925, 13 Sept. 1961.
48 UNA S/213/3/4, A2143, Linner to Narasimhan, 1218Z, 14 Sept. 1961.
49 Magennis Papers, report by Carroll.
50 UNA S/766/9/10, statement attributed to Raja by BBC radio newsreel, 0713, 14 Sept. 1961.
51 RH RW 261/5, Katanga situation, Serial 13, 14 Sept. 1961.
52 TNA FO 371/154889, Memorandum on events in Katanga, September 1961.
53 NAI DFA 305/384/31, Uneireann to Estero, 0105, 17 Sept. 1961.
54 UNA S/822/1/4, HQ Sector-A to HQ Katanga Cmd, 14 Sept. 1961.
55 Ibid., O1611, HQ Katanga Cmd to ONUC Leopoldville, 0925Z, 14 Sept. 1961. The Jat Regiment, often referred to as the 'Jats', is an infantry regiment in the Indian Army.
56 UNA S/822/4/3, O2346, Swedish Battalion, Elisabethville to HQ ONUC Leopoldville, 1130Z, 16 Sept. 1961. These vehicles would not be despatched until 20 September.
57 UNA S/840/2/5, Swedish Battalion, Elisabethville to ONUC HQ, Leopoldville, 1620Z, 16 Sept. 1961.
58 This would be published in the official United Nations report on Morthor – Document S/4940.
59 NLS L179/162, Bunche to Hammarskjöld, 14 Sept. 1961.
60 Ibid., Hammarskjöld to Bunche, 15 Sept. 1961.
61 TNA FO 371/154959, Expanded Instructions, 14 Sept. 1961.   62 *Irish Press*, 16 Sept. 1961.
63 NAI DFA 305/384/31/I, Biggar to Cremin, 16 Sept. 1961.
64 Cpl Tadhg Quinn, A-Company, interviewed on *War stories: Congo: Jadotville* (RTÉ, 2007).
65 Interview with Brig. Gen. James Farrell and Col. Michael Shannon, Dublin, 9 Aug. 2012.
66 Quoted in Doyle, *Jadotville*, p. 51.   67 Ibid.
68 UNA S/840/2/5, undated teleprinter conversation between Leopoldville and Elisabethville.
69 35th Battalion Unit History, appendix a, p. 10.
70 Interview with Capt. Noel Carey, Dublin, August 2012.
71 UNA S/840/3/4, Raja to MacEoin, 1545, 14 Sept. 1961.
72 Quinlan to McNamee, 1630, 14 Sept. 1961, quoted in Doyle, *Jadotville*, p. 63.
73 O'Brien, *Katanga*, p. 259.   74 NAI DFA 305/384/31, report by Nolan.
75 TNA FO 1100/1, rough notes by Dunnett of situation on 14 Sept. 1961.
76 UNA S/840/2/5, teleprinter message, undated, but 14 Sept. 1961.
77 Ibid., teleprinter message from MacEoin to Raja(?), undated but 14 Sept. 1961.
78 UNA S/822/4/2, HQ Katanga Cmd to Sector-B, 1130, 14 Sept. 1961.

79 Ibid., O2385, HQ Katanga Cmd to HQ ONUC Leopoldville, 1050, 14 Sept. 1961.
80 UNA S/840/3/4, telex message Ops to MacEoin, logged 0745, 14 Sept. 1961.
81 UNA S/213/3/4, A2143, Linner to Narasimhan, 1218Z, 14 Sept. 1961.   82 Ibid.
83 UNA S/822/4/2, O2308, HQ Katanga Cmd to Sector-B and Dogra HQ, 1601B, 14 Sept. 1961.
84 TNA FO 371/154886, No. 2170, Foreign Office to Leopoldville, 14 Sept. 1961.
85 UNA S/840/2/5, teleprinter message, undated, but 14 Sept. 1961.
86 Ibid., ELLEO 0880, O'Brien to Linner, Khiari and MacEoin, 1000Z, 14 Sept. 1961.   87 Ibid.
88 *Irish Press*, 16 Sept. 1961, report filed in Elisabethville, 14 Sept. 1961.
89 UNA S/840/2/5, telexcon, 1500Z, 14 Sept. 1961.
90 UNA S/822/4/2, HQ Katanga Cmd to Sector-B, 0800, 14 Sept. 1961.
91 Ibid., O2304, Raja to Waern (HQ Katanga Cmd to HQ Sector-B), 1545Z, 14 Sept. 1961.
92 Ibid., flash message, Raja to Waern, 15 Sept. 1961.
93 The account below is based on an interview with Capt. Tommy Ryan, Newbridge, Co. Kildare, Feb. 2012. All
    unattributed quotes in this section are from this interview.
94 UNA S/840/3/4, Secret I1033, Sitrep from 141600Z to 151600Z, 16 Sept. 1961.
95 MA 35th Battalion Unit History, appendix a, p. 11.
96 NAI DFA 305/384/2 Pt V, Statement of 96798 Sgt Timothy Carey, 35th Irish Battalion, made at ONUC
    Headquarters, Leopoldville, Republic of the Congo, on 3 October 1961.
97 The 35th Battalion unit history states that the ambulance was seen to drive away immediately after the attack
    and 'there is a suspicion that the A[nti]-t[an]k w[ea]p[o]n was transported in it.' A United Nations situation
    report covering the period when Cahalane's patrol was attacked includes reference to two Irish trucks being
    damaged when they came under fire from 'a Red Cross ambulance' (UNA S/840/3/4, I1033), Sitrep from
    141600Z to 151600Z, 16 Sept. 1961). Another UN document contained a report that in Elisabethville an 'Irish
    officer saw bazooka mounted on ambulance' (UNA S/822/4/4, Aide Memoire Op Morthor, undated.). The
    British Consul General in Elisabethville informed Leopoldville on 28 September that 'the Katangans used
    ambulances to carry arms', adding that the UN did also (TNA FO 371/154888, Dunnett to Riches).
98 UNA S/803/3/5, ADJT 35th Irish Battalion to Irish Liaison Officer, Leopoldville, 0820Z, 20 Oct. 1961.
99 MA 35th Battalion Unit History, appendix a, p. 13. Radio message 0015, 15 Sept. 1961.
 1 Ibid., radio message, 0300, 15 Sept. 1961, Waern, via Dogra Battalion, to Katanga Cmd.
 2 Magennis Papers, Report on events happened into my house from 14/9/61 21 hours to 15/9/61 at 8 hours, by
    Soete.
 3 UNA S/213/3/4, A2149, Linner to Narasimhan, 15 Sept. 1961.   4 Ibid.
 5 35th Battalion Unit History, appendix a, p. 14. HQ Katanga Cmd to Waern, 0950, 15 Sept. 1961.
 6 NAI DFA 305/384/2 Pt V, Lt Col. A.G. Cullen to Maj. Gen. Collins Powell, 17 Oct. 1961.

Chapter 10. *'"Little" Katanga had checked the "big" United Nations'*

 1 UNA S/213/3/4, A2149, Linner to Narasimhan, 15 Sept. 1961.
 2 TNA FO 1100/1, No. 31216, telegram to Leopoldville, 16 Sept. 1961.
 3 UNA S/840/2/5, Continuation of teletype conversation with Elisabethville 1130 on 15 September 1961.
 4 Ibid.   5 UNA S/840/3/4, teletype sitrep for Elisabethville, 1600B, 15 Sept. 1961.
 6 UNA S/822/4/2, O2388, Sector-A to HQ Katanga Cmd, 1055B, 15 Sept. 1961.
 7 UNA S/840/3/4, Sollenberg (Air Ops, Elisabethville) to ONUC HQ, Leopoldville, 1600, 15 Sept. 1961.
 8 *Daily Telegraph*, 15 Sept. 1961.
 9 MA G2/E/55/IV, memo of telex conversation between Lt Col. Lee and General Rikhye, 14 Sept. 1961.
10 UNA S/822/4/2, FC532, MacEoin to Raja, 0858Z, 15 Sept. 1961.
11 NAI DT S16137I/61, memorandum marked seen by Aiken, 15 Sept. 1961.   12 Ibid., 15 Sept. 1961.
13 UNA S/840/2/7, FC533, MacEoin to Raja and McNamee, 1215, 15 Sept. 1961.
14 UNA S/840/2/5, O1066, Raja to MacEoin, 1630, 15 Sept. 1961.
15 Ibid., HQ Katanga Cmd to ONUC HQ Leopoldville, 1150B, 15 Sept. 1961.
16 NAI DFA PMUN 387, MacEoin to Bunche, 2133, 15 Sept 1961.
17 TNA FO 1100/1, telegram to Leopoldville (No. 31216), 16 Sept. 1961.
18 Report of the Officer in Charge of ONUC to Secretary General, addendum covering developments during
    14–15 September 1961 (S/4940/Add.3), 15 Sept. 1961.
19 'A Dublin housewife', quoted in *Guardian*, 19 Sept. 1961.
20 NAI DFA 305/384/31, No. 320, Uneireann to Estero, 15 Sept. 1961.

21 MA G2/E/55/IV/A, Quinn to Director Plans and Operations, Army HQ, Dublin, 2355, 17 Sept. 1961.
22 *Evening Mail*, 15 Sept. 1961.   23 *Evening Star*, 16 Sept. 1961.
24 NAI DT S161371/61, press statement by Lemass, 9.45pm, 15 Sept. 1961.
25 TNA FO 371/154989, Lemass to Macmillan, 19 Sept. 1961.
26 TNA FO 371/154957, Maclennan to Chadwick, 19 Sept. 1961.   27 Ibid.
28 TNA FO 371/154932, Maclennan to Chadwick, 20 Sept. 1961.   29 *Irish Times*, 18 Sept. 1961.
30 *Irish Independent*, 16 Sept. 1961.   31 *Chicago Sun-Times*, 16 Sept. 1961.
32 *Evening Star*, 16 Sept. 1961.
33 NLS L179/160, 6405, Cordier to Hammarskjöld, 15 Sept. 1961.
34 MA 35th Battalion Unit History, p. 19.
35 TNA FO 371/154886, No. 1522, Riches to Foreign Office, 16 Sept. 1961.
36 TNA FO 1100/1, No. 31216, telegram to Leopoldville, 16 Sept. 1961.
37 Ibid.   38 Magennis Memoir. Unattributed quotations in this section are from this source.
39 Ibid. Tim Magennis, a journalist with Independent Newspapers in Dublin in the late 1950s, had an appointment to the Star newspaper in Johannesburg. By mid-1961 Magennis had considerable experience in Rhodesia and Nyasaland and had become a reliable informant for visiting journalists such as Gomani.
40 ÚNA S/766/9/10, Statement made by Capt. A. Magennis, 35th Irish Battalion, on 16.9.61 (at 0950 hrs).
41 UNA S/840/2/5, O1601, Raja to Linner and MacEoin, 1835Z, 15 Sept. 1961.
42 Mullins and Nolan were not officers, but the nature of the story in light of the rumours that circulated over the coming days is of significance.
43 Capt. Ryan provided a copy of this article when interviewed in February 2012, mentioning Gomani by name.
44 RH RW 260/6, Report of conversation with friend from Kolwezi, 21 Sept. 1961.
45 Col. Bob Denard (1929–2007), born Gilbert Borgeaud, a veteran of the Algerian War, who later fought as a mercenary in Congo, Angola, Zimbabwe, Gabon and the Comoros Islands.
46 Magennis Memoir.
47 Magennis was awarded the Distinguished Service Medal with Honour for his action.
48 UNA S/840/3/4, I1034, Katanga Cmd to ONUC HQ Leopoldville, sitrep 151600B to 160800B, 16 Sept. 1961.
49 MA 35th Battalion Unit History, appendix a, p. 18.
50 UNA S/840/2/5, teletype message, ONUC Elisabethville to ONUC Leopoldville, 1930B, 16 Sept. 1961.
51 Ibid., teletype message, ONUC Elisabethville to ONUC Leopoldville, 2000B, 16 Sept. 1961.
52 Quinlan to McNamee, 0710. 15 Sept. 1961, quoted in Doyle, *Jadotville*, p. 83.
53 UNA S/840/3/4, McNamee to MacEoin, 0741, 15 Sept. 1961.
54 UNA S/840/2/7, MacEoin to Raja and McNamee, no time noted, 15 Sept. 1961.
55 UNA S/822/4/3, 35th Battalion to MacEoin, 0900B, 16 Sept. 1961.
56 UNA S/822/4/4, 'Aide Memoire Op Morthor' undated.
57 UNA S/840/3/4, I1034, HQ Katanga Cmd to ONUC HQ Leopoldville, sitrep 151600B to 160800B, 16 Sept. 1961.
58 UNA S/840/2/7, FC540, MacEoin to McNamee, 16 Sept. 1961.
59 UNA S/213/3/4, A2149, Linner to Narasimhan, 15 Sept. 1961.
60 TNA FO 1100/1, No. 31216, telegram to Leopoldville, 16 Sept. 1961.
61 MA 35th Battalion Unit History, appendix a, p. 16. Note of 2345, 15 Sept. 1961.
62 UNA S/822/4/4, Aide Memoire Op Morthor, undated.
63 UNA S/822/4/2, 'RO' to HQ Katanga Cmd, 0800, 15 Sept. 1961.
64 Waern and to Raja, 15 Sept. 1961, my thanks to Capt. Noel Carey for a copy of this document
65 UNA S/822/4/4, Aide Memoire Op Morthor, undated.
66 NAI DFA 305/384/2 Pt V, Lt Col. A.G. Cullen to Maj. Gen. Collins Powell, 17 Oct. 1961.
67 UNA S/840/2/5, Egge to Loevstad, 0700Z, 17 Sept. 1961.
68 UNA S/822/4/3, 13/B/59, RO to HQ Katanga Cmd, 1500, 16 Sept. 1961.
69 McNamee to Quinlan, quoted in Doyle, *Jadotville*, p. 119.
70 UNA S/840/2/5, O1601, HQ Katanga Cmd to ONUC HQ, Leopoldville, 1605Z, 16 Sept. 1961.
71 McNamee to Quinlan, quoted in Doyle, *Jadotville*, p. 121, 1737, 16 Sept. 1961.
72 UNA S/840/2/5, undated fragment of teleprinter message.
73 NAI DT S161371/61, GIB Statement, 6.30pm, 16 Sept. 1961.
74 See Michael Moriarty, *An Irish soldier's diaries* (Cork, 2010), pp 114–32 for details.
75 NAI DFA 305/384/2 Pt V, Lt Col. A.G. Cullen to Maj. Gen. Collins Powell, 17 Oct. 1961.
76 Quinlan to McNamee, 1930, 16 Sept. 1961, quoted in Doyle, *Jadotville*, p. 129.
77 UNA S/840/2/5, undated fragment of teleprinter message.
78 Interview with Capt. Noel Carey, Dublin, August 2012.

79 Quoted in Doyle, *Jadotville*, p. 130.
80 TNA FO 371/154886, No. 1371, (Emergency) (Secret) Alport to CRO, 0140, 17 Sept. 1961.
81 UNA S/772/3, EV 463, Hammarskjöld to O'Brien, 1325Z, 17 Sept. 1961.
82 NAI DFA PMUN 387, Boland to Cremin, 18 Sept. 1961.
83 Ibid.
84 NAI DFA 305/384/31, note by Paul Keating on London–Dublin teletype message, 1115, 16 Sept. 1961.
85 UNA S/213/3/4, daily summary of events.
86 TNA FO 371/154932, Maclennan to Chadwick, 20 Sept. 1961.
87 NAI DFA 305/384/31/1, Aiken to External Affairs, 0652, 17 Sept. 1961.
88 UNA S/840/2/5, teleprinter message, 35th Battalion to Liaison Officer, Leopoldville, 17 Sept. 1961.
89 *Irish Times*, 18 Sept. 1961.   90 Ibid.   91 UNA S/213/3/4, daily summary of events.
92 UNA S/791/43/4, Defence Forces Plans and Operations to Liaison Officer, Leopoldville, 16 Sept. 1961.
93 *Irish Times*, 17 Sept. 1961.   94 Ibid.
95 UNA S/766/9/10, HQ Sector-B to HQ Katanga Cmd, giving messages from Jadotville, 1240B, 17 Sept. 1961.
96 Ibid., Message received from Irish Battalion in Jadotville, 1325, 15 Sept. 1961.
97 Doyle, *Jadotville*, p. 138.   98 Ibid., p. 140.   99 Ibid., p. 150.   1 Ibid.
2 NAI DT S161371/61, GIB press release, 2150, 17 Sept. 1961.
3 UNA S/791/22/2, report by Paul to Linner and MacEoin, 18 Sept. 1961.
4 UNA S/822/4/4, Aide Memoire Op Morthor, undated.
5 *Irish Times*, 17 Sept. 1961.   6 Doyle, *Jadotville*, p. 151.
7 NAI DFA PMUN 387, Boland to Cremin, 26 Sept. 1961.
8 NAI DT S161371/I/61, note by Nolan, 18 Sept. 1961.
9 Ibid., Lemass to Nolan, 18 Sept. 1961.
10 Ibid., message from ONUC HQ, Leopoldville to Dept of Defence, 1133, 18 Sept. 1961.
11 NAI DT S16137J/61, minute by Nolan, 19 Sept. 1961.
12 Ibid., Government Information Bureau statement, 2000, 19 Sept. 1961.
13 NAI DFA PMUN 387, No 329, Uneireann to Estero, 20 Sept. 1961.
14 TNA FO 371/154932, Maclennan to Chadwick, 20 Sept. 1961.
15 NAI DFA PMUN 433, memorandum, 20 Sept. 1961.
16 NAI DFA 305/384/31/I, Demerre to Clerkx, 17 Sept. 1961.   17 O'Brien, *Katanga*, p. 270.
18 NAI DFA 305/384/2 Pt V, Lt Col. A.G. Cullen to Maj. Gen. Collins Powell, 17 Oct. 1961.
19 UNA S/822/4/3, Swedish Batt Elisabethville/HQ Katanga to ONUC Leopoldville, 1430Z, 18 Sept. 1961.
20 UNA S/822/4/4, Aide Memoire Op Morthor, undated.
21 MA 35th Battalion Unit History, appendix a, p. 22.
22 Magennis Papers, Operations Report: 17/9/61 to ceasefire.
23 UNA S 822/1/3, HQ Katanga Cmd, Elisabethville to ONUC, Leopoldville, 1200B, 18 Sept. 1961.
24 Ibid.   25 Ibid.   26 Ibid., note on telex message OPS 1500, 1150Z, 17 Sept. 1961.
27 Ibid., HQ Katanga Cmd, Elisabethville to ONUC, Leopoldville, 1200B, 18 Sept. 1961. The French-built AMX 13 light, tank which was then in service with the Indian army.
28 UNA S/840/3/4, A2335, HQ Katanga Cmd to ONUC HQ Leopoldville, 1015Z, 17 Sept, 1961.
29 MA 35th Battalion Unit History, appendix a, p. 19.
30 UNA S/803/3/6, McNamee to ONUC Leopoldville, 1200Z, 19 Sept. 1961.
31 MA G2/E/55/IV/A, Greer to Director, Plans and Operations, Army HQ, Dublin, 1634Z, 19 Sept. 1961.
32 MA 35th Battalion Unit History, appendix a, p. 23.
33 TNA FO 1100/1, 'Michael' to David Smith, 18 Sept. 1961.
34 Chakravorty and Prasad, *Congo operation*, p. 75.
35 TNA FO 1100/1, chronology of 17 and 18 Sept 1961 by Dunnett.
36 UNA S/803/3/6, McNamee to ONUC Leopoldville, 1200Z, 19 Sept. 1961.
37 TNA FO 1100/1, chronology of 17 and 18 Sept 1961 by Dunnett.
38 UNA S/791/43/4, McNamee to ONUC HQ Leopoldville, 1600Z, 22 Sept. 1961.
39 MA G2/E/55/IV/A, Greer to Director, Plans and Operations, Dublin, 1157, 20 Sept. 1961.
40 Nolan's death in action was formally announced in weekly routine orders on 8 Dec. 1961. He and Mullins had been announced as 'missing presumed dead' in weekly routine orders on 20 Oct. 1961 and had been struck off 35th Battalion strength on 15 Sept. 1961.
41 UNA S/840/3/4, Sitrep up to 191700B, HQ Katanga Cmd to ONUC HQ Leopoldville, 1450Z, 20 Sept 1961.
42 MA G2/E/55/IV/A, Greer to Director, Plans and Operations, 1318, 19 Sept. 1961.
43 UNA S/822/4/3, 'Operational Tasks for Units', attached to memorandum 'Operational Tasks', 19 Sept. 1961.

44 MA 35th Battalion Unit History, appendix a, p. 23.

45 UNA S/766/9/10, Message from the Force Commander to the UN forces in Katanga, 19 Sept. 1961.

46 NAI DFA PMUN 387, No 329, Uneireann to Estero, 20 Sept. 1961.

47 UNA S/822/4/3, Waern to HQ Katanga Cmd, 2255, 19 Sept. 1961.

48 MA 35th Battalion Unit History, appendix a, p. 23.   49 Ibid.

50 UNA S/772/2/3, EV 468, Linner to O'Brien, 0051Z 18 Sept. 1961.

51 UNA S/213/4, Bunche to Linner, 0240Z, 19 Sept. 1961.

52 TNA FO 1100/1, Tshombe to van Weyenberg, 0905, 19 Sept. 1961.

53 TNA FO 371/154886, Dunnett to Ritchie, 1925, 19 Sept. 1961.

54 TNA FO 371/154887, message from Lord Alport, 19 Sept. 1961.

55 TNA FO 371/154888, Dunnett to Leopoldville, 23 Sept. 1961 and UNA S/752/34/1, Summary of major events, 20/21 Sept. 1961.

56 TNA FO 1100/1, Tshombe to van Weyenberg, 0905, 19 Sept. 1961.   57 Ibid.

58 NAI DFA PMUN 387, confidential note by Cremin, 21 Sept. 1961.

59 UNA S/840/2/5, ELLEO 909, O'Brien and Raja to Linner and MacEoin, 1950Z, 21 Sept. 1960.

60 O'Brien, *Katanga*, p. 288.

61 Col. Kjellgren and Khiari were appointed by the UN on 23 September and Katangese Minister for Foreign Affairs Kimba and Gen. Muké were appointed by Tshombe on 21 September.

62 UNA S/752/34/1, Summary of major events, 21/22 Sept. 1961.

63 UNA S/772/2/3, copy of two telegrams by O'Brien, 20 Sept. 1961.   64 Ibid.

65 Dag Hammarskjöld Library, transcript of Sture Linner oral history interview, p. 36 (http://www.unmultimedia.org/oralhistory/2011/10/linner-sture/, accessed 23 Aug. 2012).

66 Wieschoff was killed with Hammarskjöld at Ndola.

67 NAI DT S16137J/61, Lemass to Nolan, 22 Sept. 1961, and attached undated draft press statement.

68 TNA FO 371/154887, Dean to Foreign Office, 23 Sept. 1961.

69 Chakravorty and Prasad, *Congo operation*, p. 81.

70 RH RW 258/6, Minutes of a meeting between the Minister of Home Affairs and President Tshombe, held at the Control Tower, Ndola Airport, 20 Sept. 1961.

71 UNA S/767/1/1, O'Brien to Khiari, 1 Nov. 1961.

72 TNA FO 371/154889, Memorandum on events in Katanga, September 1961.

Chapter 11. 'Continual and violent flux'

1 NAI DT S16137J/61, Congo Situation, 23 Nov. 1961.

2 Magennis Memoir and UNA S/840/2/5, McNamee to Irish Liaison Officer, Leopoldville, 29 Sept. 1961.

3 MA G2/E/55/IV/A, Greer to Director, Plans and Operations, Dublin, 1030, 1 Oct. 1961.

4 TNA FO 371/154890, Dunnett to Riches, 23 Nov. 1961.

5 UNA S/787/11/2, HQ Katanga Cmd: Operational Instruction No. 1, 2 Oct. 1961.

6 UNA S/766/9/10, Plan for outbreak of hostilities, 25 Sept. 1961.

7 TNA FO 371/154890, Pedler to Harvey, 7 Nov. 1961.

8 UNA S/840/2/5, Khiari to Linner, 28 Sept. 1961.

9 TNA FO 371/154888, Dunnett to Foreign Office, 6 Oct. 1961.

10 TNA FO 371/155002, Dunnett to Foreign Office, 3 Oct. 1961.

11 MA G2/E/55/IV/A, Greer to Director, Plans and Operations, Dublin, 2215, 24 Sept. 1961.

12 Ibid.   13 Magennis Memoir.   14 TNA FO 371/154890, Riches to Home, 17 Nov. 1961.

15 Ibid., Dunnett to Riches, 23 Nov. 1961.

16 TNA FO 371/154887, Dunnett to Foreign Office, 22 Sept. 1961.

17 TNA FO 371/155009, Dunnett to Foreign Office, 30 Sept. 1961.

18 TNA FO 371/154959, Welensky to Home, 4 Oct. 1961.   19 Magennis Memoir.

20 MA G2/E/55/IV/A, Greer to Director, Plans and Operations, 1400, 23 Sept. 1961.

21 UNA S/840/2/5, McNamee to ONUC HQ Leopoldville, 1652Z, 24 Sept. 1961.

22 Ibid., ELLEO 934, O'Brien to Linner and MacEoin, 1110Z, 27 Sept. 1961. This telex gives further details from Mulabaka's letter about the movement of Rhodesian forces into Katanga, but it does not include the section regarding Mullins and Nolan. Mulabaka's information on the Rhodesians was sent to the UN Secretariat on Khiari's instructions.

23 UNA S/816/16/2, handwritten letter, Mulabaka to O'Brien, 23 Sept. 1961. The date on this handwritten document has been overwritten to read 23 Sept. and this date is used on all copies of the document, including

that in O'Brien's papers. The document is initialled read on 27 Sept. by an unknown hand. It is unclear from sources consulted how badly injured, if at all, Nolan was in the ambush at Radio College.

24 UNA S/840/2/5, O'Brien to MacEoin, 1730Z, 28 Sept. 1961.
25 There is no evidence to link the arrival of this information with Mulabaka's letter.
26 Magennis Memoir.
27 UNA S/840/2/5, McNamee to Irish Liaison Officer, Leopoldville, 0655Z, 29 Sept. 1961.
28 MA G2/E/55/IV/A, Greer to Director, Plans and Operations, Dublin, 1030, 1 Oct. 1961.
29 UNA S/840/2/6, McNamee to Irish Liaison Officer, Leopoldville, 1745Z, 5 Oct. 1961.
30 Magennis Memoir. Unattributed quotes in this section are from this source.
31 The second man did not identify himself, but he may have been Khiari's Sri Lankan legal advisor.
32 Considine never told Magennis what he was asked or what answers he gave about what he had seen at Radio Katanga.
33 NAI DT S 16137J/61, Lemass to Nolan, 23 Sept. 1961.
34 NAI DFA PMUN 450, Boland to Cremin, 6 Oct. 1961.
35 UNA S/822/4/5, Kjellgren to Khiari and MacEoin, 2000Z, 5 Oct. 1961.
36 UNA S/805/15/2, Secret report by Purfield, stamped seen by UN Military Information, undated. See also the official report to MacEoin dated 19 Oct. 1961 (UNA S/805/16/1).
37 On 16 October Purfield and McKeever, accompanied by Capt Carroll, along with two Irish civilians Charles Kearney and Hamish Mathieson, were arrested by Gendarmerie in the vicinity of Camp Massart while observing Gendarmerie movements and establishing whether Irish prisoners were at the camp.
38 UNA S/840/2/6, O2378, Paul to MacEoin and Quinn, 1300Z, 7 Oct. 1961.
39 NAI DFA 305/384/31/II, Boland to Cremin, 30 Oct. 1961.
40 RH RW 260/6, Tshombe to Welensky, 16 Oct. 1961.
41 TNA FO 371/155009, Dean to Foreign Office, 16 Oct. 1961.
42 UNA S/803/3/6, McNamee to Director, Plans and Operations, Army HQ, Dublin, 20 Oct. 1961. Thank you to Comdt Victor Laing for a copy of this document.
43 Commune Albert is approximately two kilometres south of where the abandoned armoured car was located.
44 UNA S/803/3/6, McNamee to Director, Plans and Operations, Army HQ, Dublin, 20 Oct. 1961.
45 Magennis Memoir.   46 Ibid.   47 Ibid.
48 NAI DFA PMUN 183, Cremin to Thant, 30 Nov. 1964.
49 Ibid., O'Croidheain to McCann, 12 Nov. 1964.
50 A comprehensive Defence Forces investigation into the deaths of Mullins and Nolan reported in 2010. Details can be found in Riegel and O'Mahony, *Missing*, pp 217-30.
51 TNA FO 371/154890, Dunnett to Riches, 23 Nov. 1961.
52 NAI DFA PMUN 441, Boland to Cremin, 21 Nov. 1961.
53 Ibid.   54 Ibid.   55 NAI DT S16137I/61, Aiken to Thant, 27 Nov. 1961.
56 NAI DFA PMUN 441, Boland to Cremin, 21 Nov. 1961.
57 Britain and France abstained in the vote and the United States voted in favour, though with great reluctance.
58 Quoted in Hoskyns, *Congo*, p. 444.   59 UNA S/789/9/2, Raja to MacEoin, 1225Z, 29 Nov. 1961.
60 *Daily Telegraph*, 26 Nov. 1961.
61 UNA S/219/7/15, General observations of the Force Commander and Dr O'Brien on the implementation of paragraphs 4 and 5 of the Security Council resolution of 24 November, undated.
62 UNA S/209/9/9, Bowitz to Rikhye, 27 Nov. 1961.
63 NAI DFA 305/384/31/II, No. 436, Uneireann to Estero, 28 Nov. 1961.
64 UNA S/789/9/2, Raja to MacEoin, 1225Z, 29 Nov. 1961.
65 TNA FO 371/154890, Dunnett to Foreign Office, 29 Nov. 1961.   66 Ibid.
67 UNA S/822/1/2, FC 714, Acting Force Commander to Raja, 1427Z, 30 Nov. 1961.
68 Ibid., O 2364, Acting Force Commander to Raja, 1700B, 30 Nov. 1961.
69 RH RW 259/1, Welensky to Home, 12 Oct. 1961.
70 NAI DFA PMUN 450, Boland to Cremin, 6 Oct. 1961.
71 Ibid., Boland to Cremin, 8 Oct. 1961.   72 Ibid.
73 TNA FO 371/154957, Dean to Stevens, 3 Nov. 1961.
74 Ibid., Stevens to Dean, 10 Nov. 1961.
75 UCDA P104/7043, O'Brien to Aiken, 8 Nov. 1961.
76 Ibid., O'Brien to Aiken, 8 Nov. 1961.
77 UNA S/209/10/2, Linner to Bunche, 6 Nov. 1961.
78 UNA S/219/7/15, O'Brien to Bunche, 18 Nov. 1961.

79 TNA FO 371/155009, Irish Interests in the Congo, 30 Nov. 1961.
80 TNA FO 371/155106, Dean to Foreign Office, 24 Nov. 1961.
81 UNA S/219/7/15, O'Brien to Bunche, 18 Nov. 1961.
82 NAI DFA PMUN 450, O'Brien to Aiken, 25 Nov. 1961.
83 O'Brien, *Same age*, p. 245 and p. 253.
84 NAI DFA P12/16/B/1, Cremin to Boland, 30 Nov. 1961.
85 O'Brien, *Katanga*, p. 319.   86 Ibid.
87 Brian Urquhart, *A life in peace and war* (New York, 1987), p. 179.
88 O'Brien, *Same age*, p. 258. Knightly returned in a Volkswagen borrowed from Capt. Art Magennis.
89 NAI DT S16137I/61, Unofficial reply to press inquiries, 29 Nov. 1961.
90 *Daily Mail*, 30 Nov. 1961.   91 O'Brien, *Same age*, p. 260.
92 O'Brien, *Katanga*, p. 326. In press conferences following his resignation O'Brien rejected suggestions that Dublin had come under pressure to secure his resignation on policy grounds.
93 Ibid., p. 327.   94 NAI DFA PMUN 437, Thant to Aiken, 30 Nov. 1961.
95 NAI DFA PMUN 450, press statement, 1 Dec. 1961.
96 See O'Brien, *Katanga*, pp 326-30.
97 NAI DT S16137I/61, Nolan to Lemass, 4 Dec. 1961.
98 *Daily American*, 2 Dec. 1961.
99 At this stage MacEntee had already resigned, but O'Brien did not know.
1   Quoted in the *Sunday Press*, 3 Dec. 1961.
2   UNA S/219/7/15, O'Brien to Bunche, 4 Dec. 1961.
3   MacEoin agreed to remain as Force Commander until 31 March 1962. This was accepted by Dublin on 19 December.
4   NAI DT S16137I/61, Cremin to Aiken, 7 Dec. 1961.
5   Ibid., message to Maclennan, attached to Cremin to Nolan, 7 Dec. 1961.
6   TNA PREM 11/3398, Maclennan to Clutterbuck, 8 Dec. 1961 and Mills to de Zulueta, 11 Dec. 1961.
7   NAI DFA PMUN 450, Cremin to Aiken, 20 Dec. 1961.
8   NAI DT S16137I/61, Macmillan to Lemass, 13 Dec. 1961.
9   *Le Monde*, 8 Dec. 1961.
10 *Irish Times*, 4 Dec. 1961.
11 TNA FO 371/155099, Maclennan to Chadwick, 4 Dec. 1961.

Chapter 12. *The point of no return*

1   Quote in Brian Urquhart, *Ralph Bunche: an American life* (New York, 1993), p. 350.
2   *Irish Times*, 4 Dec. 1961.
3   UNA S/822/1/2, O1621, Raja to Acting Force Commander, 1230B, 1 Dec. 1961.
4   UNA S/822/5/6, O2392, Raja to Force Commander, 0750B, 1 Dec. 1961.
5   UNA S/822/2/5, ELLEO 332, Ivan Smith to Linner, 10 Dec. 1961.
6   Ibid., ELLEO 335, Ivan Smith to Linner, 10 Dec. 1961.   7 Ibid.
8   Hoskyns, Congo, p. 451, quoting the *New York Times* of 4 Dec. 1961.
9   UNA S/822/1/2, O2309, Raja to Force Commander, 1950B, 3 Dec. 1961.
10 UNA S/822/5/6, O2301, HQ Katanga Cmd to all Sectors, 1230B, 3 Dec. 1961.
11 Hoskyns, *Congo*, p. 450.   12 UNA S/772/2/5, ELLEO 247, Ivan Smith to Linner and Ho, 3 Dec. 1961.
13 TNA FO 371/154891, Dunnett to Foreign Office, 4 Dec. 1961.   14 Hoskyns, *Congo*, p. 451.
15 NAI DFA 305/384/2/V, No. 451, Uneireann to Estero, 4 Dec. 1961.
16 HQ Company, elements of A-Company and the Armoured Car Group. B-Company had deployed to Albertville in November. C-Company was sent to Nyunzu in November and to Niemba in December. They were repatriated in late December.
17 Magennis Memoir.   18 Ibid.
19 Col P.J. Hally to the Advance Party, 36th Battalion, *Sunday Independent*, 19 Nov. 1961.
20 NAI DT S16137J/61, Lemass to Aiken, 13 Oct. 1961.
21 Ibid., draft cabinet minute (GC 10/1), 17 Oct. 1961.
22 UNA S/822/5/6, O2352, Raja to Linner, MacEoin and Air Commander, 2115B, 4 Dec. 1961.
23 Magennis Memoir.   24 *Times*, 8 Dec. 1961.
25 TNA FO 371/154961, Nehru to Macmillan, 8 Dec. 1961.

26 TNA FO 371/154891, No. 2345, Dean to Foreign Office, 5 Dec. 1961.

27 Ibid., No. 2367, Dean to Foreign Office, 5 Dec. 1961.

28 Ibid., No. 2358, Dean to Foreign Office, 5 Dec. 1961.

29 Ibid., Nos. 1944 and 1947, Riches to Foreign Office, 6 Dec. 1961.   30 Magennis Memoir.

31 Ibid. Magennis understood from Barrett that Kane had agreed to this command structure.

32 Ibid.   33 It was unclear to Magennis what orders Salaria expected to receive.

34 When the fighting had ceased the Irish hoped to remove the Gendarmerie armoured car as a trophy, but their Ford armoured cars proved unable to tow the heavier Gendarmerie vehicle.

35 TNA FO 371/154892, No. 557, Dunnett to Foreign Office, 5 Dec. 1961.

36 Unnamed Indian Lieutenant reported in *Guardian*, 6 Dec. 1961.

37 TNA FO 371/154892, No. 557, Dunnett to Foreign Office, 5 Dec. 1961.

38 Magennis Memoir. Indian sources suggest that Salaria and his colleagues intended to vanquish the murder in Elisabethville of Major Ajit Singh and his driver by Gendarmerie the night Urquhart was abducted.

39 UNA S/772/2/5, ELLEO 330, Ivan Smith to Linner, Ho and Caruthers, 10 Dec. 1961.

40 Salaria was posthumously awarded the Param Vir Chakra, the Indian Army's highest wartime medal. His citation says that he killed 40 Gendarmerie and took out two armoured cars in the attack. The UN reported 30 dead at the old airfield and 36 plus two mercenaries killed at roadblock. The official UN report said 38 plus 2 mercenaries. Magennis saw 8 dead and Quinlan saw 34 dead.

41 Magennis Memoir.   42 TNA FO 371/154892, No. 563, Dunnett to Foreign Office, 8 Dec. 1961.

43 *Guardian*, 8 Dec. 1961.

44 NAI DFA PMUN M13/6/3, memorandum of situation in Elisabethville as of 7 Dec. 1961.

45 This point is made in more detail in Hoskyns, *Congo*, pp 455–6.

46 MA, 36th Battalion Unit History, p. 2.   47 Magennis Memoir.

48 MA 36th Battalion Unit History, p. 3.

49 UNA S/822/1/5, FC 734, MacEoin to Raja, 0837Z, 7 Dec. 1961.

50 Security Council document S/4940/Add.18, 20 Dec. 1961.

51 UNA S/772/2/5, Elisabethville to Omnipress New York, 8 Dec. 1961.

52 TNA FO 371/154893, Riches to Stevens, 8 Dec. 1961.   53 *Guardian*, 7 Dec. 1961.

54 TNA FO 371/154892, No. 563, Dunnett to Foreign Office, 8 Dec. 1961.

55 MA 36th Battalion Unit History, p. 54.

56 TNA FO 371/154892, No. 566, Dunnett to Foreign Office, 8 Dec. 1961.

57 Observer, 10 Dec. 1961.   58 NAI DFA 305/384/31/III, Boland to Cremin, 12 Dec. 1961.

59 *Irish Independent*, 11 Dec. 1961.   60 *New York Times*, 12 Dec. 1961.

61 UNA S/213/3/5, ELLEO 313, Ivan Smith to Linner, 9 Dec. 1961.

62 UNA S/772/2/5, Elisabethville to Omnipress New York, 8 Dec. 1961.

63 *Irish Independent*, 11 Dec. 1961.   64 UNA S/213/3/5, L307, Linner to Thant, 9 Dec. 1961.

65 Magennis Memoir.   66 Ibid.   67 Ibid.

68 NAI DFA 305/384/31/III, note from Keating to O'Tuathail, 13 Dec. 1961. The statement was sent to Lemass.

69 Ibid., Boland to Cremin, 13 Dec. 1961.   70 Ibid.

71 Ibid., No. 462, Boland to Cremin, 13 Dec. 1961.

72 UNA S/772/2/5, ELLEO 343, Ivan Smith and Raja to Linner, 11 Dec. 1961.

73 Ibid., ELLEO 349, Ivan Smith to Ho and Carruthers, 11 Dec. 1961.

74 Ibid., ELLEO 360, Ivan Smith to Linner, 12 Dec. 1961.

75 Ibid., ELLEO 361, Ivan Smith to Linner, 12 Dec. 1961.

76 Ibid., ELLEO 384, Ivan Smith to Linner, 13 Dec. 1961.

77 TNA FO 371/154893, No. 585, Dunnett to Foreign Office, 14 Dec. 1961.

78 UNA S/357/23/25, US Mission to United Nations note to press correspondents, 15 Dec., 1961.

79 TNA FO 371/154893, No. 3436, Ormsby-Gore to Foreign Office, 16 Dec. 1961.

80 Ibid., No. 582, Dunnett to Foreign Office, 13 Dec. 1961.

81 UNA S/772/2/5, ELLEO 374, Ivan Smith to Linner, 13 Dec. 1961.

82 Ibid., ELLEO 362, Ivan Smith to Linner, 12 Dec. 1961.   83 *Irish Press*, 13 Dec. 1961.

84 UNA S/772/2/5, ELLEO 395, Ivan Smith to Ho, 14 Dec. 1961.

85 Security Council document S/4940/Add.18, 20 Dec. 1961.

86 TNA FO 371/155009, No. 586, Dunnett to Foreign Office, 14 Dec. 1961.

87 UNA S/213/3/5, L321, Linner to Thant, 10 Dec. 1961.

88 MA, 36th Battalion Unit History, Operation Instruction No. 14, p. 60.

89 MA 36th Battalion Unit History, p. 7.   90 UNA S/213/3/5, L321, Linner to Thant, 10 Dec. 1961.

91 Ibid., L418, Linner to Thant, 16 Dec. 1961.

92 UNA S/822/5/7, Statement of actions fought 10–15 December 1961.

93 UNA S/772/2/5, ELLEO 401, Ivan Smith to Linner, 15 Dec. 1961.

94 35th Battalion units played a relatively minor role in Unokat. Between 12 and 18 December they secured a portion of Route Charlie at White Piers Cross Roads to block movement between the airport and the city.

95 UNA S/772/2/5, ELLEO 428, Ivan Smith to Bunche, Linner, Ho and Carruthers, 16 Dec. 1961.

96 MA 36th Battalion Unit History, p. 77.   97 Ibid., p. 7.

98 NAI DFA PMUN 445, Report – Transport Section, 36th Irish BN ONUC, Period, 21.11.61 to 14.5.62, by Capt Patrick J. Cotter, Battalion Transport Officer.

99 The report by the OC A-Company of the action at the Tunnel in the 36th Battalion Unit History explained that the 84mm recoilless rifle 'must be used well forward and used aggressively, at the side of the Platoon Commander. It has taken over the role of the 60mm Mortars in attack, it is lighter and more portable and quicker into action' (MA 36th Battalion Unit History, p. 76).

1 MA 36th Battalion Unit History, p. 77. Dan Harvey's 'A' Company action (Dunboyne, 2012) gives a detailed account of the 'Battle of The Tunnel' using interviews with veterans.

2 UNA S/772/2/5, ELLEO 427, Ivan Smith to Bunche, Linner, Ho and Carruthers, 16 Dec. 1961.

3 MA 36th Battalion Unit History, p. 10.   4 Ibid.

5 TNA FO 371/155005, No. 2003, Riches to Foreign Office, 18 Dec. 1961.

6 UNA S/822/1/5, Waern(?) to MacEoin, 18 Dec. 1961.   7 MA 36th Battalion Unit History, p. 10.

8 Observer, 23 Dec. 1961.

9 NAI DFA PMUN 441 (M/13/6/3 pt2), No. 469, Uneireann to Estero, 19 Dec. 1961. Seen by Lemass.

10 Hoskyns, Congo, p. 456.   11 TNA FO 371/155005, No. 2003, Riches to Foreign Office, 18 Dec. 1961.

12 NAI DFA 305/384/31/III, Statement by UN Congo Force Commander, 19 Dec. 1961.

13 NAI DFA 305/384/31/III, Statement by UN Congo Force Commander, 19 Dec. 1961.

14 TNA FO 371/154894, No. 616, Dunnett to Foreign Office, 22 Dec. 1961.

15 TNA FO 371/154962, Codel 74, Welensky to Home, 22 Dec. 1961.

16 MA 36th Battalion Unit History, p. 18.

17 UNA S/772/2/5, ELLEO 531, Ivan Smith to Granville and Fletcher, 21 Dec. 1961.

18 Ibid., Ivan Smith to Bunche, Linner, Ho and Carruthers, 18 Dec. 1961.

19 TNA FO 371/154991, No. 625, Dunnett to Foreign Office, 23 Dec. 1961.

20 TNA FO 371/154894, No. 645, Dunnett to Foreign Office, 26 Dec. 1961.

21 Observer, 24 Dec. 1961.   22 TNA FO 371/154894, No. 631, Dunnett to Foreign Office, 24 Dec. 1961.

23 UNA S/772/2/5, ELLEO 616, Ivan Smith to Linner, Ho and Carruthers, 26 Dec. 1961.

24 Urquhart recalled that it was 'surprisingly easy to re-establish contact with Tshombe and Munongo, who seemed anxious to come to terms' (A life in peace and war (New York, 1987), p. 187).

25 Ibid.

Conclusion. 'Deliver us from E-ville'

1 See Doyle, Heroes, and Power, Siege.

Bibliography

PRIMARY SOURCES

Ireland

National Archives of Ireland, Dublin
Department of Foreign Affairs
    Permanent Mission to the United Nations
    Confidential Reports
    300 Series Registry Files – especially 305/384 sub-series

Department of the Taoiseach
    S series files

Military Archives, Cathal Brugha Barracks, Rathmines, Dublin
    32nd Battalion Unit History
    33rd Battalion Unit History
    35th Battalion Unit History
    36th Battalion Unit History
    Files relating to the 35th Battalion

University College Dublin Archives Department
    Frank Aiken papers (P104)
    Conor Cruise O'Brien papers (P82)

Personal Papers
    Captain Noel Carey (in owner's possession)
    Col. Jim Condon (Military Archives)
    Col. Phelim Connolly (in owner's possession)
    Comdt Liam Donnelly (in owner's possession)
    Brig. Gen. James Farrell (in owner's possession)
    Comdt Art Magennis (in owner's possession)
    Col. Terence O'Neill (in owner's possession)
    Brig. Gen. Patrick Purcell (in owner's possession)
    Capt. Tommy Ryan (in author's possession)

Unpublished Memoirs
    Lt Col. Seán Hennessey 'UN Service'
    Comdt Art Magennis 'My Congo'
    Tpr John O'Mahony 'On our way. To the Congo and Back'

Sweden
National Library of Sweden, Stockholm
　　Dag Hammarskjöld Private Papers (L179)

United Kingdom
Bodleian Library of Commonwealth and African Studies, Oxford (Rhodes House)
　　Sir Roy Welensky Papers

National Archives, Kew, London
　　Colonial Office Papers
　　Dominions Office Papers
　　Foreign Office Papers

United States of America
United Nations Archives, New York
　　ONUC papers
　　　　Force Commander, Leopoldville
　　　　Elisabethville Branch Office

Online Primary Sources
Dag Hammarskjöld Library, New York
　　United National Oral History Project
　　　　Sture Linner interview
　　　　F.T. Liu interview

Central Intelligence Agency
　　Electronic Reading Room (www.foia.cia.gov)
　　　　Weekly intelligence summaries concerning the Congo and Katanga

Printed Primary Sources

Foreign relations of the United States, 1961–1963, Vol. XX, Congo Crisis (Washington, 1994)
Ireland at the United Nations. Speeches by Mr Frank Aiken (Dublin, 1960–2)
Livre blanc du gouvernement Katangais sur les événements de Septembre et Decembre 1961
　　(Elisabethville, 1962)
United Nations Operations in Katanga 1961. *Evidence published June* 1962 (Salisbury, 1962)
Chakravorty, B., and S.N. Prasad, (eds), *Armed Forces of the Indian Union: the Congo operation*
　　1960–63 (Delhi, 1976)

SECONDARY SOURCES

Books
Butcher, Tim, *Blood River: a journey to Africa's broken heart* (London, 2007)
Dayal, Rajeshwar, *Mission for Hammarskjöld* (Princeton, NJ, 1976)
Devlin, Larry, *Chief of station, Congo* (New York, 2007)
de Witte, Ludo, *The assassination of Lumumba* (London, 2001)

Dorr, Noel, *Ireland at the United Nations, memories of the early years* (Dublin, 2010)

Doyle, Rose (with Leo Quinlan), *Heroes of Jadotville* (Dublin, 2006)

Durch, William J. (ed.), *The evolution of UN peacekeeping: case studies and comparative analysis* (London, 1993)

Gavshon, Arthur L., *The last days of Dag Hammarskjöld* (London, 1963)

Hammarskjöld, Dag, *Markings* (London, 1988)

Harvey, Dan, *A-Company action: the battle of the Tunnel, 16th December 1961* (Dunboyne, 2012)

Hempstone, Smith, *Katanga report* (London, 1962)

Hoskyns, Catherine, *The Congo since independence* (London, 1965)

Ishizuka, Katsumi, *Ireland and international peacekeeping operations, 1960–2000* (London, 2004)

James, Alan, *Peacekeeping in international politics* (London, 1990)

James, Alan, *Britain and the Congo crisis, 1960–63* (London, 1996)

Kalb, Madeline G., *The Congo cables: the cold war in Africa from Eisenhower to Kennedy* (New York, 1982)

McCaughren, Tom, *The peacemakers of Niemba* (Dublin, 1966)

Moriarty, Michael, *An Irish soldier's diaries* (Cork, 2010)

O'Brien, Conor Cruise (as Donat O'Donnell), *Maria Cross* (New York, 1952)

O'Brien, Conor Cruise, *To Katanga and back* (London, 1962)

— *The United Nations: sacred drama* (London, 1968)

— *Murderous angels* (Boston, 1968)

— *Memoir: my life and themes* (Dublin, 1998)

O'Brien, Máire Cruise, *The same age as the state* (Dublin, 2003)

O'Donoghue, David, *The Irish army in the Congo, 1960–1964* (Dublin, 2006)

Ó Foghlú, Seán, *No white feather* (Dunboyne, 2011)

O'Neill, John Terence, and Nicholas Rees, *United Nations peacekeeping in the post-cold war era* (Abington, 2005)

O'Sullivan, Kevin, *Ireland, Africa and the end of empire* (Manchester, 2013)

Parsons, Anthony, *From cold war to hot peace: UN interventions, 1947–1994* (London, 1995)

Power, Declan, *Siege at Jadotville* (Dunshaughlin, 2005)

Riegel, Ralph and John O'Mahony, *Missing in action: the fifty-year search for Ireland's missing soldier* (Cork, 2010)

Scott, Ian, *Tumbled house: the Congo at independence* (London, 1969)

Skelly, Joseph M., *Irish diplomacy at the United Nations, 1945–1965: national interests and the international order* (Dublin, 1997)

Skold, Nils, *Mid FN i Kongo: Sveriges medverkan i den fredsbevarande operationen, 1960–1964* (Stockholm, 1994)

Smith, Raymond, *Under the blue flag* (Dublin, 1980)

Tavares de Sá, Hernane, *The play within the play: the inside story of the UN* (New York, 1966)

Thant, U, *View from the UN* (New York, 1978)

United Nations, *The blue helmets* (New York, 1990)

Urquhart, Brian, *A life in peace and war* (New York, 1987)

Urquhart, Brian, *Ralph Bunche: an American life* (New York, 1993)

Urquhart, Brian, *Hammarskjöld* (London, 1994 edition)

Verrier, Anthony, *International peacekeeping: United Nations forces in a troubled world* (London, 1981)

von Horn, Carl, *Soldiering for peace* (London, 1966)

Welensky, Roy, *Welensky's 4000 days* (London, 1964)
Whelan, Diarmuid, *Conor Cruise O'Brien: violent notions* (Dublin, 2009)
Williams, Susan, *Who killed Hammarskjöld?* (London, 2011)

Articles and chapters
—, 'Report on a battle', *An Cosantóir*, 22:3 (Mar. 1962), 144–6
Bunworth, R.W., 'Niemba recalled', *An Cosantóir*, 40:10 (Oct. 1980), 283–7
Burke, Edward, 'Ireland's contribution to the United Nations mission in the Congo (ONUC): keeping the peace in Katanga' in Michael Kennedy and Deirdre McMahon (eds), *Obligations and responsibilities: Ireland and the United Nations, 1955–2005* (Dublin, 2005), pp 117–153
Considine, Michael, 'Cavalry in the Congo', *An Cosantóir*, 22:10 (Oct 1962), 525–9
D.N.B., 'The train stopped at Niemba', *An Cosantóir*, 22:5 (May 1962), 226–32
Doyle, E.D., 'Signals in Katanga and Kivu - Part 1', *An Cosantóir*, 21:10 (Oct. 1961), 489–501
—, 'Signals in Katanga and Kivu - Part 2', *An Cosantóir*, 21:11 (Nov. 1961), 554–565
Harris, H.E.D., 'Operation "Sarsfield": the Irish Army in the Congo, 1960', *An Cosantóir*, 21:8 (Aug. 1961), 394–406
Hinchy, R.A., 'Early days in Kamina', *An Cosantóir*, 21:1 (Jan. 1961), 1–10
MacDonald, Patrick, 'Intelligence in United Nations operations', *An Cosantóir*, 27: 11 (Nov. 1967), 592–4
Magennis, A.J., 'Cavalry in the Congo and Cyprus', *An Cosantóir*, 36:1 (Jan. 1976), 25–31
O'Neill, John Terence, 'The Irish Company at Jadotville, Congo, 1961: soldiers or symbols?', *International Peacekeeping*, 9:4 (Winter 2002), 127–44
Power, Declan, 'Lessons from the Congo', *Defence Forces Review* (2008), 23–32

Interviews
Tpr Mick Boyce (by Comdt Art Magennis and Col. Dick Heaslip); Kilbeheny, September 2005
Capt. Noel Carey, Dublin, August 2012
Comdt Liam Donnelly, Dublin, October 2012
Brig. Gen. James Farrell, Dublin, August 2012
Comdt Art Magennis; Blackrock, Co. Dublin, 2010–13
Tpr Bill Maher, by phone from Canada, September 2010
Col. Terry O'Neill, Dublin and Athlone, 2010–13
Brig. Gen. Patrick Purcell, Dublin, February 2011
Brig. Gen. Tom Quinlan, Dublin, January 2013.
Capt. Tommy Ryan, Newbridge, February 2012
Col. Michael Shannon, Dublin, August 2012
Tpr Fred Sheehy (by Comdt Art Magennis and Col. Richard Heaslip), Kilbeheny, September 2005

Radio and television programmes and films
War stories: Congo: Niemba (RTÉ television, 2008)
War stories: Congo: Jadotville (RTÉ television, 2008)
Congo: an Irish affair (Akajava Films, 2011)
Jadotville (RTÉ radio, 2004)

Index

Numbers in *italics* below refer to plate numbers in the illustrations section.